First World War
An anthology

ONE WEEK L

MANCHESTER
UNIVERSITY PRESS

FOR MAISIE SMITH

Women's writing
of the
First World War
An anthology

edited by
ANGELA K. SMITH

Manchester University Press
Manchester and New York
distributed exclusively in the USA by St. Martin's Press

While copyright as a whole and of all editorial matter is vested in Angela K. Smith, copyright of all other material belongs to the respective authors, translators, institutions and publishers as acknowledged, and no editorial or documentary material may be reproduced wholly or in part without the express permission in writing of both author and publisher.

Published by Manchester University Press
Oxford Road, Manchester M13 9NR, UK
and Room 400, 175 Fifth Avenue, New York, NY 10010, USA
http://www.man.ac.uk/mup

Distributed exclusively in the USA by
St. Martin's Press, Inc., 175 Fifth Avenue, New York, NY 10010, USA

Distributed exclusively in Canada by
UBC Press, University of British Columbia, 6344 Memorial Road, Vancouver, BC, Canada V6T 1Z2

British Library Cataloguing-in-Publication Data
A catalogue record for this book is available from the British Library

Library of Congress Cataloging-in-Publication Data applied for

ISBN 0 7190 5072 3 *hardback*
      0 7190 5073 1 *paperback*

First published 2000

06 05 04 03 02 01 00   10 9 8 7 6 5 4 3 2 1

Typeset in Minion
by Northern Phototypesetting Co. Ltd, Bolton
Printed in Great Britain
by Bookcraft (Bath) Ltd, Midsomer Norton

Contents

Illustrations

The photographs have been reproduced courtesy of the Imperial War Museum and the Mary Evans Picture Library.

Acknowledgements

Many people have provided support and inspiration during the compiling of this book. Primarily I am grateful to Jenny Hartley who was influential from the beginning of the project and offered me much valuable advice. I would also like to thank Helen Poskitt for her assistance with the preparation of the manuscript and her patience as a reader, Louise Jackson, Alan Munton and Matthew Frost for their help and advice. And Jim Sargent for his continual understanding and support.

The staff at Roehampton Institute Library, the University of Plymouth Library, the Departments of Printed Books and Documents at the Imperial War Museum, the Fawcett Library, London Guildhall University and the Liddle Collection, University of Leeds have been consistently helpful.

Permission to reprint material in this book is gratefully acknowledged:

Elizabeth von Arnim: extract from *Christine*. London: Macmillan & Co, 1917. Reprinted by kind permission of Ann E. Hardham.

Lady Cynthia Asquith: extracts from *Diaries 1915–18*. London: Hutchinson, 1968. Reprinted by permission of Hutchinson.

Enid Bagnold: extracts from *A Diary Without Dates*. London: Virago, 1978 (first published 1918); *The Happy Foreigner*. London: Virago, 1987 (first published 1920). Reprinted by permission of William Heinemann.

Vera Brittain: extracts from *Testament of Youth*. London: Virago, 1992 (first published 1933). Reprinted by kind permission of Mark Bostridge and Rebecca Williams, her literary executors and Victor Gollancz Ltd. Extract from *Honourable Estate*. London: Victor Gollancz, 1936. Reprinted by kind permission of Mark Bostridge and Rebecca Williams, her literary executors.

Mary Ann Brown: extract from the papers of Mary Ann Brown, Department of Documents, the Imperial War Museum, reprinted by kind permission of Mrs Evelyn Cleverly OBE.

G. K. Brumwell: extract from the papers of Mrs G. K. Brumwell, the Liddle Collection, University of Leeds, reprinted by permission of Peter Liddle.

Emily Chitticks: extracts from the papers of Miss Emily Chitticks, Department of Documents, the Imperial War Museum, reprinted by kind permission of Mrs Rosina Wool.

Hilda Craven: extracts from the papers of Hilda Craven, the Liddle Collection, University of Leeds, reprinted by permission of Peter Liddle.

Margaret Fawcett: extracts from *The First World War Papers of Margaret Fawcett*, Pietermaritzburg: Wyllie Desktop Publishing, 1993, ed. Audrey Fawcett Cahill, reprinted by kind permission of Audrey Fawcett Cahill.

A. T. Fitzroy: extracts from *Despised and Rejected*. London: GMP, 1988 (first published 1918). Reprinted by permission of the C. W. Daniel Company Ltd.

Nell Hague: extract from the papers of Nell Hague, the Liddle Collection, University of Leeds, reprinted by permission of Peter Liddle.

Radclyffe Hall: extracts from *The Well of Loneliness*. London: Virago, 1982 (first published 1928). Reprinted by permission of Weidenfeld & Nicolson Ltd.

Cecily Hamilton: extracts from *William an Englishman*. London: Skeffington & Son Ltd, 1919. Reprinted by kind permission of Lady Patricia Bower.

Peggy Hamilton: extract from *Three Years or the Duration: Memoirs of a Munition Worker 1914–18*. London: Peter Owen, 1978. Reprinted by permission of Peter Owen Ltd, London.

Patricia Hanbury: extracts from the papers of Patricia Hanbury, the Liddle Collection, University of Leeds, reprinted by permission of Peter Liddle.

Winifred Holtby: extract from *The Crowded Street*. London: Virago, 1981 (first published 1924). Reprinted by kind permission of Marion Shaw.

F. Tennyson Jesse: 'The Sinews of War – France' from *The Englishwoman*, no. 87, March 1916. Reprinted by kind permission of the Hospital of St John & St Elizabeth.

Winifred Kenyon: extract from the papers of Winifred Kenyon, Department of Documents, the Imperial War Museum, reprinted by kind permission of Ann Mitchell.

Phyllis Lunn: extract from the papers of Phyllis Lunn, the Liddle Collection, University of Leeds, reprinted by permission of Peter Liddle.

Elizabeth A. Macleod and Mary L. Macleod: extracts from the papers of the Macleod Family, the Liddle Collection, University of Leeds, reprinted by permission of Peter Liddle.

Catherine Marshall: 'Women and War' from *Militarism Versus Feminism*. London: Virago, 1987 (first published 1915). Reprinted by kind permission of George T. Marshall and R. Frank Marshall.

Ernestine Mills: 'Real Food Economy' from *The Englishwoman*, no. 89, May 1916. Reprinted by kind permission of Irene Cockcroft.

Christabel Pankhurst: 'The War' from *The Suffragette*, 7 August 1914; 'Women and the War': a speech delivered at the London Opera House, 8 September 1914. Published as a pamphlet by WSPU, Lincoln's Inn, London. Reprinted by kind permission of Dr Richard Pankhurst.

E. Sylvia Pankhurst: extract from *The Home Front*. London: Hutchinson, 1987 (first published 1932); 'The Military Service Bill' from *The Woman's Dreadnought*, vol. II, no. 43. Saturday 15 January 1916; 'Insults To Soldiers' Wives and

Mothers' from *The Woman's Dreadnought*, 14 November 1914; 'The East End Air Raid' from *The Woman's Dreadnought*, vol. II, no. 12, Saturday 5 June 1915, reprinted by kind permission of Dr Richard Pankhurst.

Eleanora B. Pemberton: extract from the papers of Eleanora B. Pemberton, Department of Documents, the Imperial War Museum, reprinted by kind permission of Giles Pemberton.

Irene Rathbone: extracts from the papers of Irene Rathbone, Department of Documents, the Imperial War Museum; *We That Were Young*. London: Virago, 1988 (first published 1932). Reprinted by kind permission of Mrs Pat Utechin.

May Sinclair: extracts from *A Journal of Impressions in Belgium*. London: Hutchinson & Co., 1915; *The Tree of Heaven*. London: Cassell & Co., 1917. Reprinted by permission of Cassell PLC.

Helen Zenna Smith: extracts from *Not So Quiet ... Stepdaughters of War*. London: Virago, 1988 (first published 1930). Reprinted by permission of The Estate of the Late Evadne Price and A. M. Heath & Co. Ltd.

Mabel St Clair Stobart: extract from the papers of Mrs Mabel St Clair Stobart, Department of Documents, the Imperial War Museum. Reprinted by kind permission of Eric St Clair Stobart.

Baroness de T'Serclaes: extracts from *Flanders and Other Fields*. London: George G. Harrap & Co. Ltd, 1964. Reprinted by permission of Eric Dobby Publishing Ltd.

Muriel Thompson: extract from the papers of Muriel Thompson, the Liddle Collection, University of Leeds. Reprinted by permission of Peter Liddle.

Beatrice Morwenna Trefusis: extracts from the papers of B. M. Trefusis, the Liddle Collection, University of Leeds. Reprinted by permission of Peter Liddle.

Beatrice Webb: extracts from *Beatrice Webb's Diaries 1912–1917*. London: Longmans Green & Co., 1952. Reprinted by permission of the Archives Division, British Library of Political and Economic Science.

Virginia Woolf: extracts from *The Diary of Virginia Woolf, Volume 1, 1915–19*. London: Hogarth Press, 1977. Reprinted by permission of the Executors of the Virginia Woolf Estate and the Hogarth Press.

Every effort has been made to trace all of the copyright owners, but if any have been omitted please contact the publisher. Apologies are offered to those whom it has proved impossible to identify.

Abbreviations

DORA	The Defence of the Realm Act, 1914
FANY	First Aid Nursing Yeomanry
NCF	No-Conscription Fellowship
NUWSS	National Union of Women's Suffrage Societies
QAIMNSR	Queen Alexandra's Imperial Military Nursing Service Reserve
TFNS	Territorial Forces Nursing Service
VAD	Voluntary Aid Detachment
WAAC	Women's Army Auxiliary Corps
WSPU	Women's Social and Political Union

Introduction

There are all sorts of things going round & round inside my heart which I
would love to relieve myself by expressing – queer longings, passionate &
strange, which sometimes I feel I *must* give vent to or burst! Give a feeling a
form & it will cease to hurt. (Irene Rathbone, *Diary*, 15 July 1918)

The primary aim of this anthology is to reclaim the Great War as an arena
of female experience, and to rediscover some of the written material
which articulates that experience. History has gendered the Great War as
male. The haunting images of trench warfare which seem to epitomise the
conflict represent the years of suffering for hundreds of thousands of
men. Many of these impressions have achieved their lasting effect
through the continuing popularity of 'classic' men's war texts: Erich
Maria Remarque's *All Quiet on the Western Front*,[1] Robert Graves's *Good-
bye To All That* and Siegfried Sassoon's *Memoirs of George Sherston* and
Edmund Blunden's *Undertones of War* among others.

But, engrossing though these texts are, they actually constitute the
experience of a distinct minority of the population. For a great many
non-combatant men, and all women, this historical impression of the
War is a misrepresentation of the experience of 1914–18. What this
majority actually did, how they actually felt, has for many years been
obscured by the overriding horror of the life of the trench soldier. This
anthology goes some way towards redressing the balance.

The world of the summer of 1914 is often identified as the setting for the
final blaze of a lingering Victorianism. Perhaps because it was a particularly idyllic summer, perhaps because Britain at least believed itself to be

---

[1] *All Quiet on the Western Front* was first published in 1929 and immediately became an
international best seller. *Goodbye To All That* was first published in 1929. Sassoon's semi-
autobiographical narrative of the war was published in *Memoirs of a Fox-hunting Man*
(1928), *Memoirs of an Infantry Officer* (1930), and *Sherston's Progress* (1936). They appeared
in one edition in 1937. Edmund Blunden's *Undertones of War* was first published in 1928.

on top of the world. Indeed its Empire stretched right around it. After the War all this would change. The Empire would begin to disintegrate, the extreme optimism of the early years of the century would vanish. Arguably then, the declaration of war on 4 August 1914 marked the end of much of the society and culture of the nineteenth century.[2] The sheer size of the disaster in human terms rendered obsolete much of the ideology upon which the prewar world had been based. The heavy artillery and machine guns of the Western Front clearly demonstrated the vulnerability of man in a way which had to undermine the sense of superiority which the technological innovations of the nineteenth century had inspired. Effectively, the vision caved in on itself.

But in many ways the dreams of those summer days, depicted so convincingly in works such as May Sinclair's *The Tree of Heaven* (1917), Vera Brittain's *Testament of Youth* (1933) and Siegfried Sassoon's *Memoirs of a Fox-hunting Man* (1928), were already hollow.[3] The social and political world had been in a state of flux for several decades. The Labour Movement which had found an effective leader in Keir Hardie had been growing throughout the nineteenth century, and many demands for electoral reform had already been met. Although the notion of a Welfare State was still a distant one, social reform had been the goal of a number of diverse organisations, from the trade unions to the Fabian Society, which found voice through writers like George Bernard Shaw and Sidney and Beatrice Webb.[4] The Education Acts of the 1880s ensured that every individual had access to elementary education and the majority of the population became literate for the first time.

The Women's Movement too, had been growing since the middle of the

---

[2] The history and circumstances surrounding the outbreak of the Great War have been discussed in many books. See for example: J. M. Winter, *The Experience of World War* (London: Guild, 1988); J. M. Winter, *Sites of Memory Sites of Mourning: The Great War in European Cultural History* (Cambridge: Cambridge University Press, 1995); J. M. Bourne, *Britain and the Great War 1914–1918* (London: Edward Arnold, 1989); Stephen Constantine et al., eds, *The First World War in British History* (London: Edward Arnold, 1995); James Joll, *The Origins of the First World War*, (Harlow: Longman, 1984); A. J. P Taylor, *English History 1914–1945* (Oxford: Clarendon Press, 1965); Trevor Wilson, *The Myriad Faces of War: Britain and the Great War 1914–1918* (Cambridge: Polity, 1986); Niall Ferguson, *The Pity of War* (London: Penguin, 1998).

[3] This myth of a golden age is perpetuated in Paul Fussell, *The Great War and Modern Memory* (Oxford: Oxford University Press, 1977). For a good account of its demolition see Samuel Hynes, *A War Imagined* (London: The Bodley Head, 1990).

[4] The Fabian Society was a socialist society which began in the 1880s as the Fellowship of the New Life. Among its prominent members were G. B. Shaw and Sidney and Beatrice Webb. For more information see Samuel Hynes *The Edwardian Turn of Mind* (Princeton: Princeton University Press, 1968).

nineteenth century. By 1900 Britain could boast a large number of independent suffrage societies all campaigning for the same thing: votes for women. In 1897 many of these small societies had amalgamated to form the National Union of Women's Suffrage Societies (NUWSS) under the leadership of Millicent Fawcett, giving the movement the potential for much greater impact. But the governments of the new century had greater cause for concern over the alternative branch of the women's movement, the Women's Social and Political Union (WSPU), led by the Pankhursts, which advocated acts of terrorism as a means to obtain its goals. Although only a small percentage of women campaigners were suffragettes rather than the less belligerent suffragists, the WSPU was capable of causing considerable disruption and had brought the Woman Question to the forefront of British politics.[5]

Although the women campaigners had not yet managed to obtain the vote, the position of women in society had begun to change. Increasingly women were able to gain access to a university education, and, as a result, some of the professions had opened their doors to women in the later years of the nineteenth century. Significantly, in terms of the Great War, the medical profession became a pioneering institution for the advancement of women, with the first British woman doctor, Elizabeth Garrett, added to the British Medical Register in 1869. By 1914 there were enough women doctors to make a significant impact on the care of the wounded throughout Europe, as well as thousands of career nurses who could be called upon during the crisis.

For most women, however, life in 1914 was not very different from the lives their mothers led. Few middle-class or upper-class women expected to work, and marriage was the goal. For many of these women the War provided the opportunity to become involved in a completely different world as they took on the variety of jobs, all voluntary and unpaid, which were deemed appropriate for respectable young ladies. The reality was often a far cry from the appropriate, as shy and protected Edwardian women came face to face with the horrors of the battlefield as Voluntary

---

[5] Members of the NUWSS are referred to as suffragists. This distinguishes them from their much more militant sisters, the suffragettes, members of the WSPU, who were prepared to employ more physical or violent tactics to ensure that their message was heard. For further information on the women's suffrage movement see: Sandra Stanley Holton, *Feminism and Democracy: Women's Suffrage and Reform Politics in Britain 1900–1918* (Cambridge: Cambridge University Press, 1986); Jill Liddington and Jill Norris, *One Hand Tied Behind Us: The Rise of the Women's Suffrage Movement* (London: Virago, 1978); Ray Strachey, *The Cause* (London: Virago, 1989) (first published 1928); Martin Pugh, *Women and the Women's Movement in Britain 1914–1959* (Basingstoke: Macmillan, 1992).

Aid Detachment (VAD) nurses in hospitals and as ambulance drivers in the First Aid Nursing Yeomanry (FANY)[6]

For working-class women the most common course of action before the War was to go into service, although in some areas industry already employed women in high numbers. For many of these women the War provided different opportunities. In 1915 Emmeline and Christabel Pankhurst, working in conjunction with Lloyd George, led a campaign to enable women to work in munitions factories. Although there was a crisis in the munitions industry, with supply unable to meet demand due to a depleted workforce, the work was deemed too dangerous for women. The War, and the pressure applied through activities like the Great Procession of Women or the Right to Serve March, which took place on 15 July 1917, forced the government to reconsider. With the opening of this, and other industries involved in the production of wartime materials, to a female workforce, working-class women were able to earn more money than ever before; much more than they could in service. At the same time services like the Women's Army Auxiliary Corps (WAAC), which dealt with many of the army's more domestic responsibilities, offered another alternative kind of well-paid work.[7]

Many other working-class women took over their husbands' jobs when they enlisted. Others filled the vacancies left by men in public service industries, on trams and buses, or working on the land.[8] The departure of many thousands of men from their traditional roles, and their replacement by women, added to the general psychology of confusion which the War introduced to society. Nothing was permanent any more, nothing predictable. Many of the rules of gender around which that society had been constructed were being bent and broken. Women chose or were forced, in many instances for the first time, to leave their homes and enter the world of men, and it was bound to offer them a very different taste of life.

---

[6] The Voluntary Aid Detachment was formed in 1909 to fill 'gaps' in the service provided by existing territorial forces, such as 'clearing hospitals and transports facilities'. For more information see Anne Summers, *Angels and Citizens* (London: Routledge, 1988). The First Aid Nursing Yeomanry was formed in 1914. For more information see Summers, *Angels and Citizens*.

[7] The Women's Army Auxiliary Corps was formed in 1917 to provide overseas workers to perform many support tasks for the army. For more information see Arthur Marwick *Women at War 1914–1918* (London: Fontana, 1977).

[8] For further information on the history of women's changing roles during the Great War see Gail Braybon and Penny Summerfield, *Out of the Cage: Women's Experiences in Two World Wars* (London: Pandora, 1987); Marwick, *Women at War*.

The Great War changed the lives of thousands of women. We know this not only because we can see the facts and figures presented by history books, but because they themselves chose to write about it, to record their responses to such cathartic experience. There could be many explanations for the need to do this, and they vary according to the type of writing adopted by an individual.

This anthology contains a diverse range of material. It is quite unorthodox in that I have chosen to position extracts from fictional writings alongside documentary texts and more personal pieces taken from women's private diaries and letters. This presents multiple motives for writing as well as multiple types of text. I have structured the anthology in this way for a number of reasons, not the least of which is that by limiting it to one specific type of writing I would reduce the opportunity to present the widest possible field of experience. At the same time, the boundaries between fiction and non-fiction are very difficult to define in war writing. Most of the famous men's war texts are based on very personal experience, but not all claim to be direct autobiography. Similarly, Irene Rathbone's 1932 novel *We That Were Young* is based directly on her own war experiences, some of which are recorded in detail in her diaries, now held in the Imperial War Museum archive. But it also incorporates the experiences of her friends, and explores issues such as sexuality which remained out of bounds for the younger Rathbone. Autobiography itself, a form adopted by many war writers, is a much debated genre. Many autobiographical theorists doubt that it is possible to write an objective, 'factual' life story because of the ambiguities of memory and point of view.[9]

In addition, many of the documentary texts included here are written with a specific audience or message in mind and may be coloured accordingly. Both May Sinclair and Mrs Humphry Ward were signatories of C. F. G. Masterman's 'Author's Manifesto' in which they pledged to support the war through their writing.[10] Mrs Humphry Ward's propaganda book

---

[9] For further discussion of autobiography theory, specifically women's autobiography, see: Shari Benstock, ed., *The Private Self: Theory and Practice of Women's Autobiographical Writings* (London: Routledge, 1988); Estelle Jelinek, *Women's Autobiography* (Bloomington and Indianapolis: Indiana University Press, 1980); Sidonie Smith, *The Poetics of Women's Autobiography: Marginality and the Fictions of Self-representation* (Bloomington and Indianapolis: Indiana University Press, 1987); Liz Stanley, *The Auto/biographical I* (Manchester: Manchester University Press, 1992).

[10] C. F. G. Masterman was head of the War Propaganda Bureau. He enlisted a number of literary figures to help in the production of propagandist material, all of whom signed the 'Author's Manifesto' which appeared in the *New York Times* on 18 September 1914. For further details see, Peter Buitenhuis, *The Great War of Words: Literature as Propaganda 1914–18 and After* (London: Batsford, 1987).

England's Effort (1916) takes the form of a series of letters to 'an American friend', Theodore Roosevelt, and was designed to illustrate the war for the American people. The USA was still a neutral nation at the time of the book's publication. While the images she presents are clearly not fiction, it is apparent that they give only one side of the story.

May Sinclair's *A Journal of Impressions in Belgium* (1915) is based on her experience as secretary and publicist to a motor ambulance corps. Sinclair was not a successful member of the team and was sent home after only seventeen days. There is an emotion and a romanticism about her journal which does not reflect this. Indeed it seems to be based on the way Sinclair wishes the War to be, rather than on actual 'truth'. Sinclair very much wanted to experience the 'glory' of a War in which she believed, and this noticeably influences her depiction of events in Belgium.[11]

Many professional women writers adopted the War as a subject for their work, presenting a wide variety of social and political viewpoints. From the propagandist ideas of Mrs Humphry Ward to the pacifist writing of E. Sylvia Pankhurst, from the good social advice of Ernestine Mills to the front line experience of Flora Sandes and the political fiction of A. T. Fitzroy, the war presents women with many different slates to write upon. Published autobiographical records, essays and fiction all play a large part in creating a written collage of the war from the point of view of women, and indeed fiction, despite its 'imaginary' status, is often the most influential type of writing, reaching the widest audience. I would therefore argue that the contemporary fictional presentations of the war reproduced in this anthology provide an important part of the overall picture. They supply many of the images which had a lasting impact and were, at the time, available to all. By placing the different genres in context with each other, we can make our own judgements about 'truth' and 'impression' from the multi-layered evocation of experience which is produced.

Often war fiction carried as strong a political message as the documentary writing which was overtly designed as propaganda. May Sinclair's *The Tree of Heaven* (1917) is fiercely patriotic, echoing her Masterman associations, while Mary Agnes Hamilton's *Dead Yesterday* (1916) is distinctly pacifist in outlook. Rose Allatini, writing under the pseudonym A. T. Fitzroy, produced *Despised and Rejected* in 1918 as an

---

[11] For further information see Suzanne Raitt, 'Contagious Ecstasy: May Sinclair's War Journals' in Suzanne Raitt and Trudi Tate, eds, *Women's Fiction and the Great War* (Oxford: Clarendon Press, 1997). Also Raitt's forthcoming biography of Sinclair, to be published by Oxford University Press.

attack on the conscription law, but it also emphasised the plight of minority groups or causes in society: homosexuals, Jews, the Irish. The novel was banned shortly after its publication as it was found to be in breach of the Defence of the Realm Act.

Other texts, some fictional, others not, seem intent on capturing the experience for the benefit of future generations. Enid Bagnold's *A Diary Without Dates*, published in 1918, is in part, a record of her own working life at the Royal Herbert Hospital at Woolwich, but the generic tone of the narrative does more to illustrate the atmosphere of the hospital and cause the reader to empathise with the wounded who are forced to inhabit it. Bagnold also asked her mother to keep all the letters she wrote home from France where she worked after the war as a FANY driver, chauffeuring army officials across the abandoned battlefields in 1919. These letters became the basis for her 1920 novel *The Happy Foreigner*, which attempts to present an idea of the rebirth of hope in the wasteland of the aftermath. Mary Borden's written fragments, three of which are included here, come from *The Forbidden Zone* published in 1929. Each one is an attempt to capture with words a moment, an emotion, an experience unique to the Great War. The influence of modernism is clear in her style, which conveys these sentiments effectively, giving us, the future readers, a picture postcard of the war itself.[12]

In addition to more established writers I have also drawn on the works of private individuals. Archives around the country such as those in the Imperial War Museum and the Liddle Collection held at the University of Leeds contain a wealth of material, in the form of women's memoirs, diaries and collections of letters which deal with all aspects of the experience of war, and give unique insights into the way women used that experience to influence their writing. It is clear that a great many 'ordinary' women[13] felt the need to record their personal view of the war as they lived it. I have tried to select a variety of women, whose experiences are varied and interesting, drawn from as many walks of life as possible. Despite the fact that most women were literate by the time of the Great War, it is very difficult to find personal writing by working-class women,

---

[12] Mary Borden moved in what later became known as modernist circles in the years before the outbreak of war. She was a friend and patron to Wyndham Lewis. Their relationship developed into an affair in 1915. For further information see Jeffrey Meyers, *The Enemy: A Biography of Wyndham Lewis* (London: Routledge & Kegan Paul, 1980).

[13] Jenny Hartley draws attention to the inaccuracy of the term 'ordinary'. See Introduction, Jenny Hartley, *Hearts Undefeated: Women's Writing of the Second World War* (London: Virago, 1994).

perhaps because of the severe demands on their time.[14] However Emily Chitticks[15] did work, probably in service, and I have included several more unusual women including Mére Marie Georgine,[16] a nun in a Belgian convent, and Phyllis Lunn,[17] a Scarborough schoolgirl.

For many of these women, writing might have provided a much-needed outlet for emotion. 'Give a feeling a form & it will cease to hurt', Irene Rathbone wrote as she tried to exorcise the pain of four years of war. For many, the feeling is almost too hard to express: 'The whole thing is too ghastly to write about', Mary Brown writes as she witnesses the evacuation of Gallipoli, but she says just enough to allow us to fill in some of the gaps ourselves.[18] Generally, however, these women's diaries and letters do not dwell on the sorrow, the loss, the grieving that war brings, even if the emotion is there between the lines.[19] Often it is the excitement of the war which comes across instead; the promise of something different. On 15 June 1915, Ethel Bilborough, a middle-aged civilian of Chislehurst, Kent, began her diary thus:

> This is going to be my war diary. I don't mean that it's to be political, or literary, or anything of that kind, but it will merely be my own personal impressions, and I shan't even touch on the fringe of the vast problem as to what has caused the greatest war that has ever been known in history, or as to what will be likely to terminate it all.
>
> It seems to me that everyone who happens to be alive in such stirring epoch-making times ought to write *something* of what is going on! Just think how interesting it would be to read years hence! When peace once more reigns supreme, and everything has settled down to its usual torpid routine of dullness(!)[20]

As with so many contemporary women's diaries, she trivialises her own perspective. The diary *is* both political and literary, and captures the spark of excitement that she felt at being able to record 'such stirring epoch-

---

[14] For more information regarding working-class women in the Great War see Sharon Ouditt's work in *Fighting Forces, Writing Women* (London: Routledge, 1994) and 'Tommy's Sisters: the Representation of Working Women's Experience', in Hugh Cecil and Peter H. Liddle, eds, *Facing Armageddon* (London: Leo Cooper, 1996).

[15] The correspondence of Emily Chitticks and her fiancé Private William Martin is held in the Imperial War Museum.

[16] Mére Marie Georgine's diary is held in the Imperial War Museum.

[17] Phyllis Lunn's account of the bombing of Scarborough is held in the Liddle Collection, housed in the Brotherton Library at the University of Leeds.

[18] Mary Brown's dairies are held in the Imperial War Museum.

[19] As Jenny Hartley has noted, 'In men's war writing women mourn, but grief seems to be strangely absent from women's war writing' (Hartley, *Hearts Undefeated*: 7).

[20] Ethel Bilborough's diary is held in the Imperial War Museum.

making times'. As Bilborough's dairy continues through the war years, a sense of sadness does begin to emerge, even though she herself never has cause for personal grief. Other emotions are more apparent: anger, fear, exhilaration. It is not clear who she imagines will read her diary as she fills it with thoughts, opinions and ephemera. Luckily for us, it has been preserved so that Mrs Bilborough can at last find the readers she deserves.

This anthology focuses primarily on writing which was published or produced during the years 1914–18. But it also includes a selection of important works published later, which provide further insights to the period and useful points of comparison. Most of the texts included here are out of print; many have been since first publication. Much of this work forms part of the 'missing link' in women's writing between the latter part of the nineteenth century and the 1920s; a link which is now gradually being rediscovered by feminist literary researchers[21] I have included full documents where possible, and otherwise tried to select pieces of fiction or diary/letter entries which will present a self-contained text to the reader. Although the original spelling, capitalisation etc. have been retained, I have corrected a few obvious spelling mistakes.

By presenting this mixture of fiction and non-fiction, it has been possible to document a more representative impression of the Great War as it was lived, worked and fought by women, who are so often excluded from official versions. These fascinating and varied texts have been pieced together to create an overall impression of the experience of war on a scale which seems impossible prior to the twentieth century.

[21] For further information see Claire Tylee, *The Great War and Women's Consciousness* (London: Macmillan, 1990); Sharon Ouditt, *Fighting Forces, Writing Women* (London: Routledge, 1994); Dorothy Goldman, ed., *Women and World War 1: The Written Response* (London: Macmillan, 1993); Raitt and Tate, eds, *Women's Fiction and the Great War* (Oxford: Clarendon Press, 1997).

Part I

THE BEGINNING

As I write a dreadful war-cloud seems about to burst and deluge the peoples of Europe with fire, slaughter, ruin – this then is the World as men have made it, life as men have ordered it. (Christabel Pankhurst, *The Suffragette*, 7 August 1914)

[handwritten margin note: Feminism blaming men]

When the German army invaded Belgium on 3 August 1914, war was inevitable. The crisis in Europe had been deepening since the assassination of the Austro-Hungarian Archduke Franz Ferdinand in Sarajevo on 28 June 1914, but the politics were complicated, and the imminent danger of military conflict remained distant to many people in Britain.[1] Ultimately, however, the invasion of Belgium, a nation without the army or the technology to defend itself against German militarism, pushed the British and French governments to issue an ultimatum and to declare war on Germany.

In Britain the declaration prompted many different responses, ranging from Beatrice Webb's philosophical acceptance to Lady Kate Courtney's clear anguish. For Christabel Pankhurst, still embedded in her own war with the government, the declaration of war meant something completely different; the failure of patriarchal society. Her impassioned piece, written for *The Suffragette* (7 August 1914), in fact addresses the issue of women's subjugation rather than the War itself. In those early days, perhaps before the extent of the danger became clear, the War provided a useful weapon with which to attack male government. As we shall see, within a month Christabel had significantly changed her approach to the War and her public statements to her devoted followers.

---

[1] For details of the politics which led to the outbreak of the First World War see J. M. Winter, *The Experience of World War 1* (London: Guild, 1988); J. M. Bourne, *Britain and the Great War 1914–1918* (London: Edward Arnold, 1989); James Joll, *The Origins of the First World War* (Harlow: Longman, 1984); A. J. P. Taylor, *English History 1914–1945* (Oxford: Clarendon Press, 1965).

Elizabeth von Arnim's presentation of the beginning of the War in Berlin, from *Christine* (1917), presents an impression of a people hungry for war. Christine's letter to her mother describes a rude and ignorant crowd responding to an address from the Kaiser. Christine herself is over-awed by the emotion of the moment and a fear of what it will bring. She excuses the German people, but is alarmed that they are being led into a dreadful situation, manipulated by the Kaiser and his generals. The crowd could so easily become a mob. Later on in the book it does, as Christine, now an enemy alien, struggles to leave the country and rejoin her mother in Britain.

Although Christine does meet some sympathetic Germans (the intel-lectual teacher, the romantic officer), the book acts as an indictment of a people gone sour. The mob mentality is equally apparent in novels which describe the outbreak of war in Britain. The streets of London are star-tlingly similar to the streets of Berlin in May Sinclair's *The Tree of Heaven* (1917). Sinclair's novel is a patriotic one, but there is something sinister about the celebrating crowds seen through the eyes of her pacifist char-acter, Michael Harrison. There is a hint of madness about them, the repeated imagery of the sea suggesting a movement out of control. Later in the novel, Michael rejects his pacifist views and finds fulfilment on the battlefields of Flanders, but these early sections present an ambiguity which is often out of line with the patriotic intention. The same scenes are witnessed by Daphne Leonard and Nigel Strode in Mary Agnes Hamil-ton's *Dead Yesterday* (1916), but from Daphne's unshakably anti-war per-spective they are even more sinister.

The celebration of the outbreak of the War, the enthusiasm felt by so many people, seems astonishing with hindsight. But Britain had not been involved in a major European war since the Crimea in the 1850s and the nation's confidence was high. Those who recorded it seem to have cap-tured the jubilation even if it is tempered by their own reservations, and the weeks that followed the declaration brought horror stories which for many people more than justified the decision to go to war.

By invading Belgium, Germany provided the Allies with a 'propaganda advantage'.[2] The idea of a tiny defenceless country at the mercy of a war machine was much exploited, particularly in the early months of the War, drawing on an already established tradition of the use of atrocity stories

---

[2] See Peter Buitenhuis, *The Great War of Words: Literature as Propaganda 1914–18 and After* (London: B. T. Batsford Ltd, 1987).

in wartime. The newspapers were filled with images of mutilated babies, defiled nuns and general carnage which inspired many people to support the War.[3] Although some of the most powerful campaigns about Belgium took place in 1915, following the Bryce Report, it is difficult to verify many of the stories.[4]

The newspaper stories and the steady flow of Belgian refugees certainly convinced some of the population of the truth of the allegations. Ethel Bilborough wrote in her diary on 15 June 1914: 'The poor brave little Belgium was drawn in, and Germany began to show her poisonous fangs, and the poor Belgians were driven right and left, homeless and destitute, and their homes pillaged and burnt.' The sentiment is echoed by Gertrude Holland, who worked with a ambulance unit in Belgium in the first few months of the war.[5]

But others who were on the spot describe the Belgium experience in different ways. Mère Marie Georgine, a nun in a Belgian convent, saw the German invasion at first hand; indeed, when the convent was adopted by the German army as its headquarters, she became its host. Her diary (written in English) is particularly interesting because it tries to give a very objective representation. While she is clearly concerned for the welfare, even the lives, of the local civilians, the wounded Belgians and the nuns, she is not blind to the fear of the German soldiers themselves, highlighting their insecurity as 'the enemy' in a foreign land. The nun fears the Germans and at the same time feels sorry for them. Rarely are both sides so eloquently put, especially by a virtual prisoner of war.

Mary Borden's opening sketch, 'Belgium', presents a very different perspective. Here is an impersonal landscape of mud and iron, a few bored and despairing soldiers, impotent, drab and broken. Borden coaxes us into the wasteland, 'Come, I'll show you', making us part of the ruin. She appeals to all the senses, showing us how we would see the destruction, hear the distant 'growling' of the war and feel the earth tremble if we were really present. This is Belgium, 'a broken fragment of a nation', waiting without hope for the end of the War. There are no civilians here, no life, only aimless soldiers and an anonymous king. Individuals no longer matter. Belgium barely exists.

---

[3] See Trudi Tate, *Modernism, History and the First World War* (Manchester: Manchester University Press, 1998).

[4] The Report of the Committee on Alleged German Outrages, chaired by Lord Bryce, was published in early 1915 and aimed at influencing American as well as British public opinion. For further information see Buitenhuis, *Great War of Words*.

[5] Gertrude Holland's war memoirs are held in the Imperial War Museum.

May Sinclair's *A Journal of Impressions in Belgium* attempts to convey how this wilderness has been created. Sinclair tells of how she is able to make a rare outing as a war correspondent, following the ambulance on its way to find the wounded. But what is most noticeable about Sinclair's tone is not the way she captures the atmosphere of Belgium but her sense of excitement at being part of a great adventure. She lacks the objectivity of a war correspondent, hinting instead at the reasons why her trip to Belgium was not a success.[6]

But if Sinclair's 'impression' of Belgium differs from those of Borden and Holland and Mère Marie Georgine, the place described by Emily Hobhouse in her article for *The Woman's Dreadnought* (14 October 1916) is quite unrecognisable. *The Woman's Dreadnought* was a pacifist publication produced in the East End from the offices of Sylvia Pankhurst. There could be obvious political reasons why Hobhouse might choose to show a Belgium that was much less war-ravaged than the press would have people believe. It is another type of propaganda. Far from being ruined, Belgium is barely touched, suggesting that there has been a lot of fuss about nothing; catching the patriotic propagandists out.

It is difficult to say which representation, if any, is true. What this selection does show is the prominent place held by 'poor brave little Belgium' in the public imagination. This is further demonstrated by the success of Cicely Hamilton's 1919 novel *William an Englishman* which won the Femme Vie Heureuse prize for that year. The novel tells the story of William Tully and his campaigning feminist wife, Griselda, who are caught in Belgium, where they are honeymooning, at the outset of the War. The events that they witness, including the execution of civilians, and their own experience, specifically Griselda's rape and subsequent death, have a profound effect of William's life. The novel combines many of the images of Belgium recorded here, adding a further dimension through fiction. William struggles with pacifist sentiments which are not adequate when the War enters his life on a personal level. Yet militarism can not be condoned either. The novel presents a number of moral dilemmas which, in some ways, can be embodied in the complex and ambiguous situation of Belgium.

---

[6] See Suzanne Raitt, 'Contagious Ecstasy: May Sinclairs War Journals' in Suzanne Raitt and Trudi Tate, eds, *Women's Fiction and the Great War* (Oxford: Clarendon Press, 1997).

1

The outbreak of war

balance

Christabel Pankhurst
The War

As I write a dreadful war-cloud seems about to burst and deluge the peoples of Europe with fire, slaughter, ruin – this then is the World as men have made it, life as men have ordered it.

A man-made civilisation, hideous and cruel enough in time of peace, is to be destroyed.

A civilisation made by men only is a civilisation which defies the law of nature, which defies the law of right Government.

This great war, whether it comes now, or by some miracle is deferred till later, is Nature's vengeance – is God's vengeance upon people who held women in subjection, and by doing that have destroyed the perfect human balance. Just as when the laws governing the human body are defied we have disease, so when the law of right government is defied – the law that men and women shall co-operate in managing their affairs – we have a civilisation-imperfect, unjust, savage at its best and fore-doomed to destruction.

Had women been equal partners with men from the beginning, human civilisation would have been wholly different from what it is. The whole march of humanity would have been to a point other than we have reached at this moment of horrible calamity.

There are men who have a glimmering idea of something better, but only by the help of women could civilisation have been made other than cruel, predatory, destructive. Only by the help of women as citizens can the World be saved after the holocaust is ended.

In the coming days it is the enfranchised women – for women must and will be enfranchised – who will save the race. For that which has made men for generations past sacrifice women and the race to their lusts

is now making them fly at each other's throats, and bring ruin upon the world.

Women of the W.S.P.U., there will be much suffering for women in this war. The price of war as of all tragedy is mainly paid by women.

Women of the W.S.P.U., we must protect our Union through everything. It has great tasks to perform. It has much to do for the saving of humanity.

Let us in everything strive unceasingly that the World may learn from the tragedy by which it is menaced, that for the sake of the human race, for the sake of the divinity that is in the human race, women must be free.

Elizabeth von Arnim
from
Christine

BERLIN,
Before Breakfast, Sat. Aug. 1st, 1914.

MY BLESSED LITTLE MOTHER,

I've seen a thing I don't suppose I'll forget. It was yesterday, after the news came that Germany had sent Russia an ultimatum about instantly demobilizing, demanding an answer by eleven this morning. The sensation when this was known was tremendous. The Gräfin was shaken out of her calm into an exclamation of joy and fear, – joy that the step had been taken, fear lest Russia should obey, and there be no war after all.

We had to shut the windows to be able to hear ourselves talk. Some women friends of the Gräfin's who were here – we had no men with us – instantly left to drive by back streets to the Schlossplatz to see the sight it must be there, and the Gräfin, saying that we too must witness the greatest history of the world's greatest nation in the making, sent for a taxi – her chauffeur has gone – and prepared to follow. We had to wait ages for the taxi, but it was lucky we had to, else we might have gone and come back and missed seeing the Kaiser come out and speak to the crowd. We went a long way round, but even so all Germany seemed to be streaming towards the Lindens and the part at the end where the palace is. I don't expect we ever would have got there if it hadn't been that a cousin of the Gräfin's, a very smart young officer in the Guards, saw us in the taxi as it was vainly trying to cross the Friedrichstrasse, and flicking the obstructing policemen on one side with a sort of little kick of his spur, came up all amazement and salutes to inquire of his most gracious cousin what in the world she was doing in a taxi. He said it was hopeless to try to get to the Schlossplatz in it, but if we would allow him to escort us on foot he would be proud – the gracious cousin would permit him to offer her his arm, and the young ladies would keep close behind him.

So we set out, and it was surprising the way he got us through. If the crowd didn't fall apart instantly of itself at his approach, an obsequious policeman – one of those same Berlin policemen who are so rude to one if one is alone and really in need of help – sprang up from nowhere and made it. It's as far from the Friedrichstrasse to the Schlossplatz as it is from here to the Friedrichstrasse, but we did it very much quicker than we did the first half in the taxi, and when we reached it there they all were, the drunken crowds – that's the word that most exactly describes them – yelling, swaying, cursing the ones in their way or who trod on their feet, shouting hurrahs and bits of patriotic songs, every one of them decently dressed, obviously respectable people in ordinary times. That's what is so constantly strange to me, – these solid burghers and their families behaving like drunken hooligans. Somehow a spectacled professor with a golden chain across his black waistcoated and impressive front, just roaring incoherently, just opening his mouth and hurling any sort of noise out of it till the veins on his neck and forehead look as though they would burst, is the strangest sight in the world to me. I can imagine nothing stranger, nothing that makes one more uncomfortable and ashamed. It is what will always jump up before my eyes in the future at the words German patriotism. And to see a stout elderly lady, who ought to be presiding with slow dignity in some ordered home, hoarse with shouting, tear the feathered hat she otherwise only uses tenderly on Sundays off her respectable grey head and wave it frantically, screaming *hochs* every time a prince is seen or a general or one of the ministers, makes one want to cry with shame at the indignity put upon poor human beings, at the exploiting passions, in the interests of one family.

The Gräfin's smart cousin got us to some steps and stood with us, so that we should not be pushed off them instantly again, as we would have been if he had left us. I think they were the steps of a statue, or fountain, or something like that, but the whole of whatever it was was so covered with people, encrusted with them just like one of those fly-sticks is black with flies, that I don't know what it was really. I only know that it wasn't a house, and that we were quite close to the palace, and able to look down at the sea beneath us, the heaving roaring sea of distorted red face, all their mouths wide open, all blistering and streaming in the sun.

The Gräfin, who had recovered her calm in the presence of her inferiors of the middle classes, put up her eyeglasses and examined them with interest and indulgence. Helena stared. The cousin twisted his little moustache, standing beside us protectingly, very elegant and slender and nonchalant, and remarked at intervals, '*Fabelhafte Enthusiasmus, was?*'

It came into my mind that Beerbohm Tree must sometimes look on like that at a successful dress rehearsal of his well-managed stage crowds, with the same nonchalant satisfaction at the excellent results, so well up to time, of careful preparation.

Of course I said '*Colossal*' to the cousin, when he expressed his satisfaction more particularly to me.

'*Dreckiges Volk, die Russen,*' he remarked, twisting his little moustache's ends up. '*Werden lernen was es heisst, frech sein gegen uns. Wollen sie blau und schwartz dreschen.*'

You know German, so I needn't take its peculiar flavour out by transplanting the young man's remarks.

'*Oh pardon – aber meine Gnädigste – tausendmal pardon –*' he protested the next minute in a voice of tremendous solicitude, having been pushed rather hard and suddenly against me by a little boy who had scrambled down off whatever it was he was hanging on to; and he turned on the little boy, who I believe had tumbled off rather than scrambled, with his hand flashing to his sword, ready to slash at whoever it was had dared push against him, an officer; and seeing it was a child and therefore not *satisfactionsfahig* as they say, he merely called him *infame* and *verfluchte Bengel* and smacked his face so hard that he would have been knocked down if there had been room to fall in.

As it was, he was only hurled violently against the side of a man in a black coat and straw hat who looked like an elderly confidential clerk, so respectable and complete with his short grey beard and spectacles, who was evidently the father, for he instantly on his own account smacked the boy on his other ear, and sweeping off his hat entreated the Herr Lieutenant to forgive the boy on account of his extreme youth.

The cousin, whom by now I didn't like, was beginning very severely to advise the parent jolly well to see to it, or German words to that effect, that his idiot boy didn't repeat such insolence, or by hell, etc., etc., when there was such a blast of extra noise and hurrahing that the rest of his remarks were knocked out of his mouth. It was the Kaiser, come out on the balcony of the palace.

The cousin became rigid, and stood at the salute. The air seemed full of hats and handkerchiefs and delirious shrieking. The Kaiser put up his hand.

'Majestät is going to speak,' exclaimed the Gräfin, her calm fluttered into fragments.

There was an immense instantaneous hush, uncanny after all the noise. Only the little boy with the boxed ears continued to call out, but not patriotically. His father, efficient and Prussian, put a stop to that by seizing his head, buttoning it up inside his black coat, and holding his arm tightly over it, so that no struggles of suffocation could get free. There was no more noise, but the little boy's legs, desperately twitching, kicked their dusty little boots against the cousin's shins, and he, standing at the salute with his body rigidly turned towards Majestät, was unable to take the steps his outraged honour, let alone the pain in his shins, called for.

I was so much interested in this situation, really absorbed by it, for the little boy unconsciously was getting quite a lot of his own back, his little boots being sturdy and studded with nails, and the father, all eyes and ears for Majestät, not aware of what was happening, that positively I missed the first part of the speech. But what I did hear was immensely impressive. I had seen the Kaiser before, you remember; that time he was in London with the Kaiserin, in 1912 or 1913 I think it was, and we were staying with Aunt Angela in Wilton Crescent and we saw him driving one afternoon in a barouche down Birdcage Walk. Do you remember how cross he looked, hardly returning the salutations he got? We said he and she must have been quarrelling, he looked sulky. And do you remember how ordinary he looked in his top hat and black coat, just like any cross and bored middle-class husband? There was nothing royal about him that day except the liveries on the servants, and they were England's. Yesterday things were very different. He really did look like a royal prince out of a picture book, a real War Lord, – impressive and glittering with orders flashing in the sun. We were near enough to see him perfectly. There wasn't much crossness or boredom about him this time. He was, I am certain, thoroughly enjoying himself, – unconsciously of course, but with that immense thrilled enjoyment all leading figures at leading moments must have: Sir Galahad, humbly glorying in his perfect achievement of negations; Parsifal, engulfed in an ecstasy of humble gloating over his own worthiness as he holds up the Grail high above bowed adoring heads; Beerbohm Tree – I can't get away from theatrical analogies – coming before the curtain on his most successful first night, meek with happiness. Hasn't it run through the ages, this great humility at the moment of supreme success, this moved self-depreciation of the man who has pulled it off, the 'Not unto us, O Lord, not unto us' attitude, – quite genuine at the moment, and because quite genuine so extraordinarily moving and impressive? Really one couldn't wonder at the people. The Empress was there, and a lot of officers and princes and people, but it was the Emperor alone that we looked at. He came and stood by himself in front of the others, He was very grave, with a real look of solemn exaltation. Here was royalty in all its most impressive trappings, a prince of the fairy-tales, splendidly dressed, dilated of nostril, flashing of eye, the defender of homes, the leader to glory, the object of the nation's worship and belief and prayers since each of its member was a baby, become visible and audible to thousands who had never seen him before, who worshipped him by faith only. It was as though the people were suddenly allowed to look upon God. There was a profound awe in the hush. I believe if they hadn't been so tightly packed together they would all have knelt down.

Well, it is easy to stir a mob. One knows how easily one is moved oneself by the cheapest emotions, by something that catches one on the sentimental side, on that side of one that through all the years has still stayed clinging to one's mother's knee. We've often talked of this, you and I, little mother. You know the sort of thing, and have got that side yourself, – even you, you dear objective one. The three things up to now that have got to me most on that side, got me on the very raw of it – I'll tell you now, now that I can't see your amused eyes looking at me with that little quizzical questioning in them – the three things that have broken my heart each time I've come across them and made me only want to sob and sob, are when Kurwenal, mortally wounded, crawls blindly to Tristan's side and says, '*Schilt mich nicht dass der Treue auch mitkommt,*' and Siegfried's dying '*Brunhild, heilige Braut,*' and Tannhäuser's dying '*Heilige Elisabeth, bitte fur mich.*' All three German things, you see. All morbid things. Most of the sentimentality seems to have come from Germany, an essentially brutal place. But of course sentimentality is really diluted morbidness, and therefore first cousin to cruelty. And I have a real and healthy dislike for that Tannhäuser opera.

But seeing how the best of us – which is you – have these little hidden swamps of emotionalness, you can imagine the effect of the Kaiser yesterday at such a moment in their lives on a people whose swamps are carefully cultivated by their politicians. Even I, rebellious and hostile to the whole attitude, sure that the real motives beneath all this are base, and constitutionally unable to care about Kaisers, was thrilled. Thrilled by him, I mean. Oh, there was enough to thrill one legitimately and tragically about the poor people, so eager to offer themselves, their souls and bodies, to be an unreasonable sacrifice and satisfaction for the Hohenzollerns. His speech was wonderfully suited to the occasion. Of course it would be. If he were not able to prepare it himself his officials would have seen to it that some properly eloquent person did it for him; but Kloster says he speaks really well on cheap, popular lines. All the great reverberating words were in it, the old big words ambitious and greedy rulers have conjured with since time began, – Wives, Little Ones, God again – lots of God.

Perhaps you'll see the speech in the papers. What you won't see is that enormous crowd, struck quiet, struck into religious awe, crying quietly, men and women like little children gathered to the feet of, positively, a heavenly Father. 'Go to your homes,' he said, dismissing them at the end with uplifted hand, – 'go to your homes and pray.'

And we went. In dead silence. That immense crowd. Quietly, like people going out of church; moved, like people coming away from communion. I walked beside Helena, who was crying, with my head very high and my chin in the air, trying not to cry too, for then they would have been more than ever persuaded that I'm a promising little German, but I did desperately want to. I could hardly *not* cry. These cheated people! Exploited and cheated, led carefully step by step from babyhood to a certain habit of mind necessary to their exploiters, with certain passions carefully developed and encouraged, certain ancient ideas, anachronisms every one of them, kept continually before their eyes, – why, if they *did* win their murderous attack on nations who have done nothing to them, what are they going to get individually? Just wind; the empty wind of big words. They'll be told, and they'll read it in the newspapers, that now they're great, the mightiest people in the world, the one best able to crush and grind other nations. But not a single happiness *really* will be added to the private life of a single citizen belonging to the vast class that pays the bill. For the rest of their lives this generation will be poorer and sadder, that's all. Nobody will give them back the money they have sacrificed, or the ruined businesses, and nobody can give them back their dead sons. There'll be troops of old miserable women everywhere, who were young and content before all the glory set in, and troops of dreary old men who once had children, and troops of cripples who used to look forward and hope. Yes, I too obeyed the Kaiser and went home and prayed; but what I prayed was that Germany should be beaten – so beaten, so punished for this tremendous crime, that she will be jerked by main force into line with modern life, dragged up to date, taught that the world is too grown up now to put up with the smashings and destructions of a greedy and brutal child. It is queer to think of the fear of God having to be kicked into anybody, but I believe with Prussians it's the only way. They understand kicks. They respect brute strength exercised brutally. I can hear their roar of derision, if Christ were to come among them to-day with His gentle, 'Little children, love one another.'

YOUR CHRIS

Beatrice Webb

A Strange London on Sunday

August 5th, – It was a strange London on Sunday: crowded with excursionists to London and baulked would-be travellers to the continent, all in a state of suppressed uneasiness and excitement. We sauntered through the crowd to Trafalgar Square where Labour, Socialist, pacifist demonstrators – with a few Trade Union flags – were gesticulating from the steps of the monuments to a mixed crowd of admirers, hooligan war-mongers and merely curious holiday-makers. It was an undignified and futile exhibition, this singing of the Red Flag and passing of well-worn radical resolutions in favour of universal peace. We turned into the National Liberal Club: the lobby was crowded with men, all silent and perturbed. Sidney went up into the smoking room and brought down Massingham and Hammond. Both these men were bitter and depressed. We argued with them that if Belgian neutrality was defied we had to go to war – they vehemently denied it. On Monday the public mind was cleared and solidified by Grey's speech. Even staunch Liberals agree that we had to stand by Belgium. But there is no enthusiasm about the war: at present it is, on the part of England, a passionless war; a terrible nightmare sweeping over all classes – no one able to realise how the disaster came about.

The closing of the Bank for four days and the paralysis of business (no one seems to know whether the closing is limited to banks and many businesses have stopped because there is no money to pay wages) gives the business quarters of London a dispirited air. Every train that steams out of London, every cart in the street, is assumed to be commandeered by the Government for the purposes of war. Omnibuses and taxi-cabs are getting sparse. There is strained solemnity on every face – no one has the remotest idea of what is going to happen now that we are actually at war with Germany. Personally I have an un-comfortable conviction that Germany is terribly efficient – overpoweringly efficient in its army. As for its navy, who knows what will prove to be the winning factor in strategy or arms? And there is complete uncertainty as to what is the ultimate issue before the civilised world. To the Englishman of to-day it seems the survival of France, Belgium and Holland. To the Englishman of to-morrow it may seem a mistaken backing up of the Slav against the Teuton. Even if we realise that the mistake was due to the unbearable insolence of the Prussian autocracy, we may live to regret it. If we are beaten at sea as well as the French on land it will mean compulsory military service and a long submission to discipline. The 'Servile State' will be on us as vengeance for our past disorder – the 'Webbs' won't be in it figuratively, I mean – actually they may be helping to run it. There never has been a war in which the issues are so blurred and indistinct – we English, at any rate, are quite uncertain who ought to win from the standpoint of the world's freedom and man's spiritual development. The best result would be that every nation should be soundly beaten and no one victorious. That might bring us all to reason.

August 6th, – It is difficult not to feel distracted with depression and anxiety. There is still no enthusiasm for the war but a good deal of quiet determination: even such pacifists as the Courtneys agreeing that we had to stand by Belgium. If this little race had not been attacked the war would have been positively unpopular – it could hardly have taken place. The Government have played a bold hand, far more radically collectivist than we could have hoped for. The retirement of John Burns (no one notices Lord Morley's resignation) from the Government and of J. R. MacDonald from the Chairmanship of the Labour Party are both desirable events. Sidney is busy devising plans for increasing employment during the war. If only we could hear of a decisive naval victory, we could settle back to our work.

The *Statesman's* financial position, with no advertisements, the rising price of paper, is serious. The young men are naturally intent on keeping alive their source of livelihood, but our four available capitalists are not likely to want to pay up. The Fabian Research Department and the new offices of the Fabian Society are commitments, and even the Shaw course of lectures are a big speculation.

Lady Kate Courtney
A Terrible Week

August 9th 1914.

A terrible week – and it has come. On August 3rd, Bank Holiday, news papers, which were very late at Parmoor, brought us and Alfred up to London too late to hear Grey's statement in Commons. A fateful statement – well made and so convincing to most Lib. and Lab. opponents of war that only a few remained to raise any questions whatever. 'A united front!' 'All parties – all men!'

Lord Crewe declined to make any statement in Lords, simply referring to Grey. L[eonard]. raised a voice against being committed to a policy without having a statement of it and of the reasons. There was a hubbub at first, and L. stood facing a hostile House, while I noticed Lord Morley sat looking utterly depressed, with his head bent down, I thought in disapproval of his friend. L. persisted, and finally got his one sentence out. It was an ordeal, and made me anxious. Came away very sad.

Tuesday morning Graham Wells called on behalf of a quickly got up Neutrality Committee to ask L.'s help. L. dictated an appeal to go to Grey and the press. This went with his and Bryce's signatures first, and others followed, many M.P.'s coming in after it was obviously too late. The proposed German violation of Belgian neutrality was the rock on which all the anti-war feeling shipwrecked. That we could not stand, and I shared that feeling, but hoped – no German soldier yet in Belgium.

But Grey had sent an ultimatum to Germany expiring midnight, Tuesday. Huge crowds stayed up to hear result, and about 2.30 Wednesday morning I heard parties passing our house singing patriotic songs, and my hopes grew faint. Sure enough we had declared war, and now further action for peace is hopeless for a season.

Stephen Hobhouse appears to have gone out and got somewhat knocked about. The streets are full of crowds – not mafficking badly – on the whole serious. All the peace papers, even 'Manchester Guardian,' sorrowfully admit war must come, and Belgium is an excuse, if not a good and sufficient reason.

Still names keep coming in to L's protest!! Basil Williams had come on that Tuesday to the Lords to act sort of Sec. We had tea – Lord Farrer joined us and Lord Shuttleworth.

Resignation Morley, John Burns and C. P. Trevelyan. The latter two are unexpectedly fine – both so much to lose. J.B. may again be a leader of working people.

Banks closed. Some anxiety as to money and food until Government measures had reassured people. Anxiety too about Mary Meinertzhagen in the Caucasus. No news for three weeks – probably only delays and stoppages by post.

Friday afternoon – a great revulsion of feeling about Grey's negotiation. White paper comes out, and Aneurin Williams calls to point out a despatch of last Saturday to Goschen at Berlin as enclosed. A terrible revelation – too late – concealed absolutely from the Commons in Monday's statement, and yet what a difference the knowledge of it would have made. So we might have had peace – safeguarding Belgium and French coast towns and possibly more – all we openly avowed asking for. Grey must have been bent on war, but realised that public opinion here must think it was for Belgium. Meanwhile Belgium has done wonders in defending Liege, and inflicting great loss on Germans who entered Belgium on the 4th. Apparent failure all along the line of German force. But the events of the war will be fully noted.

May Sinclair
from
The Tree of Heaven

An immense restlessness came over them.

At a quarter-past eight Dorothy telephoned from her club in Grafton Street. Frank had had to leave her suddenly. Somebody had sent for him. And if they wanted to see the sight of their lives they were to come into town at once. St. James's was packed with people from Whitehall to Buckingham Palace. It was like nothing on earth, and they mustn't miss it. She'd wait for them in Grafton Street till a quarter to nine, but not a minute later.

Nicky got out his big four-seater Morss car. They packed themselves into it, all six of them somehow, and he drove them into London. They had a sense of doing something strange and memorable and historic.

Dorothy, picked up at her club, showed nothing but a pleasurable excitement. She gave no further information about Frank. He had had to go off and see somebody. What did he think? He thought what he had always thought; only he wouldn't talk about it.

Dorothy was not inclined to talk about it either.

The Morss was caught in a line blocked at the bottom of Albemarle Street by two streams of cars, mixed with two streams of foot passengers, that poured steadily from Piccadilly into St. James's Street.

Michael and Dorothy got out and walked. Nicholas gave up his place to Anthony and followed with Veronica.

Their restlessness had been a part of the immense restlessness of the crowd. They were drawn, as the crowd was drawn; they went as the crowd went, up and down, restlessly, from Trafalgar Square and Whitehall to Buckingham Palace; from Buckingham Palace to Whitehall and Trafalgar Square. They drifted down Parliament Street to Westminster and back again. An hour ago the drifting, nebulous crowd had split, torn asunder between two attractions; its two masses had wheeled away, one to the east and the other to the west; they had gathered themselves together, one at each pole of the space it now traversed. The great meeting in Trafalgar Square balanced the multitude that had gravitated towards Buckingham Palace, to see the King and Queen come out on their balcony and show themselves to their people.

And as the edges of the two masses gave way, each broke and scattered, and was mixed again with the other. Like a flood, confined and shaken, it surged and was driven back and surged again from Whitehall to Buckingham Palace, from Buckingham Palace to Whitehall. It looked for an outlet in the narrow channels of the side-streets or spread itself over the flats of the Green Park, only to return restlessly upon itself, sucked back by the main current in the Mall.

It was as if half London had met there for Bank Holiday. Part of this crowd was drunk; it was orgiastic; it made strange, fierce noises, like the noises of one enormous, mystically excited beast; here and there, men and women, with inflamed and drunken faces, reeled in each other's arms; they wore pink paper feathers in their hats. Some, only half intoxicated, flicked at each other with long streamers of pink and white paper, carried like scourges on small sticks. These were the inspired.

But the great body of the crowd was sober. It went decorously in a long procession, young men with their sweethearts, friends, brothers and sisters, husbands and wives, fathers and mothers with their children; none, or very few, went alone that night.

It was an endless procession of faces; grave and thoughtful faces; uninterested, respectable faces; faces of unmoved integrity; excited faces;

dreaming, wondering, bewildered faces; faces merely curious, or curiously exalted, slightly ecstatic, open-mouthed fascinated by each other and by the movements and the lights; laughing, frivolous faces, and faces utterly vacant and unseeing.

On every other breast there was a small Union Jack pinned; every other hand held and waggled a Union Jack. The Union Jack flew from the engine of every other automobile. In twelve hours, out of nowhere, thousands and thousands of flags sprang magically into being; as if for years London had been preparing for this day.

And in and out of this crowd the train of automobiles with their flags dashed up and down the Mall for hours, appearing and disappearing. Intoxicated youths with inflamed faces, in full evening dress, squatted on the roofs of taxi-cabs or rode astride on the engines of their cars, waving flags.

All this movement, drunken orgiastic, somnambulistic, mysteriously restless, streamed up and down between two solemn and processional lines of lights, two solemn and processional lines of trees, lines that stretched straight from Whitehall to Buckingham Palace in a recurrent pattern of trees and lamps, dark trees, twilit trees, a lamp and a tree shining with a metallic unnatural green; and, at the end of the avenue gilded gates and a golden-white façade.

The crowd was drifting now towards the Palace. Michael and Dorothea, Nicholas and Veronica, went with it. In this eternal perambulation they met people that they knew; Stephen and Vera; Mitchell, Monier-Owen; Uncle Morrie and his sisters. Anthony, looking rather solemn, drove past them in his car. It was like impossible, grotesque encounters in a dream.

Outside the Palace the crowd moved up and down without rest; it drifted and returned; it circled round and round the fountain. In the open spaces the intoxicated motor-cars and taxi-cabs darted and tore with the folly of moths and the fury of destroyers. They stung the air with their hooting. Flags, intoxicated flags, still hung from their engines. They came flying drunkenly out of the dark, like a trumpeting swarm of enormous insects, irresistibly, incessantly drawn to the lights of the Palace, hypnotised by the golden-white façade.

Suddenly, Michael's soul revolted.

'If this demented herd of swine is a great people going into a great war, God help us! Beasts – it's not as if *their* bloated skins were likely to be punctured.'

He called back over his shoulders to the others.

'Let's get out of this. If we don't I shall be sick.'

He took Dorothy by her arm and shouldered his way out.

The water had ceased playing in the fountain.

Nicholas and Veronica stood by the fountain. The water in the basin was green like foul sea-water. The jetsam of the crowd floated there. A small child leaned over the edge of the basin and fished for Union Jacks in the filthy pool. Its young mother held it safe by the tilted edge of its petticoats. She looked up at them and smiled. They smiled back again and turned away.

It was quiet on the south side by the Barracks. Small, sober groups of twos and threes strolled there, or stood with their faces pressed close against the railings, peering into the barrack yard. Motionless, earnest and attentive, they stared at the men in khaki moving about on the other side of the railings. They were silent, fascinated by the men in khaki. Standing safe behind the railing, they stared at them with an awful sombre curiosity. And the men in khaki stared back, proud, self-conscious, as men who know that the hour is great and that it is their hour.

'Nicky,' Veronica said, 'I wish Michael wouldn't say things like that.'

'He's dead right, Ronny. That isn't the way to take it, getting drunk and excited, and rushing about making silly asses of themselves. They *are* rather swine, you know.'

'Yes; but they're pathetic. Can't you see how pathetic they are? Nicky, I believe I love the swine – even the poor drunken ones with the pink paper feathers – just because they're English; because awful things are going to happen to them, and they don't know it. They're English.'

'You think God's made us all like that? He *hasn't*.'

They found Anthony in the Mall, driving up and down, looking for them. He had picked up Dorothy and Aunt Emmeline and Uncle Morrie.

'We're going down to the Mansion House,' he said, 'to hear the Proclamation. Will you come?'

But Veronica and Nicholas were tired of crowds, even of historic crowds. Anthony drove off with his carload, and they went home.

'I never saw Daddy so excited,' Nicky said.

But Anthony was not excited. He had never felt calmer or cooler in his life.

He returned some time after midnight. By that time it had sunk into him. Germany *had* defied the ultimatum and England *had* declared war on Germany.

He said it was only what was to be foreseen. He had known all the time that it would happen – really.

The tension of the day of the ultimatum had this peculiar psychological effect that all over England people who had declared up to the last minute that there would be no War were saying the same thing as Anthony and believing it.

Mary Agnes Hamilton
from
Dead Yesterday

They passed out of the station into the street, crowded with jostling people, full of hurrying traffic. On the pavement as they emerged lay posters of the evening papers, and a row of boys held damp copies, snatched from them by the people as they streamed by. On each poster – yellow, green, white, pink – were the same words filling the space with all the emphasis of the three repeated lines of heavy leaded capitals – 'England's Ultimatum to Germany.' Daphne stared at them, the letters dancing before her eyes. The mist cleared, but it was no dream. On each the same – 'England's Ultimatum to Germany.'

Nigel had hailed a taxi; but Daphne stood staring, unaware that he was waiting for her with the door held open. The words suddenly made clear to her how little before she had realised. All the time, stunned as she was, unbelief had lived; she had secretly hoped. Even the soldiers in the station had not killed her hope. But there it stared at her, monstrous, real, the truth.

In the taxi Nigel talked, but Daphne hardly took in what he said. She heard, but the words said nothing. For the first time in all her experience she was with Nigel and hardly conscious of him. They emerged from then Strand into the open space of Charing Cross, and it was solid with people: people, packed in, filled the square, sat on the lions and on the base of the column. Up St. Martin's Lane, Pall Mall and Northumberland Avenue it stretched, the unbroken mass, blocking the way. Hundreds and thousands of men and women: a sea of straw hats: waiting. To and fro it swayed, but the movement was on top of, did not break up, the solid mass. Nigel leaned forward, his eyes bright; but Daphne felt suddenly afraid – though the crowd was silent its silence was more alarming than noise. The taxi stopped opposite the station.

'We might as well get out here,' Nigel said. 'We can get across to the

Ship on foot. We'll have something to eat there. You must be very hungry.'

Daphne looked round her while he paid the man. She was not hungry; food seemed absurd. But she was frightened and, suddenly, she thought of her mother and wanted to be at home. She began to murmur something of this, but Nigel did not hear her.

'Hang on to my arm, tight,' he said. 'We'll get across in time. It's rather thrilling a big crowd like this, don't you think? You'll never see such a sight again. It's a great thing to have seen it.' He looked about him, his head a little thrown back. Daphne said nothing, but held his arm as she was told. She felt helpless, helplessly dumb: not thrilled, only afraid. Nigel, whose height gave him an advantage in enabling him to see, was clever in pushing his way, catching sight of the least opening, going with the general movement. Daphne clung to him. She looked at the people whom they jostled as they made their way through, and wondered what they were like, what they were feeling; shrinking into herself as young men made loud remarks, or laughed at jokes which she heard but did not understand. Most of the people seemed to be silent. On the back of one of the lions a girl was standing, wrapped in a Union Jack and with a cap of Liberty on her head. She was surrounded by a group of young men and girls all shouting and laughing, and every now and then she burst into song – music hall patter song, varied by the 'British Grenadiers' – the others joining in the chorus. But their noise and hilarity was in marked contrast to the apathetic gloom of the mass of the people. They looked as if they had always stood there and would always go on standing there.

'Nigel, what are they all waiting for?' she asked as they paused on an island.

'To hear the reply to our ultimatum, I suppose: the declaration of war.'

'War with Germany?'

Nigel nodded. Daphne found herself staring into the faces of two sombre looking young men, held up like themselves on the island. Something in their eyes struck her as more miserably helpless than any she had yet met, and she looked at them more carefully. They were about the same height; small, with very sleek hair, one dark, the other light; little bristling moustaches and neat suits cut rather low in front. They looked like waiters; perhaps they were Germans. Of course they were Germans; she realised it in a moment. Germans in the midst of that huge crowd waiting to know whether England was going to war with Germany. She felt sorry for them, and would have spoken had she been able to think of anything to say. But nothing came. In another minute Nigel had seen his opportunity; they were struggling across Whitehall, really struggling, for the crowd was moving down to Westminster and they had to cut across it. Buffeted and bruised in flesh as well as spirit they landed on the pavement. Daphne with her hat over one eye, feeling irritated and degraded, found to her surprise that Nigel appeared exhilarated. He evidently did find a crowd 'thrilling' as he had said. It was after nine o'clock and the 'Ship' empty and quiet, an emptiness and a quiet for which Daphne was thankful. She was glad to lean back, her face away from the window, and would have been still more glad if there had not come in at it the incessant roar of the street below, which seemed now to grow louder and more menacing every moment. ...

... But when they emerged from the restaurant into Whitehall any chance of getting anywhere seemed gone. The noise which had broken in before was evidently only the forerunner of a big movement, and now, up from the Strand, from Northumberland Avenue, from Pall Mall, a vast concourse of people came that swelled out into a mob in Trafalgar Square and swept on, thence, down Whitehall; a mob of people and an indescribable inferno of sound. They were a strange and motley collection: mostly men, and men of the roughest; a few women and excited girls; a few men in miscellaneous uniforms. Every other individual seemed to be armed with some kind of instrument, mouth organs, concertinas, penny whistles, tin trumpets, gongs and combs: any and every vehicle of noise. Others carried banners, mostly battered Union Jacks. From time to time they burst into unintelligible song. Along the side of the main body of the procession, if it could be so called, there ran boys waving small flags, caps or coloured handkerchiefs. They kept up a running accompaniment in which all the others from time to time joined, of a single word – 'War. War. War.' Incessant, monotonous, sinister, that cry rang clear above all the other noises, loud and raucous as they were, until it seemed to gather them all up into itself. People standing in the crowd were by its power swept into the procession and came on with it, yelling in their turn – 'War. War. War.' As they came on down Whitehall the din was tremendous; the whole wide street seemed to have become part of the seething, hideously shouting mass, all crying, as with one hungry bloodhound throat – 'War. War. War.'

2

Belgium

Mary Borden

Belgium

Mud: and a thin rain coming down to make more mud.

Mud: with scraps of iron lying in it and the straggling fragment of a nation, lolling, hanging about in the mud on the edge of disaster.

It is quiet here. The rain and the mud muffle the voice of the war that is growling beyond the horizon. But if you listen you can hear cataracts of iron pouring down channels in the sodden land, and you feel the earth trembling.

Back there is France, just behind the windmill. To the north, the coast; a coast without a port, futile. On our right? That's the road to Ypres. The less said about that road the better: no one goes down it for choice – it's British now. Ahead of us, then? No, you can't get out that way. No, there's no frontier, just a bleeding edge, trenches. That's where the enemy took his last bite, fastened his iron teeth, and stuffed to bursting, stopped devouring Belgium, left this strip, these useless fields, these crumpled dwellings.

Cities? None. Towns? No whole ones. Yes, there are half a dozen villages. But there is plenty of mud – mud with things lying in it, wheels, broken motors, parts of houses, graves.

This is what is left of Belgium. Come, I'll show you. Here are trees drooping along a canal, ploughed fields, roads leading into sand dunes, roofless houses. There's a farm, an old woman with a crooked back feeding chickens, a convoy of motor lorries round a barn; they squat like elephants. And here is a village crouching in the mud: the cobblestone street is slippery and smeared with refuse, and there is a yellow cat sitting in a window. This is the headquarters of the Belgian Army. You see those men, lolling in the doorways – uncouth, dishevelled, dirty? They are soldiers.

You can read in their heavy jowls, in their stupefied, patient, hopeless eyes, how boring it is to be a hero.

The king is here. His office is in the school-room down the street, a little way past the church, just beyond the dung heap. If we wait we may see him. Let's stand with these people in the rain and wait.

A band is going to play to the army. Yes, I told you, this is the army – these stolid men standing aimlessly in the drizzle, and these who come stumbling along the slippery ditches, and those leaning in degraded doorways. They fought their way out of Liege and Namur, followed the king here; they are what is left of plucky little Belgium's heroic army.

And the song of the nation that comes from the horns in the front of the wine shop, the song that sounds like the bleating of sheep, can it help them? Can it deceive them? Can it whisk from their faces the stale despair, the unutterable boredom, and brighten their disappointed eyes? They are so few, and they have nothing to do but stand in the rain waiting. When the band stops playing they will disappear into the estaminet to warm their stomachs with wine and cuddle the round-cheeked girls. What else can they do? The French are on one side of them, the British on the other, and the enemy in front. They cannot go back; to go back is to retreat, and they have been retreating ever since they can remember. They can retreat no farther. This village is where they stop. At one end of it is a pigsty, at the other end is a grave-yard, and all about are flats of mud. Can the noise, the rhythmical beating of the drum, the piping, the hoarse shrieking, help these men, make them believe, make them glad to be heroes? They have no-where to go now and nothing to do. There is nothing but mud all about, and a soft fine rain coming down to make more mud – mud with a broken fragment of a nation lolling in it, hanging about waiting in it behind the shelter of a disaster that has been accomplished.

Come away, for God's sake – come away. Let's go back to Dunkerque. The king? Didn't you see him? He came out of the school-house some time ago and drove away toward the sand-dunes – a big fair man in uniform. You didn't notice? Never mind. Come away.

Gertrude Holland
A Brave Little Country

No one could possibly realise unless they had visited the spot, & worked in it as I have done what Belgium has suffered at the hands of the Germans.

This brave little country, headed by the bravest of Kings, has been slowly but surely strangled to death by the enemy, as one by one of its beautiful cities, ancient towns, picturesque villages & hamlets & even the open country has been ruthlessly savaged by fire, shell & wilful destruction.

This noble country, slowly being stifled out of existence, is now hardly more than a vast desolate sea of bricks & mortar & land damaged almost beyond repair by the people's own but necessary self-sacrifice when they flooded this beloved country to hinder the invading enemy.

That & the destruction of many beautiful bridges, let alone miles of railways, was the greatest sacrifice any country could have made.

May Sinclair
from
A Journal of Impressions in Belgium

Afternoon
Got very near the fighting this time.

Mr. L. (Heaven bless him!) took me out with him in the War Correspondent's car to see what the Ambulance was doing at Zele, and, incidentally, to look at the bombardment of some evacuated villages near it (I have no desire to see the bombardment of any village that has not been evacuated first). Mr. M. came too, and they brought a Belgian lady with them, a charming and beautiful lady, whose name I forget.

When Mr. L. told me to get up and come with him to Zele, I did get up with an energy and enthusiasm that amazed me; I got up like one who has been summoned at last, after long waiting, to a sure and certain enterprise. I can trust Mr. L. or any War Correspondent who means business, as I cannot (after Antwerp) trust the Commandant. So far, if the Commandant happens upon a bombardment it has been either in the way of duty, or by sheer luck, or both, as at Alost and Termonde, when duty took him to these places, and any bombardment or firing was, as it were, thrown in. He did not go out deliberately to seek it, for its own sake, and find it infallibly, which is the War Correspondent's way. So that if Mr. L. says there is going to be a bombardment, we shall probably get somewhere nearer to it than thirty kilometres.

We took the main road to Zele. I don't know whether it was really a continuation of the south-east road that runs under the Hospital windows; anyhow, we left it very soon, striking southwards to the right to find what Mr. L. believed to be a short cut. Thus we never got to Zele at all. We came out on a good straight road that would no doubt have led us there in time, but that we allowed ourselves to be lured by the smoke of the great factory of Schoonard burning away to the south.

For a long time I could not believe it was smoke we saw and not an enormous cloud blown by the wind across miles of sky. We seemed to run for miles with that terrible banner streaming on our right to the south, apparently in the same place, as far off as ever. East of it, on the skyline, was a whole fleet of little clouds that hung low over the earth; that rose from it; rose and were never lifted, but as they were shredded away, scattered and vanished, were perpetually renewed. This movement of their death and re-birth had a horrible sinister pulse in it.

Each cloud of this fleet of clouds was smoke from a burning village.

At last, after an endless flanking pursuit of the great cloud that continued steadily on our right, piling itself on itself and mounting incessantly, we struck into a side lane that seemed to lead straight to the factory on fire. But in this direct advance the cloud eluded us at every turn of the lane. Now it was rising straight in front of us in the south, now it was streaming away somewhere to the west of our track. When we went west it went east. When we went east it went west. And wherever we went we met refugees from the burning villages. They were trudging along slowly, very tired, very miserable, but with no panic and no violent grief. We passed through villages and hamlets, untouched still, but waiting quietly, and a little breathlessly, on the edge of their doom.

At the end of one lane, where it turned straight to the east round the square of a field, we came upon a great lake ringed with trees and set in a green place of the most serene and vivid beauty. It seemed incredible that the same hour should bring us to this magic stillness and peace and within sight of the smoke of war and within the sound of guns.

At the next turn we heard them.

We still thought that we could get to Schoonard, to the burning factory, and work back to Zele by a slight road. But at this turn we had lost sight of Schoonard and the great cloud altogether, and found ourselves in a little hamlet Heaven knows where. Only straight ahead of us, as we looked westwards, we heard the guns. The sound came from somewhere over there and from two quarters; German guns booming away on the south, Belgian [? French] guns answering from the north.

Judging by these sounds and those we heard afterwards, we must have been now on the outer edge of a line of fire stretching west and east and following the course of the Scheldt. The Germans were entrenched behind the river.

In the little hamlet we asked our way of a peasant. As far as we could make out from his mixed French and Flemish, he told us to turn back and take the road we had left where it goes south to the village of Baerlaere. This we did. We gathered that we could get a road through Baerlaere to Schoonard. Failing Schoonard, our way to Zele lay through Baerlaere in the opposite direction.

We set off along a very bad road to Baerlaere.

Coming into Baerlaere, we saw a house with a remarkable roof, a steep-pitched roof of black and white tiles arranged in a sort of chequer-board pattern. I asked Mr. L. if he had ever seen a roof like that in his life and he replied promptly. 'Yes; in China.' And that roof – if it *was* coming into Baerlaere that we saw it – is all that I can remember of Baerlaere. There was, I suppose, the usual church with its steeple where the streets forked and the usual town hall near it, with a flight of steps before the door and a three-cornered classic pediment; and the usual double line of flat-fronted, grey-shuttered houses; I do seem to remember these things as if they had really been there, but you couldn't see the bottom half of the houses for the troops that crowded in front of them, or the top half for the shells you tried to see and didn't. They were sweeping high up over the roofs, making for the entrenchments and the batteries beyond the village.

We had come bang into the middle of an artillery duel. It was going on at a range of about a mile and a half, but all over our heads, so that though we heard it with great intensity, we saw nothing.

There were intervals of a few seconds between the firing. The Belgian [? French] batteries were pounding away on the left quite near (the booming seemed to come from behind the houses at our backs), and the German on the right, further away.

Now, you may have hated and dreaded the sound of guns all your life, as you hate and dread any immense and violent noise, but there is something about the sound of the first near gun of your first battle that, so far from being hateful or dreadful, or in any way abhorrent to you, will make you smile in spite of yourself with a kind of quiet exultation mixed very oddly with reminiscence,[1] so that, though you first impression (by no means disagreeable) is of being 'in for it,' your next, after the second and the third gun, is that of having been in for it many times before. The effect on you nerves is now like that of being in a very small sailing-boat in a very big-running sea. You climb wave after high wave, and are not swallowed up as you expected. You wait, between guns, for the boom and the shock of the next, with a passionate anticipation, as you wait for the next wave. And the sound of the gun when it comes is like the exhilarating smack of the wave that you and your boat mean to resist and do resist when it gets you.

You do not think, as you used to think when you sat safe in your little box-like house in St. John's Wood, how terrible it is that shells should be hurtling through the air and killing men by whole regiments. You do not think at all. Nobody anywhere near you is thinking that sort of thing, or thinking very much at all.

At the sound of the first near gun I found myself looking across the road at a French soldier. We were smiling at each other.

When we tried to get to Schoonard from the west end of the town we were stopped and turned back by the General in command. Not in the least abashed by this contretemps, Mr. L., after some parley with various officers, decided not to go back in ignominious safety by the way we came, but to push on from the east end of the village into the open country through the line of fire that stretched between us and Zele. On our way, while we were about it, he said, we might as well stop and have a look at the Belgian batteries at work – as if he had said we might as well stop at Olympia and have a look at the Motor Show on our way to Richmond.

At this point the unhappy chauffeur, who had not found himself by any means at home in Baerlaere, remarked that he had a wife and family dependent on him.

Mr. L. replied with dignity that he had a wife and family too, and that we all had somebody or something; and that War Correspondents cannot afford to think of their wives and families at these moments.

Mr. M.'s face backed up Mr. L. with an expression of extreme determination.

---

[1] I have heard a distinguished alienist say that this reminiscent sensation is a symptom of approaching insanity. As it is not at all uncommon, there must be a great many lunatics going about.

The little Belgian lady smiled placidly and imperturbably, with an air of being ready to go anywhere where these intrepid Englishmen should see fit to take her.

I felt a little sorry for the chauffeur. He had been out with War Correspondents several times already, and I hadn't.

We left him and his car behind us in the village, squeezed very tight against a stable wall that stood between them and the German fire. We four went on a little way beyond the village and turned into a bridle path across the open fields. At the bottom of a field to our left was a small clump of willows; we had heard the Belgian guns firing from that direction a few minutes before. We concluded that the battery was concealed behind the willows. We strolled on like one half of a picnic party that has been divided and is looking innocently for the other half in a likely place.[2] But as we came nearer to the willows we lost our clue. The battery had evidently made up its mind not to fire as long as we were in sight. Like the cloud of smoke from the Schoonard factory, it eluded us successfully. And indeed it is hardly the way of batteries to choose positions where interested War Correspondents can come out and find them.[3]

So we went back to the village, where we found the infantry being drawn up in order and doing something to its rifles. For one thrilling moment I imagined that the Germans were about to leap out of their trenches and rush the village, and that the Belgians [? French] were preparing for a bayonet charge.

'In that case,' I thought, 'we shall be very useful in picking up the wounded and carrying them away in that car.'

I never thought of the ugly rush and the horrors of it. It is extraordinary how your mind can put away from it any thought that would make life insupportable.

But no, they were not fixing bayonets. They were not doing anything to their rifles; they were only stacking them.

It was then that you thought of the ugly rush and were glad that, after all, it wouldn't happen.

You were glad – and yet in spite of that same gladness, there was a little sense of disappointment, unaccountable, unpardonable, and not quite sane.

---

[2] Except that nobody had any time to attend to us, I can't think why we weren't all four of us arrested for spies. We hadn't any business to be looking for the position of the Belgian batteries.

[3] More than likely our appearance there stopped the firing.

Emily Hobhouse
In Belgium

I entered Belgium from Switzerland by way of Herbesthal. I went prepared to see a devastated country. My long sojourn in South Africa after the Anglo-Boer War had taught me what to expect when soldiers have done their work with fire and sword. My sympathy with non-combatants made me wish to know how the Belgians fared in a similar state of things.

The train threaded its way through the pretty wooded country which lies between the frontier and Liege. The invading army had passed that way. Full of desire to see all the havoc it had wrought, I went from side to side eagerly scanning both landscapes, till some German nuns apologetically filled the compartment and limited my outlook. It was a glistening June morning after rain, and all was verdant, flowery and tranquil – everything seemed normal. Presently we came upon the village of Dolhain lying below in its valley. As far as one could see looking down upon it (and I can only speak of what I saw, not of what I did *not* see) the village was in its usual condition. Smoke rose gently from the chimneys, gardens were blooming, and no trees seemed to be cut down.

My escort cried: 'Now I will show you a ruined house' – and there immediately beyond Dolhain, on a crag over-hanging the village, was the once-familiar sight of a roofless house with gaping windows. The first mark of war.

I saw nothing more till we reached Liege. A considerable part of this town is visible from the line, but I could detect nothing much unusual – certainly there had been no general destruction, only occasional ruin here and there – and as we glided through the more level country towards Brussels there was nothing to note, with the exception of Louvain, which I shall refer to in a moment. The crops promised well, and, superficially, all looked fair. We were in a German train, the express from Berlin to Lille, and it ran well. The railways are manned throughout by Germans, for I understand the Belgians, with one accord, refused, very naturally, to undertake this service. Notices were posted in German, and the names of stations were changed to German forms – a curious work of supererogation beloved of armies of occupation, as I have elsewhere noted.

Brussels and Antwerp

We ran into Brussels. The station is very military in its arrangements and system of passports, &c., but the beautiful city is just of old. Her cathedral, her old square, with its richly gilded medieval architecture, her churches and palaces, her treasures of art and science, all are intact. Even the lion of Waterloo – further afield – said to have been removed for its metal, stands safe on its pyramid. Life, though chilled by the presence of the stranger and his rule, goes on; only – and this is a big exception – industrial activity is paralysed. The blockade has stopped the passage in Belgium of all raw material, and this is bringing grievous consequences.

My first trip was to Antwerp. As one neared the town, isolated houses in that populous district were to be seen more or less ruined, and many had already been repaired. Here, as everywhere, I marvelled that there was no indication of wholesale and complete destruction. The armies had fought in that vicinity and buildings here and there had suffered, while others close at hand were untouched. The village and church of Duffel had received hard blows, and further on stray houses in the outskirts of Antwerp gaped to the sky.

Much that I had planned to do that day in Antwerp was prevented by a tempest of wind and rain; still I was able to drive and walk over the most important parts of the town. It was difficult to realise that it had suffered bombardment. The cathedral is intact, and prolonged scrutiny with the naked eye failed to detect an injury which [I had heard] marks the exterior. The Royal Palace, the chief thoroughfares, the fine old Square, with its medieval gabled buildings, were unharmed. We came upon destruction in the Shoe Market; there a complete block, though of no great extent or value, had been entirely demolished by shells. The outlying parts of the city I could not visit owing to the torrential rain, but I saw the long line of docks, deserted and silent, where grass grows green between the flags and rusty rails. Years ago I saw those docks teeming with life and shipping, but no vessel enters now. War has killed commerce.

A town bombarded as was Antwerp for three days and two nights must have shown many shell-holes and shell craters. No doubt these were quickly filled in, for I saw no sign of them. Probably also the suburbs show more wreckage than appears in the centre.

Malines

Malines, the scene of fighting and bombardment, has suffered proportionately far more. We took the tram straight for the cathedral, whose
lovely old tower, seen afar from the tram, had been re-assuring. There was
a sad bit of structural damage to a western gable and buttresses, and
sundry lesser injuries to the exterior. Architects might recognise deeper
injuries, I can only speak as a superficial observer. Inside the aspect was
deplorable, chiefly on account of the ruin of the rare old windows. These,
shivering under concussion, had crashed down in a thousand pieces,
strewing the ground within and without with jewel-like fragments of
varied hue. We gathered a few to treasure reverently, inclined to cry over
them with the helpless feeling that clings to things that can never be put
together again. As Bernard Shaw wrote: 'You can have glorious wars or
glorious cathedrals, but you can't have both.' Malines, however, still has
her Cathedral which can be repaired probably with ease, but the coloured
glory of her Flemish glass is already only a memory. Shells have dealt
more harshly with the precincts of the Cathedral. There several old buildings of interest and value have been demolished, leaving mere skeleton
walls. Somewhat further on I passed a block of considerable extent completely levelled. Men were at work here in the debris evidently planning
reconstruction; I remarked it as the only instance seen by me in the town.
The other large church of Malines seemed to have escaped all structural
injury, but there also a good deal of old glass had fallen from the shaken
windows, and the holes were already filled with plain glass. Service was
being held; nevertheless, I found the verger in a side aisle. I was anxious
to learn from him the fate of the Rubens which I recollected having seen
in the church. He pointed to the red curtain behind which it once hung,
and told me the picture had been removed for safety before the tide of
war reached their town – he was not certain, but he believed it was in
London. There were several gutted houses in the long street leading to the
station and in some of the adjacent streets. Also in and around the station
square numerous houses, themselves intact, had their window-panes
broken, and these were boarded up or covered with sacking. The glass
roof of the station was riddled with holes through which the rain dripped
upon us.

Louvain

Interest, of course, centres in Louvain,[1] where I spent a day of inspection, as careful as the untoward weather would permit. One's first feeling was one of profound astonishment that the greater part of the town showed no sign of war at all. This is a town of some 44,000 inhabitants, and 38,000 are living there as usual. The absent 6,000 included men serving in the Belgian Army. I walked and drove about the town for several hours, and believe I saw it pretty thoroughly. There are three centres of destruction – first, the Station Square, of which every house is wrecked, together with the Rue de la Gare; these were mainly small restaurant hotels and shops; secondly, the Place du Peuple, in which some, but not nearly all, the houses were gutted; and thirdly, the Old Market, a large oblong square, in which a good many houses, but by no means all, had been destroyed. Fronting on the Old Market came one end of the world-famous Library, which was burnt the night of August 25th, four or five days after the Germans had entered Louvain. Of this nothing remains but the walls and gable end. One hoped there may be foundation for the rumour that some of the more precious manuscripts were put in safety.

Stories abound as to the origin of this fire, a disaster not at all surprising with burning houses near at hand, and a pile of tents and canvases belonging to the booths of the market folk. A study of the spot may incline one to accept the view compounded from several, but it would be folly to make up one's mind as to the truth till the war is over and evidence can be brought by eye-witnesses from each side. (Strenuous efforts were being made to subdue the flames, in which Belgians and Germans worked together.) Nevertheless, the bell turret and roof of the Cathedral caught fire, and these were destroyed before the flames were got under, the molten bells crashing into the nave below. There in the nave I found a sad-looking verger, who showed me the mass of refuse, charred beams, piles of metal, and broken glass. After nearly two years the smell of fire was still very strong. A new roof had already been put on, though of a lower pitch and probably temporary; the nave was boarded off, and Mass was being held in the choir and transepts. Here I drew aside and watched while Belgian citizens and German soldiers knelt side by side in prayer. I

---

[1] The 'destruction of Louvain' is, therefore, a *fiction*. This is probably well-known to the directors of the *Times*. Yet only the other day the *Times* again spoke of Louvain as being destroyed. In a Leader in its issue of October 23rd, it said: 'In the autumn of 1914, Louvain, the nursery of Belgian piety and learning, was *wantonly destroyed*, and the Library, which was its especial pride, was reduced to ashes.' That the *Library* was destroyed is true: that it was wantonly destroyed is almost certainly untrue: that Louvain itself was destroyed is false.

came across many similar instances of good feeling elsewhere between the German common soldiers and the Belgian peasantry. That sight bore within it the germs of the future, and I felt it would live longer in my memory than anything else I had seen in Louvain. I gathered a few jewels from the dust here also, and stole away feeling that the possibility of universal brotherhood still lives.

A fine picture which hung in the Cathedral was saved by the German officers, who carried it out and placed it in safety. They also, I was told, dynamited two or three houses to prevent the flames from passing to the Hotel de Ville. This unique building is unscathed. Curiously enough, being a sight-seer not of sights as in normal times, but of No sights or Destruction, I passed it lightly by as a thing of lesser interest! Everywhere I sought only ruins.

The other churches of Louvain are uninjured, but as we drove about the town now and again one came across a house which had suffered. On the further side of the station the suburb of Kesselloo presents a dismal sight; the majority of its houses are destroyed. Altogether it is thought an eighth of Louvain has suffered.

Charleroi

I spent Whit-Sunday in Charleroi – an ugly coal-mining town. The journey lay through pretty undulating country which looked fair and prosperous, crops promising well, and gardens blooming. Here and there a cottage had been repaired, but I could detect no ruin till we reached Charleroi itself. I had given up looking for wholesale devastation, but there in the streets leading up from the station some thirty or forty houses had suffered in varying degree, and, again, in one of the boulevards, a section of perhaps 300 or 400 yards had been wrecked. We walked and trammed about for several hours, but found no other material sign of war. The people were busy with an exhibition and sale of handicrafts produced by the lads of the Industrial School. I went in and bought some objects tied up with Belgian colours.

Aerschot

Another day was spent at Aerschot – a small town of some 8,000 inhabitants. I heard it computed that perhaps the tenth part is destroyed, but if so, the ruin must be almost entirely in an out-lying part across the river. I saw considerable wreckage there. In the Market Square very few houses are wrecked, and the Bürgermeister's is quite untouched, with the exception of two bullet-holes which had pierced the panes of one window. It was there that Captain Stengel met his death. We walked about the narrow, picturesque streets and found them in normal condition. The church had sustained no injury, except to the western door. This had evidently been burnt, because the walls close by were blackened and a couple of pictures on the adjacent wall had caught fire and their charred frames and canvases hung mournfully in place. Judging from a third of similar character, these pictures, fortunately did not seem to be of artistic value, though doubtless prized locally. The doorway was boarded up and the church was in full use.

Such details become wearisome, and I have perhaps said enough to show that our Allies can take comfort in the thought that, at any rate, the towns mentioned above are not so badly injured as commonly supposed. Probably at the moment of their hurried flight the flames, the smoke, and the debris newly fallen gave a terrible aspect to familiar streets. Now that is removed a clearer idea of the extent of the damage can be formed.

Dinant is, I am told, far more seriously destroyed, owing to much street fighting with the 'Garde Civique,' but unfortunately, a tempest of rain and wind prevented my visit, and the same reason prohibited excursions to the little villages of Vise, Andennes, &c, which I was especially anxious to see, believing from hearsay that these are really on a par with many Boer villages I had seen – viz., every building, public and private, levelled with the ground.

General condition

I have heard it computed by a neutral who has had special facilities for observation, that the houses destroyed in Belgium can perhaps be estimated roughly at 15,000 out of a total of over 2,000,000. Comparing these figures with South Africa, the only standard of devastation that I have experience of for comparison, it would seem that the Belgians have escaped fairly well from the talons of war. For in the Boer Republics 30,000 farms alone were burnt, besides towns and villages in which every building, churches included, was levelled to the ground, and this out of a very small total. This consideration helps us to realise that we are all Huns in turn. If only for the sake of the Belgians, one wishes that peace could be negotiated and their country thus protected from the further destruction consequent upon the air raids now proceeding dropping bombs on Bruges, Ghent, Aerschot, and Brussels.

I will not here speak of the under fed condition of the industrial section of the people, since I have called attention to it elsewhere. The blockade is mainly responsible for this, and it is a very strong additional reason for urging negotiations.

Nor will I speak of the population generally, except to say this. It is a second time I have seen a people in the grip of that agony – the agony of submission to a rule which, however good in itself, is the rule of the conqueror and foreigner. Perhaps the strongest thing one could say on that point is to register one's belief that the last German officials, as they turn their backs upon Belgium, will depart filled with a thankfulness far exceeding that of the Belgians who watch them go.

Mère Marie Georgine
German occupation

Aug. 23rd [1914]

I shall not get much written even now after this long pause in my diary. I have perhaps 20 minutes at my disposal unless something unforeseen occurs which is generally the case at present, and the events since I last wrote would in themselves make a book – of horrors. I told you that the Gs. [Germans] were passing – well, they have been passing on and off ever since. The first alarm came where I left off writing and made the dash up above.

M. Mathilde burst into the room saying she was afraid perhaps someone was at the window as there was a dreadful German down below who insisted on making the round of the house to see if we had soldiers or arms hidden. I rushed off at once to the Moyennes to see that they were alright and crossing the salle des fêtes I saw some half dozen of them fully armed in the middle of those poor frightened villagers who had taken refuge here.

They went all over the house everywhere absolutely even into the cloisters, cells, infirmary. cellars etc. etc., had cupboards opened to be sure nothing was hidden in them and eventually went away declaring themselves satisfied but leaving a sick man apparently badly wounded in the throat.

Sept. 4th [*1914*]

Excuse writing. I have a gathered finger. So much has happened that I
have quite lost count of time and the order in which they (the events)
took place but I will endeavour to continue now for half an hour to the
music of the cannon which is booming away somewhere close at Malines
we think. Towards evening they arrived again and insisted upon setting a
guard for the house. The two parlours by the door had to be emptied and
mattresses placed. Then they insisted on making a second round of the
house. Half the people had already gone to bed. The second section was
full of poor folk with screaming babies trying to sleep on straw or mattresses and two dormitories of people of better class. They made all the
men get up and assemble in the salle des fêtes. You never saw such a state
of mind as we were all in. Nobody knew what was going to happen. I don't
think they quite knew themselves but were frightened at seeing so many
men and feared for themselves during the night. At first there was a talk
of sending them all away to their respective dwellings, but that of course
was quite impractical, as many of them have no longer a roof to call their
own and in any case they would have been killed or made prisoners on
the way. Finally they decided to keep everyone (men of course) for the
night in the salle des fetes under guard. Two soldiers fully armed in the
salle itself and three on the bridge. Every two hours the guard changed.
You can imagine that nobody felt like going to bed, even the children were
told to lie down fully dressed in case of alarm. One officer took off his
boots, put on light shoes so that he could not be heard and thus equipped
paraded the house wherever he felt inclined all night. Delightful wasn't
it!!! Meanwhile our poor dying soldier had expired at midday, and one of
the nuns at 5 p.m. to add to our other troubles. The German soldiers
buried the soldier early next morning. They departed but the march past
continued. In the afternoon – oh I had forgotten to tell you two of the
most appalling incidents of this first visit. They went to the presbytery, an
officer and some men fully armed, knocked at the door and when nobody
opened they broke it in. They found their way to the room where M. le
Curé was with his sister, his servant and the Curé of Wygmael and stood
over them with pistols cocked saying they had the right to kill them as it
was the priests who excited the people against them. Finally they changed
their tactics and insisted on his taking down the Belgian flag which was
still floating in the church. Naturally it was not his doing, but was placed
there by the commune so they brought him here under guard to fetch the
clerc who had the key of the tower and then the two had to go up with
armed soldiers behind them to take down the flag. During the night the

whole sky was lit up by the burning of the factory, La Corbeille at Wespelaer. They had found powder or ammunition of some sort there and burnt it down in revenge. The horrors committed at Wespelaer defy description and the poor Curé had aged 20 years when we last saw him bringing a poor cancerous woman whom they had shot (after killing her mother and brother) here to be looked after. The poor creature had been two days in a ditch unable to get help. The Gs. saw her but would do nothing and no one else dared to venture out of doors.

Sept. 17th [1914]
So much has happened since I last wrote that I really hardly know myself. Everything is jumbled up in my memory. We really seem to be absolutely the centre of the German operations and have never been without German soldiers in the house since that first day. I am now writing in the ambulance where I am keeping watch until midnight and there are two sentinels outside the door in the little ones' playground. As every pane of glass is smashed they might just as well be inside as far as I am concerned. We have been so dreadfully busy in the ambulance that I have been quite unable to keep as I had intended a sort of diary for you. I did not even see office or anything for days together. I will try now to continue events in their chronological order but I am afraid I shall not succeed. The next day in the afternoon arrived a soldier to say that we had to lodge 60 officers, Germans of course. As there was no help for it we prepared a dormitory. They are all the same in one respect. They go about in abject terror of their lives knowing that they are in the enemy's country. The burgomaster had made himself scarce so they took the poor Curé prisoner and he slept all night guarded by fully-armed soldiers and next morning said his Mass in between two soldiers for fear he escaped. He was held responsible for the whole village and was told that if anyone shot at a soldier he would be the first one shot. Poor man, he was in a state and it is no idle threat they make, for they have done frightful things pretending that civilians had shot at soldiers when they had done no such thing. One family here had their house burnt down because some B. [Belgian] soldiers had hidden behind it – which they had a perfect right to do – then a G. soldier fired on them in the garden. The father and a boy of 12 were both wounded in the shoulder, the mother had a bayonet wound on her face and the little girl of 7 was shot in the back of her leg high up so badly that in spite of all we could do she died after about a week. Those four we had here to take care of, but besides that two girls of 17 and 18 were killed as well as the baby of two which the mother was holding in her arms. The

uncle lived next door and three or four of his sons were killed at the same time. Well, these gentlemen had a general – a very important one it appears – with them and required 2 salles one for writing etc., and one for the council of war or something of the sort. It was their etal Major (whatever that may be in English) I believe. During the night more illuminations and fireworks. Poor folks kept pouring in with bundles containing all they had been able to save, sent off by the Germans who immediately burnt down their houses. As I said before we already had a number of people here. Well, the soldiers broke open the doors of the houses pillaged everything and destroyed what they could not carry away. They broke into the poor school and lodged there the night doing as much damage as they could. Unfortunately the straw which had been put there for our soldiers and the lamps were still there so they had a splendid time on the whole and opened cupboards carrying off or tearing all the clothes prepared for the prizes and left the place in a filthy mess which I will not attempt to describe to you in detail – it was too low. We have had such frequent repetitions of that kind of thing that I will not attempt to describe each one in detail – indeed I couldn't if I would.

I wonder if you got my P.C.. A Dutch delegate brother of one of our old pupils passed here and offered to send letters for us by Holland but we thought letters too dangerous, they might compromise him or us and one cannot be too careful nowadays. I told you that the house had been badly damaged by cannon in a skirmish between the Bs at Wespelaer and the Gs on this side of the canal. They stay here always to keep the bridge as it is the road they use to go to Louvain, but it is very rare that we have the same troops more than a day or two. I think it was August 28 and then the wounded began to arrive. We already had 13 or 14 but by the next morning we had over 50 and some dreadful cases. They brought two dead Gs. and buried them right away in the garden, then they brought a man who had had his arm shot right off – awful it was – and another man shot through the lungs. In the afternoon we were giving extreme unction to a Pole shot through the head when they announced 7 Belgians badly wounded, poor fellows they were in such a state that we gave them the last sacraments as they arrived with the least possible ceremony for fear they did not live till the end. Of the 7 we only succeeded in saving one – two died that same evening. You can believe that we were pretty busy in the ambulance after that. Several died of course, but many began to get convalescent when an extra objectionable lot of men arrived apparently commanded by an army doctor. He was terrified for his life and tried to hide it by a great deal of bluster. He stationed sentinels all over the house and nobody might move from where they were while he once more searched the house from attic to cellar. I had just slipped out of the ambulance into the garden to try to say Vespers and get a little fresh air at the same time. When I came back I found a sentinel (in front of the door) who refused to let me enter. I thought the wisest thing to do was to pretend I didn't understand though his gestures were significant enough. I was laughing and trying to explain in my German that I absolutely must go to my sick – he trying to be polite and do his duty at the same time though he felt it was idiotic and showed it when one of the convalescent Germans who knew me perfectly by sight came along and I called him to the rescue. Naturally he could do nothing but try to explain what I wouldn't understand and finally he passed though saying to his comrade 'I can pass anyhow'. 'Of course' laughed the other which I pretended to understand as meant for me and slipped through at the same time the sentinel conveniently turning his back and pretending not to see. I don't mind admitting now that my heart went pit-a-pat in spite of my laughing exterior and I did not feel at all sure that I should not get a bullet in my back or something of the kind. The search was made for ages, cupboards, boxes etc., had to be opened and it was 8 o'clock instead of 6 when we were eventually able to think of supper. Next day he packed off all the Germans and Poles (pupils) and took with him as prisoners 23 of our convalescent Belgian soldiers – oh we did feel sick, but what could we do! We shan't forget his passage here in a hurry. He insisted on sleeping in the ambulance with two others as he was a doctor but stipulated absolutely that the door of the corridor should be locked and nobody but nuns be allowed to pass during the night. Of course in the ambulance we are always two at least during the night and more when necessary and just then we had several critical cases. We had a vicaire from some parish in Antwerp who got stranded here with two Seminarists trying to walk back from Louvain for trains and posts are quite things of the past so far as we are concerned. He, the priest, acts as chaplain in the ambulance and has proved invaluable for nights together he slept on a mattress on the ground ready for sick calls and we insisted that he had to be there that night too as it was absolutely necessary. Finally we obtained that much. The day after that man left the ambulance from Brussels sent 5 motors to fetch some of our men and we sent 16 I think so that our numbers were considerably diminished and eventually we were left with only 7 very badly wounded.

After that arrived a lot of sailors they were here quite a long time – a week I should think – because of the Naval Victory of the English at Heligoland. We knew no details but they said there was nothing for them to do at sea just then which was a good. sign and they hate the English so whole-heartedly that that is another good sign. They had with them 2 doctors. The principal was a particularly nice man. He brought with him 4 Belgian prisoners badly wounded and 2 Germans and tended them like a father. On the Friday we heard the cannon quite close all day long. It was at Werchter and Wackerzeel and no end of damage was done. Several wounded were brought in amongst others 3 or 4 officers who were put in a room apart. Next morning at about 4 began our turn. I never wish to live through the like again. The Germans had taken their stand behind the farm buildings so far as I can make out and the Belgians must have known that they had had their headquarters here. In any case they made our convent the aim of their cannon balls with dire results. The whole community spent the day in the cellars with a few exceptions. I remained in the ambulance with two others and I can assure you I never wish to spend another such day. As far as I can make out, the object of the affair was to bring down the belvedere as we call it – that little watch tower by the big reservoir.

Cecily Hamilton
from
William an Englishman

William's eye was caught and held by the oiled swiftness, the mechanical simultaneousness of the movement; he stared at the line of uniforms, now rigidly inactive again, till a hand from behind gripped his collar and impelled him urgently sideways. One of his captors had adopted this simple method of informing him that way must be made for those about to issue from the door of the sentry-guarded house. He choked angrily and brought up against the wall – to which Griselda, taking warning, had hastily backed herself. He was still gasping when the little procession came out; a soldier leading it, a couple more with bayonets fixed – two civilians walking together – a couple more soldiers with bayonets fixed and last of all an officer, a fattish, youngish, mustachioed man whom the sentries stiffened to salute. He came a little behind his men, paused on the step and stood there framed in the doorway with his hand resting on his sword, the embodiment of conscious authority; the others, the two civilians and their guard, went on to the middle of the road. There, in the middle of the road, they also halted – the soldiers smartly, the captives uncertainly – and William saw the two civilians clearly.

One was a short and rotund little man who might have been sixty to sixty-five and might have been a local tradesman – nearly bald and with drooping moustaches, rather like a stout little seal. Essentially an ordinary and unpretentious creature, he was obviously aiming at dignity; his chin was lifted at an angle that revealed the measure of the roll of fat that rested on his collar, and he walked almost with a strut, as if he were attempting to march. Afterwards William remembered that he had seen on the little man's portly stomach some sort of insignia or ribbon; at the time it conveyed nothing to him, but he was told later that it was the outward token of a mayor. He remembered also that the little man's face was pale, with a sickly yellow-grey pallor; and that as he came down the steps with his head held up the drooping moustache quivered and the fat chin beneath it twitched spasmodically. There was something extraordinarily pitiful about his attempt at a personal dignity which nature had wholly denied him; William felt the appeal in it even before he grasped the situation the meaning and need of the pose.

The man who walked on his left hand was taller and some years younger – middle-aged, slightly stooping and with slightly grizzled hair and beard. He belonged to an ordinary sedentary type, and William, thinking him over later, was inclined to set him down a schoolmaster, or perhaps a clerk. He wore steel-rimmed eye-glasses and his black coat was shiny on the back and at the elbows; he had none of his fellow's pomposity, and walked dragging his feet and with his eyes bent on the ground. He raised them only when, as they halted in the middle of the road, the respectable woman in black called out something – one word, perhaps his name – came up to him and caught him by the shoulder. He answered her quickly and very briefly – with hardly more than a word – and for a second or two after he had spoken she stood quite still, with her hand resting on his shoulder. Then, suddenly, her sallow face contorted, her thin mouth writhed and from it there came a cry that was too fierce to be called a groan and too hoarse to be called a scream; she flung herself forward on the neck of the grizzled man and her lean black arms went round it. He tried to speak to her again, but she silenced him by drawing down his head to her breast; she held it to her breast and pressed it there; she rocked and swayed a little from side to side, fondling the grizzled hair and kissing it to a stream of broken endearment. Her grief was animal, alike in its unrestraint and its terrible power of expression; convention fell away from her; in her tidy dress and with her dowdy hat slipping to one

shoulder she was primitive woman crooning over her dying mate. ...
When she was seized and drawn away from her man, her curved fingers
clung to his garments. Two soldiers held her and she writhed between
them choking out a hoarse incoherent appeal to the officer standing in
the frame of the doorway with his hand on the hilt of his sword; she went
on crying herself hoarser as her captors urged her further down the street
and at last, in mercy to those who looked on, out of sight through an open
doorway. William had his hands to his ears when the door shut. No one,
in spite of the persistence of her cries, came out into the street to inquire
the cause of her grief; but it seemed to William afterwards that he had
been aware here and there of furtive faces that appeared at upper windows.

While they forced the dowdy woman away from him her man stood
motionless, turned away from her with his bead bent and his eyes on the
ground, so that he started when a soldier came up behind him and tapped
him sharply on the arm. The soldier – he had stripes on his sleeve and
seemed a person of authority – held a handkerchief dangling from his
hand; and, seeing it, the grizzled-haired captive removed his steel-
rimmed eye-glasses.

'Don't look,' said William under his breath. 'Griselda, don't look.'

For the first time mortal fear had seized him by the throat and shaken
him. He knew now that he stood before death itself, and the power to
inflict death, and his heart was as water within him. His wife was beside
him – and when he realized (as he did later on with shame) that the spasm
of terror in those first moments of comprehension had been stronger
than the spasm of pity, he excused it by the fact of her presence. His fear
in its forecast of evil took tangible shape. Griselda at his elbow had her
eyes and her mouth wide open; she was engrossed, fascinated – and he
was afraid, most horribly afraid, that in her amazement, her righteous
pity, she might say or do something that would bring down wrath upon
them. He remembered how bold she had been in the face of a crowd, how
uplifted by sacred enthusiasm! ... He plucked her by the sleeve when he
whispered to her not to look – but she went on staring, wide-eyed and
wide-mouthed, for the first time unresponsive to his touch and the sound
of his voice.

They bandaged the eyes of the two prisoners – the rotund pompous
little mayor and the man who might have been a schoolmaster. All his life
William remembered the look of the rotund mayor with a bandage covering him from forehead to nose-tip and his grey moustache quivering
beneath it – a man most pitifully afraid to die, yet striving to die as the sit-

uation demanded. And he remembered how, at the moment the bandage was knotted on the mayor's head, there stepped up to him quietly the stout old woman who had stood praying on the further side of the road with her eyes fixed upon the door. She held up a little crucifix and pressed it to the quivering grey moustache. ... Griselda clutched William by the wrist and he thought she was going to cry out.

'Don't, darling, don't!' he whispered. 'Oh, darling, for both our sakes!' ...

He did not know whether it was his appeal or her own terror and amazement that restrained her from speech – but she stood in silence with her fingers tightened on his wrist. He wished she would look away, he wished he could look away himself; he tried for an instant to close his eyes, but the not seeing was worse than sight, and he had to open them again. As he opened them a car roared by raising a smother of dust; but as the cloud of its passage settled he saw that the two blindfolded men were standing with their backs to a blank wall – a yellow-washed, eight-foot garden wall with the boughs of a pear-tree drooping over it. It was opposite the yellow-washed wall, across the road, that the file of soldiers was drawn up; the captives were facing the muzzles of their rifles and the red-faced boy-officer had stationed himself stiffly at the farther end of the file. The dust settled and died down – and there followed (so it seemed to William) an agony of waiting for something that would not happen. Long beating seconds (three or four of them at most) while two men stood upright with bandaged eyes and rifles pointed at their hearts; long beating seconds, while a bird fluted in the pear-tree – a whistle-note infinitely careless. ... And then (thank God for it!) a voice and a report that were as one. ... The man with the grizzled hair threw out an arm and toppled with his face in the dust; the mayor slid sideways against the wall with the blood dribbling from his mouth.

With the conviction that no one was heeding his comings and goings, a certain amount of assurance came back to William Tully, and as the way cleared before him he set off down the street without any attempt at concealment. By house to house visitation he sought for his wife through the village; it was there she had been taken from him, and he thrust back the deadly suspicion that she need not have remained in the place where she had disappeared from his sight.

There was not a closed door in the length of the street, and nowhere was his entrance barred; the call to arms had temporarily cleared the houses of the invaders quartered in them, and he ran from one doorway to another unhindered, calling on Griselda as he entered, looking into every room, and then out to repeat the process. The two first houses were empty from garret to cellar, but with signs of having been left, recently and hurriedly, by the soldiers billeted therein; odds and ends of military kit were scattered about, chairs overturned and left lying; and in one room, a kitchen, on a half-extinguished fire, a blackened frizzle of meat in a frying-pan filled the air with a smell of burning. The third house he thought likewise empty; downstairs there was the same litter – overthrown furniture and food half eaten on the table; but opening the door of an upper room he came on a woman with three children.

The woman started to her feet as the door opened, a child hugged to her bosom and other two clinging to her skirt; and William had a passing impression of a plump, pallid face with lips apart and wide, wet eyes, half-imploring and half-defiant. One of the children was crying – its mouth was rounded in a roar – but you heard nothing of its vigorous plaint for the louder din without. William made a gesture that he meant to be reassuring, shut the door and ran back into the street.

He went in and out desperately, like a creature hunted or hunting; and, having drawn blank in house after house, the deadly thought refused to be thrust and kept under. If they had taken her away, she might be ... anywhere! East or west, gone in any direction, and leaving no clue for her following. Anywhere in a blind incomprehensible world, where men killed men and might was right, and life, as he knew it from his childhood up, had ended in an orgy of devilry! He went on running from house to house, while shells screamed and burst and guns clattered by, and no man gave heed to his running or the tumult and torture of his fears. Upstairs and down and out again – upstairs and down and out.

He was nearing the end of the street when he found her at last; in the upper back room of a little white house some yards beyond the building in flames and not far from the spot where they had seen the hostages die. She was alone and did not move when he flung the door open; crouched in a corner with her head on her knees, she neither saw nor heard him. For an instant it seemed to him that his strength would fail him for gladness, and he staggered and held to the door; as the giddiness passed he ran to her, babbling inaudible relief, and pulled the hands from her face. He had an instant's glimpse of it, white and tear-marked, with swollen lips and red eyes; then, as his arms went round her and he had her up from the floor, it went down on his shoulder and was hidden. He felt her clinging to him, trembling against him, sobbing against him while he held her – and all his soul was a passion of endearment and thankfulness. ... So for

a minute or two – perhaps longer – they clung to each other, reunited:
until William, his sense of their peril returning, sought to urge his wife to
the door.

She came with him for a step or two, her head still on his shoulder;
then, suddenly, she shivered and wrestled in his arms, thrust him from
her, rushed back to the end of the room and leaned against it, shaking
with misery. Her arm was raised over her hidden face and pressed against
the wall; and he saw what he had not seen before, that the sleeve was torn
and the flesh near the wrist bruised and reddened. He saw also – his eyes
being opened – that it was not only her hair that was tumbled; all her
dress was disordered and awry. There was another tear under the armpit
where the sleeve had given way and the white of her underlinen showed
through the gap. ... His heart cried out to him that she had struggled
merely as a captive, had been restrained by brute force from escaping –
but his own eyes had seen that she turned from him as if there was a barrier between them, as if there was something to hide that yet she wished
him to know. ... For a moment he fought with the certainty, and then it
came down on him like a storm: for once in his life his imagination was
vivid, and he saw with the eyes of his mind as clearly as with the eyes of
his body. All the details, the animal details, her cries and her pitiful
wrestlings; and the phrase 'licentious soldiery' personified in the face of
the man who had been Griselda's gaoler. Round and roughly good-
humoured in repose with black eyebrows and a blue-black chin. ... He
caught her by the hands and said something to her – jerked out words
that stammered and questioned – and she sobbed and turned her face
from him again. ... After that he could not remember what he felt or how
long he stood in the middle of the room, oblivious of danger and staring
at her heaving shoulders and the tumbled hair that covered them; but it
seemed to him that he talked and moved his hands and hated – and did
not know what to do.

In the end there must have come to him some measure of helpless
acquiescence, or perhaps he was quieted and taken out of himself by the
need of giving help to Griselda. After how long he knew not he found
himself once more with his arms around her; she let him take her hand,
he kissed it and stroked her poor hair. This time she came with him when
he led her to the door, and they went down the stairway together. Near the
street door she hesitated and halted, and he saw she had something to say.

'Where are we going?' she asked, with her lips to his ear. 'Can we get
away?'

He told her he thought so, that now was the time when they might slip away unnoticed – trying to encourage her by the assumption of a greater confidence than he felt. Fortune favoured them, however, and the assumption of confidence was justified; though the bombardment had slackened as suddenly as it had begun, the remnant of German soldiery left in the place was still too much occupied with its own concerns to interfere with a couple of civilians seeking safety in the rear of the fire-zone, and no one paid any heed to them as they made their way along the street. They turned inevitably west-ward – away from the guns – down the road they had come that morning: two hunted, dishevelled little figures, keeping well to the wall and glancing over their shoulders. The crush of wagons, of guns and men, had moved forward and out of the village, which, for the moment, seemed clear of all but noncombatants – save for the ubiquitous cyclist who dashed backwards and forwards in his dust. An ambulance was discharging its load at a building whence waved the Red Cross, and near at hand, but out of sight, a battery was thudding regularly; but of the few uniformed figures in the street itself there was none whose business it was to interest himself in their movements. They hurried on, clinging to each other and hugging the wall – except when a heap of fallen brickwork, a derelict vehicle or other obstacle forced them out into the road.

They were almost at the entry of the village when they came upon such an obstacle: the upper part of one of the endmost houses had evidently been struck by a shell, for a large slice of roof and outside wall had crumbled to the pathway below. It had crumbled but recently, since the dust was still clouding thickly above the ruin and veiling the roadway beyond it; hence, as they skirted its borders, it was not until he was actually upon them that they were aware of a motor-cyclist speeding furiously out of the dusk. The roar of the battery a few yards away had drowned the whirr of his machine, and Griselda was almost under it before she had warning of its coming. The stooping rider yelled and swerved, but not enough to avoid her; she went down, flung sideways, while the cyclist almost ran on to the heap of rubble on his right – then, recovering his balance, dashed forward and was lost in the dusk. Save for that momentary swerve and stagger, he had passed like a bolt on his errand, leaving Griselda crumpled in the road at William's feet. To his mind, no doubt, a mishap most luckily avoided.

Griselda lay without moving, her face to the dust, and for one tortured moment William thought the life beaten out of her; but when he raised her, her lips moved, as if in a moan, and as he dragged her for safety to the side of the road she turned her head on his arm. He laid her down while he ran for water from the river; panted to its brim, soaked his handkerchief for lack of a cup, brought it back and pressed it to her forehead. Her eyes, when she opened them, were glazed with pain and her lips drawn tightly to her teeth; when he wanted to raise her to a sitting position she caught his hand thrust it from her and lay with her white face working. So she lay, for minutes that seemed hours, with her husband kneeling beside her. … Men passed them but stayed not; and once, when William looked up, a car was speeding by with helmeted officers inside it – too intent on their own hasty business of death to have so much as a glance to spare for a woman in agony of bodily pain and a man in agony of mind.

The night had come down before Griselda was able to move. With its fall the near-by battery was silenced and the distant thunder less frequent; so that William was able to hear her when she spoke and asked him to lift her. He sobbed for joy as he lifted her, gently and trembling lest he hurt her; she sat leaning on his arm, breathing painfully and telling him in jerks that it was her side that pained her most – her left side and her left arm, but most of all her side. At first she seemed dazed and conscious only of her sufferings – whimpered about them pitifully with intervals of silence – but after ten minutes or so she caught his sleeve and tugged it.

'Let's get away. Help me up!'

He suggested that she should rest a little longer, but she urged him with trembling, 'Let's get away!' and he had perforce to raise her. In spite of the fever for flight that had taken possession of her she cried out as he helped her to her feet and stood swaying with her eyes shut and her teeth bitten hard together. He would have lain her down again, but she signed a 'No, no!' at the attempt and gripped at his shoulder to steady herself; then, after a moment, guided his arm round her body, so that he could hold her without giving unnecessary pain.

'You mustn't press my side – I can't bear it. But if you put your hand on my shoulder –'

They moved away from the village at a snail's pace, Griselda leaning heavily on her husband. Behind them at first was the red light from burning houses; but as they crawled onwards the darkness of the valley closed in on them until, in the sombre shadow of the cliff, William could only distinguish his wife's face as a whitish patch upon his shoulder. When she groaned, as she did from time to time, he halted to give her relief, but she would never allow him to stand for more than a minute or two; after a few painful breaths there would come the tug of her fingers at his coat that was the sign to move forward again. Once or twice she whispered to know if any one were coming after them, and he could feel her whole body a-quiver with fear at the thought.

Barred in by cliff to right and river to left, they kept perforce to the road – or, rather, to the turf that bordered it. The traffic on the road itself had not ceased with the falling of night; cars were coming up and guns were coming up and the valley was alive with their rumble – and at every passing Griselda shrank and her fingers shivered in their grip upon William's sleeve.

'Can't we get away from them?' she whispered at last. 'Right away and hide – can't we turn off the road?'

He said helplessly that he did not know where, until they reached the entrance to their valley. 'It's all cliff – and the river on the other side.'

She had known it without asking; there was nothing for it but to drag herself along. To both the distance was never-ending; Griselda's terror of recapture communicated itself to her husband, and he shivered even as she did at the rattle of a passing car. Instinctively they kept to the shadow, stumbling in its blackness over the uneven ground below the cliff. Once, when a couple of patrolling horse-men halted near them in the roadway, they crouched and held their breath during an eternity of dreadful seconds while they prayed that they had not been noticed. It seemed to William that his heart stopped beating when one of the horsemen walked his beast a yard or two nearer and flashed a light into their faces; but the man, having surveyed them, turned away indifferently and followed his comrade down the road. That was just before they came to the gap in the heights that led into the valley of silence.

As they entered it for the last time, in both their minds was the thought that they might find it barred to them; and the beating of their hearts was loud in their ears as they crept into its friendly shadow.

'The woods,' Griselda whispered.

They turned into the woods and took cover; and, with a yard or two, the blackness under the trees had closed in on them, blotting out all things from sight. They halted because they could see to walk no further.

'Let me down,' Griselda said – and her husband knew by the gasp in her voice that she was at the end of her powers of endurance. He explored with an outstretched hand for a tree trunk and lowered her gently to the ground with her back supported against it; she panted relief as he sat down beside her and groped for her fingers in the darkness. ... So they sat holding to each other and enveloped in thickest night.

The guns had died down altogether, and the rumble from the road, though almost continuous was dulled – so that William could hear his wife's uneven breathing and the stealthy whisper of the trees. He sat holding Griselda's hand and staring into the blackness, a man dazed and confounded; who yesterday was happy lover and self-respecting citizen and to-day had suffered stripes, been slave and fugitive, learned the evil wrought on his wife.

Thinking on it afterwards, he wondered that he had closed an eye; yet he had sat in the darkness but a very few minutes when, swiftly and without warning he fell into a heavy sleep.

Part II

ATTITUDES TO THE WAR

Many cultural and social attitudes in 1914 were still very much influenced by certain political ideologies of the nineteenth century. The 'Rule Britannia' ethos born of one hundred years of imperialism projected a state of public self-confidence and national superiority through the growing media. As the outbreak of the War was welcomed by many, jubilation quickly turned to oration and action in towns across the country. Many people, like Beatrice Trefusis,[1] applauded 'the end of apathy' as thousands of young men lined up to enlist and the British Expeditionary Force landed safely on the shores of France. The national patriotic spirit was animated by all the excitement. Britain's most recent military history was filled with success stories and it was often claimed that the War would be over and won by Christmas.

But it was not, and the excitement of 1914 led to the stalemate of 1915 and bloody battles like the Somme (1916) and Passchendaele (1917). As the years passed, and the young men kept dying to no effect, the propagandists had to work hard to convince the public that all would be well. And the public, even the most patriotic, may have needed all the convincing they could get, as Ethel Bilborough's sombre response to the execution of Edith Cavell illustrates. By the time May Sinclair published her patriotic novel *The Tree of Heaven* (1917), the British people had suffered a great deal, but as yet there was no end in sight. Sinclair's passionate insistence on an all-consuming love for England was vital to the patriotic cause. Her protagonists, Anthony and Francis Harrison, convince themselves that no sacrifice is too great, even the lives of their sons. There must have been many thousands of parents across the country in need of that kind of conviction, and Sinclair was exploiting this common bond to reinforce her arguments of belief in the War.

---

[1] Beatrice Morwenna Trefusis's journal is held in the Liddle Collection housed in the Brotherton Library, University of Leeds.

Some writers and campaigners maintained an enthusiasm for the War throughout the years of the conflict. As the British Army mobilised in the summer of 1914, other organisations were equally determined to 'do their bit'. The Suffrage Movement, which had reached its zenith by 1914, was finally divided by the outbreak of the war. The WSPU, led by Emmeline and Christabel Pankhurst, suspended its militant activities and took up the patriotic cause with equal fervour. The NUWSS, whose tactics had always been more subtle, favouring diplomacy rather than violence, took the milder course of supporting the war effort but not the War, regarding it as a new arena within which women could prove themselves worthy of the vote.[2]

Christabel Pankhurst's rousing speech, delivered on 8 September 1914 and published shortly afterwards, illustrates how the fervour was transferred from one cause to the other without any apparent complication. For Christabel, the new war simply becomes an extension and an expansion of the old one, equally worthy and fraught with danger. The militancy of the WSPU can be only an advantage as she uses the suffering of Belgium and France to inspire the men of Britain to enlist. Despite the fact that the democratic British government had seen fit to force her into exile, Christabel admits that they represent a freedom worth fighting for, although her positive response to the 'revolutionary' nature of the Russians may seem rather ironic given the nature of her mother's later electioneering comments. The common cause is, by definition, the woman's cause and she is able to make a continuing case for improvements to women's rights, although the call for the vote takes a back seat for a while. It is this citizenship, held by most men, that she calls upon them to protect, with a view to it being expanded to women in the future.[3] After all, a war *must* bring some good.

On 5 April 1918, Emmeline Pankhurst's rallying cry, 'War Until The Victory!', illustrates how the WSPU had managed to maintain its momentum during the years that followed. Communicating through its mouth-

---

[2] For further information on the Women's Suffrage Movement see Sandra Stanley Holton, *Feminism and Democracy: Women's Suffrage and Reform Politics in Britain 1900–1918* (Cambridge: Cambridge University Press, 1986); Jill Liddington and Jill Norris, *One Hand Tied Behind Us: The Rise of the Women's Suffrage Movement* (London: Virago, 1978); Ray Strachey, *The Cause* (London: Virago, 1989) (first published 1928); Martin Pugh, *Women and the Women's Movement in Britain 1914–1959* (Basingstoke: Macmillan, 1992).

[3] The Representation of the People Act of 1918 granted the vote to all men and to women of property over the age of thirty. This was a step in the right direction but in fact excluded many of the women who had worked so hard as nurses, ambulance drivers and factory operatives during the war, proving that they were 'worthy' of the vote.

piece, *Britannia*, the Pankhursts and their supporters were able to use many of the wartime changes to the social infrastructure to continue their fight for women's rights whilst fully supporting the government and the war. 'Magnificent Patriotism' had created a vast army of women workers, a small number of whom would be able to vote in the forthcoming general election. This small number included the leaders of the WSPU so they had nothing to lose by continuing their emphatic support.

But not all former WSPU campaigners were able to support the War. Having already turned her back on the beliefs of her mother and sister, Sylvia Pankhurst rejected the war completely, believing that only pacifism could be synonymous with the women's cause in a war created by a conservative patriarchal culture.

Sylvia, the renegade sister, spent the war years working in the East End, fighting for the rights of working-class women and children left to survive there while their men were away. She campaigned with as much vigour as her mother and sister, but for the opposite cause, although never losing sight of the notion of 'women's rights'. For her pains she earned the disdain of many more patriotic members of society, as the Macleod sisters demonstrate when they recount a bitter exchange between Sylvia and some wounded soldiers during a public meeting.

Sylvia is unlikely to have been daunted by such heckling. Her absolute dedication to the cause of peace is articulated in her retrospective account of the organisation of the Women's Peace Conference at The Hague on 28 April 1915, taken from her 1932 account of the war years *The Home Front*.[4] Sylvia, like most of the potential British delegates to the Conference, was unable to obtain the necessary visa to travel. But she had a great deal of other work to do running kitchens in the East End, lobbying the government for their various causes and supporting Keir Hardy in his work for the trade unions. The Conference was presided over by Jane Addams, an American woman with a long history of social reform.[5] An internationally respected figure, her status as a neutral gave her access to the representatives of all the governments of Europe as well as an oppor-

[4] For more information on the women's peace movement see Gertrude Bussey and Margaret Tims, *Pioneers for Peace: Women's International League for Peace and Freedom 1915–1965* (Oxford: Alden Press, 1980); Anne Wiltsher, *Most Dangerous Women* (London: The Women's Press, 1985)

[5] Jane Addams (1860–1935) was an American feminist social campaigner who founded the Hull House Social settlement in Chicago – a settlement for immigrants to the USA. She was President of the Women's International League for Peace and Freedom from it's foundation, following the Hague Conference in 1915, until her death.

tunity to meet some leading social figures in Britain. Lady Kate Courtney and Beatrice Webb both recorded in their diaries their resposes to meeting her, and speak of her and her views with respect. Unfortunately, however, the Peace Conference itself did nothing to halt the ongoing war.

There were some campaigners in the Women's Movement, among them Catherine Marshall, who felt unable to support the war on any level, believing that the notion of war was so alien to the biological and social make-up of women that it must be prevented or ended as soon as possible. This is a view that has continued even to the latter part of the twentieth century, as the women's peace camp at Greenham Common in the 1980s testifies.[6] Marshall's essay 'Women and War' was first published in 1915 as a part of the peace campaign and sets out her views very clearly.

Catherine Marshall was also active in the organisation and running of the No Conscription Fellowship, which was set up in November 1915 in anticipation of the Military Service Act which became law in January 1916. The aim of the fellowship was help conscientious objectors to avoid military service. Initially the Act applied only to single men between the ages of eighteen and forty-one, but was extended in May 1916 to include married men.[7]

Inevitably, conscription was a very emotive issue, bound to inspire strong opinions both in support and in opposition. Ethel Bilborough, in the fortunate position of having no one to be conscripted, makes her support very clear in her diary, echoing a popular media sentiment of the day with her references to 'cowards and slackers'. Perhaps not unsurprisingly, Sylvia Pankhurst takes a very different view in her article on 'The Military Service Bill' written for *The Women's Dreadnought* (15 January 1916), the official mouthpiece of the East End pacifist movement. Her language is powerful and insistent: 'The Bill is apologised for on the ground that it applies to a limited number of men only, but if it applied to one [single human being] only, it should be fought, until it has been destroyed.' There can be no doubt as to whom she considers responsible for this outrage: 'It appears to us as peculiarly mean that middle-aged politicians, from their position of well-paid security, should be endeavouring to exercise compulsion against the young lads who are still under the legal age of maturity and may not vote.' The power is in the hands of the few, they are using

---

[6] See Lynne Segal, *Is the Future Female?* (London: Virago, 1987).
[7] See Claire Tylee, *The Great War and Women's Consciousness* (London: Macmillan, 1990): 119.

it to exploit those with no power at all, and there is a particular danger to those who are under age.

The article also attacks the military tribunals which were set up to decide the fate of those conscientious objectors who stood by their opinion. Pankhurst sows a seed of doubt as to the justice of the proposed system and questions the right of the authorities to sit in judgement of other men's principles, particularly in light of the harsh sentences which they are able to pass. Lady Kate Courtney's diary account of one such tribunal seems to reinforce Pankhurst's opinion. And when Pankhurst writes, 'TRUE Conscientious objectors to war service will in most cases refuse to take any contributory part in warfare, however remote', she could be speaking of Courtney's Stephen, facing a sentence of hard labour for his beliefs.

I have placed Courtney's rather sad diary entry next to an extract from A. T. Fitzroy's novel *Despised and Rejected*, in which the hero, Dennis Blackwood, faces judgement in the House of Commons for his own pacifist beliefs. The tribunal is described from the point of view of Antoinette De Courcy, a young woman who is love with Dennis, despite her understanding of his clandestine love for another man. Dennis represents the marginal hero in a number of ways (as indeed does Antoinette, herself troubled by questions of sexuality and identity), but he does not lack conviction when called upon to defend himself. Fitzroy's argument concerning the oppression of these minorities is reinforced when the judges reach their inevitable verdict, and it is no surprise that Dennis finds another supporter in a elderly former suffragette. Although part of a wider story, the set piece captures the atmosphere of despair surrounding the tribunal very effectively, and Dennis's 'otherness' may also have a foundation in fact. After witnessing the National Convention of the No Conscription Fellowship Beatrice Webb observed, 'Among the 2,000 were many diverse types. The intellectual pietist, slender in figure, delicate in feature and complexion, benevolent in expression, was the dominant type. These youths were saliently conscious of their own righteousness.' She could be describing Dennis Blackwood; and he does not impress her.

Attitudes to the patriotic cause, the pacifist movement and conscription have their basis in the politics of the individual. But attitudes towards human relationships tend to operate on a much more personal level, even though they may be influenced by contemporary social ideas. The Great War both created and destroyed relationships, many of which were considered unorthodox at the time. For the young of 1914 the pace of life suddenly accelerated. Whereas, formerly, long engagements would have been quite normal, with the Western Front swallowing young men at an alarming rate, there was no time to lose. May Sinclair's heroine Dorothea in *The Tree of Heaven* pays the ultimate price for putting off her marriage to Frank Drayton, believing she has more important things to do. 'I could bear it if I hadn't wasted the time we might have had together. All those years – like a fool – over that silly suffrage.' (Sinclair, *The Tree of Heaven*: 276) So she weeps after her fiancé is killed in the retreat from Mons.

Real-life stories are no less tragic. The poignant letters of Emily Chitticks tell the story of her all-too-brief relationship with her fiancé William Martin before his death in action in March 1917. Chitticks wrote several letters to Martin after his death because it took days for the news to reach her. Rather uncannily, she wrote these letters in red, continually expressing her concern at not having heard from him, as though with some kind of sinister unconscious premonition. The sense of pain at their immediate separation, coupled with the underlying knowledge that it could become permanent, is always present. Emily Chitticks never married.

For the young Vera Brittain, the separation from her fiancé Roland is equally difficult, but Brittain, writing years later, having since married someone else, is able to elaborate and evaluate, developing her feelings for the reader. She can write consciously of a sexual temptation which Chitticks would not have been able to acknowledge, while her inclusion of their immature poetry tends to romanticise the piece. Brittain lost her fiancé a few months later. She also lost her brother later on in the War. Lady Cynthia Asquith writes of the loss of a brother in 1916, but, although her own pain is apparent in her words, she represents the event through its impact on her sister-in-law, his widow. This is interesting in several ways. On the one hand it appears to give a external account of another person dealing with grief, suggesting that, although many sub-sidiary people come and go, they are unable to help. She also illustrates the extreme danger of entertaining hope where none exists. Perhaps most significantly, by addressing the issue through her sister-in-law Asquith is able to keep her own grief at bay, almost as a kind of transferral of anxi-ety. By throwing herself into the concerns of others she can escape for a short while, but it cannot last: 'Not till I was left alone did I feel the full pain for myself – Letty's had parried it.' In the end each person has to con-front their loss in their own individual way.

The accelerated pace of life caused many young people to address issues of sexuality sooner than they perhaps would have done before the War. Victorian society had condemned sex before marriage, particularly for women, and this was the code of practice inherited by the youth of the Great War. But, as Vera Brittain suggests, the imminent threat of death seemed to offer different life choices to many of those involved:

> We sat on the sofa till midnight, talking very quietly. The stillness, heavy-laden with the dull oppression of the snowy night, became so electric with emotion that we were frightened of one another, and dared not let even our fingers touch for fear that the love between us should render what we both believed to be decent behaviour suddenly unendurable.

While Brittain and her lover manage to resist temptation and maintain 'decent behaviour', others were not so determined. Diaries, however, rarely testify to this and it is better to turn to fiction to gain an understanding of how some women may have felt. In G. B. Stern's *Children of No Man's Land* (1919), heroine Deb Marcus lives on the fringes of a radical group who believe in free love, but she is unable to invest whole-heartedly in their ideas, remaining a 'demi-maid', a girl who both does and does not commit sexually. In the extract included here, she witnesses the tragic results of the influence of her friends on a much younger woman, Nell Redbury, who, having become pregnant by her fiancé, is left to face the scandal alone after he is killed in action. In fiction, the idea of the sexual woman induced by the War is very often distanced, confined to marginal characters, so that the experience may be explored without 'ruining' the heroine. In Irene Rathbone's *We That Were Young*, the central character, Joan Seddon, watches the decline of her nursing colleague, Phyllis 'Thrush' Shirley, who gives in to temptation before her betrothed leaves for the Front.[8] Through fiction, Rathbone and Stern are able to explore dilemmas without relating it to a personal experience which, for many women, may have been difficult to contemplate.

In *Rules of Desire*, Cate Haste argues, 'Though the war heightened emotional feelings and accelerated the decline of old taboos and conventions, there is little evidence of a dramatic breakdown in codes of sexual behaviour'.[9] Whilst it seems likely that most women at home or on active service probably honoured the moral codes of their upbringing, in fiction at least, sex can be used to argue an alternative case. Helen Zenna Smith

---

[8] 'When the boy you adore is going out to those awful trenches again you give him everything he wants – and you don't know whether it's him or you who's wanting it most' (Rathbone, [1932] 1988: 140).

[9] Cate Haste, *Rules of Desire* (London: Chatto & Windus, 1992): 43.

(a pseudonym for novelist Evadne Price) wrote *Not So Quiet ... Step-daughters of War* (1930) as a 'female' response to Erich Maria Remarque's *All Quiet on the Western Front*. One of the primary aims of the novel is to suggest that the war could be as gruelling and traumatic for women as for men. By emulating Remarque's narrative style and placing her women ambulance drivers within set pieces comparable to those inhabited by the soldiers in Remarque's original, Smith suggests strong parallels between their respective experiences. The episode in *Not So Quiet* in which Helen sleeps with Robin, uses sex to reinforce this notion of shared experience. Just as Paul Baumer finds temporary comfort in the arms of a French peasant, so Helen is able to lose her terrible memories as she dances towards her liaison with Robin:

> He is clean and young and straight and far removed from the shadow pro-cession I watch night after night, the procession that came to me early this morning and wakened me shrieking in the presence of a compartmentful of shocked strangers. He is so gay, so full of life, this boy who is holding me closely in his arms ... he could never join that ghostly parade.

Jane Marcus has suggested that 'Helen Zenna Smith is writing to clear the volunteers of the charge of lesbianism'.[10] She is referring specifically to the section of Radclyffe Hall's *The Well of Loneliness* (1928), included here, in which Stephen Gordon finds love during her time as an ambulance driver in France. Smith *is* rather unsympathetic in her treatment of lesbianism, but it is represented in the novel. It is possible to find many examples of homosexuality, both male and female, in Great War literature. Hall writes of the blossoming of a relationship between women; Fitzroy describes the consummation of a relationship between men. Vera Brittain, in her 1936 novel *Honourable Estate*, gives an account of a sister learning of her brother's homosexuality by reading a letter after his death. The poignant letter to Ruth Allendyne from her beloved brother high-lights many of the sufferings of those on the margins of what is accept-able, forced to face up to their difference by the immediacy of the War. It also completely encompasses the pain and suffering of love, separation and sexuality at a time when nothing seemed certain any longer.

The final extract in this chapter, 'Women and Wives', is taken from *Backwash of War* (1916), a collection of sketches written by an American nurse, Ellen La Motte, who worked in a French military field hospital in

---

[10] Jane Marcus, 'Corpus/Corps/Corpse: Writing the Body in/at War', in H. M. Cooper et al., eds, *Arms and the Woman: War, Gender and Literary Representation* (Chapel Hill and London: University of North Carolina Press, 1987): 124–67.

Belgium from 1915 onwards. The book was published in America, but suppressed elsewhere until after the War because its unflinching representations of hospital life were considered bad for morale. Indeed 'Women and Wives' reveals both a tragedy and a hypocrisy in separation as her detached narrative voice describes the roles of women, spiritual and physical, in the lives of the men in the front line. The distinction between women and wives is disturbing, and the overall picture of women's place, or at least the men's perception of it, at the battle front is not an attractive one.

3
Patriotism

Beatrice M. Trefusis

The Good of the Empire

About September 12th 1914

Recruits are pouring in in overwhelming numbers.

In spite of the already heavy casualty lists, & inevitable distress in this country – I can't help feeling that it is all a most splendid tonic for us all, both individually & collectively. Nothing else could so have drawn the Empire together – this 'loosely woven' Empire – as the German's like to think it. Every colony & every person is anxious to 'do their bit.' India's magnificent response makes one thrill. Ireland – right at the beginning – sunk her troubles in the common cause.

One gets down to realities.

In the last weeks my feelings have changed. I seem to see that it is just *this* that we were all in need of. Here & now is an end to apathy – to insincerity – to selfishness – for the time being anyhow.

This is going to be the biggest thing in our lives, for some of us. It is calling out fine qualities. We are up against something bigger than any of us in this generation have ever known. It is a tremendous test. The horrors & suffering, thoughts which obsessed me so much at first – seem now small in comparison with the tremendous power for good to the whole Empire. It is a fine thought – this whole Empire rising as one man to fight not so much for material things, but for honour & spiritual progress – against a doctrine of militarism & material force. It gives rise to some big thoughts. Cynics would say, of course, that we are merely fighting for self interest & to defend our material possessions. So we may be – *consciously*. But what does the Empire stand for in the world of spiritual things?

I have become prouder of England than I ever was before. She has risen to the occasion. After all, we are not so hopelessly amateurish. I hear that the equipping and dispatching of the Expeditionary Force was a master piece of organisation. War was declared on the 5th Aug & by the 16th the Expeditionary force was safely landed in France without a single casualty or untoward occurrence – thanks, of course, largely to our fleet.

Christabel Pankhurst
Women and the War

Preface

One reason why this pamphlet has been published is that it is felt to be right that women whose future liberty, no less than that of men, is at stake, shall assume such a share as is justly theirs of the moral responsibility for the present war.

It is for women, too, to do their part in appealing to the national unity and love of country, that have been assailed, though, happily, not destroyed by the evil and unjust laws that for the well-being of the State must, when the war ends, be swept away.

Because of the danger in which the country stands, and because of the terrible cost in suffering and in life that the war imposes, the militant women have, for the time, ceased from their warfare. They cannot, however, forget, and the public must not forget, how closely related is the question of women's vote with the war, and with the national safety. To be silent on this matter would be contrary to the national interest.

It is natural and it is right that the militant women should say: 'Why were we not enfranchised even five years ago – in 1909 when, as Mr Churchill has reminded us, the present war with Germany very nearly broke out?' Then, instead of being engrossed, as inevitably we have been engrossed, in the struggle for citizenship, we could have taken our part as citizens in safeguarding the country against danger.

If the time and energy that of late years have been devoted to fighting against the Suffragettes had been devoted to preparing to fight against the Germans, it would have been better for their country.

Urgently do the women of the W.S.P.U. reinforce the appeal for new recruits for the new Army that is soon to fight side by side with the brave soldiers who, on the field of battle, are already distinguishing themselves and protecting those at home.

Remember that the entire manhood of France has learnt to defend and is defending the national freedom! In our own country there is surely as great a readiness to learn and to serve.

The war is showing the utter helplessness of a population – however great it may be in number, and however intelligent and brave – unless it is trained and armed for self-defence.

Every man who prepares himself for the fight is helping to save the country from humiliation and ruin of defeat, and is helping to make its voice stronger when the day comes for making terms of peace.

A speech delivered at the London Opera House, September 8th, 1914

Ladies and Gentlemen: It is very good to be back in one's own country again, amongst one's own friends. But I think my exile would have continued a little longer had things gone in the war as by many people we were told they would go when first the fighting began.

Had the country been as fully prepared for this war as it might have been, the war-worn W.S.P.U. could well have afforded to go into hospital for a little while, just as other war-worn, wounded soldiers do. I, myself, after a somewhat strenuous exile, should greatly have enjoyed a rest during the two or three months which some people suggested were all that were needed to see this thing through. As for those of our people – my mother and other women who have been under fire, who have been in the fighting line during the past few years – they did indeed need the repose which we thought it might be possible for them all to have.

The country in danger

But every day it has become to us more and more apparent that our country is in danger, and that it is necessary for all sections to unite, in order that we may be strong as we have never been strong before; and therefore we Suffragettes believe that it is our duty to do all we can to rouse the individual citizen to fight for the freedom and the independence of this country and this Empire.

We think that, as militant women, we may perhaps be able to do something to rouse the spirit of militancy in men. We know by experience that there are times and seasons when peace can be observed, and that there are other times and seasons when, for the sake of peace, there must be fighting. We know, too, how necessary it is that, supporting the actual fighters, there shall be the whole country with them in spirit, with them unitedly, with them heart and soul. For if a country is engaged in warfare, then the whole people must, each one playing his or her part, be at one in that warfare.

The politicians are declaring it to be necessary that the country shall be educated as to the causes of this war; not only that the women shall be educated – not only we women politically ignorant, politically incapable as some have called us – but the men, the electors, the rulers of our Empire, these men also need education, we are told, as to the causes of a war in which the country is already engaged. Well, some of us have already formed our opinion as to what the causes of this war are. I am going to give you what I believe to be the opinion of the most thoughtful women in the country.

The case of Belgium

We have been told that we are fighting to preserve the neutrality of Belgium. We are. And I have been amazed to find, in some unexpected quarters, a very strange indifference to this question of the neutrality of Belgium. There are some people who seem to care not much more than a German statesman might, for the existence of 'scraps of paper,' and the solemn engagements written thereupon. It seems to me that such indifference to the neutrality of Belgium is akin to the shameful indifference which certain of our countrymen have come to feel where the rights of free speech and of a free Press are concerned. There are some things that never grow old with time, and just as our rights as free citizens of this country never become out of date, neither do such matters as the independence and the neutrality of gallant Belgium.

To fight for Belgium! That to a Suffragette seems indeed a great cause, because this little country has withstood and has fought an enemy infinitely stronger than itself in the physical sense, without ever counting whether success was or was not possible; without ever considering whether its fighting forces were small or large. Never forget that that is the spirit in which some of your own citizens, the militant women, have been fighting for a long time.

The land of ideas and ideals

It is said we are fighting for the sake of France. That again is a great, a glorious cause! It must be remembered that France is (or will be some day, when its women are emancipated), one of the greatest of all democracies. French civilisation is one of the finest civilisations in the world. We have

comparison between wspu & the army.

not heard just lately so much of the culture of France as of German culture it is true (I have my suspicions of persons or nations who boast too loudly of their culture), but if we would fight for culture, then we must fight for France. To all who know that great country, France is the land of ideas and of ideals. Prince Von Bülow, in his book on German and international politics, says, with a certain contempt, that 'it is a characteristic trait of the French people to put psychic needs before material needs.' If that be true, then for that reason alone it is to the interest of the whole world that France shall be maintained in her integrity and in her independence. Yet as we know the object of the Germans is utterly to crush France, they regret that they did not crush her more completely in the war of 1870. This time they are determined, if they can, to beat her to the very ground. So awful a tragedy must be averted. It has been said, and said most truly, that everyone has two countries – his own and France; and so in fighting for France, we are fighting for that which is infinitely precious to ourselves.

To save this country

But we are not only fighting for Belgium. We are not only fighting for France. Do not let us lay too much stress on those two ideas; we are fighting for our own sake, for our own safety. We are fighting for our own existence as a nation, as an Empire – and that in truth is the main and root cause of the war. The Germans are hacking their way to us through the bodies of the Belgians, through the bodies of the French. Let us face the fact that France and Belgium are fighting for us, and that these two countries are at present making a sacrifice greater than ours. It is only because of a geographical accident that we have not already suffered the fate of the Belgian people.

It is said for the Germans, 'You British think you have a gift for Empire. They have the same gift for Empire.' We cannot share that view, because we find that there is no country in the world which does not dread the thought of German rule; no people under British rule, however hardly Britain may have treated them in the past – Britain is getting wiser now – who would exchange our rule for that of Germany. We have no right to surrender to Germany, people who claim to remain under the British flag.

For a very long time, a great many people in this country have tried to close their eyes to the undoubtedly hostile intentions of the German Government – and you cannot for practical purposes distinguish between the German Government and the German people. The prime and supreme object of the present war is to destroy the British Empire and put a German Empire in its place.

The woman's point of view

Now, from a woman's point of view, the defeat of our country and the victory of Germany would be a calamity. It is unnecessary for me to tell you whether or not I am satisfied, whether or not the W.S.P.U. is satisfied, with the position which women hold in Great Britain to-day. You know very well what our opinions are on that point, for we have expressed them in deeds as well as words. Therefore you will not misunderstand me, then, when I say that (if we except Scandinavia), it is in the English-speaking countries, it is under the British flag and under the Stars and Stripes, that women's liberty is greater, that women's position is higher, that women's influence and political rights are more extended that in any other part of the world. And I think that no one in this hall will quarrel with me when I say that of the great European countries, that country in which women's position is lowest and most hopeless, is Germany. Therefore, if the women of the world are to preserve and to increase the liberty they already enjoy, this country of ours must be victorious in the present war. The world domination that Germany seeks to win would mean the abasement of women, would mean a disastrous check to women's progress towards equal citizenship. Obviously, the might-is-right principle upon which German policy is now based is altogether contrary to the principle upon which women's claim to citizenship depends.

Women have already won the vote in Australia and in New Zealand; and in Great Britain the only remaining obstacle to their enfranchisement is the resistance that has until now been made to their just demands by a handful of politicians. Very well, then; upon the preservation of our Empire depends the enfranchisement of the women of the Empire. And more than that, the help which we as British women can give to women in other lands largely depends upon the influence and power which our country enjoys. We have a mission to fulfil, a mission of liberation amongst the women of all countries of the world, and more particularly in the East. Therefore, we women are determined that the British citizenship for which we have fought in the past, for which we are prepared to fight again, for which we are prepared to die as readily as any soldier now fighting on the battlefield – we are determined that that citizenship shall be preserved from destruction at the hand of Germany.

Democratic government at stake

Picture our position at the present time. This is war in which most literally, most plainly, our existence as a nation, as an Empire, is at stake: that is to say, that very foundation upon which we have been basing our fight as women, the very citizenship for which we have been striving, may crumble before we have achieved it.

I want to say to Socialists, to advanced Liberals, and to all those people who may not have warmed to the fight as yet, that the whole system of democratic government for men as well as women is at stake. The triumph of Germany would lead to the extinction of democratic and constitutional government. Democratic and constitutional government has been already destroyed in Germany itself and replaced by a military tyranny. The same thing would happen in every other land in which German power prevailed. That being so, Progressives, Liberals, and Socialists should be as impassioned for British victory in this cause as the militant women can possibly be.

What of Russia?

The thought that is at the back of some minds is this: What of Russia? It is a thought that has to a large extent been put there by the Germans themselves. We have all heard of the tactics whereby the immediate enemy tries to place us in such deadly fear of one who may be, or may not be, an enemy later on, that we forget to escape the present danger by which we are menaced. We militants have often been urged: 'Do not fight so-and-so because so-and-so may treat you worse.' Let us take one danger at a time, and cope with that! I tell you frankly that it amazes me to find some men, some British men, talking as though all they have to do is to choose whether they will be swallowed by Germany or by Russia.

It is the business of the people of this country to defend their citizenship, to defend their independence, to defend their position in the world against all comers – and either to live victorious or die victorious; but never to surrender.

Do not let the remoter danger, if it be a danger at all, so paralyse you that you fall a prey to the foe that is at your gates. As a woman, I have more fear of Germany than I have of Russia, and I have more hope of Russia than I have of Germany.

The feeling about Russia that some of you have depends upon what you have heard of Russia's treatment of reformers. Suffragettes are the last people to say a word in favour of coercion, for they know too much about it. But I would remind you that before any man in this country has the right to criticise the use of coercion in Russia, he must remember the offence of torture, of forcible feeding committed here, at the expense of women, and he must expiate that offence.

It is not for those in our more western country, this country which, though it has boasted democratic institutions for hundreds of years, has yet tortured women rather than enfranchise them – it is not for this country to be self-righteous when it speaks of a country further East, not so old, not so schooled in the ways of democracy.

The spirit of rebellion

I will tell you why I have hope of Russia. It is because in that country there lives the spirit of rebellion. It is because you have there an indocile people – a people who are prepared to fight for liberty. The spirit of the Russians is a guarantee that liberty will live and triumph.

It is when you have a people such as that of Germany, who know not how to rebel; a people who have submitted to the deprivation of constitutional rights in the manner that, I am sorry to say, the German people have done; it is then that you have reason to fear their Government.

Yes, and those very men who profess distrust of Russia, seem to be ready enough that Russia shall help to win our victories. For it is they who would not believe in the German peril, who would not allow this country to be prepared, who wanted a smaller Navy, and would not have a larger Army.

There are some who say that war is never right, and think that women should under all circumstances stand for peace. But surely it is obvious that submission to our German enemies, who do not believe in peace, and think that our love of peace is a sign of decadence, would mean the greatest victory of war that war has ever had.

I agree with the Prime Minister

I agree with the Prime Minister – and I hope he will never again in the future disagree with me where our agitation for the vote is concerned – that brutality must not be allowed to triumph over freedom. We suffragettes believe in peace with honour; peace that is based on mutual respect.

The kind of peace that we believe in is that which we hope will prevail while the world lasts between ourselves and the United States of America. It is peace based upon an agreement that we will regulate our disputes, not by violence, but by reason and mutual concession. But you cannot have peace between two people, two parties, or two countries unless they are like of mind in desiring peace, and unless each respects the other, and wishes the other's welfare. And therefore we say that to talk of serving the cause of peace by yielding to German pretensions and German atttack would be absolutely preposterous.

What we must do, and what this country must always be strong enough to do, not only now but in the future, is to ensure the peace of the world on fair and honourable terms, terms which must take into consideration the rights and value to us all of the small nations. We must be strong enough to restrain the German and any other disturber of the world's peace.

We, in this country, have always been kept very much in the dark about foreign politics. We are called an insular people, and successive Governments have done their best to make, and keep us insular. It seems to me that this war will have the effect of breaking down our insularity. It will, it must bring us closer to the other peoples of the world. I believe that we shall be better citizens, that we shall better solve our national problems when we know more of other countries, and when we know more of the people of those countries. I hope that henceforward the newspapers will tell us more about foreign lands; more about what the people there are thinking and doing. Then we shall not, as now, be in a position of having to be educated at the thirteenth hour as to what a war is being fought about.

We were not strong enough

It has always been said by the people who oppose the enfranchisement of women, that women, if they had any power, would use that power for the ruin and weakness of the state. What an extraordinary idea! especially in a country in which for some years gone by the most fighting element, the most actively patriotic element, has been represented by women. Everybody is talking now of the causes of war. There is one great cause, and that is that we were not strong enough to make the enemy afraid to attack us. It is not women; it is men who are responsible for that.

I admire more than I can say the courage of the men who are now volunteering to go through their brief training and then out to face the enemy. It is in that light that we really know, and really respect our countrymen; it is there that they are showing us their stronger and their more admirable qualities. As one who has had something to do with organisation, I admire exceedingly also those men who so loyally and so courageously are undertaking, at this short notice, to carry through the stupendous and almost superhuman task of creating an army, when the need of that army has already become a most urgent and most tragic one. They do not say as they might have said to the Government and the electors, 'We told you beforehand that you were not prepared. We told you beforehand that you were not strong enough.' They bravely get to work.

Perhaps nobody in this country realises as the Suffragettes realise it, what are the difficulties of creating a great army at this late hour. When one reads in the newspapers of people waiting hours to be enrolled; of people offering services which are not instantly utilised, as an organiser one says: 'My criticism is not of those who at a moment's notice have had to devise the necessary machinery, my criticism is rather of those others who did not make ready in time.'

It is very easy to say, when we are in the midst of war, that people must learn how to defend their country; it is more practical to learn to defend it before the war begins. And then the need for fighting may never arise.

Problems of national defence

I cannot help thinking that if women had had the vote five years ago, if they had been asked to give their serious consideration to these problems of National Defence, if they had had before them the facts that they ought to have had before them, they could and would have saved the situation.

Women realise with especial clearness what this most terrible and devastating war means, not only to the combatants but to the so called noncombatants, and above all to women. We know that women of Belgium and France have had to suffer more than the newspapers have told, and more than the newspapers dare ever tell. We say that if money, time and energy spent in time of peace can prevent the happening of such horrors, then they will be well spent.

You may say we cannot afford to prepare and ensure ourselves against war. We can still less afford to *have* war! We cannot afford to lose some of the strongest and bravest of our citizens on the battlefield. We cannot afford to have our people starved as the result of war. If, living at the present rate, we cannot afford to ensure against war, then let there be less luxury, and less difference between the life of the rich and the life of the poor. Though we have to live more simply we must defend ourselves, and we must defend the interests of which we are the guardians against any and every attack, no matter from what quarter it may come.

A nation marches on its stomach

Now, a word upon another aspect of the question. We are constantly reminded that an army marches upon its stomach; but no less true is it

that the *Nation* marches upon its stomach. It is said that if we were to give
employment to all those women who, owing to the war, are unemployed
in London to-day, £50.000 a week for London alone would be required
even if they were paid only 10s. a week. This brings one to an important
point! When the men are asked to join the army, the answer many of them
make is: 'What of our wives, what of our children?' Now, how long have
we of the W.S.P.U. asked that women shall be economically independent!
How many times have we said that the married woman ought to have an
income of her own! How often have we told you that if you want the
country to be prosperous, you must organise and utilise the productive
energy of women as well as of men, so that they may not be in the position of being a burden to the country! Why is it that every woman who
wants to earn her living, and is physically fit to do so, has not a trade in
her fingers, so that she could step into the place that her husband leaves
vacant, or pursue some occupation of her own? It is a serious weakness to
our country that women should be economically dependent upon others.
As it is, men are prevented from enlisting because of the women who are
dependent upon them. Then there are the thousands and thousands of
women out of employment. You cannot give them work? If you cannot
give them work, you must give them food.[1]

Share and share alike

I should like to see everyone of us, no matter what our means, put upon
a food allowance as the soldiers are. When these men are risking their life
for the country, the rest of us ought to be in a sense living as they do. I
mean that we ought not to consent, some to eat much, some to eat nothing. The winter is coming on, and the Prime Minister tells us that we are
only at the beginning of a protracted struggle. Should we not all be happier if we knew that the elementary needs of existence, food and shelter,
were guaranteed to everybody? You are asking young men of position and
education to enlist in the ranks, and you are right in doing that, for there
should be no class distinction on the battlefield, and there are no class distinctions in death. But if there are to be no class distinctions at the front,
why should there be class distinctions at home where the question of
bread and butter is concerned?

We must not ignore the fact – a word here to the rich – that the patriotism has been very nearly starved out of some people. But we cannot

---

[1] The necessary State machinery for the provision of relief and work exists. To put it in
effective motion is all that remains to be done.

put all the blame for this on the rich. The majority of the electors are working men, and certain reformers and Socialists and advanced politicians would be better engaged in the constructive work of insisting upon due provision being made for those who are in need, than in trying to dim the flame of patriotism in this time of crisis.

Should women fight?

I suppose some of you will ask whether the Suffragettes think that women ought to take part in the fighting. The answer to that is that women are just as ready as men to do what is needed for the sake of their country. The Suffragettes have always put country first, and self second. Unless they had done so, they would never have made the fight of the past years.

So, our position with regard to women fighting is this. If we are needed in the fighting line, we shall be there. If we are needed to attend to the economic prosperity of the country, we shall be there. What it is best in the interests of the State to do, women will do. But it must be clearly understood that if women do not actually take part in the fighting, that argues no inferiority, that argues no diminution of their claim to political equality. It simply means that men and women in co-operation decide the task which, in the interests of the whole, it is most necessary that they shall do. You must remember that if the men fight, the women are the mothers. Without the mothers you have no nation to defend. Therefore we never have admitted – we never shall admit – that even though we do not take part in the actual fighting we are not equally important from the point of view of citizenship. It is well known that you cannot maintain more than a certain proportion of your citizens in the fighting line. For every one who fights you must have a number of non-combatants to feed him, to clothe him, and to prevent the State for which he is fighting from crumbling into ruins. One thing is certain. You are not now utilising to the full the activities of women. In France, from which country I have just come, the women, while all the able-bodied men are at the front, are able to keep the country going, to get the harvest, to carry on the industries. It is the women who prevent the collapse of the nation while the men are fighting the enemy.

Go forth to meet the enemy

The appeal that has to be made, and the appeal that we are now making to men, is not an appeal that they shall wait till the enemy has set foot on our soil. It is not an appeal to drive the invader into the sea. It is an appeal to go where the invader now is, it is an appeal to make less terrible than it has been hitherto the burden which has fallen upon our Allies, and upon our comparatively few British soldiers at the front. More and more it becomes clear that there must be no waiting until the German is here; that the most practical thing to do is to go out and meet him and beat him on the other side of the Channel.

You read in a Liberal newspaper the other day these words about what our defeat in this war might mean: –

'The German army presses on, and your home, your country, these quiet streets, are in peril. You must help England now if you want to save her.

'There is no doubt about it, and it is possible. It is possible that, unless you strike a blow now, the last days of our free nation may be upon us.

'If Germany should beat us, you will be a colonist of Prussia. Your children will be taught German and compelled to speak it; your boys will be German conscripts. You will be taxed to keep up the German army, which will keep you down.'

I think on the whole we would rather be taxed to keep up an army of our own. Better be trained and ready to fight to maintain our national independence than be in rebellion as we should be under alien rule.

We read again: –

'… You will lose your free speech, your vote, your free newspapers, your right to organise.'

Well, we women do not possess all those blessings yet, but we are going to share them, and therefore we demand that they be maintained in existence until we are able to enter into possession of them.

If you lost your citizenship!

To those of us women who have fought for British citizenship, it is perhaps more precious than it is to men who have had it from their birth, without raising a finger either to win it or to protect it. Men! if you were to lose your citizenship, you would know its value then.

No man who is not physically incapable of fighting has any right to sit still while the rights of himself and his country-women are in the balance. That is the position.

We have lived so long free from war, at any rate from war menacing our existence as a nation, that it requires a tremendous mental agility to realise that we are in danger now; but if you were on the other side of the British Channel you would realise it. The war is not a cinematograph show – something to see pictures of, to read about. It must not be a thing for the descendants of the people here to read of with grief and humiliation. They must not know of it as people to whom our country is but a memory and but a name.

The Germans maintain that Britain is played out; that we are an old civilisation, too old to live any longer.

Why empires have fallen

Perhaps some few of our own people have become obsessed with the idea that, like the empires of the past, we must fall and give place to others. No, no, no! Other Empires fell because they had in them the seeds of decay. They were cursed by the existence of slavery, they were cursed by the subjection of women, and all the evils, moral and physical, that the subjection of women brings with it. No wonder those Empires fell. No wonder they died.

But the British Empire at this moment is being re-born. How can we tell that? (A voice: By the life in the women.) Yes, by the life in the women. The brains, the energy, the patriotism of the women are being offered in the service of the Empire, and this is one of the chief signs and means of its regeneration. Also we have the magnificent answer which men are now making to the call of national defence.

No, my friends, we may not be cultured, but we are very much alive we British people. We may not be so profound in our thought and in our learning as some other people profess to be! but we have the political genius; we know how to rule, and we know how to govern ourselves; and that is why we are especially fitted for the fulfilment of our very great responsibilities, our National responsibility, our Empire responsibility. We do not know everything, we cannot do everything, but we know, and we can do those things that are essential to us and to our work in the world.

Patriotism from the Suffragettes' point of view is by no means out of date. We have no use for that vague cosmopolitanism which is detached from love of one's own country. Our love for another country is absolutely worthless unless we love our own.

The world is with you

You will never coerce the patriotism out of Suffragettes. We do not identify our country with people who may have despitefully used us. We identify our country with everything that is great. We believe that our Empire is not worn out. We have a tremendous belief in British civilisation.

We militant women understand so clearly and so well how the man of an age for military service feels at this time. He is wondering if it is really his duty to take his life in his hands and go out to the war. The militants have, at one time or other, had a choice to make which was not so very different from that. It is true that we never had to face the sudden blow of the enemy which may lay you dead in an instant; but you must remember that, on the other hand, you men who decide to fight have a wonderful backing; everybody is wishing you well; everybody is urging you forward; everybody is supporting you. When we Suffragettes began our fight we had public opinion against us, and, as you all know, that is harder to face than the guns of the enemy.

As to physical danger, Suffragettes see things in this way: – Life is very short at the best, and none of us can escape death. The fighters are not called upon to exchange eternal life on this planet for death. We must all die, and the belief of the Suffragette is that as we have got to die, happy are those among us, men or women, who can buy something as they die; who can exchange their life for something more precious. Those who die for their country, whether it be in a political struggle, or whether it be in an international struggle, are most blessed of all mankind.

Those who go out and do the actual fighting, they at least have the joy of knowing, 'I have done my share. I have discharged my duty.'

The most awful thought that can come to any one of us, the keenest torture that we can suffer, is the thought that *we might have done more*. If at the end of this war there is any man who feels 'I might have done more,' he will be much to be pitied. We need never pity those who go down doing their duty.

The great occasion

Many a man has thought that no great occasion would ever come to him; no occasion on which he could show what was in him; no duty would ever come to him which would enable him to lose himself in some great task, in some great object. Well, such an occasion has come to the men of this country now. Horrible though the war is, looked at from one point of view, there is always that which ennobles it.

With all my heart and mind I believe that as a nation we need feel no remorse on account of this war. We had to do it, we had to fight. And as we have to do it, let us do it well; let us do it bravely and successfully. Not that success is the greatest thing! If ever the day should come when this Empire had to go under, when all it means had to be blotted out, we would die game, we would die nobly, and not until every drop of British blood had been poured out. It is in that spirit we militant women, whom some of you have misunderstood and unjustly condemned, have humbly tried to fight and work ever since our crusade for liberty began. It is the spirit which British men, as well as women, always show when they are at their best, that they are showing now, that will bring the nation to victory. Be sure of this: There are none who more fully understand, none who more wholly admire the bravery of the soldiers who have faced fearful odds in battle, than do the militant women, who themselves know something of the discipline of warfare.

The good that war will bring

Sooner or later this war will end in victory, and when that day comes women who are paying their share of the price will claim, will insist upon being brought into equal partnership as enfranchised citizens of this country.

If the war does nothing else it will do this. It will sweep away, it must and shall sweep away, the superstition, the narrowness, the jealousy, the suicidal folly which have made of our country two opposing camps – the enfranchised men in one, and voteless women in the other.

The events of this time are a proof that even in the province of national defence, even in the province of Imperial policy, the women's counsel is needed as well as the men's. Men citizens have been brought face to face with their own mistakes at this crisis. The country is paying heavily for it – the women and the men of France and Belgium have had to pay for it in blood and tears. But if through this you can learn to be wiser in the future, if through this you can learn to take the precaution of putting at the service of the State all the powers of women as well as of men – women's common sense, women's foresight, women's judgement, women's patriotism, all their moral, mental, and spiritual force, then the price will not have been paid in vain.

Elizabeth A. and Mary L. Macleod
On Sylvia Pankhurst

May 14th 1916
We came across a crowd in the Backs, and there was Sylvia Pankhurst standing on a seat, and holding forth on her twaddly opinions. It was a violent Anti-Compulsion, Stop the War at once speech, but the crowd were not having any. After proving (to herself) the evils of conscription in

other countries, she said tragically 'And now England has had conscription forced on her.' 'Hooray' from the crowd. 'And if we use the same arguments against it as we did before the war we are liable to be had up under the Defence of the Realm Act.' 'Hooray-Ay': On the subject of Protection, 'We shall never have protection if I can help it' – Roars of derision. 'This is an unjust war, a war in which Capitalists are exploiting labour for their own ends, and the soldiers and industrious poor are suffering for the greed of the government. We must stop the war at once' – and more twaddle to the same effect. After having proved her case to her own satisfaction, she invited questions. The first from a wounded Scotsman from Huntly, who sat down on the seat beside her.

McKinna: Why aren't you making munitions?

S. Pankhurst: My friends because I don't believe in the war; I have other far more important things to do. I work 14 hours a day and I like it.

A voice: How many a day do you talk?

2nd wounded soldier: If everyone was like you and refused to make munitions, what sort of condition do you suppose you'd be in when the Germans landed in Cambridge?

S. Pankhurst: My friends if everyone refused to make munitions, there would be peace at once, and as for the belief that the Germans could then come to Cambridge and ill treat women and children, it is not founded in fact.

2nd wounded soldier: If you want peace so much why don't you go to Germany, where the war came from, and ask for it?

Call of 'Oh we don't want to lose you but we think you ought to go.'

S. Pankhurst: My friends,

Voice: I beg your pardon.

S. Pankhurst: That's not a question.

Voice: No you said 'My friends', and I said I beg your pardon.

Another voice: You're an enemy.

S. Pankhurst: (sweetly) Well, I may not be your friend, but I have no enemies. You are my friend.

Voice: That's nice of you, I'm sure.

S. Pankhurst: I believe that we can only have peace with righteousness by persuading the people of England, Germany is ready for peace: she does not want Belgium now, she's asking for something else.

2nd wounded soldier: She'll get it too.

She then said that the men who had been fighting had been merely wasting time: the crowd promptly gave three cheers for the wounded, and next for all soldiers. As soon as she alluded to peace again, there were shouts of 'Get the war finished first.'

She began again that this war was bigger that the Boer war, but no more just (cries of Shame and Rot.) She asked the second wounded soldier what he was fighting for?

2nd wounded soldier: For, to whop the Germans – was the answer.

After a few vain attempts to the audience she said: Well I am disappointed that a seat of learning like Cambridge knows no better than to support such an unjust war and will therefore declare this meeting closed. (Much applause).

The chief of the Independent Liberal Party here, Mr Huckle then mounted the seat and was greeted with a roar of 'Sit down, throw him in the river. He's running like the Cam. Blow your nose.'

After much fumbling he produced a grubby handkerchief. 'Why khaki?', from the crowd. In spite of all his glares he could not make himself heard and so had to descend. W.S.2 next got up amidst cheers, but S. Pankhurst having something else to say he politely let her up in his place. This was to appeal for funds (pennies) for her Milk for Babies Fund in E. London. After her other sentiment she didn't get much. Finally W.S.2 got up on the seat again and said: 'I wasn't here at the beginning, so don't know all she said but what me and thousands of my comrades went out and got wounded for was to whop the Germans and what I say is let's do that and get the war finished and then think about peace.' (Prolonged cheers). Then as an after thought: 'I wish I'd been a conscientious objector, but it's too late now.' Laughter and cheers, and the meeting dispersed. Altogether a very entertaining afternoon, and we hope it will give Sylvia Pankhurst a lesson.

May Sinclair
from
The Tree of Heaven

After Drayton's death Frances and Anthony were sobered and had ceased to feed on illusions. The Battle of the Marne was fought in vain for them. They did not believe that it had saved Paris.

Then came the fall of Antwerp and the Great Retreat. There was no more Belgium. The fall of Paris and the taking of Calais were only a question of time, of perhaps a very little time. Then there would be no more France. They were face to face with the further possibility of there being no more England.

In those months of September and October Anthony and Frances were changed utterly to themselves and each other. If, before the War, Frances had been asked whether she loved England, she would, after careful consideration, have replied truthfully, 'I like England. But I dislike the English people. They are narrow and hypocritical and conceited. They are snobbish; and I hate snobs.' At the time of the Boer War, beyond thinking that the British ought to win, and that they would win, and feeling a little spurt as of personal satisfaction when they did win, she had had no consciousness of her country whatsoever. As for loving it, she loved her children and her husband, and she had a sort of mild, cat-like affection for her garden and her tree of Heaven and her house; but the idea of loving England was absurd; you might just as well talk of loving the Archbishopric of Canterbury. She who once sat in peace under the Tree of Heaven with her *Times* newspaper, and flicked the affairs of the nation from her as less important that the stitching on her baby's frock, now talked and thought and dreamed of nothing else. She was sad, not because her son Nicholas's time of safety was dwindling week by week, but because England was in danger; she was worried, not because Lord Kitchener was practically asking her to give up her son Michael, but because she had found that the race was to the swift and the battle to the strong, and that she was classed with her incompetent sisters as too old to wait on wounded soldiers. Every morning she left her household to old Nanna's care and went down to the City with Anthony, and worked till evening in a room behind his office, receiving, packing, and sending off great cases of food and clothing to the Belgian soldiers.

Anthony was sad and worried, not because he had three sons, all well under twenty-seven, but simply and solely because the Government persisted in buying the wrong kind of timber – timber that swelled and shrank again – for rifles and gun-carriages, and because officials wouldn't listen to him when he tried to tell them what he knew about timber, and because the head of a department had talked to *him* about private firms and profiteering. As if any man with three sons under twenty-seven would want to make a profit out of the War; and as if they couldn't cut down everybody's profits if they took the trouble. They might cut his to the last cent so long as we had gun-carriages that would carry guns and rifles the would shoot. He knew what he was talking about and they didn't.

And Frances said he was right. He always had been right. She who had once been impatient over his invariable, irritating rightness, loved it now. She thought and said that if there were a few men like Anthony at the head of departments we should win the War. We were losing it for want of precisely that specialised knowledge and that power of organisation in which Anthony excelled. She was proud of him, not because he was her husband and the father of her children, but because he was a man who could help England. They were both proud of Michael and Nicholas and John, not because they were their sons, but because they were men who could fight for England.

They found that they loved England with a secret, religious, instinctive love. Two feet of English earth, the ground that a man might stand and fight for, became, mysteriously and magically, dearer to them than their home. They loved England more than their own life or the lives of their children. Long ago they had realised that fathers do not beget children nor mothers bear them merely to gratify themselves. Now, in September and October, they were realising that children are not begotten and born for their own profit and pleasure either.

Ethel Bilborough
On Edith Cavell

20th October 1915, Wednesday.
Tragedies follow each other in quick succession now-a-days. Just now all England is boiling with wrath at the cold blooded murder of one of our British nurses in Belgium. Edith Cavell her name was, and she has been sheltering and befriending English & French soldiers in Belgium and helping them rejoin their regiments. Of course she knew she was defying German law! A very risky thing to attempt! She was imprisoned, tried, and almost before anyone knew anything about it, she was calmly shot in the night, or rather at 2 o clock in the morning. What a ghastly time to be executed!

She was very brave and heroic, and declared she was 'happy to die for her country', but poor soul! her courage failed her at the thought of those deadly six rifles awaiting her, and as she walked to the place of execution she fainted. The courageous noble minded(!) Hun who was in charge, calmly drew his revolver and shot her dead where she lay. What a glorious triumph for Germany! to shoot a poor fainting hospital nurse! – a woman who had given all her life to the care of others!

... Still, I think it all being rather *over* done, and *we* shouldn't like a German woman in England getting her countrymen (who were prisoners) back to the Fatherland! But we shouldn't shoot her like a dog for all that.

Emmeline Parkhurst

War Until the Victory!

A stirring message to our women, by Mrs Pankhurst, who gives a stirring Easter message on women's duty in the crisis of the War

Easter has always meant so much to the women in Christian countries, but this Easter, fraught as it is with anxiety and danger to our loved ones at the front, should be for us a time of spiritual uplifting and increased resolution to devote ourselves to the services of our country.

This is the message I would convey through the 'Empire News' to the million women munition workers of this country, who are playing a noble part in the great campaign.

The newly formed Women's Party is out to fight the German propagandists, who are trying to undermine the patriotism of our industrial workers. It is war to the knife, and the odds are on the women.

The time has now arrived when the women must come to the rescue on the Home Front. Many of the best men have died, and of those who live the best are in the fighting line.

Of those who remain, some are past active service, some are maimed and weakened in the struggle. Unfortunately, there remains a remnant – those who have been unwilling to serve, though they cling to any emoluments that war gives them, and are using their industrial and political power to the injury of their country.

Our mighty force

The women are a mighty force, intact and unimpaired. I have no doubt we will be equal to the task which now falls upon us at this critical hour.

The first duty of enfranchised women is to wage unceasing war against

British Bolshevists. They are now insidiously at work in the industrial world assisting Germany by fomenting unrest, and are using the machinery af trades unionism to bring about strikes.

The present war situation must convince even those who have most extreme sentimental objections to war that our existence as a nation is at stake.

But there are still people preaching the theory of peace negotiation, which shows, after the result of the Brest negotiations, they must be under some sinister influence and, consciously or unconsciously, are enemies of their country and their country's cause.

Magnificent patriotism

The great army of women munition makers are solid against these diabolical moves. During my present campaign I have addressed thousands of women in such great munition centres as Birmingham, Coventry, Manchester, and the Clyde. Not one pacifist have I met.

The scenes have been magnificent in their patriotism. I have asked great bodies of women what they would do if the men downed tools. The reply has been a great chorus of 'Let them. We will do their work.'

Everywhere the women are unanimous in their determination to 'carry on' while husbands, sons, brothers, and sweethearts are in the trenches. And they have three uppermost thoughts or desires: –

1. To win the war.
2. They want the comb-out, so that the healthy young men who have not fought at all should be sent to fight in the place of sending back the men who have been wounded several times.
3. They realise the horrors which they themselves would have to endure if this country were invaded.

Now it has been said of the British race that we are at our best in times of stress and adversity. I agree. But I do not think there is wisdom in concealing even the hardest facts from the people.

Much will depend on the next few weeks of warfare, according to those best able to judge.

Munitions first

The soldiers, we know, will do their part. It is for women on the Home Front to do their share in upholding the national courage and to stimulate the national determination to provide our armies with the munitions to carry us to victory.

The women are just as important as the men in the trenches. They have the power to save the country.

If it rested with them there would be no half-measures with the Germans and their Kaiser. They will do all that is asked of them – and more.

The Women's Party has been formed to unite the women to fight for victory and national security, and afterwards to wage a campaign of social reform to secure better housing, better education, greater security for mothers and infants, and a system of industrial organisation which will give good conditions of work, short hours, good wages, and at the same time greater efficiency and increased national wealth.

War till victory

As an organisation we have no political interests to serve, no axes to grind. We hope to play an important part in the next General Election in every constituency.

The line we shall take in the election will be a patriotic one. The candidates who are out wholeheartedly to win the war will get our support, irrespective of politics.

'War till victory, followed by a peace imposed upon the Germans,' is our motto.

4
Pacifism

Sylvia Pankhurst
The Women's Peace Conference

War grew daily more terrible. The miseries of a winter in the trenches were followed by frantic efforts to break through the opposing lines, in which thousands of lives were lost without result. On the shores of the Dardanelles poor fellows were dying in attempting the impossible, the blockade was tightened – submarine warfare intensified. Behind the great offensive, Peace efforts were feebly striving. News filtered through that there had been a Truce in the Trenches on Christmas Day, that British and German soldiers had thrown down their arms to fraternise, exchanging little keepsakes and comforts, rejoicing in the respite from slaughter their mutual confidence had won for them, finding themselves as brothers in their adversity. This brief manifestation of human solidarity, banned from official reports, was never permitted to recur.

Vain efforts were being made to resurrect the Socialist International. The Dutch Socialists had given hospitality to the Secretary of the International Socialist Bureau, Camille Huysmans, a Belgian. It was their hope that on neutral soil he would be able to perform the difficult task of resuscitation. The difficulties were great, and Huysmans unequal to the task. The officials of the Majority Socialist Parties in belligerent nations maintained, until the end of the War, their refusal to meet the Socialists of the countries with which the capitalist Governments of their countries were in conflict.

The Socialist Parties of the northern neutral countries had met at Copenhagen in January 1915 and had issued a manifesto denouncing the War as a product of Capitalist imperialism and its secret diplomacy, and calling on the Socialists of the belligerent nations to be active for peace, and to work with renewed energy to conquer political power. The leaders who controlled the Socialist parties of the belligerent nations were in no mood to second such a pronouncement. Under the auspices of the British Section of the International Socialist Bureau, a conference, which was supposed to represent the Socialist movements of Britain, France, Belgium and Russia, issued a declaration strongly supporting the cause of the Allied Governments, and declaring the Socialists of their countries 'inflexibly resolved to fight until victory is achieved.' When this manifesto was condemned at the I.L.P. conference, J. R. MacDonald, who had been a party to it, characteristically replied that it was a compromise. He urged his critics to 'be very careful to remember the date on which it was passed.'

Across the ruins of the International came the voice of Karl Liebknecht, demanding on the floor of the Prussian Landtag the democratisation of the franchise and of foreign policy.

'Democratic control by the people would have prevented the War. ... Away with the hypocrisy of civil peace! On with the international class struggle for the emancipation of the working class and against the War!'

His words thrilled round the world, evoking the heartbeat of a multitude. Brave Karl Liebknecht!

Already on December 2nd, 1914, he had voted against the War Credits in the German Reichstag. No British Socialist was ready to follow his example. On March 10th, 1915, Liebknecht repeated his negative. We learnt with joy that on March 18th several thousand women, who had organised secretly with this intent, had appeared before the Reichstag, shouting for peace. Karl Liebknecht from a window in the Reichstag had addressed them. As punishment he was ordered to the Front – to his death his friends feared. He had been joined by Ledebour, Ruhle, Mehring, Clara Zetkin and Rosa Luxemburg in a manifesto calling for an immediate peace, without annexations, which would secure political and economic independence to every nation, disarmament, and the compulsory arbitration of international disputes. At Christmas Liebknecht had conveyed a message to the I.L.P. in London appealing for a new Socialist International.

In March a conference of Socialist women, summoned by Clara Zetkin, the International Secretary of the Women's Socialist Organisation, and one of the leaders of the German Social Democratic Party, met secretly in Berne. It was attended by delegates from both factions of warring nations, who met in their old fraternity, to utter a call for the speedy ending of the

War, and a peace which should impose no humiliating condition on any nation. Unheralded and unchronicled, little was heard of the event. Women Socialists of all countries had overcome the nationalist hysteria of war time, which held the male leaders of the International in its grip. Clara had planned this conference with Rosa Luxemburg. They intended to go together across the frontiers to visit the Socialists of the other nations. Then Rosa was arrested. Clara saw her in prison, then went to Holland, but was unable to pass the Belgian frontier. She sent couriers to Huysmans but he did not reply. Soon Clara was herself in prison for four months; she was ill when she came out, but she persevered with the conference. The Social Democratic leaders declared it an offence against the discipline of the Party and forbade their members to distribute the conference manifestos.

Amongst women of another milieu a movement for peace was also germinant. At Christmas Emily Hobhouse, Helen Bright Clark, Margaret Clark Gillett, Sophia and Lily Sturge, Isabella Ford, Lady Barlow and Lady Courtney of Penwith had addressed a letter to the women of Germany and Austria, urging them to join in calling for a truce. Through *Jus Suffragii*, the organ of the International Women's Suffrage Alliance, whose editor, Miss Sheepshanks, bravely upheld its internationalism, despite very great discouragement from the majority of the British Suffrage Societies, a response was received from prominent German and Austrian women.

Dr. Aletta Jacobs and other Dutch Suffragists now issued an appeal for a women's international congress at The Hague, to urge the belligerent governments to call a truce to define their peace terms; and to demand the submission of international disputes to arbitration; the democratic control of foreign policy; that no territory should be transferred without the consent of its population; the political enfranchisement of women and the inclusion of women delegates in the conference of Powers which would follow the War. The conference was to cost £1,000; the Dutch Suffragists offered a third of the sum; the German Suffragists responded with a further third. The National Union of Women's Suffrage Societies under Mrs. Fawcett, which represented British women in the International Suffrage Alliance, repudiated the Congress; but a group of seceders from that organisation met with other women's organisations, including our Federation, in conference at the Caxton Hall to answer the invitation from Holland. The delegates were enthusiastic. More than 200 of us volunteered to go to The Hague.

The Congress now began to receive tremendous publicity. The Press condemned it; prominent women assailed it. We who had agreed to go were execrated. Mrs. Fawcett declared that to talk of peace while the German armies were in France and Belgium was 'akin to treason.' Mrs. Cecil Chapman, President of the New Constitutional Society for Women's Suffrage, considered the time 'painfully inopportune' for members of the belligerent nations to confer. The W.S.P.U., which had been *hors de combat* and existing on occasional speeches by Christabel and Mrs. Pankhurst, now burst into life to oppose the Congress. The *Suffragette* reappeared on April 16th, 1915, after eight months' suspension, declaring in its leading article that it was a 'thousand times more' the duty of militant Suffragettes to fight the Kaiser for the sake of liberty, than it had been to fight anti-Suffrage Governments. Nina Boyle, in the Women's Freedom League organ, *The Vote*, attacked *Jus Suffragii* for becoming 'the mouthpiece' of the promoters of the Conference, and protested that the Women's Freedom League 'refused to ask for more legislation – even reform legislation – until women could help to control and administer it.' She marvelled that there should be Suffragists 'who imagine it possible for them … to be an international power, and set in motion reforms vaster and more quixotic than any body of men with franchise, representatives, and Cabinet Ministers in their pocket, would venture to attack at the present moment.'

With such chilling and bitter sarcasm the ardent idealism of the pioneer is ever met; yet the true pioneers fling out their golden conceptions on the world, reeking not of obstacles, serene in their faith.

From French Suffragists came equally emphatic denunciations. An American woman who considered joining the Women's International Congress Movement sent a copy of its objects to ex-President Roosevelt he condemned them as 'silly and base.'

Mrs. Astor wrote to me that she would never have invited me to her house, had she known I would offer to attend such a Congress. She added that she had learnt we were paying £1 a week in the toy factory, instead of the 10s. of the Queen Mary Rooms. Had she known it she would not have aided us. Many members of the Women's Social and Political Union, who during its inactivity had worked for our Federation, now sheered off and left us. Some even of those who had professed internationalist and pacifist views now rallied to their old allegiance to Mrs. Pankhurst and Christabel; some hesitated, uncertain what course to take. Many subscribers to our work for mothers and children withdrew. By every post came letters refusing further support. 'Subscribers are falling off like dead leaves at the end of the season!' I said to Smyth, but we held on, redoubling our efforts, that those who depended on us might not suffer. Many times, before and since, the choice came to me, whether for the sake of the work I was doing, to stay my hand and remain silent, or to speak and do what I believed to be right, knowing that through me, all else that I was prominently engaged in would suffer attack and perhaps extinction. I was guided by the opinion that freedom of thought and speech is more important than any good which can ever come of concealing one's views, and by the knowledge that in the hour of its greatest unpopularity the pioneering cause needs one most. Yet it was often hard to choose thus sternly, flying in the face of what seemed prudent, casting to the winds the result of laborious effort; hard, not on my own account; for I had shed all personal aims when I gave up painting in the years of the Suffragette struggle before the War; hard only on account of the work I was striving to do, and the people who looked to me for aid. On this occasion we weathered the storm. Smyth came forward as usual with donations and loans, writing off most of the latter, too, as donations, when she found, as financial secretary, they were too hard to repay. New workers and sub-scribers came gradually in to replace the departed.

The women of Russia, Germany, Austria, France and Belgium were permitted to proceed to the Congress; but the British Government, having directed the Press abuse. of our mission, refused to let British women go. McKenna, at one point, conceded to Miss Courtney and Miss Marshall, who were conducting the negotiations, that passports should be issued to twenty women of discretion, whom he selected from the two hundred. Some of the chosen were quite flattered by his choice: such phrases as: 'They don't mind when they feel they can really trust you' fell from their lips. It is impossible to describe the atmosphere of repression which overhung the movement. Vain efforts at diplomacy attempted, to parry opposition. In the *Dreadnought* I had written of the Women s Peace Conference at The Hague. I received a letter of protest from Miss Crystal MacMillan of the British Committee for the Congress:

> British Committee of the
> International Women's Congress.

> Dear Miss Pankhurst,
> It has been pointed out to us that in the *Woman's Dreadnought* you speak of this international Congress as a 'Peace Congress.' This is giving rise to a good deal of misunderstanding as the Congress cannot fairly be so described. The definition of the terms of peace is the only point in connection with peace on which it expresses an opinion or makes a demand. To call it a 'Peace Con-ference' gives the impression that its object is to demand peace at any price.

We shall be very glad, therefore, if you will do what you can to remove the false impression which has been created.

C. MACMILLAN.

Alas, for the caution and confidence of the chosen ladies; McKenna, for all his promises did not permit them to sail. Miss Courtney, it is true, had been too sharp for him. When he assured her: 'Of course I should have no objection to issue permits to you and Miss Marshall,' she answered 'I will take mine now,' and was allowed to proceed. The others were kept waiting expectant until the eleventh hour. On one occasion McKenna assured them that he would have issued the necessary permits to them there and then; but the official whose duty it was to affix his signature to the documents had left the office for the night. It would be quite out of order for himself, or anyone save that particular official to sign. On their final visit he assured the chosen ladies that he would assuredly have let them travel at last; but, to his great regret, 'the boats had stopped running' on account of a great event of which they would certainly read in the Press. No notice of the event ever appeared. The ladies declared they had been tricked. The rest of us were curtly and frankly informed that no permits to attend the Congress were being issued.

Having no illusion that I might receive a permit I had drafted a series of resolutions to be sent to the Congress. These covered the abolition of secret and sectional treaties and alliances and the creation of a permanent peace treaty uniting all nations; the abolition of national armies and navies; the democratisation of the international Court of Arbitration and the extension of its scope. I showed the resolutions to Keir Hardie; he took the sheets from me eagerly. 'This is important,' he said, in his forceful way, and urged me to propose that a committee be appointed by the Congress to consider such proposals. 'Then something may come of it,' he said. We did not know that the American delegates to the Congress, amongst whom was Emmeline Pethick Lawrence, had held a preliminary conference on their voyage from New York and had worked out a similar programme.

I saw little of Keir Hardie in those days, so burdened I was by the volume and stress of our work. He had sunk into a great sadness. Whenever we met I found him ill and suffering. I left him heavy with anxiety. As I waited in Bishopsgate for the Old Ford 'bus, a thought, tragic and luminant, seized me - not my thought it seemed, but one from without, which assailed me. In a flash I realised the long struggle sustained in the advanced countries, through many generations, to waken the masses that they might gain control of their national Parliaments: I saw them at last make entry into the citadel, only to find it empty, the power gone – removed to an international Government, wherein the dead-weight of backward peoples would strangle all progress for generations to come. Was this the truthful augur of Internationalism? Was it thus that privilege and poverty would be buttressed in their ancient reign? Profound melancholy closed down on me. How static was this poverty, cruel and stultifying, with which we warred!

All schemes for international arbitration and agreement seemed empirical. The belief flared up insistent that only from a society re-created from the root, replacing the universal conflict of to-day by universal co-operation, could permanent peace arise. Yearning for the golden age of the coming equalitarian society, I passed, in thought, to the extremist pole, whereat all save a world-embracing social rebirth and reconstruction seemed mere trumpery. Then the daily fight with misery and hardship recalled me to do what I could for each of these poor ones.

The Women's Congress met in due course. Jane Addams, whom John Burns had described as America's finest citizen, presided over the gathering. She declared it the most deeply moving she had ever known. Historically it is to be regretted that the net demand for a truce made in the original appeal from Dutch women did not find a place in the final verdict of the Congress. Yet the belligerent governments were asked 'to put an end to this bloodshed and begin peace negotiations.' The neutral governments were urged to form a council offering continuous mediation, which should invite suggestions for a settlement of the conflict from each of the belligerent nations and should itself submit to them reasonable proposals for peace. Envoys were appointed to urge these demands. Jane Addams, Dr. Aletta Jacobs, and Rosa Genoni of Italy, for her country had not yet entered the War, went as neutrals to the belligerent Governments Rosika Schwimmer of Hungary, and others of the belligerent countries, visited the neutrals. It was probably the unique position of Jane Addams in American regard which induced Asquith and Grey to receive the envoys of this Congress which British women had not been permitted to attend.

In France the envoys had audience of Delcasse and Viviani, and of Davignon, on behalf of the Belgian Government at Havre; in Italy of Sonnino, Salandra and the Pope, in Berlin of von Bethmann Holiweg, in Vienna of Count Sturgkh, in Budapest of Count Tiza and Baron Burian. Everywhere they received fair words of encouragement to no purpose.

The European neutrals would gladly have undertaken the proposed mediation; they were suffering too much from the British blockade to be other than anxious to take every step which might bring the War to a close; but all neutral effort was rendered ineffective by the refusal to participate of America, the only powerful neutral. President Wilson referred the envoys to his special factotum, Colonel House, and to Robert Lansing, Counsellor of the Department of State, then assistant to W. J. Bryan in United States foreign affairs. House, who regarded peace negotiations on America's behalf as his own particular province, dismissed the appeal of the Women's Congress for neutral mediation as 'utterly impracticable.' Mediation by a group of neutral nations did not appeal to him; he desired mediation by Wilson and America, to their everlasting glory, and to ensure an adequate share for American interests in exploiting the undeveloped territories of the world. He was by no means a pacifist of Jane Addams's gentle type.

From the Women's Congress at The Hague arose a permanent organisation. A British Section, termed the Women's International League, was formed in the autumn. As at the preliminary Conference, all the women's organisations working for Peace were invited to send delegates Suffragists, Socialists, Labourists and Quakers being thus represented. I was elected to the Executive. The majority of its London members were seceders from Mrs. Fawcett's National Union of Suffrage Societies. The work, therefore, assumed a cautious and moderate tone. Our Federation delegates were out-voted, when we proposed that the title should be the Women's International Peace League, and that women of foreign citizenship, resident in Britain, should be admitted to membership of the British Section. Mrs. Swanwick opposed the proposition on the ground that 'a great deal of mud' would be cast at the organisation. Even the British wives of aliens were excluded.

The non-militant Suffragists felt the fierce opposition to our Peace efforts more sharply than Suffragettes and Socialists, who had already borne the brunt of championing unpopular causes.

The organisation was from the first overshadowed by the tremendous magnitude of its task. It worked many degrees below the high-keyed enthusiasm of the Hague Conference. It carried no fiery cross; but tried, in a quiet way, sincerely, if at times haltingly, to understand the causes of war, and to advance the causes of Peace by negotiation, and the enfranchisement of women. From time to time it expressed itself by resolution in careful phrases; from time to time it held a public meeting, from which notorious people were, as a rule, prudently excluded. All Peace work laboured under the weight of harsh adversity. The less could be accomplished, alas, the more lengthy, were the sittings of the Committee. They lasted from 10 a.m. to 6 p.m. It seemed almost like undertaking the labours of Penelope, when I essayed to induce the Executive to call a week's Conference to debate such international questions, then to the fore, as the Freedom of the Seas, Disarmament, the Self-Determination of Oppressed Nationalities and so on! Protracted as the task was, it was accomplished at length! When I returned to the East End after these lengthy sittings, to find myself obliged to cut out sleep, and work forty-eight hours, with scarcely a break, to cope with the arrears which had accumulated during my absence, I often told my East End colleagues I should prefer to resign from the W.I.L. 'Oh, do stay there and leaven them!' Norah Smyth and others urged me: but I did so reluctantly. In the East End we were equally powerless to stay the hideous progress of the War; but we could alleviate some of its miseries. To me it was essential to be able to voice my opinions spontaneously, and without fear or favour. To trim one's statements, in order to conciliate influential opinion, oppressed me with a sense of insincerity.

Lady Kate Courtney
On Jane Addams

May 18th 1915

Came back from Cambridge to a busy week with the meetings and parties in connection with the Hague Women's Congress, centring round Jane Addams, the well-known and well-loved American philanthropist, who had presided. A fine attractive personality. Outwardly a stoutish elderly lady with pleasant homely voice and manner, but full of goodness and shrewdness and reality. She and Dr Jacob, the Dutch organiser, and a Signora Genoni, an Italian pacifist, were the delegates for here, and saw the P.M. and Sir Edward Grey, and besides Committee Meeting and party, we had a fine public meeting in Kingsway Hall. Every speech good, and no foolish, excitable word. I was surprised, after the Lusitania, at our success, numbers and quality.

Friday last she was to have dined here with Pages, Lord Chancellor,

Hoovers, Alfred and Miss Robertson, who stayed the night, but was off back to Holland en route for Berlin!!

Saturday: President Wilson's note to Germany very good. L., asked by the 'New York World' to telegraph his opinion, did it, in spite of his rule not to respond to newspapers. ...

Meanwhile there have been horrible anti-German riots in London and elsewhere, and the Govt. are interning more men, and our Emergency Committee is again overwhelmed. We had got slacker. That Lusitania brutality has carried people off their balance. S. Webb, who is generally pretty calm, is hardened against Germany, and the 'New Statesman' has a preposterous article on the terms of peace which might have been in the 'Daily Mail.' Violence meets violence, and so it goes on. There were protests against the riots and retaliation with poisonous gas, but Asquith's answer is evasive, and how different in tone to General Botha's rebuke to their rioters! It is humiliating, and he is the one successful British General too! And yet we triumph in our Boer friend's good repute, and think of less than fifteen years ago when an hotel in London refused him entry.

Beatrice Webb

On Jane Addams

June 22nd. – Jane Addams, with whom we stayed at Hull House, Chicago, on our first world tour, dined with us last night. Since we knew her seventeen years ago she has become a world celebrity – the most famous woman of the U.S.A. representing the best aspects of the Feminist Movement and the most distinguished elements in the social reform movement. Some say that she has been too much in the limelight of late and that she is no longer either so sane or so subtle in her public utterances. But to us she seemed the same gentle, dignified, sympathetic woman, though like the rest of us she has lost in brilliancy and personal charm – the inevitable result of age, personal notoriety, and much business. Her late mission to the governments of the world, as the leading representative of the neutral women at the Hague Conference, has brought her into still greater prominence. She and one or two other women of neutral countries were charged with the 'Peace Mission' to the Governments of

Germany, Austria, Hungary, Italy, France, Belgium and England. She had found Sir Edward Grey politely encouraging, expressing his own personal pacific sentiments, but saying nothing about his Government.

The French Ministers were decidedly hostile – the most hostile of all the Governments – to any 'Peace manoeuvres'; the Italians were boys with a new toy; the Hungarians were deliberately oncoming; they showed no hatred of England or Russia; disclaiming all responsibility for the treatment of Belgium, 'that is Germany's affair', and suggesting that it might be quite easy for them to make a separate peace with Russia; they had beaten her, they were ready to make friends. As for the rest of the war, it did not concern them. The Hungarian Government even permitted a public meeting at which the women delegates pleaded for peace. The Austrians, on the other hand, were nervous and depressed but pretended complete confidence and refused to commit themselves. Jane Addams was most interesting in her description of Berlin. To outward seeming everything was prosperous and easy, the whole population united and confident. But there was a grimness, a restrained misery that manifested itself in bitterness against England and the U.S.A. They had thrashed Russia and if they chose to sacrifice the men they could break through in France: Italy was negligible. In spite of this appearance of brutal self-confidence the Chancellor and Foreign Secretary were far more willing to listen to peace proposals and even to encourage her to promote peace than any of the other Governments. Bethmann-Hollweg was terribly distressed at the loss of life: he had lost his son: every family was in mourning; they could win, but at what a cost! The longer the war lasted the more difficult it would be to persuade the military party to give up Belgium: the sooner peace came the more reasonable Germany could afford to be. Though Jane Addams did not herself suggest it, I should gather that Germany feels herself to be at the top of her fortunes and would be glad to entertain proposals before another winter in the trenches. Bethmann-Hollweg even suggested that there might be a conference of neutral powers with representatives of the belligerents. They would not accept the U.S.A. as arbiter and looked to Sweden or Spain as the initiator of peace. No one in Berlin seemed in the least concerned about the effect, on American public opinion, of the sinking of the Lusitania. 'The Americans cannot fight,' remarked Sudicum [Sudekum] contemptuously, 'their opinion of our doings is really of no account.'

Jane Addams herself thinks it inconceivable that the U.S.A. should come into the war, and she clearly sees little or no difference between British and German policy, either before or during the war – at least that is the impression she leaves on our minds. Her great thesis to us was 'the neutrality of the seas'.

Jane Addams
The War Conscience

I was sharply reminded of an obvious division between high tradition and current conscience in several conversations I held during the European War with women who had sent their sons to the front in unquestioning obedience to the demands of the state, but who, owing to their own experiences, had found themselves in the midst of that ever-recurring struggle, often tragic and bitter, between two conceptions of duty, one which is antagonistic to the other.

One such woman who had long been identified with the care of delinquent children and had worked for years towards the establishment of a children's court, had asked me many questions concerning the psychopathic clinic in the juvenile court in Chicago, comparing it with the brilliant work accomplished in her own city through the co-operation of the university faculty. The national government itself had recently recognised the value of this work, and at the outbreak of the War was rapidly developing a system through which the defective child might be discovered early in his school career, and not only saved from delinquency, but such restricted abilities as he possessed might be trained for the most effective use.

'Through all these years,' this mother said, 'I had grown accustomed to the fact that the government was deeply concerned in the welfare of the least promising child. I had felt my own efforts so identified with it that I had unconsciously come to regard the government as an agency for nurturing human life, and I had apparently forgotten its more primitive functions. I was proud of the fact that my son held a state position as professor of industrial chemistry in the university, because I knew that the research in his department would ultimately tend to alleviate the harshness of factory conditions, and to make for the well-being of the working classes in whose children I had become so interested.

'When my son's regiment was mobilised and sent to the front I think it never occurred to me any more than it did to him to question his duty. His professional training made him a valuable member of the aviation corps, and when in those first weeks of high patriotism his letters reported successful scouting or even devastating raids, I felt only a solemn satisfaction.

'But gradually through the months when always more of the people's food supply and constantly more men were taken by the government for its military purposes, when I saw the state institutions for defectives closed, the schools abridged or dismissed, women and children put to work in factories under hours and conditions which had been prohibited years before, when the very government officials who had been so concerned for the welfare of the helpless were bent only upon the destruction of the enemy at whatever cost to their fellow citizens, the state itself gradually became for me an alien and hostile thing.

'In response to the appeal made by the government to the instinct of self-preservation, the men of the nation were ardent and eager to take any possible risks, to suffer every hardship, and were proud to give their lives in their country's service. But was it inevitable, I constantly asked myself, that the great nations of Europe should be reduced to such a primitive appeal? Why should they ignore all the other motives which enter into modern patriotism and are such an integral part of devotion to the state that they must in the end be reckoned with?

'I am sure that I had reached these conclusions before my own tragedy came, before my son was fatally wounded in a scouting aeroplane, and his body later thrown overboard into a lonely swamp. It was six weeks before I knew what had happened, and it was during that period that I felt very strongly the folly and waste of putting men, trained as my son had been, to the barbaric business of killing.

'This tendency in my thinking may have been due to a hint he had given me in the very last letter I ever received from him of a change that was taking place within himself. He wrote that whenever he heard the firing of a huge field gun, he knew that the explosion consumed years of the taxes which had been slowly accumulated by some hard-working farmer or shop-keeper, and that he unconsciously calculated how fast industrial research could have gone forward had his department been given once a decade the costs of a single day of warfare, with the command to turn back into alleviation of the industrial conditions the taxes which people had paid.

'He regretted that he was so accustomed to analysis that his mind would not let the general situation alone, but wearily went over it again and again; and then he added that this War was tearing down the conception of government which had been so carefully developed during this generation in the minds of the very young men who had worked hardest to fulfil that conception.

'Although the letter sounded like a treatise on government, I knew there was a personal pang somewhere behind this sombre writing, even though he added his old joking promise that when their fathers were no longer killed in industry he would see what he could do for my little idiots.

'At the very end of the letter he wrote, and they were doubtless the last words he ever penned, that he felt as if science herself in this mad world had also become cruel and malignant. I learned later that it was at this time that he had been consulted in the manufacture of asphyxiating gases, because the same gases are used in industry, and he had already made experiments to determine their poisonousness in different degrees of dilution. The original investigation with which he had been identified had been carried on that the fumes released in a certain industrial process might be prevented from injuring the men who worked in the factory.

'I know how hard it must have been for him to put knowledge acquired in his long efforts to protect normal living to the brutal use of killing men. It was literally a forced act of prostitution.'

As if to free her son's memory from any charge of lack of patriotism, after a few moments she continued: 'These modern men of science are red-blooded, devoted patriots, facing dangers of every sort in mines and factories and leading strenuous lives, in spite of the popular conception of the pale anaemic scholar, but because they are equally interested in scientific experiments wherever they may be carried on, they inevitably cease to think of national boundaries in connection with their work.

'The international mind which really does exist, in spite of the fact that it is not yet equipped with adequate organs for international government, has become firmly established at least among scientists. They have known the daily stimulus of a wide and free range of contacts, they have become inter-penetrated with the human consciousness of fellow scientists all over the world.

'I hope that I am not a whining coward. My son gave his life to his country as many another brave man has done, but I do envy the mothers whose grief is at least free from this fearful struggle of opposing ideals and traditions. My old father, who is filled with solemn pride over his grandson's gallant record and death, is most impatient with me. I heard him telling a friend the other day that my present state of mind was a pure demonstration of the folly of higher education for women; that it was preposterous and more than human flesh could bear to combine an intellectual question on the function of government with a mother's sharp agony over the death of her child.

'He said that he had always contended that women, at least those who bear children, had no business to consider questions of this sort, and that the good sense of his position was demonstrated now that such women were losing their children in war. It was enough for women to know that government waged war to protect their firesides and to preserve the nation from annihilation; at any rate, she should keep her mind free from silly attempts to reason it out. "It's all Berta von Suttner's book and other nonsense that the women are writing," he exploded at the end. ... At times I feel immeasurably old, and in spite of my father's contention that I am too intellectual, I am consciously dominated by one of those overwhelming impulses belonging to women as such irrespective of their mental training in their revolt against war. After all, why should one disregard such imperative instincts? We know perfectly well that the trend of a given period in history has been influenced by habits of preference and instinctive actions founded upon repeated and unnoticed experiences of an analogous kind; that "desires to seek and desires to avoid" are in themselves the very incalculable material by which the tendencies of an age are modified.

'The women in all belligerent countries who feel so alike in regard to the horror and human waste of this War, and yet refrain from speaking out, may be putting into jeopardy the power inherent in human affairs to right themselves through mankind's instinctive shifting toward what the satisfactions recommend and the antagonisms repulse. The expression of such basic impulses in regard to human relationships may be most important in this moment of warfare which is itself a reversion to primitive methods of determining relations between man and man or nation and nation.

'Certainly women in every country, who are now under a profound imperative to preserve human life, have a right to regard this maternal impulse as important as was the compelling instinct evinced by primitive women, when they made the first crude beginnings of society by refusing to share the vagrant life of man because they insisted upon a fixed abode in which they might cherish their children. Undoubtedly, women were then told that the interests of the tribe, the diminishing food supply, the honour of the chieftain, demanded that they leave their particular caves and go out in the wind and weather without regard to the survival of their children. But at the present moment the very names of the tribes and the honours and glories which they defended are forgotten, while the basic fact that the mothers held the lives of their children above all else, insisted upon staying where the children had a chance to live, and cultivated the earth for their food, laid the foundation of an ordered human society.

'My son used to say that if I should forget all the science I did not know I should think more clearly. Undoubtedly, I am putting it badly, and my scientific knowledge is certainly irregular, but profound experiences such as we are having in this War throw to the surface of one's mind all sorts of opinions and half-formed conclusions. The care for conventions, for agreements with one's friends is burned away. One is concerned to express only ultimate conviction, even though it may differ from all the rest of the world. This is true in spite of the knowledge that every word will be caught up in an atmosphere of excitement and of that nervous irritability which is always close to grief and to moments of high emotion.

'In the face of many distressing misunderstandings, I am, nevertheless, certain that if a majority of women in every country would clearly express their convictions, they would find that they spoke, not for themselves alone, but for those men for whom the War has been a laceration, "an abdication of the spirit." Such women would doubtless formulate the scruples of certain soldiers whose "mouths are stopped by courage," men who months ago with closed eyes rushed to the defence of their countries, but are now fighting behind a "thick wall of certitudes" over which they dare not look.

'It may also be true that as the early days of this war fused us all into an overwhelming sense of solidarity until each felt absolutely at one with all his fellow-countrymen, so the sensitiveness to differences is greatly intensified and the dissenting individual has an exaggerated sense of isolation. I try to convince myself that this is the explanation of my abominable sense of loneliness which is almost unendurable.

'I have never been a feminist, and have always remained quite unmoved by the talk of the peculiar contribution women might make to the state, but during the last dreadful months, in spite of women's widespread enthusiasm for the War and their patriotic eagerness to make the supreme sacrifice, I have become conscious of an unalterable cleavage between militarism and feminism. The militarists believe that government finally rests upon a basis of physical force, and in a crisis such as this militarism, in spite of the spiritual passion in war, finds its expression in the crudest forms of violence.

'It would be absurd for women even to suggest equal rights in a world governed solely by physical force, and feminism must necessarily assert the ultimate supremacy of moral agencies. Inevitably, the two are in eternal opposition.

'I have always agreed with the feminists that, so far as force plays a great part in the maintenance of an actual social order, it is due to the presence of those elements which are in a steady process of elimination; and, of course, as society progresses the difficulty arising from woman's inferiority in physical strength must become proportionately less. One of the most wretched consequences of war is that it arrests these beneficent social processes and throws everything back into a coarser mould.

'The fury of war enduring but for a few months or years may destroy slow-growing social products which it will take a century to recreate – the "consent of the governed," for instance ... But why do I talk like this? My father would call it one of my untrained and absurd theories about social progress and the functions of government concerning which I know nothing, and that, at any rate, I have no right to discuss the latter in this time of desperate struggle. Nevertheless, it is better for me in these hideous long days and nights to drive my mind forward even to absurd conclusions than to let it fall into one of those vicious circles in which it goes round and round to no purpose.'

Catherine Marshall
Women and War

When within the course of a few short days last summer the nations of Europe (like climbers roped together on a dangerous precipice when the leader slips) were one after another engulfed in the great tragedy of war, I suppose the first thought in the minds of most of us women was a sense of shattering horror at the choice with which the men were confronted. The situation as it appeared to most British men was that either their country must fail to keep her pledged word, must turn a deaf ear to the cry of Belgium in her agony, or they – the whole manhood of the nation – must go forth to kill and be killed; to suffer, and, still worse, to inflict, all the horrors of war; to do violence to the whole spirit of civilisation, the whole teaching of Christianity.

Close upon this first thought, and the great flame of pity and tenderness it called forth in our hearts for the men who had this terrible choice to make, there came a crushing sense of our responsibility and guilt – the guilt of the peoples – in having permitted such a tragedy to come to pass. It is true that the peoples have not wanted war; but they have not willed peace. They had been content if their rulers have avoided *making war*; they have not insisted that they should, positively and constructively, *make peace* – make conditions that promote mutual trust and co-operation instead of acquiescing in conditions that promote mutual suspicion and enmity. If the peoples had cared enough for peace they would have known no rest until they had established such relations between the civilised countries as would have made a disaster like the present war impossible. For the choice with which our men are faced today need not have been the only choice; the sacrifices each nation is making need not have been necessary sacrifices. Honour demands, truly, that a nation shall keep its word, that it shall not leave in the lurch a neighbour whom it had led to count on its support. But honour does *not* demand that destruction or bloodshed shall be the only means of fulfilling these obligations. It is only because we have neglected to provide other means that we found ourselves last August confronted with the choice between breaking our faith with our neighbour or violating the law of Christ and of human brotherhood.

And for this lack of will to peace, this acquiescence in conditions which made possible, if not inevitable, the cataclysm in which we are now involved, we women realised at last that we share the responsibility; and in that fact lies, I believe, the great hope for the future, the source from which the peace forces will be able to draw new motive-power. The mother-heart of womanhood has been stirred to its depths; and it is a womanhood whose sense of responsibility has been developed, whose mind has been educated, whose capacity for co-operation has been trained by the Women's Movement, with all that it has meant of awakening and enlightenment, and the widening of sympathy.

And what contribution has this awakened womanhood to offer for the solution of the great problems of reconstruction that the civilised world has got to face?

Women in all countries have proved the value of their service in relieving the suffering and mitigating the material evils caused by war; and the most valuable qualities they have brought to this work have been the qualities of imagination, of faith, of dauntless love; their habit of regarding people under all circumstances as human beings, and not merely as ciphers in an Army estimate or a Census return; their experience as mothers and as heads of households, in presiding over the mutual relations of the separate human units of which a family or a household is composed, adjusting the claims and needs of its various members, with their different temperaments, their different stages of growth, in such a way that each may develop all his powers to the full and use them for the common good of all. In some instances, women's very inexperience has been of value; it has made them refuse to be daunted by difficulties which to men, tired and discouraged by former failures, had appeared unsurmountable.

I believe that all these qualities are just as much needed for the work of creating a new social fabric as for the patching and mending of the existing fabric on which the war has wrought such destruction. I believe that just as women can do much for the healing of the physical wounds which men are inflicting on one another, so they can do much also for the healing of the deeper and more disastrous spiritual wounds which nation is inflicting on nation. I believe that women, if they turn their minds in that direction, are more likely than men to find some other way of settling international disputes than by an appeal to force, partly because that is an appeal which is not open to them as women, and they have, therefore, never been accustomed to rely upon it. (It is interesting to trace the analogy between the position of women and that of the smaller nations in this respect.) I believe that the experience and habits of mind which women acquire as mothers of families and as heads of households might, if applied to a wider field, throw new light on the problems of the great human family of nations, and help to build up a better system of international relations which would make impossible the repetition of such a tragedy as that in which we are now involved.

But above all I believe that on women rests a large share of the responsibility for providing the motive-power which alone can make all these things possible, and without which the most perfect machine in the world will not work. And I believe that this motive-power is to be found in the deep horror of war which has entered for the first time into the soul of an organised women's movement. Women, thousands of individual women, have known that horror indeed only too well in the past; for war, to women, is pre-eminently an outrage on motherhood and all that motherhood means; the destruction of life and the breaking up of homes is the undoing of women's work as life-givers and home-makers. But in former great wars there was not an organised women's movement to give expression to the passion of horror in the women's hearts, to be fired by it to co-operative action. Today there is such a women's movement, organised, articulate, in almost all the belligerent and most of the neutral countries.

And I believe the great call to the women's movement, if we have ears to hear and courage and faith and love enough to respond to it, is that we should face and visualise the full horrors of war, accepting our share of responsibility as those who might have helped, had we cared enough, to save the world from this tragedy.

I believe that this is the share which we, as women and non-combatants, are called upon to take in making this truly a 'war to end war', to 'put an end to militarism' – in ensuring that the sacrifices our men are making shall not have been in vain.

Let us look steadfastly at war and the consequences of war, with our women's eyes – our mother's eyes – and tell the world what we see. Let us look honestly and courageously, 'les yeux bien ouverts, les yeux qui veulent voir', shirking none of the pain and the horror, refusing to be blinded by glamour. (There is no glamour about the wrecked homes of Belgium and E. Prussia. If we succeed in carrying out our threat to stop food supplies from reaching Germany there will be no glamour for the women who see their children and their invalids and their old people dying of starvation.) We must not shut our eyes to any of the wickedness of it; we must let the pity and the shame of it enter deep into our hearts and rouse a passionate determination that these things shall never be again.

It is by this deliberate opening of our hearts to all the pain and suffering, this sharing in the sense of responsibility and sin, that even the simplest and humblest of us may attain the power and the wisdom to build up the new world of our dreams. This is the great truth taught in the legend of Parsifal, 'der reine Thor, durch Mitleid wissend' – the pure-hearted fool who, through compassion, through sharing in the suffering and sin of the world, attained wisdom and understanding. It was not enough that he should see and pity physical suffering; he grieved over the swan he had killed, but he did not understand. It was not enough that he should see the repentance of another; he was permitted to witness the mystery of the Holy Grail and the agony of Amfortas, but still he did not understand; he looked on as a fool, blindly from outside. It was only when he himself participated in the greatest suffering of all – the sense of sin – that enlightenment came. That sense entered his heart in an agonising flash; he knew, he understood. From that moment his path lay clear before him. He went out to his task in the world, and he became worthy not only to receive and understand the mystery of the Grail, but to be its keeper, to administer its blessing to others.

Let us too seek this knowledge and understanding. Let us not try to escape any of the agony of remorse that it will bring; for out of that agony a new hope will be born, a new force will arise in the world. In this way, and I believe in this way only, can we truly follow in the steps of Him who came 'to bring light to them that walk in darkness and in the shadow of death, and to guide our feet into the way of peace.'

5

Conscription

Ethel Bilborough

Conscription in England Has Come!

5th March 1916:

Conscription in England has come! One can hardly realise it, things have come about so gradually. Voluntary recruiting did well, but not well enough, and the slackers *had* to be got somehow, so thanks to Lord Derby's scheme all those who wouldn't enlist will be *made* to. But the government have felt their way to this great step very cautiously, very guardedly, and have made absurd concessions relating to men bearing arms who may have 'conscientious' objections to war! and endless exemptions are being made. On these lax lines of course things are not working, & *far* more stringent rules must be enforced if we are to get the necessary men. Naturally every coward and slacker thinks fighting is 'wrong'! and the most ludicrous reasons are being put forward by men who want to get exemption owing to their 'conscientious'(?) scruples! The other day a man who said he was an artist, claimed exemption on the grounds that he 'could not mutilate anything so beautiful as the human form'!!

Only the single men have been called up so far, but compulsory service is soon to be put into practice for the young married men also.

Sylvia Pankhurst
The Military Service Bill

A week has passed since the issue of Lord Derby's statement and the introduction of the Conscription Bill, for which the statement is supposed to be the excuse.

The Derby figures are merely a patchwork of guesses, and this was generally admitted after Sir John Simon's speech of January 3rd.

Nevertheless, the Government still takes its stand upon Lord Derby's statement, and makes no attempt to justify its resort to compulsion by the production of definite figures. This is one of the most amazing pieces of bluff and effrontery committed even by this Government.

But it is our desire to say frankly, and indeed to proclaim the truth as widely as we can, that *no* figures, however large, could reconcile us to Conscription, or could mitigate in the slightest degree our passionate determination to oppose it with all the energy at our command.

The present Conscription bill does not go so far as some of the advocates of all-round compulsion would like, but it goes further than most of them have dared to hope, and infinitely too far for us!

The Bill is apologised for on the ground that it applies to a limited number of men only, but if it applied to one [single human being] only, it should be fought, until it has been destroyed.

It is pretended that though compulsion is unjust, there is no harm in making conscripts of the unmarried men. What a dishonest piece of absurdity!

It is merely an excuse for attacking one set of men at a time, under cover of the individual selfishness which makes bodies of people fail to realise their collective solidarity, instead of facing the opposition of married and unmarried men together.

The principle of compulsion is wholly bad, and every clause of the Bill appears to contain a special blot of its own.

Mothers and fathers, who realise that a lad under twenty is, and should be, but a child still in many ways, will keenly resent the fact that the conscript age begins at 18, especially when it is realised that according to present War Office practices a boy of 17 and three quarters, whose physique appears to be equal to that of 19, may be counted officially as 19. Soon we are likely to find that a boy of 16, whose physique appears to be that of 18, may be called up as a conscript.

It appears to us as peculiarly mean that middle-aged politicians, from their position of well-paid security, should be endeavouring to exercise compulsion against the young lads who are still under the legal age of maturity and may not vote.

The conscience clause is merely a sham, as Mr Asquith clearly showed when he indicated that those whose conscientious objections are accepted may be compelled to do mine sweeping and other 'duties which are very important to the prosecution of the war'.

One well-known objector has aptly replied to Mr Asquith in declaring that conscientious objectors could only agree to undertake mine sweeping if they might sweep up British mines as well as others, as all mines are dangerous to life.

TRUE Conscientious objectors to war service will in most cases refuse to take any contributory part in warfare, however remote.

The Bill does not define the tests which shall satisfy the Military Service Tribunal that an objection is conscientious, and the spirit of the Bill and of the Government offer no reason for believing that the test intended is the plain unvarnished statement of the objector that his conscience tells him that for one reason or another he ought not to attest. Any other method than this would certainly be manipulated by the authorities, and any pretence that the men are to be put to non-combatant service, (even if conscientious objectors could assent to it) would certainly be disregarded when the men got to the front.

The penalty to be imposed on those who resist military service is not stated in the Bill. Presumably, it would be death, as the men would be under military law.

The composition of the Military Service Tribunals, which the Bill proposes to set up, is thoroughly unsatisfactory, and the members of the local Tribunals, the Appeal tribunal and the Central Tribunal, are to be chosen in an entirely arbitrary way, and without any reference whatsoever to the votes or the wishes of the people.

The Bill provides that the King, which, of course means the Government, may make regulations by Order in Council, in regard to the procedure of these Tribunals. This provision opens the door to still further autocracy.

There is nothing in the Bill to prevent the men who may be forced to attest under it, but who remain in civil employment, from being held under the dominance of military rule.

There is nothing in the Bill to prevent the men who are being forced to attest under it from being used, against their will, to act as strike breakers and blacklegs by military order.

This Bill is another link in the chain of compulsion, in which the Government is striving to entangle us. We must resist at every point, instead of allowing ourselves to be gradually betrayed. Mr Birrell said in the debate on the Bill 'we must take care that in Ireland we don't force the [pace] thereby revealing that though [the] steps must be slower, Ireland also is to be put under compulsion as soon as possible'. Yet the Irish Members have decided to withdraw their opposition to the Bill and merely to abstain from voting.

The Labour Members in the Government are hesitating to obey the mandate of the Trade Union Congress; determined action by these men might already have killed the Bill, the working people, who are always the sufferers under the compulsion, will remember this in time to come.

The Government, which has continually refused to prevent profiteering in food and freight charges, has now audaciously issued from its Committee on Production as statement to certain trade unions that 'any further advances in wages (other than advances following automatically from existing agreements) should be strictly confined to the adjustment of local conditions, where such adjustments are proved to be necessary.'

And this they say is a war for *freedom!* Meanwhile the price of bread goes up!

Beatrice Webb
The No-Conscription Fellowship

April 8th. – The Friends' Meeting House in Devonshire House Hotel – a large ugly circular hall with a big gallery running round it – was packed with some 2,000 young men – the National Convention of the No-Conscription Fellowship. The entries to the meeting were discreetly held by stalwart policemen of the City Division. The assembly, presided over by Clifford Allen, was good-tempered and orderly. The Chairman was a monument of Christian patience and lucid speech – his spiritual countenance, fine gentle voice and quiet manner serving him well as the President of a gathering of would-be martyrs for the sacred cause of Peace. For it became clear in the course of the meeting, that what the Fellowship is standing for, is not the right to refuse military service, but the inauguration, first in England and then in the world, of a strike against war by the armies – actual and potential – of all warring peoples. This was brought

out by the enthusiastic denunciation of any alternative service, however
free from military considerations. They wanted to smash militarism; they
intended, in fact, to use the conscience clause to nullify the Conscription
Act. 'The only alternative service which we will accept, as work of national
importance, is the energetic continuance of our agitation for peace' –
summed up Clifford Allen, in defiant tones amid deafening applause.

Among the 2,000 were many diverse types. The intellectual pietist,
slender in figure, delicate in feature and complexion, benevolent in
expression, was the dominant type. These youths were saliently conscious
of their own righteousness. That they are superior alike in heart and intelligence to the 'average sensual man' is an undoubted fact: ought one to
quarrel with them for being aware of it? And yet the constant expression,
in word and manner, of the sentiment avowed by one of them – 'We are
the people whose eyes are open' – was unpleasing. There were not a few
professional rebels, out to smash the Military Service Act, because it was
the latest and biggest embodiment of authority hostile to the conduct of
their own lives according to their own desires. Here and there were mis-
guided youths who had been swept into the movement because 'conscientious objection' had served to excuse their refusal to enlist and possibly
might save them from the terrors and discomforts of fighting – pasty-
faced furtive boys, who looked dazed at the amount of heroism that was
being expected from them. They were obviously scared by the unanimity
with which it was decided 'to refuse alternative service'; and they will certainly take advantage of the resolution declaring that every member of
the Fellowship must follow his own conscience in this matter. On the
platform were the sympathisers with the movement – exactly the persons
you would expect to find at such a meeting – older pacifists and older
rebels – Bertrand Russell, Robert Trevelyan, George Lansbury, Olive
Schreiner, Lupton, Stephen and Rosa Hobhouse, Dr. Clifford, C. H.
Norman, Miss Llewelyn Davies and the Snowdens: the pacifist predominating over the rebel element. The speeches in the afternoon might have
been delivered at any gathering of persons dissenting from the verdict of
the bulk of their fellow-citizens because they felt themselves possessed of
a higher standard of morality. 'You are made of the stuff of Prophets', tes-
tified Philip Snowden.

The muddled mixture of motives – the claim to be exempt from a given
legal obligation, and the use of this privilege as a weapon against the carrying out of the will of the majority – marred the persuasive effect of this
demonstration of the No-Conscription Fellowship. The first argument
advanced by all the speakers was, 'I believe war to be an evil thing; killing

our fellow men is expressly forbidden by my religion, and by the religion, by law established, of my country. Under the Military Service Act *bona fide* conscientious objectors are granted unconditional exemption: I claim this exemption.' But this plea did not satisfy the militant majority. They declared their intention to defy the Act, so that the Act should become inoperative, even if all the conscientious objectors, on religious grounds, should be relieved from service. They *want* to be martyrs, so as to bring about a revulsion of feeling against any prosecution of the war. They are as hostile to voluntary recruiting as they are to conscription. If the Government decided to rely on the recruiting sergeant, they would send a missionary down to oppose him. These men are not so much conscientious objectors as a militant minority of elects, intent on thwarting the will of the majority of ordinary citizens expressed in a national policy.

Now it seems clear that organised society could not continue to be organised, if every citizen had the right to be a conscientious objector to some part of our social order, and insisted that he should be permitted not only to break the law himself but to persuade other citizens to break it. Moreover, when the conscientious objection is to carrying out an unpleasant social obligation like defending your country or paying taxes, conscience may become the cover for cowardice, greed or any other form of selfishness. Hence the State, in defence, must make the alternative to fulfilling the common obligation sufficiently irksome to test the consciences of the objectors. A wise statesman will make the test sufficiently severe to turn back the slackers without inflicting too great a punishment on the genuine dissenters. If the test is administered with kindliness and equity, public opinion will uphold both the law and the exemptions granted on grounds of conscience. But the public will not tolerate any use of a conscience clause for the express purpose of defeating the law.

Has this movement a future? Will it be a ferment, or one of the ferments, which will bring about a revulsion of feeling, here and on the Continent, against compulsory service? Or will it peter out like the passive resistance to the education rate, or the still feebler refusal to conform to the Insurance Act? It has the great quality of youthfulness. Personally, I think it is doomed to failure, assuming that the Act is administered with any degree of equity and good nature. (A big assumption!) The majority of conscientious objectors will not survive the test of alternative employment even if they survive the mingled coaxing and duress that will be attempted in a barrack yard to get them into uniform. ...

Lady Kate Courtney
The Western Tribunal Appeal Court

January 9th 1916

Penzance. A curious sunrise! The sky covered with grey clouds might break into colour, but as the minutes went on between 8 o'c. and 8.30 I gave up hope – the dead grey remained. I had ceased to look seaward, and when a blaze like a ship on fire caught the corner of my eye and turning round there it was, a globe of living fire – five minutes' glory and the grey cloud swallowed it – but I am cheered and hope it may be a good omen.

For indeed the outlook seemed very bleak – a bitter contest against conscription added to the fierce war, perhaps beginning of social strife which we fear will follow this war. I felt last night some understanding of people taking their own lives in despair. But that burst of sunrise gives fresh hope. And, indeed, for me there is much happiness as long as I have Leonard, and one feels selfish in realizing that.

On 4th [April 1916] an old Quaker fetched me from the Emergency Committee to go into the Western Tribunal Appeal Court, Mr Neld a K.C. and M.P. presiding, and it certainly was a disgusting scene from a point of view of justice – a farce – brow-beating argument, any that would serve, and no understanding of the young men's position, some of them simple, shy workmen, others with more thought out views, but all seemed in earnest. A Church of England man was told he could not be a consc. objector as there was an article of the 39 sanctioning war. Another was asked where specially 'Christ' opposed war, and [was] told love for enemies was an abstract proposition, and he must be practical. An appeal to the law of Christ brought a remark that the Law of Christ was not the question, but the Act of Parliament, and a reference to W. Long's circular (L.G.Bd.) was scornfully put aside with: 'We have nothing to do with circulars but only statute.' Objection to take the military oath was met with: 'You have no need to, you are already enrolled and presumed to have taken it.' Socialists came off specially badly – could not apparently have consciences, and to have joined the No Consc. Fellowship or the O.R. was clearly a crime. One socialist said he had two Austrian friends who were members of the Int. Soc. as he was, and when war was imminent they made a compact with him that neither he nor they would fight. The Austrians remained here and were interned, and he could not break the compact. Whereupon the military representative got up and said: 'This man has made a compact with the enemy and comes within the law.' I am bound to say the K.C. demurred to this, but what an insight into the militarist mind! To have kept two of the enemy, and men who had been trained too, as against one untrained townsman was disloyalty. The whole object of the war seems now to be to kill more Germans than we lose, and yet two to one out of action peacefully is a crime. Very typical of the military anti-pacifist attitude.

November 20th 1916

And my dear Stephen has faced the consequences of his determined opposition to military service. The Court Martial came off last Wedn. Leonard insisted on going down to Warminster for it, though Stephen deprecated his doing so. We slept the night at the Bath Arms (not too well on a hard bed – what must not a plank one be!) We, Rosa with us, took motor to Longbridge Barracks, and there, on the skirts of a wood full of late autumn tints, were the huts and soldiery. Stephen emerged – it was early, before 9 o'c. – looking a gentleman, in spite of no collar and unpolished boots and shabby clothes, calm and unperturbed. The proceedings were tedious, a repetition of the formal evidence of refusal to put on a uniform by several witnesses unchallenged, and all taken down in writing instead of short-hand. Major Churt, the President, was fair and courteous. Stephen read a simple, short and dignified statement, and Leonard was allowed to speak as to character – not altogether relevant some of it to the actual charge, but I was glad he got it in, and grateful to him for going. The two young people were much helped in their trial, and it did good to the other C.O.'s also. But of course the result was a foregone conclusion: 'Deemed a soldier, they disobeyed orders.' The sentence we now hear is 6 months hard labour, and S. has gone to Wormwood Scrubs, where it is said there is the largest Quaker Meeting for Worship in England. Perhaps an exaggeration this – but there will hardly be a more living one.

A. T. Fitzroy
from
Despised and Rejected

'Clear the court!'

The people were hustled out into one of the long stone corridors of the House of Commons, and the door closed upon them. Behind the door the fate of two applicants for exemption was being decided. Antoinette groaned at the delay. Dennis had been called for 2.30 that afternoon, but it was nearly 4 o'clock now, and so far only five out of the twelve cases had been heard. The fact that one did not know in what order they were to be heard, added to the suspense of waiting. In the first case there had only been a brief interval between the applicant's statement and the delivery of judgment. The spectacled, obviously highly-strung young man had appealed on socialist grounds. His speech was both virile and vehement, and he quoted Tolstoy and Wells and Karl Marx and Philip Gibbs in a breathless cockney voice that told of self-education and the night-school. When he had finished, he still stood tense and rigid, although he had the Board's permission to be seated. And when the blow fell – 'Appeal dismissed. Applicant passed for Foreign Service' – he crumpled up quite suddenly into his chair in a way that made Antoinette's throat feel tight.

The two next appeals had been decided in much the same manner; but the last two had evidently presented greater difficulties and were now being considered behind closed doors.

In the corridor a crowd of men and women, friends and supporters of the applicants, were huddled together, talking in low voices. Amongst them there were representatives of both pacifist and militarist newspapers, a plain-clothes detective, and two policemen. There was only one bench, and that was occupied by a youth in khaki and three white-faced women in black. The others had to stand, shifting restlessly to and fro, yet not daring to move too far from those doors that might open again at any moment. People who had never met before drifted into whispered conversation with each other, linked together by an outlook and an anxiety common to them all.

An elderly woman was talking to Dennis, and Antoinette was glad that his attention was engaged. His behaviour to her had been entirely aloof and impersonal ever since Alan's arrest. Perhaps he thought – thus she interpreted his mood – that if he was less aloof and impersonal he would be guilty of treachery towards Alan. Even now, though she had accompanied him here, and was outwardly quite in the picture – 'the woman at his side' – there was no intimacy between them. She knew well enough who it was who really 'stood by' him.

She heard the woman say to Dennis: 'I shall *will* you to get total exemption. I am a great believer in will-power, aren't you? If they offer you Non-Combatant Service, I do hope you won't take it! Yes, I've been to prison three times – look!' She lowered her voice to a whisper and pointed to the suffragette badge she wore inside her jacket. Then, turning to Antoinette: 'I shall will him to get off for both your sakes, my dear. ...'

Antoinette thanked her gravely.

The doors were flung open again, and the people pressed back into the court, struggling to regain their old places on the benches that ran, three deep, along the walls. Would it be Dennis's turn now to face those twenty-five men upon whom his fate depended?

Judgement was delivered upon the previous applicants. Then a name was called: not Dennis's. The young man in khaki stepped forward and took his place at the desk, and a murmur of astonishment went through the crowd at the sight of his uniform. He stated that when the military authorities had come to remove him, he had told them that he had an appeal pending, but they had taken no notice.

There were groans of 'Shame. ...' 'A disgrace!' which were instantly quelled. The Chairman declared that the man must be put back into civilian ranks before his case could be heard.

The next applicant claimed exemption on the grounds that he was the sole support of his mother, his grandmother and a paralysed sister. His father was dead, and his brother had been killed in the war. While the Chairman enquired into the details of the circumstances, Antoinette looked at the woman who had accompanied the applicant; the mother, probably. Her hands were clenched in her lap, her eyes fixed imploringly upon the Chairman's face. Impossible to tell from the perfect impartiality of his manner in which direction he was biassed, if at all. Antoinette found herself following that case, as she had followed most of the others: not impersonally, but as if all her own hopes and longings centred in the desire that the man should get his exemption. She shared the breathless painful suspense of the mother, and the feeling that the agony was being unnecessarily prolonged, when judgement was for a moment deferred, and the next man called.

This one stated that he had religious scruples against the taking life. In

proof of this he had relinquished his post with a firm of motor-tyre man-
ufacturers on discovering that they were working for the Government. He
put his case badly, halting and stammering; but his underlying determination seemed to be inflexible.

'The Lord said: "*Thou shalt not kill.*"'

Here the Military Representative, to whose smooth fat face and sneer-
ing expression Antoinette had taken an instantaneous dislike, rose to his
feet and asked the applicant with affected politeness if he were aware that
one or two of the Germans – yes, let us say one or two of them – had
already broken that commandment, and that it was his duty to his country to retaliate?

'If the Germans do wrong, sir, I can't help it. I can't get beyond the
words of God.'

'You wish to interpret them in the manner most convenient to yourself.
Since you are so well up in the Bible, what about the passage that demands
"*An eye for an eye*"?'

'The God of vengeance may have demanded that, sir – never the God
of Love.'

'Ask the Germans how much the God of love enters into their calculations!' sneered the Military Representative; 'it must be obvious to every
normal intellect that we were never meant to love hordes of barbarians
like those we have at present to combat.'

The man hesitated; fumbled for words; opened his mouth once or
twice; then: 'But the laws of the Almighty weren't meant to hold good
only in times of peace, sir!'

A ripple of laughter and applause ran through the crowd and was
severely reprimanded. The applicant was told that exemption would be
granted to him if he returned to his employment with the Government-
firm, or took up other work of national importance. He shook his head
in answer to both suggestions, and his appeal was dismissed.

And then Dennis's name was called. ... They were both actually to go
through it now, he and she; no longer mere spectators of other people's
anguish and suspense. She would have liked to touch his hand and whisper 'Good luck ...' as the other women did to their men, but he did not
even glance down at her as he passed by, with sombre, preoccupied gaze
and furrowed brow. He took his place. She could see him in profile – if she
looked. But at first she could not bear to look, knowing him there before
the twenty-five, defenceless and at bay. Nor did she take in the meaning
of his words when he began to speak.

With all her faculties and thoughts concentrated upon the final issue, she sat tense and rigid – as Dennis must have sat through Alan's tribunal. Alan had been in prison for three months already. If they offered him release now, at the price of abandonment of his principles, she wondered if he would accept it. Gladly, perhaps how gladly. … Always at Miss Mowbray's one heard tales of the things that were being done to the conscientious objectors in prison. Could those fat, bald-headed old gentlemen who sat there in judgement really be callous enough to condemn Dennis to things of that sort?

The Chairman was saying: 'So you think all warfare is wrong: I daresay a good many people share that view, but most of them are fighting all the same, realising that that is the only way to end this particular war.'

Dennis replied: 'It is my firm belief that I should not in any way be benefiting humanity by taking part in this war, as I am convinced that there is no such thing as a "war to end war," and that victory would only lead to successive wars, each more terrible than the last; also that the solution of international disputes should be sought in arbitration and diplomacy, rather than in bloodshed.'

The old gentleman sitting nearest to Dennis truculently demanded if he had held these views previous to August, 1914.

'Certainly,' he answered.

'How can you prove that? Have you ever written or stated in public anything of the sort before 1914?'

'No; but most of my friends were acquainted with my views. I'm afraid I can't offer you any more definite proof. You must take my word for it.'

The old gentleman grunted, and relapsed into silence. Antoinette hoped and thought that this was the end, but immediately another interlocutor rose in place of the first.

'Does the applicant not differentiate between a righteous war, a war of self-defence – and one waged for gain and greed, with the sole object of crushing smaller nations?'

'I'm afraid I can't think of any war as a righteous war – war in all its essentials being so profoundly unrighteous. And as to the comparison of the respective war-aims of the Allies and of Germany – who can say at this stage that England is only fighting to avenge Belgium, and with no view to conquest of enemy territory or extension of power? What about the conquest of German colonies in East Africa? The French say they won't make peace till they've got Alsace-Lorraine back. Have they the right to it? Alsace-Lorraine was German territory before ever it became French – before they got it back again in 1870.'

'Yes, yes, young man, you're not here to teach us history,' the first speaker cut him short, and the second rejoined: 'Nor to give us your highly unpatriotic views of your country's war-aims. It's your business to fight for your country, not to criticise it.'

'If I am sent out to kill, surely I have the right to question the cause that requires me to convert myself into a murderer.'

'"Right or wrong, my country" – that's the line for every true Briton to take up.'

'I am a humanitarian before I am a "true Briton," then, if either the "right" or the "wrong" of my country involves the deliberate slaughter of human beings.'

The suffragette who had spoken to them in the passage signified her approval of this by nodding and smiling across at Antoinette. The girl flushed. Her man was making a good fight, and she was proud of him, even while she knew that she had no right to think of him as her man, and hence no right to her pride. But she could almost have wished that he were being just a little less vehement: it was obvious that the general attitude was hostile towards him; only the Chairman still appeared impartial, as he said: 'You categorically refuse in any way to help carry on the war?'

'I do. I want to help to stop the war, and all possibility of future wars. My justification for being here is my confirmed belief that I am doing more towards that end by adhering to my refusal to fight than by unthinkingly and unquestioningly going out to kill.'

Again there was a murmur of applause; and a moment's silence followed. Antoinette glanced from one to the other of the men's faces; she longed to tackle each of the twenty-five separately, to beseech and implore him to be merciful. She tried to pick out at least one, whose physiognomy held a promise of tolerance or understanding; but there seemed to be an absurd family-likeness between them: they all looked pompous, comfortable, overfed; and at the present moment, righteously indignant. These old men had lived their lives; they would neither be called upon to shed their blood for their country, nor to go to prison, if they upheld opposing views; they had probably sent their sons to the war, but of themselves no personal sacrifice would be demanded. They were old – they were safe – and what right had they to send young men to kill each other? What right to sit in judgement upon one with all the potentialities of life still before him? To decree whether he was to be allowed to act according to his principles, or faced with the alternative of being forced to violate them or cast into prison?

Like the suffragette, Antoinette tried to 'will' them into the required frame of mind. Perhaps some of her 'willing' was having its effect. That moment's silence could surely be taken as a good sign?

But already the unctuous tones of the Military Representative had terminated the silence.

'The applicant is so very anxious to end the war at all costs: does he realise that there are not two ways but only one way in which he can help to do so?'

'I've declared the reasons for my unwillingness to take the one way,' returned Dennis.

Another endless-seeming pause; looks and inaudible remarks exchanged between the old gentlemen.

Antoinette held her breath.

'*Total exemption granted*' – could not all her wishing or 'willing' force the Chairman to speak those words? He was about to speak now:

'Clear the court!'

With sighs of exasperation at the renewed delay, the people rose and crowded into the passage again. The young man's mother was crying. The reporters scribbled ceaselessly in their notebooks.

The suffragette was congratulating Dennis. 'You made a splendid stand, splendid, but they're prejudiced against the "conscience" men; it's easy to see that.'

Yes, he had made a splendid stand, but Antoinette would have liked him to come to her for reassurance ... to whisper to her in the crowd: 'I was all right, wasn't I?'

He evidently had no need of her reassurance. With an abstracted smile, he thanked the suffragette for her congratulations, and stood gazing out of the window, as if determined to keep unshared whatever turmoil of fear and hope might be passing in his mind. But perhaps if the words were spoken, that they both longed to hear, and the appalling strain snapped, he would turn to her. ...

The bank-clerk's mother was moaning: 'If only they'd be quick and tell us – can't they see we need him more than the army does?'

But the present Board showed no signs of 'being quick.' A man carrying a tray laden with tea-things had just unceremoniously jostled aside the crowd and entered the court. He was followed by a boy with a very large cherry cake. The old gentlemen were going to have tea. ... Antoinette suddenly understood some of the feelings that had given rise to the French Revolution! Soon the sound of hearty laughter mingled with the rattle of cups. The old gentlemen were apparently telling each other funny stories, while the people waited outside in suspense and agony of mind.

For a weary half-hour they were still kept in the passage. Then at last the doors were flung open again.

The Chairman stated that in the case of the bank-clerk who was sole support of his family, the Board had decided to grant three months' exemption, with leave to appeal again. The decision was cheered, and the mother cried hysterically: 'Oh, thank you – thank you so much …' and was led out on her son's arm.

'In the case of Mr. Dennis Blackwood – Non-Combatant Service.'

6
Love, separation and sexuality

Emily Chitticks
from
Letters to Private Will Martin

5 October 1916.   Suffolk House, Herongate, Essex.
I was so delighted to receive your letter this morning & to hear that you arrived at Witham quite safely. You can't think dear how your letter cheered me up. I do miss you terribly Will, but it won't be for long will it dear? ...

I must try to cheer up until you come back. I am so sorry dear to hear that you are having such a hard time of it. I don't blame you dear for having that port and lemon as I am sure you were in need of it & I know very well you would not take more than was good for you. ...

Poor boy, I know you miss me as much as I do you but cheer up dear you know I love you, oh so much Will. You are everything to me dear & I don't know what I should do without you. I only wish this wretched war was over. ...

It was terrible parting from you on Tuesday Will, I am glad you did not say much to me, as I could not have borne it dear. ...

You are the only one that I have ever loved with my whole heart & soul, & if anything came to part me from you now Will, I believe it would kill me, I feel more convinced than ever that we are made for each other don't you dear? I don't say much to you about how I care for you when you are with me dear, but it is not always those that say so much that care the most. Actions speak louder than words don't they dear.

Fondest love & kisses
from your loving little girl
  X X X Emily X X X

31 October 1916.

Well my darling boy I miss you terribly. My life seems quite empty now you have gone. I nearly broke my heart dear to let you go on Saturday, & yet dear Will I am very happy now I really belong to you. You cannot imagine what happiness you gave to me on Friday dear, I did not expect it then dear, but that was what I had been hoping for darling. Of course I knew dear that you loved me, but yet I did not feel so near to you then as I do now. Really my dear I don't think I could live without you now.

11 November 1916.

How can I thank you enough for my dear little ring. I am so delighted with it dear. I wish that you were here to put it on for me. It fits nicely dear, & looks ever so neat & nice on my finger. ...

Oh my dear Will, I do wish that I was with you. I should love to be able to come & look after you, but it's no use wishing for the impossible is it dear.

20 November 1916.

So you have got your 'pack' at last. You must feel strange. I really think it a shame dear to treat you all like that. It seems so ridiculous to train you for cavalry & then turn you into infantry like that. ...

Last night in particular I could see you in my dream as plain as could be, only you looked so terribly thin & ill dear, it regular hurt me to see you & when I woke up this morning, really dear, I expected to see you coming in the room for a minute, my dream was so vivid.

26 December 1916.

I always feel more happy & cheerful dear when I get your letters. They are always so full of hope & so kind & loving. I don't know how I should get on without your letters, & I love writing to you, it seems as tho we are not so far away from each other when I am writing to you dear. ...

I had to get some books & have a good read to keep my thoughts down a bit dear.

I have had some more unpleasant dreams dear about you. One in particular I dreamt dear that you were home with me, but you had ceased to love me & treated me as cold as ice. I don't know why I dream such silly things. I wish I didn't because I know you do love me. I couldn't bear it if you didn't love me, but there I am getting despondent again. I do try to be cheerful, but it is very hard, sometimes more so than others. ...

Emily thinks I am very staid & old fashioned now not wanting to go out, but she does not understand dear does she. Perhaps she will one day, when she meets her right boy. That nice boy I told you of that used to write to her so often is killed she told me. ... I see in the papers they are talking about having all young girls for munition work so don't be surprised dear if your little girl has to go. I shan't mind very much if I can get a decent job. ... I hope dear you do not think me a funny girl for telling you all my thoughts & dreams as I do, but I must tell you, dear. I can't help it. I feel more happy when I tell you everything dear. ... Poor old Arthur says he cannot imagine my ever getting married dear. He says he has often thought of it & he can't possibly imagine it. So it seems as tho he still holds his silly ideas. He says he hopes I shall, but yet he can't imagine it. ...

March 1917.
I have just received another letter from you dear. I can't quite understand your meaning dear in one sentence. It's where you said I had guessed right & you had seen some life since. ... Do you mean Will you have been fighting. Don't keep it from me dear if you have been in the trenches. Tell me, I would rather know. I can't think what else you mean darling.

March 1917.
Oh dear Will, I feel I want to say such a lot to you darling & yet the words won't come somehow. Do you ever feel like that dear? My heart seems ready to burst with longing for you dear. What ever I shall do when you have to go right away I really don't know. It will break my heart really Will.

Returned letters

25 March 1917.
I shall be so glad when I receive your letter. It's a week now since I had the last & it seems more like a month. ... Oh my dear boy I do pray that you will be spared, if I lost you well dear I don't know what I should do. I do hope I shall hear from you soon. ... What a dreadful time you must be going through. I don't know where my brother George is, we haven't heard yet. I dreamt he was killed the other night Will I hope my dream won't come true. On several occasions I have dreamed that you were back home with me dear & the most strange thing about them, you are always in civilian clothes when I dream of you & I have never seen you in those dear. ... I hope that will come true.

Pte W. J. Martin was killed on the afternoon of Tuesday March 27th while in the performance of his duty in the front line. He was hit in the head by a sniper's bullet & never recovered consciousness before he died.[1]

6 June 1917.
Sacred to the memory of my Darling sweetheart Will the only boy I love with my whole heart & soul, who loved me so well he gave his all, his life for me. When I die I wish all his letters to be buried with me as my heart & love *are buried* in his grave in France.

Vera Brittain
from
Testament of Youth

When he had driven up in the taxi with me from the station, and we were left together in the morning-room, which looked across the snow-covered town to the sad hills beyond, the sudden effect of seeing him in my semi-invalid weakness after such agitation of mind brought me so near to crying that I couldn't prevent him from noticing it.

Fighting angrily with the tears, I asked him: 'Well, are you satisfied at last?'

He replied that he hardly knew. He certainly had no wish to die, and now that he had got what he wanted, a dust-and-ashes feeling had come. He neither hated the Germans nor loved the Belgians; the only possible motive for going was 'heroism in the abstract,' and that didn't seem a very logical reason for risking one's life.

Mournfully we sat there recapitulating the brief and happy past; the future was too uncertain to attract speculation. I had begun, I confessed to him, to pray again, not because I believed that it did any good, but so as to leave no remote possibility unexplored. The War, we decided, came hardest of all upon us who were young. The middle-aged and the old had known their period of joy, whereas upon us catastrophe had descended just in time to deprive us of that youthful happiness to which we had believed ourselves entitled.

'Sometimes,' I told him, 'I've wished I'd never met you – that you hadn't

[1] Will Martin was killed on 27 March 1917. On 6 April Emily Chitticks received a letter from his commanding officer, from which this is a quotation. The officer was killed on 2 April 1917.

come to take away my impersonal attitude towards the War and make it a cause of suffering to me as it is to thousands of others. But if I choose not to have met you, I wouldn't do it – even though my future had always to be darkened by the shadow of death.'

'Ah, don't say that!' he said. 'Don't say it will all be spoilt; when I return things may be just the same.'

'If you return,' I emphasised, determined to face up to things for both of us, and when he insisted: '"When," not "if"'; I said that I didn't imagine he was going to France without fully realising all that it might involve. He answered gravely that he had thought many times of the issue, but had a settled conviction that he was coming back, though perhaps not quite whole.

'Would you like me any less if I was, say, minus an arm?'

My reply need not be recorded. It brought the tears so near to the surface again that I picked up the coat which I had thrown off, and abruptly said I would take it upstairs – which I did the more promptly when I suddenly realised that he was nearly crying too.

After tea we walked steeply uphill along the wide road which leads over lonely, undulating moors through Whaley Bridge to Manchester, twenty miles away. This was 'the long white road' of Roland's poems, where nearly a year before we had walked between 'the grey hills and the heather,' and the plover had cried in the awakening warmth of the spring. There were no plover there that afternoon; heavy snow had fallen, and a rough blizzard drove sleet and rain in our faces.

It was a mournfully appropriate setting for a discussion on death and the alternative between annihilation and an unknown hereafter. We could not honestly admit that we thought we should survive, though we would have given anything in the world to believe in a life to come, but he promised me that if he died in France he would try to come back and tell me that the grave was not the end of our love. As we walked down the hill towards Buxton the snow ceased and the evening light began faintly to shine in the sky, but somehow it only showed us the more clearly how grey and sorrowful the world had become.

Time, so desperately brief; so immeasurably precious, suddenly seemed to be racing. At dinner that night I wore my prettiest frock, a deep blue ninon over grey satin, with a wide *chiné* sash, and afterwards, though my father kept Roland smoking and talking in the dining-room too long for my impatience, we were left to ourselves in the dim, lamplit drawing-room.

Still too much bewildered and distressed by the love that had descended upon us with such young intensity to make any coherent plans for the future – even supposing that the War allowed us to have one – we nevertheless mentioned, for the first time, the subject of marriage.

'Mother says that people like me just become intellectual old maids,' I told him.

'I don't see why,' he protested.

'Oh, well, it's probably true!' I said, rather sharply, for misery had as usual made me irritable. 'After the War there'll be no one for me to marry.'

'Not even me?' he asked very softly.

'How do I know I *shall* want to marry you when that time comes?'

'You know you wouldn't be happy unless you married an odd sort of person.'

'That rather narrows the field of choice, doesn't it?'

'Well – do you need it to be so very wide?'

The rest was fragmentary. We sat on the sofa till midnight, talking very quietly. The stillness, heavy-laden with the dull oppression of the snowy night, became so electric with emotion that we were frightened of one another, and dared not let even our fingers touch for fear that the love between us should render what we both believed to be decent behaviour suddenly unendurable.

I was still incredibly ignorant. I had read, by then, too much to have failed to acquire a vague and substantially correct idea of the meaning of marriage, but I did not yet understand the precise nature of the act of union. My ignorance, however, was incapable of disturbing my romantic adoration, for I knew now for certain that whatever marriage might involve in addition to my idea of it, I could not find it other than desirable. I realised as clearly as he did that a hereafter in which we should both be deprived of our physical qualities could mean very little to either of us; he would not be Roland without his broad shoulders, his long-lashed dark eyes, and above all the singularly attractive voice which I could never recall when he was absent.

"'I want no angel, only she,'" Olive Schreiner had written in the strange little novel which had become our Bible: "'No holier and no better, with all her sins upon her, so give her me or give me nothing.'" ... For the soul's fierce cry for immortality is this, – only this: Return to me after death the thing as it was before. Leave me in the Hereafter the being that I am to-day. Rob me of the thoughts, the feelings, the desires that are my life, and you have left nothing to take. Your immortality is annihilation, your Hereafter is a lie.'

So I, too, wanted to find no angel after the War, after the Flood, after the grave; I wanted the arrogant, egotistic, vital young man that I loved.

The next day I saw him off; although he had said that he would rather I didn't come.

In the early morning we walked to the station beneath a dazzling sun, but the platform from which his train went out was dark and very cold. In the railway carriage we sat hand in hand until the whistle blew. We never kissed and never said a word. I got down from the carriage still clasping his hand, and held it until the gathering speed of the train made me let go. He leaned through the window looking at me with sad, heavy eyes, and I watched the train wind out of the station and swing round the curve until there was nothing left but the snowy distance, and the sun shining harshly on the bright, empty rails.

When I got back to the house, where everyone mercifully left me to myself, I realised that my hands were nearly frozen. Vaguely resenting the physical discomfort, I crouched beside the morning-room fire for almost an hour, unable to believe that I could ever again suffer such acute and conscious agony of mind. On every side there seemed to be cause for despair and no way out of it. I tried not to think because thought was intolerable, yet every effort to stop my mind from working only led to a fresh outburst of miserable speculation. I tried to read; I tried to look at the gaunt white hills across the valley, but nothing was any good, so in the end I just stayed huddled by the fire, immersed in a mood of blank hopelessness in which years seemed to have passed since the morning.

At last I fell asleep for some moments, and awoke feeling better; I was, I suppose, too young for hope to be extinguished for very long. Perhaps, I thought, Wordsworth or Browning or Shelley would have some consolation to offer; all through the War poetry was the only form of literature that I could read for comfort, and the only kind that I ever attempted to write. So I turned at once to Shelley's 'Adonais,' only to be provoked to new anguish by the words:

> *O gentle child, beautiful as thou wert,*
> *Why didst thou leave the trodden paths of men*
> *Too soon, and with weak hands though mighty heart*
> *Dare the unpastured dragon in his den?*

But the lovely cadences stirred me at last to articulateness; there was no one to whom I wanted to talk, but at least I could tell my diary a good deal of the sorrow that seemed so fathomless.

'I can scarcely bear to think of him,' I wrote, 'and yet I cannot bear to think of anything else. For the time being all people, all ideas, all interests have set, and sunk below the horizon of my mind; he alone I can contemplate, whom of all things in heaven and earth it hurts to think about most.'

Certainly the War was already beginning to overshadow scholarship and ambition. But I was not ready, yet, to give in to it; I wanted very badly to be heroic – or at any rate to seem heroic to myself – so I tried hard to rationalise my grief.

'I felt,' I endeavoured subsequently to assure myself, 'a weak and cowardly person ... to shrink from my share in the Universal Sorrow. After all it was only right that I should have to suffer too, that I had no longer an impersonal indifference to set me apart from the thousands of breaking hearts in England to-day. It was my part to face the possibility of a ruined future with the same courage that he is going to face death.'

So I finished up the miserable morning by looking through some of the short verses that he had left with me, and especially one in which – as in two or three of his poems – some prophetic instinct led him to a truer knowledge of the future than the strong, dominant consciousness that felt certain of survival:

> Good-bye, sweet friend. What matters it that you
> Have found Love's death in joy and I in sorrow?
>   For hand in hand, just as we used to do,
> We two shall live our passionate poem through
>   On God's serene to-morrow.

Lady Cynthia Asquith
The Loss of a Brother

Saturday, 1st July (1916)

I don't know how to write about this awful day. I didn't expect Beb till 2.20, so had arranged to lunch with my grandmother. Was back soon after two, ran into room in high spirits. Beb said, 'I'm afraid there's bad news', and gave me an opened letter from Papa. 'The worst is true about Ego. The officer prisoners of Angora certify that he was killed at Katia ... I have wired to Guy Wyndham at Clouds. I don't know how Letty will be told. It is very cruel and we must all help each other to bear it.'

Oh God – oh God, my beautiful brother that I have loved so since I was a baby – so beautiful *through* and *through*! Can it be true that he'll never come back? At first I could only think of Letty, just the blank horror of that gripped me. Mamma's away at Clouds – that's unthinkable, too! Letty will occupy her for the first days, but afterwards I'm frightened for her.

Papa telephoned to me and I went round to Cadogan Square. Poor, poor Papa! He really proudly loved those two perfect sons. He said he had been round to Kakoo – she expected John back in the afternoon and they thought he had better tell Letty. Her mother was not coming back till nine and Diana was away. We walked round to Eaton Square together and found Kakoo in. No John, and we discussed what had better be done. Came to conclusion that if John had not arrived by five, Papa and I would go round to Letty. We telephoned and found out she would be in between five and six. I went home to Beb and waited – no message came, so after five I went to Cadogan Square and picked up poor Papa. The poignancy of what followed was so inconceivably beyond anything in my experience that I don't feel as if I could ever be unhaunted by it for a minute.

Letty was alone with the children playing the piano to them. Papa went up – I waited downstairs. The music stopped and I heard a gay 'Hulloa', then silence. I rushed up and found Letty clinging to Papa. It's indescribable – it was just like somebody in a fearful, unimaginable, physical pain. Streams of beautiful, eloquent words were torn from her heart. The children were scared. 'What has happened to you, Mummie? What is the matter with you? Will you be better in the morning?' I ran up to Sparks – she came and fetched them, and brought sal volatile and was wonderfully nice and good with Letty. We tried to make Letty go upstairs, but she wanted to stay down a little.

Papa was wonderfully sweet, and she seemed to cling to him: 'Oh Papa, it can't be true! How could God be so cruel? There was no one else in the world in the least like him – no one – I have been so wonderfully happy. His beautiful face, his smile … my Ego, come back to me. Oh God! Oh God! It's no use calling to God – nothing is any use – nothing in all the world can help him. I'm only twenty-eight – I'm so strong – I shan't die!'

Marjorie came in, perfectly self-controlled and bracing – spoke to Letty as you would a housemaid being vaccinated. 'Now, now Letty – come, come'. At last we got her to go upstairs and carried her to her room. Then she saw his photographs and the bed. She sent for the children – his two lovely little boys, and tried to make them understand. 'David, I want you to understand Poppa's – you remember what he looked like – Poppa's never coming back to us.' David said at once, 'But, I want him to …' but he didn't understand and said, 'I must go now, or I shall be late for bed'. She was afraid that they would never remember him and the children – the one platitude one clung to for her – became one of the most poignant stabs.

Papa went away and I stayed alone with her. She got quieter. John came after six and took the line that there *was* hope with her, clinging to the fact that it was not 'official'. I have *none*. Is it cruel or kind to give it to her? I think one ought to give her evidence, but not colour it with subjective optimism at all – she is so open to suggestion. Nothing could be crueller than the way it has come. Those two months of terror in which she said, 'I tried to teach myself every day and every night that he was dead, then I was swept up into Heaven, and now … this fiery Hell. I'm so tired of being brave – I was brave for two months and this is my reward.'

When I went up and joined John I found – to my alarm – that he had really tonicked and buoyed her up. Perhaps it is right to stay it a *little* by tiny hope, so that waiting for clues may be some occupation, but I am sure she mustn't be allowed to have real fundamental hope. She can't have the physical shock twice. John was angry to our not having waited for him or his mother, but personally I think Papa was the best person to tell her: he even said, 'I think she's been most brutally told.' They are an astonishing family. A dear old family doctor came – she seemed to welcome him. He left her a sleeping draught.

The mother didn't arrive till past nine – I waited till then, and Letty asked me to come back and sleep. I went back to Beb, had Bengers, and picked up a nightgown. I dropped him at Bruton Street. I just ran upstairs and kissed Mary, and Evelyn drove me to Montagu Square. Got into bed with Letty. She didn't know whether to allow herself to hope or not, and kept appealing to me. I didn't know what to say. She said, 'I can't hope a chink – I must hope altogether or not at all'. That was exactly what I was afraid of. She took the draught and went to sleep after a long time. I scarcely slept.

Sunday, 2nd July
Ghastly awakening. She began to moan in her sleep, 'Don't let me wake up to this ghastly day – I don't want to wake up'. She said, 'I've had such a wonderful dream, I dreamt that he was there.' Then the full realisation came back to her: 'Oh God, make me mad – make me mad, if I can't die!' 'Come back to me just for one minute my sweet Ego, just to tell me how to bear it, I can't bear it without you to help. You must come back and see David just once.' 'Oh God, the pain of it! I'm so frightened – I can't face

the long years. What am I to do – I haven't got the brains to cope with it? I don't believe I've got any brains – only a heart, oh such a heart. No philosophy, no religion. Ego was my religion!'

The agony of one's impotence to help. I'm not the right person for her – not spontaneous enough, too self-conscious. A sense of their utter futility makes the words die in my throat. She is so childlike in a way that I believe she is very open to suggestion, and could be helped by people. What she wants, I think, is Ettie with her extraordinary articulate *conviction* of personal immortality – I can't convey it. Martin was too sweet, seeming to understand more than David – not what had happened – but his mother's unhappiness. He kissed and patted her, 'There's a tear in both your eyes, Mummie.' She had ups and downs of hope. It is so difficult when she says, 'Is there any hope, Cynthia?' not to allow oneself to draw the sword out of her heart for a moment. Grace and Pamela came and both saw her. Pamela was very sweet. She said she would stay with her till her mother came, so I went to Beb. In the course of the morning they succeeded in buoying themselves up into *real* hope. I can't have any. Rested with Beb, and then we lunched at Queen's Restaurant. Went to see Mary H. at four, had tea with her. She was wonderfully perfect. Looked in at Letty, saw they had made her quite hopeful: she has resolved to go on as before, refusing to believe it. I think they are *wrong*, but what can one do?

Beb and I had early dinner and then he went away to Brighton. Not till I was left alone did I feel the full pain for myself – Letty's had parried it. It burst upon me now and I was in Hell. Mamma hasn't come back yet. There is still that to face. Grace rang up saying she had been full of hope, but it had been dashed to the ground – A friend of Evie's, a man called Cohen, has seen a man who was a Katia (he was taken prisoner and escaped), and he says Ego was wounded slightly and later returned to his machine gun – a shell burst quite near and none of those men could be seen again. If this is true, it explains his body not being found.

Monday, 3rd July
Breakfasted and wrote diary in bed. Papa asked me to lunch with him, and said he had begun to be hopeful yesterday, but the latest story had extinguished hope – though, on thinking it over, the story sounded improbable. Of course there is no reason why one should believe it, any more than all the other conflicting rumours, only what can be 'official' – the word the Rutlands cling to now? Nothing.

They have Letty practically back where she was *before* the good telegram about his being at Damascus, and I don't see what's to end this intolerable phase, unless perhaps Tom's first letter which may well never arrive. It is so difficult for us – they make one feel they think one a sensationalist. I can't humbug Letty. Let her have all the evidence and draw her own conclusions.

Papa telephoned to ask Cohen to come and see him at five, and showed me a wonderful letter from Mamma and a copy of one Ego had written her after Yvo's death. I think it is so perfect. ...

Began to write to Beb when Whibley walked in. I'm really glad he came, though I suppose I wouldn't have seen him on purpose. He was very, very dear and said delicious things about Ego. At five Papa telephoned and said something quite definite had come from the American Embassy, so when the motor came I went round to Cadogan Square. Buckler, special agent at the American Embassy, has been round to Papa with a telegram from the Red Crescent, saying that Coventry and Lieutenant Strickland certify that Lord Elcho was killed at Katia – that's 'official'. Poor Papa was very shattered, he must have hoped after all.

We wondered what to do about Letty, rang up her house, and asked for Kakoo who was with her. We told her and she begged us not to tell Letty anything until John did, and said she would go round to Eaton Square where he was. Papa and I came to the conclusion we had better go round and see him in case they shirked, poor things. Then he said he didn't feel he could face seeing John, he had been so irritated by him the day before, so I went by myself. I found the Duchess there and John was just taking down the same message from the telephone. Poor things, they tried still to clutch at straws, but I wouldn't let them. John wanted to see whether Buckler thought the Red Crescent authority sufficiently good, but I told him he had himself brought the message to papa. They *had* to accept. I liked John again – he looked so desperately miserable. He kissed me and said how sorry he was. The Duchess quite broke down. I suggested she should fetch a doctor and take him round to Letty – I was convinced she ought to be told that night.

Papa and I went round to Bruton Street. Poor Con was with Mary – very dear: I had dinner with Mary. I telephoned the Duchess. She said Letty had known directly she saw her face and had been terribly bad, and then they had left her with John, who seemed best able to cope with the agony part. Diana and her mother were going to sleep with her. Evelyn drove me home. Mercifully, I was utterly exhausted, so I went to sleep but couldn't stay asleep.

Helen Zenna Smith
from
Not So Quiet …

'You've just come from France, haven't you?'

I look up from the coffee I am drinking in the hotel lounge. He is a second-lieutenant, very spick and span in his new Sam Browne and well-cut uniform – 'Rather a nut,' The B.F. would label him. He is so immaculate I feel dirty immediately, despite my pre-dinner hot bath, my shampoo and hair-cut, my manicure and my newly-acquired powder-puff.

He smiles disarmingly. 'Awful cheek my coming over, but I embark to-morrow. First time out. Frightful novice.'

First time out. I avoid his laughing blue eyes. He is indeed a frightful novice … that is why his eyes are still laughing.

'Do let me talk to you,' he begs. 'I'm lonely and you seem lonely, too. I've been watching you all through dinner, wondering why you stayed in Folkestone instead of going straight through. Do talk to me. I'd love some tips first-hand from someone who's been out there. …'

I agree to talk to him … but not of the war. Anything but the war. My voice hardens. He notices it and his eyes are suddenly grave … but I do not want them to be grave. Let them smile while they can still smile, they will be grave soon enough. I make a stupid joke … the blue eyes dance again. Blue eyes, dancing like the sea on a breezy summer's day. There is a hop going in the ballroom … I hesitate, my uniform is almost in rags … he tells me it may be, but I look tophole, and my short hair is the sort of hair a fellow would like to rumple his fingers through if he dared … he clasps his hands together in mock penitence. …

He is so gay, so audacious, this boy of my own age who is so young and brimming over with life. He invents a wild fandango, and shouts with laughter at an old lady in the corner who stares disapprovingly through lorgnettes. He is clean and young and straight and far removed from the shadow procession I watch night after night, the procession that came to me early this morning and wakened me shrieking in the presence of a compartmentful of shocked strangers. He is so gay, so full of life, this boy who is holding me closely in his arms … he could never join that ghostly parade. …

Dance, dance, dance, go on dancing … press me against your breast …

talk, talk, talk, go on talking … yes, daringly drop a kiss on top of my cropped head in full view of the shocked old lady with the lorgnettes … laugh, laugh, laugh, go on laughing … yes, I will drink more champagne with you, I will smile when you smile … I will press your hand when you press mine under the table … yes, I will dance with you again till I forget I have seen you at the end of the ghostly procession that has crossed the Channel with me.

He asks me to call him Robin. I tell him my name is Nell. I wish it were something more charming.

But it is charming, as charming as its owner. Oh, yes, yes, *yes* … if I shake my head again he'll kiss me in the middle of the ballroom, and the disapproving old girl with the lorgnettes will pass out completely … he loves to see me smile. … Not unhappy as I was at dinner now, am I?

The last dance comes. The last chord crashes. He pulls me to him so roughly that I am left breathless for a second. 'The King' is played. He stands rigidly to attention, his eyes clouded for a moment. 'The King' finishes. I make a quick joke about Paris leave; he throws his head back and laughs. Easily and swiftly he laughs, this Robin who is straight and clean and whole.

We walk into the lounge slowly … bed now, he supposes, with a side-glance at me … hardly worth while undressing, embarking at five … filthy, unearthly hour to get a fellow out of bed. …

We get into the lift without speaking … our rooms are on the same floor.

At my door he kisses me, at first gently … 'a good-night kiss' … then more ardently … how strong and beautiful he is, this Robin who has not been out to hell yet … *Dear Nell* … he kisses me again … *Dear Robin.* …

Must he say good-night? … Can't he come in and talk to me after I am in bed? … I don't think him an awful rotter for suggesting it, do I? … How ingenuous he is, this Robin who kisses me so ardently, whose eyes are blue and sane. … He'll be good, honestly – well, just as good as I want him to be … he kisses me again … poor Robin, poor Robin. …

The luminous hands of my watch say four o'clock. It is pitch dark. I switch the bed-lamp on. He is deep in the abyss of sleep. … 'Time to go, Robin.'

He awakens smiling and flushed, like a child. 'Nell. …'

Then, after a while, ' You will write – promise?'

I promise.

'I feel a cad, an absolute. …'

No, no, no.

'I'm your first lover, aren't I? Why, Nell? Were you a bit in love with me, too? ...'

I nod. A lie, but it will do. But it was not only because he was whole and strong-limbed, not only because his body was young and beautiful, not only because his laughing blue eyes reflected my image without the shadow of war rising to blot me out ... but because I saw him between me and the dance orchestra ending a shadow procession of cruelly-maimed men. ...

Poor Robin, poor baby.

'I shall always treasure this, Nell; ... you're the first girl I've loved, decently; ... there have been others, but ...' he stammers boyishly, embarrassed. ... 'When I come on leave we'll dance again, won't we. ... We'll have such fun, Nell. ...'

I kiss him despairingly, the hot tears choking me. ... We will not dance again, this Robin and I; it is so pitiful; he is twenty and I am twenty-one, but he is so young. ...

Poor Robin, poor baby, poor baby.

He closes the bedroom door softly behind him.

G. B. Stern
from
Children of No Man's Land

Nell Redbury walked slowly across the lawn towards the tea-table under the yellowing chestnut tree. Arrived there, she stood, mutely awaiting interrogation; her gaze full on Gillian. ... Nobody spoke; the three elder girls felt as though nipped and held in the pincers of tragedy, and each one was afraid. ...

'I'm going to have a baby,' said Nell at last, in the stupid voice of a child repeating a lesson she has not quite understood. 'The doctor said so. Mums cried. And father said I was not to come home anymore.'

'Is that all!' Gillian almost laughed in her relief. 'Oh, you lucky little devil – no, I don't mean that – you're only a kid still yourself, and it's rather rough luck, but still – Who and where's the infant husband? I suppose it's Timothy?'

'Yes,' Nell answered gravely, but still standing a little aloof from the tea-table. 'But he's not my husband. We – I – thought you would be pleased.'

'Because I did it myself?' Her goddess became suddenly stern.

'Yes.' And once more the refrain, 'I thought you would be pleased. You said … you all said. … I've forgotten what you said,' with sudden droop to weariness.

'Whatever I said and whatever I did, wasn't for a baby like you,' Gillian brutally informed her, in a double effort to vitalise the girl's apathy and to knock her own conscience insensible. 'I may have said that where marriage is impossible, it's better to do the other thing than to brood and mope ... but in your case marriage *is* possible; possible natural and inevitable. Especially now. ... There's no earthly or heavenly reason, young Nell, why you and Timothy should put yourselves to the inconvenience of being not married and you're jolly well going to be shoved through the ceremony the very first moment he can wangle leave and come back.'

'Yes,' Nell acquiesced again. And, after a pause: 'But he won't come back. It was in the paper to-day. ... They've killed him.'

She still stood a little way off from the group at the tea-table staring with mournful enquiry at Gillian, who had broken down in a fit of wild sobbing. Then, lest she had not been understood, she repeated: 'The doctor says I'm going to have a baby. And Mums cried. And father said –'

'You needn't go home, my dear, my dear. ... You're coming to my home with me. It's all right – nothing to be frightened of – I'm going to look after you … yes, both of you –' It was Antonia who swept to Nell's side by an irresistible impulse, had gathered her strongly in her arms, and faced round on the other two with a look that challenged while it scorched.

'You're neither of you going to meddle any more where Nell is concerned – haven't you done enough harm? with your talk and your example and rubbish? – No one's business but your own what you do with your life, is it, Gillian? – is it? I knew somebody would have to suffer – ancient law – on those who break the laws – and you go scot free, and this poor kiddie. ... Oh, *damn* your splendid freedom, and your new era, and your mix-up and mess-up of everything that's clear and right – time-tested Progress – is *this* your statue of progress?' She pointed to Nell Redbury, now crumpled forlornly against the older girl's tense erect body. ...

'No use ranting at me, Antonia; I'm terribly responsible in this case,' Gillian acknowledged. 'And of course it's my business, not yours, to take Nell home and look after her –'

'With Theo about the place?'

Gillian was silent. And Deb interposed: 'She's better with Antonia, Jill.'

I can't give her shelter, worse luck –' Samson, she knew, would show no mercy in this crisis.

Gillian said softly, 'If Theo can help. …' She found it difficult to put into words her conviction that Nell was only eighteen, and it might be warmth to her frozen emotions to have it conveyed – even by Theo Pandos – that men were still in the world and still desiring her … a wintry gleam of promise for the future.

But it was heartless to translate her meaning in front of Nell, whose chubby serious young lover was only just dead. … And Antonia's wrath swept out again like a banner in the wind:

'Theo – *help*? isn't he as promiscuous as the rest of you – as Deb, as Cliffe … with your love-making all over the place … sex discussed just for the fun of it. … Deb prattling about the waste of her young limbs – we haven't forgotten that talk, Nell and I. … Nell hasn't forgotten it to some purpose. … Let's all live our own lives – let's all live somebody else's. … Well, it's been a merry puddle-party while it lasted! Come on, Nell,' her voice sank to inexpressible tenderness. Without a backward glance, she supported the quivering, clinging form of the younger girl across the lawn and through the garden gate. 'Taxi!' they heard her clear call. And the responding grate of wheels against the kerb.

Their departure was one little aspect of the war: woman perforce dependent upon the manlier woman … while out in France the fatal shrapnel bullets ripped through the staggering 'planes. …

A. T. Fitzroy
from
Despised and Rejected

'Such decent chaps they were,' said Alan reflectively, 'we had a most delightful conversation. They don't really want to arrest me in the least. Not with any conviction. Still, they're coming to discharge their painful duty at 8 a.m. to-morrow morning. Don't look so wretched, Dennis. I'm glad to be really up against it at last.'

Dennis made no answer. He was mentally calculating how many hours of freedom still remained to Alan. It was 2 a.m.. Not many hours more.

'And they're mistaken if they think that imprisonment can make me forswear my creed, or declare that I believe in war as a means of regeneration of nations, or that the duties of citizenship lie in taking the lives of other citizens, rather than in trying to promote pacific relations between them. Benny was complaining the other day that we're so few, and I know some of us have ratted on that score alone, given up the battle because they think it's no use against such odds. Being in the minority doesn't imply being in the wrong. But capitulating means admitting that we believe that black is white, just because the majority says so. Poor devils all over Europe are being told that black *is* white, and are dying in proof of it. Dying gallantly and splendidly and wastefully for the sake of a lie.'

'And when we try to assert our truth, we're condemned to the death-in-life of prison.'

'I wouldn't call it so much death-in-life, as so many years that a benighted State unlawfully robs out of our lives, and it's our business to prove that even that theft can't daunt us.'

'You needn't be afraid that I shall let it daunt me.' To logic and commonsense and humanity; to every argument, reason and motive that had hitherto impelled Dennis to take up his stand as a pacifist, was now added the greatest of all these – love. 'A couple of weeks hence I expect I shall be safely under lock and key too.'

Alan grinned. 'Locked up because we're considered a danger to humanity. ... Almost humorous, isn't it?'

'Well, at least we shall both be going through the same hell, Alan.'

'The same hell, and the same good fight; I think we fought side by side before now. In ancient Greece, perhaps, or Rome. Sometimes I have dreams ... and in those dreams you are always my comrade in battle, my comrade in love.'

'And always will be, Alan, always. ...'

'You're sure, Dennis – sure that it will be, when we come out on the other side of this infernal tunnel?' There was a note of anxious pleading in the boy's voice. For all his keen determination and courage, he looked suddenly even younger than he was – as young as he had looked that night at Crannack.

'Alan ...' Dennis dug the nails into the palms of his hands as he tried to master the choking sob that rose in his throat. But at that note in Alan's voice all his laboriously built-up self-control and restraint gave way. ...

The Square was very still, flooded in the cold bluish light of the moon. The two stood a moment in silence on Dennis's door-step.

Then Alan smiled up at his friend. 'Good-night, Dennis. ...'

'Good-night, boy. ...' He tightened the pressure of his hand round Alan's arm. 'If only I could keep you safe. ...'

'Nothing matters now,' murmured Alan, 'I'm glad it's been like this – the last time. ...'

Radclyffe Hall
from
The Well of Loneliness

A stump of candle in the neck of the bottle flickered once or twice and threatened to go out. Getting up, Stephen found a fresh candle and lit it, then she returned to her packing-case upon which had been placed the remnants of a chair minus its legs and arms.

The room had once been the much prized salon of a large and prosperous villa in Compiègne, but now the glass was gone from its windows; there remained only battered and splintered shutters which creaked eerily in the bitter wind of a March night in 1918. The walls of the salon had fared little better than its windows, their brocade was detached and hanging, while a recent rainstorm had lashed through the roof making ugly splotches on the delicate fabric – a dark stain on the ceiling was perpetually dripping. The remnants of what had once been a home, a child's wooden horse, added to the infinite desolation of this villa that now housed the Breakspeare Unit – a Unit composed of Englishwomen, that had been serving in France just over six months, attached to the French Army Ambulance Corps.

The place seemed full of grotesquely large shadows cast by figures that sat or sprawled on the floor. Miss Peel in her Jaeger sleeping-bag snored loudly, then choked because of her cold. Miss Delme-Howard was gravely engaged upon making the best of a difficult toilet – she was brushing out her magnificent hair which gleamed in the light of the candle. Miss Bless was sewing a button on her tunic; Miss Thurloe was peering at a half-finished letter; but most of the women who were herded together in this, the safest place in the villa and none too safe at that be it said, were apparently sleeping quite soundly. An uncanny stillness had descended in the town; after many hours of intensive bombardment, the Germans were having a breathing-space before training their batteries once more on Compiègne.

Stephen stared down at the girl who lay curled up at her feet in an army blanket. The girl slept the sleep of complete exhaustion, breathing heavily with her head on her arm; her pale and rather triangular face was that of someone who was still very young, not much more than nineteen or twenty. The pallor of her skin was accentuated by the short black lashes which curled back abruptly, by the black arched eyebrows and dark brown hair – sleek hair which grew to a peak on the forehead, and had recently been bobbed for the sake of convenience. For the rest her was slightly tip-tilted, and her mouth resolute considering her youth; the lips were well-modelled and fine in texture, having deeply indented corners. For more than a minute Stephen considered the immature figure of Mary Llewellyn. This latest recruit to the Breakspeare Unit had joined it only five weeks ago, replacing a member who was suffering from shell-shock. Mrs. Breakspeare had shaken her head over Mary, but in these harassed days of the German offensive she could not afford to remain short-handed, so in spite of many misgivings she had kept her.

Still shaking her head she had said to Stephen: 'Needs must when the Boches get busy, Miss Gordon! Have an eye to her, will you? She may stick it all right, but between you and me I very much doubt it. You might try her out as a second driver.' And so far Mary Llewellyn had stuck it.

Stephen looked away again, closing her eyes, and after a while forgot about Mary. The events that had preceded her own coming to France began to pass through her brain in procession. ...

Stephen's thoughts stopped abruptly. Someone had come in and was stumping down the room in squeaky trench boots. It was Blakeney holding the time-sheet in her hand – funny old monosyllabic Blakeney, with her curly white hair cropped as close as an Uhlan's, and her face that suggested a sensitive monkey.

'Service, Gordon; wake the kid! Howard – Thurloe – ready?'

They got up and hustled into their trench coats, found their gas masks and finally put on the helmets.

Then Stephen shook Mary Llewellyn very gently: 'It's time.'

Mary opened her eyes: 'Who? What?' she stammered.

'It's time. Get up, Mary.'

The girl staggered to her feet, still stupid with fatigue. Through the cracks in the shuttered the dawn showed faintly.

The grey of a bitter, starved-looking morning. The town like a mortally wounded creature, torn by shells, gashed open by bombs. Dead streets – streets of death – death in streets and their houses; yet people still able to sleep and still sleeping.

1 Sylvia Pankhurst

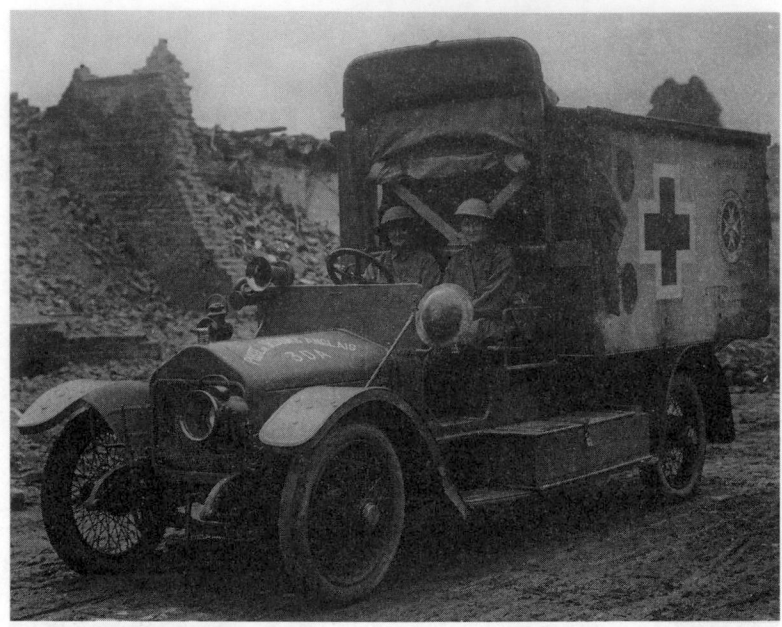

2 The two 'Women of Pervyse' driving their motor ambulance through the ruins of Pervyse, 30 July 1917

3 Air raid damage, Chambers Street, E. London. Airship raids of 13/14 October 1915

4 Dr Elsie Inglis

5 Ward in the Duchess of
Westminster's (No. 1 Red
Cross) Hospital at Le
Touquet, 18 June 1917

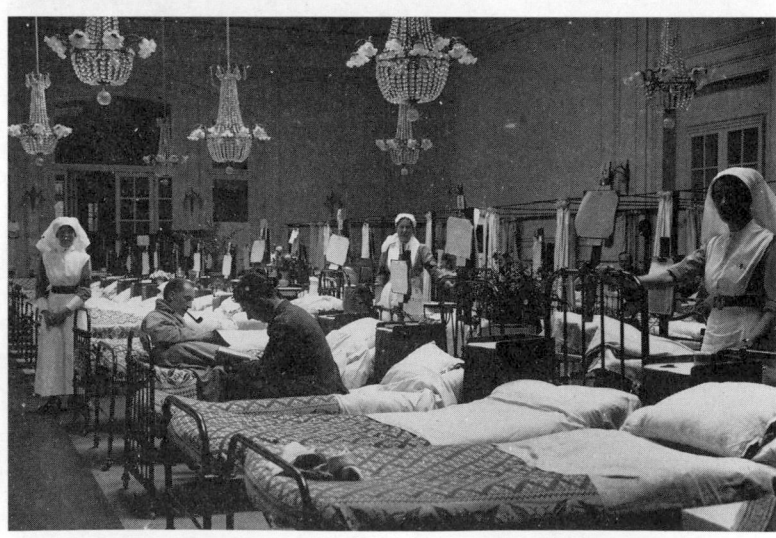

6 First Aid Nursing Yeomanry at St Omer. Ambulance drivers attending to their cars, 28 February 1918

7 Women of the Land Army, thistle hoeing

9 Men and women workers in a shell-filling factory

8 Women workers operating a shell-case-forming machine in the New Gun Factory, Royal Arsenal, Woolwich, May 1918

'Stephen.'

'Yes, Mary?'

'How far is the Poste?'

'I think about thirty kilometres; why?'

'Oh, nothing – I only wondered.'

The long stretch of an open country road. On either side of the road wire netting hung with pieces of crudely painted rag – a camouflage to represent leaves. A road bordered by rag leaves on tall wire hedges. Every few yards or so a deep shell-hole.

'Are they following, Mary? Is Howard all right?'

The girl glanced back: 'Yes, it's all right, she's coming.'

They drove on in silence for a couple of miles. The morning was terribly cold; Mary shivered. 'What's that?' It was rather a foolish question for she knew what it was, only too well!

'They're at it again,' Stephen muttered.

A shell burst in a paddock, uprooting some trees. 'All right, Mary?'

'Yes – look out! We're coming to a crater!' They skimmed it by less than an inch and dashed on, Mary suddenly moving nearer to Stephen.

'Don't joggle my arm, for the Lord's sake, child!'

'Did I? I'm sorry.'

'Yes – don't do it again,' and once more they drove forward in silence.

Farther down the road they were blocked by a farm cart: 'Militaires! Militaires! Militaires!' Stephen shouted.

Rather languidly the farmer got down and went to the heads of his thin, stumbling horses. 'Il faut vivre,' he explained, as he pointed to the cart, which appeared to be full of potatoes.

In the field on the right worked three very old women; they were going with a diligent and fatalistic patience. At any moment a stray shell might burst and then, presto! little left of the very old women. But what will you? There is war – there has been war so long – one must eat, even under the noses of the Germans; the bon Dieu knows this. He alone can protect – so meanwhile one just goes on diligently hoeing. A blackbird was singing to himself in a tree, the tree was horribly maimed and blasted; all the same he had known it the previous spring and so now, in spite of its wounds, he had found it. Came a sudden lull when they heard him distinctly.

And Mary saw him: 'Look,' she said, 'there's a blackbird!' Just for a moment she forgot about war.

Yet Stephen could now very seldom forget, and this was because of the girl at her side. A queer, tight feeling would come round her heart, she would know the fear that can go hand in hand with personal courage, the fear for another.

But now she looked down for a moment and smiled: 'Bless that blackbird for letting you see him, Mary.' She knew that Mary loved little wild birds, that indeed she loved all the humbler creatures.

They turned into a lane and were comparatively safe, but the roar of the guns had grown much more insistent. They must be nearing the Poste de Secours, so they spoke very little because of those guns and after a while because of the wounded.

The Poste de Secours was a ruined auberge at the crossroads, about fifty yards behind the trenches. From what had once been its spacious cellar, they were hurriedly carrying up the wounded, maimed and mangled creatures who, a few hours ago, had been young and vigorous men. None too gently the stretchers were lowered to the ground beside the two waiting ambulances – none too gently because there were so many of them, and because there must come a time in all wars when custom stales even compassion.

The wounded were patient and fatalistic, like the very old women back in the field. The only difference between them being that the men had themselves become as a field laid bare to a ruthless and bloody hoeing. Some of them had not even a blanket to protect them from the biting cold of the wind. A Poilu with a mighty wound in the belly, must lie with the blood congealing on the bandage. Next to him lay a man with his face blown away, who, God alone knew why, remained conscious. The abdominal case was the first to be handled, Stephen herself helped to lift his stretcher. He was probably dying, but he did not complain inasmuch as he wanted his mother. The voice that emerged from his coarse, bared throat was the voice of a child demanding its mother. The man with the terrible face tried to speak, but when he did so the sound was not human. His bandage had slipped a little to one side, so that Stephen must step between him and Mary, and hastily readjust the bandage.

'Get back to the ambulance! I shall want you to drive.'

In silence Mary obeyed her.

And now began the first of those endless journeys from the Poste de Secours to the Field Hospital. For twenty-four hours they would ply back and forth with their light Ford ambulances. Driving quickly because the lives of the wounded might depend on their speed, yet with every nerve taut to avoid, as far as might be, the jarring of the hazardous roads full of ruts and shell-holes.

The man with the shattered face started again, they could hear him above the throb of the motor. For a moment they stopped while Stephen listened, but his lips were not there ... an intolerable sound.

'Faster, drive faster, Mary!'

Pale, but with firmly set, resolute mouth, Mary Llewellyn drove faster.

When at last they reached the Field Hospital, the bearded Poilu with the wound in his belly was lying very placidly on his stretcher; his hairy chin slightly upward. He had ceased to speak as a little child – perhaps, after all, he had found his mother.

The day went on and the sun shone out brightly, dazzling the tired eyes of the drivers. Dusk fell, and the roads grew treacherous and vague. Night came – they dared not risk having lights, so that they must just stare and stare into the darkness. In the distance the sky turned ominously red, some stray shells might well have set fire to a village, that tall column of flame was probably the church; and the Boches were punishing Compiègne again, to judge from the heavy bombardment. Yet by now there was nothing real in the world but that thick and almost impenetrable darkness, and the ache of the eyes that must stare and stare, and the dreadful, patient pain of the wounded – there had never been anything else in the world but black night shot through with the pain of the wounded.

On the following morning the two ambulances crept back to their base at the villa on Compiègne. It had been a tough job, long hours of strain, and to make matters worse the reliefs had been late, one of them having had a breakdown. Moving stiffly, and with red rimmed and watering eyes, the four women swallowed large cups of coffee; then just as they were they lay down on the floor, wrapped in their trench coats and army blankets. In less than a quarter of an hour they slept, though the villa shook and rocked with the bombardment.

There is something that mankind can never destroy in spite of an unreasoning will to destruction, and this is its own idealism, that integral part of its very being. The ageing and the cynical may make wars, but the young and the idealistic must fight them, and thus there are bound to come quick reactions, blind impulses not always comprehended. Men will curse as they kill, yet accomplish deeds of self-sacrifice, giving their lives for others; poets will write with their pens dipped in blood, yet will write not of death but of life eternal; strong and courteous friendships will be born, to endure in the face of enmity and destruction. And so persistent is this urge to the ideal, above all in the presence of great disaster, that mankind, the wilful destroyer of beauty, must immediately strive to create new beauties, lest it perish from a sense of its own desolation; and this touched the Celtic soul of Mary.

For the Celtic soul is the stronghold of dreams, of longings come down the dim paths of ages; and within it there dwells a vague discontent, so that it must for ever go questing. And now as though drawn by some hidden attraction, as though stirred by some irresistible impulse, quite beyond the realms of her own understanding, Mary turned in all faith and innocence to Stephen. Who can pretend to interpret fate, wither his own fate or that of another? Why should this girl have crossed Stephen's path, or indeed Stephen hers, if it came to that matter? Was not the world large enough for them both? Perhaps not – or perhaps the event of their meeting had already been written upon tablets of stone by some wise if relentless recording finger.

An orphan from the days of her earliest childhood, Mary had lived with a married cousin in the wilds of Wales; an unwanted member of a none too prosperous household. She had little education beyond that obtained from a small private school in a neighbouring village. She knew nothing of life or of men and women; and even less did she know of herself, of her ardent, courageous, impulsive nature. Thanks to the fact that her cousin was a doctor, forced to motor over a widely spread practice, she had learnt to drive and look after his car by filling the post of an unpaid chauffeur – she was, in her small way, a good mechanic. But the war had made her much less contented with her narrow life, and although at its outbreak Mary had not been quite eighteen, she had felt a great longing to be independent, in which she had met no opposition. However, a Welsh village is no field for endeavour, and thus nothing had happened until by a fluke she had suddenly heard of the Breakspeare Unit via a local parson, an old friend of its founder – he himself had written to recommend Mary. And so, straight from the quiet seclusion of Wales, this girl had managed the complicated journey that had finally got her over to France, then across a war-ravaged, dislocated country. Mary was neither so frail not so timid as Mrs. Breakspeare had thought her.

Stephen had felt rather bored just at the prospect of teaching the new member her duties, but after a while it came to pass that she missed the girl when she was not with her. And after a while she would find herself observing the way Mary's hair grew, low on the forehead, the wide setting of her slightly oblique grey eyes, the abrupt sweep back of their heavy lashes; and these things would move Stephen, so that she must touch the girl's hair for a moment with her fingers. Fate was throwing them continually together, in moments of rest as in moments of danger; they could not have escaped this even had they wished to, and indeed they did not wish to escape it. They were pawns in the ruthless and complicated game of existence, moved hither and thither on the board by an unseen hand, yet moved side by side, so that they grew to expect each other.

'Mary, are you there?'

A superfluous question – the reply would be always the same.

'I'm here, Stephen.'

Sometimes Mary would talk of her plans for the future while Stephen listened, smiling as she did so.

'I'll go into an office, I want to be free.'

'You're so little, you'd get mislaid in an office.'

'I'm five foot five!'

'Are you really, Mary? You feel little somehow.'

'That's because you're so tall. I do wish I could grow a bit!'

'No, don't wish that, you're all right as you are – it's you, Mary.'

Mary would want to be told about Morton, she was never tired of hearing about Morton. She would make Stephen get out the photographs of her father, of her mother whom Mary thought lovely, of Puddle, and above all of Raftery. Then Stephen must tell her of the life in London, and afterwards of the new house in Paris; must talk of her own career and ambitions, though Mary had not read either of her novels – there had never been a library subscription.

But at moments Stephen's face would grow clouded because of the things she could not tell her; because of the little untruths and evasions that must fill up the gaps in her strange life-history. Looking down into Mary's clear, grey eyes, she would suddenly flush through her tan, and feel guilty; and that feeling would reach the girl and disturb her, so that she must hold Stephen's hand for a moment.

One day she said suddenly: 'Are you unhappy?'

'Why on earth should I be unhappy?' smiled Stephen.

All the same there were nights now when Stephen lay awake even after her arduous hours of service, hearing the guns that were coming nearer, yet not thinking of them, but always of Mary. A great gentleness would gradually engulf her like a soft sea mist, veiling reef and headland.

She would seem to be drifting quietly, serenely towards some blessed and peaceful harbour. Stretching out a hand she would stroke the girl's shoulder where she lay, but carefully in case she should wake her. Then the mist would lift: 'Good God! What am I doing?' She would sit up abruptly, disturbing the sleeper.

'Is that you, Stephen?'

'Yes, my dear, go to sleep.'

Then a cross, aggrieved voice: 'Do shut up, you two. It's rotten of you, I was just getting off! Why must you always persist in talking!'

Stephen would lie down again and would think: 'I'm a fool, I go out of my way to find trouble. Of course I've grown fond of the child, she's so plucky, almost anyone would grow fond of Mary. Why should I have affection and friendship? Why should I have a real human interest? I can help her find her feet after the war if we both come through – I might buy her a business.' That gentle mist, hiding both reef and headland; it would gather again blurring all perception, robbing the past of its crude, ugly outlines. 'After all, what harm can it do the child to be fond of me?' It was so good a thing to have won the affection of this young creature.

The Germans got perilously close to Compiègne, and the Breakspeare Unit was ordered to retire. Its base was now at a ruined chateau on the outskirts of an insignificant village, yet not so very insignificant either – it was stuffed to the neck with ammunition. Nearly all the hours that were spent off duty must be passed in the gloomy, damp-smelling dug-outs which consisted of cellars, partly destroyed but protected by sandbags on heavy timbers. Like foxes creeping out of their holes, the members of the Unit would creep into daylight, their uniforms covered with mould and rubble, their eyes blinking, their hands cold and numb from the dampness – so cold and so numb that the starting up of motors would often present a real problem.

At this time there occurred one or two small mishaps; Bless broke her wrist while cranking her engine; Blakeney and three others at a Poste de Secours, were met by a truly terrific bombardment and took cover in what had once been a brick-field, crawling into the disused furnace. There they squatted for something over eight hours, while the German gunners played hit as hit can with the tall and conspicuous chimney. When at last they emerged, half stifled by brick-dust, Blakeney had got something into her eye, which she rubbed; the result was acute inflammation.

Howard had begun to be irritating, with her passion for tending her beautiful hair. She would sit in the corner of her dug-out as calmly as though she were sitting at a Bond Street hairdresser's; and having completed the ritual of brushing, she would gaze at herself in a pocket mirror. With a bandage over her unfortunate eye, Blakeney looked more like a monkey than ever, a sick monkey, and her strictly curtailed conversation was not calculated to enliven the Unit. She seemed almost entirely bereft of speech these days, as though reverting to species. Her one comment of life was: 'Oh, I dunno ...' always said with a jaunty rising inflection. It meant everything or nothing as you chose to take it, and had long been her panacea for the ills of what she considered a stupid creation. 'Oh, I dunno ...' And indeed she did not; poor, old, sensitive, monosyllabic Blakeney. The Poilu who served out the Unit's rations – cold meat, sardines, bread and sour red Pinard – was discovered by Stephen in the very act of attempting to unload an aerial bomb. He explained with a smile that the Germans were sly in their methods of loading: 'I cannot discover just how it is done.' Then he showed his left hand – it was minus one of the fingers: 'That,' he told her, still smiling, 'was caused by a shell, a quite little shell, which I was also unloading.' And when she remonstrated none too gently, he sulked: 'But I wish to give this one to Maman!'

Everyone had begun to feel the nerve strain, except perhaps Blakeney, who had done with all feeling. Shorthanded by two, the remaining members of the Unit must now work like veritable niggers – on one occasion Stephen and Mary worked for seventy hours with scarcely a respite. Strained nerves are invariably followed by strained tempers, and sudden, hot quarrels would break out over nothing. Bless and Howard loathed each other for two days, then palled up again, because of a grievance that had recently been evolved against Stephen. For everyone knew that Stephen and Blakeney were by far the best drivers in the Breakspeare Unit, and as such should be shared by all the members in turn; but poor Blakeney was nursing a very sore eye, while Stephen still continued to drive only with Mary. They were spendidly courageous and greathearted women, every one of them, glad enough as a rule to help one another to shoulder burdens, to be tolerant and kind when it came to friendships. They petted and admired their youngest recruit, and most of them liked and respected Stephen, all the same they had now grown childishly jealous, and this jealousy reached the sharp ears of Mrs. Breakspeare.

Mrs. Breakspeare sent for Stephen one morning; she was sitting at a Louis Quinze writing-table which had somehow survived the wreck of the chateau and was now in her gloomy official dug-out. Her right hand reposed on an ordnance map, she looked like a very maternal general. The widow of an officer killed in the war, and the mother of two large sons and three daughters, she had led the narrow, conventional life that is common to women in military stations. Yet all the while she must have been filling her subconscious reservoir with knowledge, for she suddenly blossomed forth as leader with a fine understanding of human nature. So now she looked over her ample bosom not unkindly, but rather thoughtfully at Stephen.

'Sit down, Miss Gordon. It's about Llewellyn, whom I asked you to take on as a second driver. I think the time has now arrived when she ought to stand more on her own in the Unit. She must take her chance like every- one else, and not cling quite so close – don't misunderstand me, I'm most grateful for all you've done for the girl – but of course you are one of our finest drivers, and fine driving counts for a great deal these days, it may mean life or death, as you yourself know. And – well – it seems scarcely fair to the others that Mary should always go out with you. No, it certainly is not quite fair to the others.'

Stephen said: 'Do you mean that she's to go out with every one in turn – with Thurloe for instance?' And do what she would to appear indiffer- ent, she could not quite keep her voice from trembling.

Mrs. Breakspeare nodded: 'That's what I do mean.' Then she said rather slowly: 'These are strenuous times, and such times are apt to breed many emotions which are purely fictitious, purely mushroom growths that spring up in a night and have no roots at all, except in our imaginations. But I'm sure you'll agree with me, Miss Gordon, in thinking it our duty to discourage anything in the nature of an emotional friendship, such as I fancy Mary Llewellyn is on the verge of feeling for you. It's quite natural of course, a kind of reaction, but not wise – no, I cannot think it wise. It savours a little too much of the schoolroom and might lead to ridicule in the Unit. Your position is far too important for that; I look upon you as my second in command.'

Stephen said quietly: 'I understand. I'll go at once and speak to Blak- eney about altering Mary Llewellyn's time-sheet.'

'Yes, do, if you will,' agreed Mrs. Breakspeare; then she stooped and studied her ordnance map, without looking again at Stephen.

If Stephen had been fearful for Mary's safety before, she was now ten times more so. The front was in a condition of flux and the Postes de Sec- ours were continually shifting. An Allied ambulance driver had been fired on by Germans, after having arrived at the spot where his Poste had been only the previous evening. There was very close fighting on every sector; it seemed truly amazing that no grave casualties had so far occurred in the Unit. For now the Allies had begun to creep forward, yard by yard, mile by mile, very slowly but surely; refreshed by a splendid transfusion of blood for the youthful veins of a great child-nation.

Of all the anxieties on Mary's account that now beset Stephen, Thurloe was the gravest; for Thurloe was one of those irritating drivers who stake all on their own inadequate judgement. She was brave to a fault, but inclined to show off when it came to a matter of actual danger. For long hours Stephen would not know what had happened, and must often leave the base before Mary had returned, still in doubt regarding her safety.

Grimly, yet with unfailing courage and devotion, Stephen now went about her duties. Every day the risks that they all took grew graver, for the enemy, nearing the verge of defeat, was less than ever a respecter of persons. Stephen's only moments of comparative peace would be when she herself drove Mary. And as though the girl missed some vitalizing force, some strength that had been hitherto hers to draw on, she flagged and Stephen would watch her flagging during their brief spell together off duty, and would know that nothing but her Celtic pluck kept Mary Llewellyn from a breakdown. And now, because they were so often parted, even chance meetings became of importance. The might meet while preparing their cars in the morning, and if this should happen they would draw close together for a moment, as though finding comfort in nearness. ...

Events gathered momentum. By June of that year 700,000 United States soldiers, strong and comely men plucked from their native prairies, from their fields of tall corn, from their farms and their cities, were giving their lives in defence of freedom on the blood-soaked battlefields of France. They had little to gain and much to lose; it was not their war, yet they helped to fight it because they were young and their nation was young, and the ideals of youth are eternally hopeful.

In July came the Allied counter-offensive, and now in her moment of approaching triumph France knew to the full her great desolation, as it lay revealed by the retreating armies. For not only had there been a holocaust of homesteads, but the country was strewn with murdered trees, cut down in their hour of most perfect leafing; orchards struck to the ground, an orgy of destruction, as the mighty forces rolled back like a tide, to recoil themselves – incredulous, amazed, maddened by the outrage of the coming disaster. For mad they must surely have been, since no man is a more faithful lover of trees than the German. ...

All roads of thought seemed to lead back to Mary; and these days, in addition to fears for her safety, came a growing distress at what she must see – far more terrible sights than the patient wounded. For everywhere now lay the wreckage of war, sea-wrack spewed up by a poisonous ocean – putrefying, festering in the sun; breeding corruption to man's seed of folly. Twice lately, while they had been driving together, they had come upon sights that Stephen would have spared her. There had been that shattered German gun-carriage with its stiff, dead horses and its three dead gunners – horrible death, the men's faces had been black like the faces of negroes, black and swollen from gas, or was it from putrefaction? There had been the deserted and wounded charger with its fore-leg hanging as though by a rag. Near by had been lying a dead young Uhlan, and Stephen had shot the beast with his revolver, but Mary had suddenly started sobbing: 'Oh, God! Oh, God! It was dumb – it couldn't speak. It's so awful somehow to see a thing suffer when it can't ask you why!' She had sobbed a long time, and Stephen had not known how to console her.

And now the Unit was creeping forward in the wake of the steadily advancing Allies. Billets would be changed as the base moved slowly from devastated village to village. There seldom seemed to be a house left with a roof, or anything much beyond its four walls, and quite often they must lie staring up a the stars, which would stare back again, aloof and untroubled. At about this time they grew very short of water, for most of the wells were said to have been poisoned; and this shortage of water was a very real torment, since it strictly curtailed the luxury of washing. Then what must Bless do but get herself hit while locating the position of a Poste de Secours which had most inconsiderably vanished. Like the Allied ambulance driver she was shot at, but in her case she happened to stop a bullet – it was only a flesh wound high up in the arm, yet enough to render her useless for a moment. She had had to be sent back to hospital, so once again the Unit was short-handed.

It turned hot, and in place of dampness and the cold, came days and nights that seemed almost breathless; days when the wounded must lie out in the sun, tormented by flies as they waited their turn to be lifted into ambulances. And as though misfortunes attracted each other, as though indeed they were hunting in couples, Stephen's face was struck by a splinter of shell, and her right cheek cut open rather badly. It was neatly stitched up by the little French doctor at the Poste de Secours, and when he had finished with his needle and dressings, he bowed very gravely: 'Mademoiselle will carry an honourable scar as a mark of her courage,' and he bowed yet again, so that in the end Stephen must also bow gravely. Fortunately, however, she could still do her job, which was all to the good for the short-handed Unit.

On an autumn afternoon of blue sky and sunshine, Stephen had the Croix de Guerre pinned on her breast by a white-haired and white-moustached general. First came the motherly Mrs. Claude Breakspeare, whose tunic looked much too tight for her bosom, then Stephen and one or two other members of the valiant and untiring Unit. The general kissed each one in turn on both cheeks, while overhead hovered a fleet of Aces; troops presented arms, veteran troops tried in battle, and having the set look of war in their eyes – for the French have a very nice taste in such matters. And presently Stephen's bronze Croix de Guerre would carry three miniature stars on its ribbon and each star would stand for a mention in despatches.

That evening she and Mary walked over the fields to a little town not very far from their billets. They paused for a moment to watch the sunset, and Mary stroked the new Croix de Guerre; then she looked straight up into Stephen's eyes, her mouth shook, and Stephen saw that she was crying. After this they must walk hand in hand for a while. Why not? There was no one just then to see them.

Mary said: 'All my life I've been waiting for something.'

'What was it, my dear?' Stephen asked her gently.

And Mary answered: 'I've been waiting for you, and it's seemed such a dreadful long time, Stephen.'

The barely healed wound across Stephen's cheek flushed darkly, for what could she find to answer?

'For me?' she stammered.

Mary nodded gravely: 'Yes, for you. I've always been waiting for you; and after the war you'll send me away.' Then she suddenly caught hold of Stephen's sleeve: 'Let me come with you – don't send me away, I want to be near you. … I can't explain … but I only want to be near you, Stephen. Stephen – say you won't send me away. …'

Stephen's hand closed over the Croix de Guerre, but the metal of valour felt cold to her fingers; dead and cold it felt at that moment as the courage that had set it upon her breast. She stared straight ahead of her into the sunset, trembling because of what she would answer.

Then she said very slowly: 'After the war – no, I won't send you away from me, Mary.'

Vera Brittain
from
Honourable Estate

MY DEAREST Jill,

To-night I am writing you a long letter because there is a stunt on to-morrow and I don't expect to come out of it alive. In fact I may as well be honest with you and tell you that I don't mean to come out of it. You were always the one person in the family with whom I could be quite honest, and that is why I'm going to tell you one or two things about this War that I would like you to remember. I have kept it all out of letters before, but this is the last I shall ever write you, and I want you to know.

As I couldn't get a letter like this past the Censor I am giving it to Meury, the American lance-corporal I told you about who got the D.M.C., to put into your hands if ever he goes to England. You may think it queer my not giving it to an officer, Val and Eric are the only officers I know really intimately now. When you have read this you will understand why it is no use for Val to have it, and Eric is so often tight nowadays that if I gave it to him the chances are you would never get it at all. Meury is not only the pluckiest chap in the platoon but awfully efficient as well, so I feel this letter is more likely to reach you through him than anyone else out here.

When we first joined up I probably gave you the impression that every-thing was splendid. The battalion was encamped in lovely country, and I got quite fond of a lot of the chaps who seemed so different from the ordi-nary Tommy. We were all going to be fine fellows and heroes, and see the world and have a glorious time.

Well, the real thing isn't like that at all. If you had seen men with their faces blown in or their bowels running out and kids of seventeen gone stark staring mad and gibbering for their mothers, you would know it isn't. I wonder how much you are told about the true facts of the fighting here? We never have any real rest from it, as the so-called rest camps get shelled almost as much as the fire-trenches. There's not a spot on the bloody Peninsula where there's no risk of getting shot. Do people at home realise from the colossal casualty lists anything of what this hell is, or don't they get published? Anyhow you can take it from me there is no marching and singing patriotic songs and cheering our brave boys out here. It's all blood and bones and decaying bodies and chaps turned to

skeletons with dysentery and one long eternal insufferable stink. The
whole place reeks of defunct Turks and Australians, especially when they
swell up and burst in the sun. These rotting corpses simply breed flies and
so do the filthy Turk trenches, whatever we do to scavenge ours. I can't
believe we have only been here two months for it feels like two years. All
this foul bayonet fighting makes me sick. I can't stick ripping out another
man's guts and I can stick even less the people who say they like it. Besides,
whatever we do in that way is no good anyhow as there never seem to be
any reinforcements to follow up our attacks.

But I'm not only trying to tell you what war does to people's bodies,
even though it does tear their insides out and emasculate them and mutilate the most intimate parts of their persons for the public gaze. What's
even worse is what it does to your mind. At first there's the appalling
monotony and the hideous obscene language and the ever-lasting drills
and parades, and thick-headed old sergeants without a scrap of education
or humanity teaching you to shove you bayonets into men's stomachs by
working you into a hysterical frenzy over sacks of straw. After a few weeks
nobody seems to care 2*d*. about pictures or decent books; it's all cards and
girls and whisky and what sort of harlot you're going to pick up when you
next get a pass. By the time you get to the front you've got nothing left in
the way of philosophy or religion to help you face death or stick the sights
or bear up under the smells. There's no way of forgetting what you can't
prevent and can't avoid, except through the whisky bottle, and whatever
you do the only rule is expediency and not getting found out.

When we were first in camp old Eric, who is not a fighter anyhow, soon
fell for the girls and the whisky, but Val and I thought we might have some
use for our intellects when the War was over and we didn't want the rot
to get us if we could help it. We have never cared for getting drunk and
going with prostitutes, so when life got really intolerable we decided that
the only thing to do was to be everything we possibly could to one
another. You will know what I mean if you remember the conversation we
had in the bicycle shed years ago about Val having to leave Ludborough. I
don't know how much you know nowadays and I shall never know what
you think of this letter, but I tell you that if it hadn't been for Val I should
never have stuck this damned War as long as I have.

There was no trouble at all to begin with, but soon after we got here and
were always crowded together some swinish fellows began to talk. A few
days ago the C.O. sent for me and told me that next time we are out of the
line there will probably be an enquiry – which of course might mean a
court-martial and expulsion from the Army. Well, I don't intend to let it

come to that and nor does Valentine. We don't feel we have done anything wrong or harmed anyone, but after the hell I have been through already I can't face the hullabaloo and the public disgrace and the scenes there would be at home, especially as our beautiful respectable family would take care I didn't live it down and forget it, or make a success of any career even if I had the chance. Knowing so well what the Allendyenes are I can't confront Father and Mother with the fact that their son is what they would call vicious and immoral instead of a virtuous patriotic hero. So we have decided to quit. Please try to forgive me and not to think too badly of me. Life has been so ghastly at times that it is difficult to explain every thing properly.

I think that's all I have to say, except just this – that if you ever get married and have a son, don't, whatever you do, let them make him fight in a war. Don't let them cheat him into thinking it's all fine and glorious, but tell him the truth as I have tried to tell you.

And now, Jill darling, I'm afraid it will have to be goodbye. I wish I could have talked to you once more but it was not to be. I got out your photograph just now and looked at it, because I shan't ever see you again. But if there is anything after death and I can find a way, I promise I will try to come back and watch over you.

In life and in death, dearest Jill.
Your ever loving
JACK.

Ellen La Motte
Women and Wives

A bitter wind swept in from the North Sea. It swept in over many miles of Flanders plains, driving gusts of rain before it. It was a biting gale by the time it reached the little cluster of wooden huts composing the field hospital, and rain and wind together dashed against the huts, blew under them, blew through them, crashed to pieces a swinging window down at the laundry, and loosened the roof of Salle I. at the other end of the enclosure. It was just ordinary winter weather, such as had lasted for months on end, and which the Belgians spoke of as vile weather, while the French called it vile Belgian weather. The drenching rain soaked into the long, green winter grass, and the sweeping wind was bitter cold, and the howling of the wind was louder than the guns, so that it was only when the wind paused for a moment, between blasts, that the rolling of the guns could be heard.

In Salle I. the stove had gone out. It was a good little stove, but somehow was unequal to struggling with the wind which blew down the long, rocking stove pipe, and blew the fire out. So the little stove grew cold, and the hot water jug on the stove grew cold, and all the patients at that end of the ward likewise grew cold, and demanded hot water bottles, and there wasn't any hot water with which to fill them. So the patients complained and shivered, and in the pauses of the wind, one heard the guns.

Then the roof of the ward lifted about an inch, and more wind beat down, and as it beat down, so the roof lifted. The orderly remarked that if this Belgian weather continued, by tomorrow the roof would be clean off – blown off into the German lines. So all laughed as Fouquet said this, and wondered how they could lie abed with the roof of Salle I., the Salle of the *Grands Blessés*, blown over into the German lines. The ward did not present a neat appearance, for all the beds were pushed about at queer angles, in from the wall, out from the wall, some touching each other, some very far apart, and all to avoid the little leaks of rain which streamed or dropped down from little holes in the roof. This weary, weary war! These long days of boredom in the hospital, these days of incessant wind and rain and cold.

Armand, the chief orderly, ordered Fouquet to rebuild the fire, and Fouquet slipped on his *sabots* and clogged down the ward, away outdoors in the wind, and returned finally with a box of coal on his shoulders, which he dumped heavily on the floor. He was clumsy and sullen, and the coal was wet and mostly slate, and the patients laughed at his efforts to rebuild the fire. Finally, however, it was alight again, and radiated out a faint warmth, which served to bring out the smell of iodoform, and of draining wounds, and other smells which loaded the cold, close air. Then, no one knows who began it, one of the patients showed the nurse photograph of his wife and child, and in a moment every man in the twenty beds was fishing back of his bed, in his *musette*, under his pillow, for photographs of his wife. They all had wives, it seems, for remember, these were the old troops, who had replaced the young Zouaves who had guarded this part of the Front all summer. One by one they came out, these photographs, from weather-beaten sacks, from shabby boxes, from pillows, and the nurse must see them all. Pathetic little pictures they were, of common, working-class women, some fat and work-worn, some thin and work-worn, some with stodgy little children grouped about them, some without, but all were practically the same. They were the wives of these men in the beds here, the working-class wives of working-class men – the soldiers of the trenches. Ah yes, France is democratic. It is the Nation's war, and all the men of the Nation regardless of rank, are serving. But some serve in better places than others. The trenches are mostly reserved for men of the working class, which is reasonable, as there are more of them.

The rain beat down, and the little stove glowed, and the afternoon drew to a close, and the photographs of the wives continued to pass from hand to hand. There was much talk of home, and much of it was longing, and much of it was pathetic, and much of it was resigned. And always the little, ugly wives, the stupid, ordinary wives, represented home. And the words home and wife were interchangeable and stood for the same thing. And the glories and heroisms of war seemed of less interest, as a factor in life, than these stupid little wives.

Then Armand, the chief orderly, showed them all the photograph of his wife. No one knew that he was married, but he said yes, and that he received a letter from her every day – sometimes it was a postcard. Also that he wrote to her every day. We all knew how nervous he used to get, about letter time, when the *vaguemestre* made his rounds, every morning, distributing letters to all the wards. We all knew how impatient he used to get, when the *vaguemestre* laid his letter upon the table, and there it lay, on the table, while he was forced to make rounds with the surgeon, and could not claim it until long afterwards. So it was from his wife, that daily letter, so anxiously, so nervously awaited!

Simon had a wife too. Simon, the young surgeon, German-looking in appearance, six feet of blond brute. But not blond brute really. Whatever his appearance, there was in him something finer, something tenderer, something nobler, to distinguish him from the brute. About three times a week he walked into the ward with his fountain pen between his teeth – he did not smoke, but he chewed his fountain pen – and when the dressings were over, he would tell the nurse, shyly, accidentally, as it were, some little news about his about his home. Some little incident concerning his wife, some affectionate anecdote about his three young children. Once when one of the staff went over to london on vacation, Simon asked her to buy for his wife a leather coat, such as English women wear, for motoring. Always he thought of his wife, spoke of his wife, planned some thoughtful little surprise or gift for her.

You know, they won't let wives come to the Front. Women can come into the War Zone, on various pretexts, but wives cannot. Wives, it appears, are bad for the morale of the Army. They come with their troubles, to talk of how business is failing, of how things are going to the bad at home, because of the war; of how great the struggle, how bitter the trials and the poverty and hardship. They establish the connecting link between the soldier and his life at home, his life that he is compelled to resign. Letters can be censored and all disturbing items cut out, but if a wife is permitted to come to the War Zone, to see her husband, there is no censoring the things she may tell him. The disquieting, disturbing things. So she herself must be censored, not permitted to come. So for long weary months men must remain at the Front, on active inactivity, and their wives cannot come to see them. Only other people's wives may come. It is not the woman but the wife that is objected to. There is a difference. In war, it is very great.

There are many women at the Front. How do they get there, to the Zone of the Armies? On various pretexts – to see sick relatives, in such and such hospitals, or to see other relatives, brothers, uncles, cousins, other people's husbands – oh, there are many reasons which make it possible for them to come. And always there are the Belgian women, who live in the War Zone, for at present there is a little strip of Belgium left, and all the civilians have not been evacuated from the Army Zone. So there are plenty of women, first and last. Better ones for the officers, naturally, just as the officers' mess is of better quality than that of the common soldiers. But always there are plenty of women. Never wives, who mean responsibility, but just women, who only mean distraction and amusement, just as food and wine. So wives are forbidden, because lowering to the morale, but women are winked at, because they cheer and refresh the troops. After the war, it is hoped that all unmarried soldiers will marry, but doubtless they will not marry these women who have served and cheered them in the War Zone. That, again, would be depressing the country's morale. It is rather paradoxical, but there are those who can explain it perfectly.

No, no, I don't understand. It's because everything has two sides. You would be surprised to pick up a franc, and find Liberty, Equality, and Fraternity on one side, on the other, the image of the Sower smoothed out. A rose is a fine rose because of manure you put at its roots. You don't get a medal for sustained nobility. You get it for the impetuous action of the moment, an action quite out of keeping with the trend of one's daily life. You speak of the young aviator who was decorated for destroying a Zeppelin single-handed, and in the next breath you add, and he killed himself, a few days later, by attempting to fly when he was drunk. So it goes. There is a dirty sediment at the bottom of most souls. War, superb as it is, is not necessarily a filtering process, by which men and nations may be purified. Well, there are many people to write you of the noble side, the heroic side, the exalted side of war. I must write you of what I have seen, the other side, the backwash. They are both true. In Spain, they bang their silver coins upon a marble slab, accepting the stamp upon both sides, and then decide whether as a whole they ring true.

Every now and then, Armand, the orderly, goes to the village to get a bath. He comes back with very clean hands and nails, and says that it has greatly solaced him, the warm water. Then later, that same evening, he gets permission to be absent from the hospital, and he goes to our village to a girl. But he is always as eager, as nervous for his wife's letter as ever. It is the same with Simon, the young surgeon. Only Simon keeps himself pretty clean at all times, as he has orderly to bring him pitchers of hot water every morning, as many as he wants. Simon has a girl in the village, to whom he goes every week. Only, why does he talk so incessantly about his wife, and show her pictures to me, to everyone about the place? Why should we all be bored with tales of Simon's stupid wife, when that's all she means to him? Only perhaps she means more. I told you I did not understand.

Then the *Gestionnaire*, the little fat man in khaki, who is purveyor to the hospital. Every night he commandeers an ambulance and drives back into the country, to a village twelve miles away, to sleep with a woman. And the old doctor – he is sixty-four and has grandchildren – he goes down to our village for a little girl of fourteen. He was decorated with the Legion of Honour other day. It seems incongruous.

Oh yes, of course these were decent girls at the start, at the beginning of the war. But you know women, how they run after men, especially when the men wear uniforms, all gilt buttons and braid. It's not the men's fault that most of the women in the War Zone are ruined. Have you ever watched the village girls when a regiment comes through, or stops for a night or two, *en repos*, on its way to the Front? Have you seen the girls make fools of themselves over the men? Well, that's why there are so many accessible for the troops. Of course the professional prostitutes from Paris aren't admitted to the War Zone, but the Belgian girls made such fools of themselves, the others weren't needed.

Across the lines, back of the German lines, in the invaded districts, it is different. The conquering armies just ruined all the women they could get hold of. Any one will tell you that. *Ces sales Bosches!* For it is inconceivable

how any decent girl, even a Belgian, could give herself up voluntarily to a
Hun! They used force, those brutes! That is the difference. It's all the difference in the world. No, the women over there didn't make fools of
themselves over those men – how could they! No, no. Over there, in the
invaded districts, the Germans forced those girls. Here, on this side, the
girls cajoled the men till they gave in. Can't you see? You must be pro-
German! Any way, they are all ruined and not fit for any decent man to
mate with, after the war.

They are pretty dangerous, too, some these women. No, I don't mean
in that way. But they act as spies for the Germans and get a lot of information out of the men and send it back, somehow, into the lines. The
Germans stop at nothing, nothing is too dastardly, too low, for the
attempt. There were two Belgian girls once, who lived together in a room,
in a little village back of our lines. They were natives, and had always lived
there, so of course they were not turned out, and when the village was
shelled from time to time, they did not seem to mind and altogether they
made a lot of money. They only received officers. The common soldiers
were just dirt to them, and they refused to see them. Certain women get
known in a place, as those who receive soldiers and those who officers.
These girls were intelligent, always asked a lot of intelligent, interested
questions, and you know a man when he is excited will answer unsus-
pectingly any question put to him. The Germans took advantage of that.
It is easy to be a spy. Just know what questions you must ask, and it is surprising how much information you can get. The thing is, to know upon
what point information is wanted. These girls knew that, it seems, and so
they asked a lot of intelligent questions, and as they received only officers,
they got a good lot of valuable information, for as I say, when a man is
excited he will answer many questions. Besides, who could have sus-
pected at first that these two girls were spies? But they were, as they found
out finally, after several months. Their rooms were one day searched, and
a mass of incriminating papers were discovered. It seems the Germans
had taken these girls from their families – held their families as hostages
– and had sent them across into the English lines, with threats of vile
reprisals upon their families if they did not produce information of value.
Wasn't it beastly! Making these girls prostitutes and spies, upon pain of
reprisals upon their families. The Germans knew they were so attractive
that they receive only officers. That they would receive many clients, of
high rank, of much information, who would readily fall victims to their
wiles. They are very vile themselves, these Germans. The curious thing is,
how they understand how to bait a trap for their enemies. In spite of

having nothing in common with them, how well they understand the nature of those who are fighting in the name of Justice, of Liberty and Civilization.

PARIS
4 May, 1916.

Part III

THE EXPERIENCE OF THE WAR

Most of the men had not washed for weeks, many had their socks sticking to their feet, all the clothes were filthy, clotted with blood and very odoriferous and it was just a joy to get them off and the poor fellows a bit clean and fairly comfortable, but it brought war home to one in a way that nothing else, short of the actual battlefield could. (Eleanora Pemberton, 2 November 1914)[1]

This section of the book, by far the longest, addresses women's direct experience of the war. This experience took many forms. Although women could not actually fight, the removal of a large percentage of the male population opened up new avenues to them, allowing them to become active in industry, commerce, other areas of professional life. Many thousands answered the call to join the nursing services, tending the wounded in Britain and abroad, or driving ambulances or other vehicles. But even those who did not take up any form of wartime occupation were unable to escape the impact of the war on their lives at home. Air raids, food shortages, wartime advertising and the profusion of khaki on the streets would all have taken effect, not to mention the horror of bereavement which hung over almost every family on the Home Front.

The British military refused to allow women to go near to the actual field of battle: officially. But some women were able to invade this 'forbidden zone',[2] despite army regulations. Mildred Aldrich was a retired American journalist, living about twenty miles outside Paris in 1914. Her close proximity to the first German 'push' gave her access to some of the sights and experiences of the early weeks of the war which were hidden to most women. Her first book, *A Hilltop on the Marne*, published in 1915,

---

[1] The war letters of Eleanora Blanshard Pemberton are held in the Imperial War Museum.

[2] 'The Forbidden Zone' was described by Mary Borden as 'the strip of land immediately behind the zone of fire' in her book of that name.

gives a detailed account of the early threat to Paris as she saw it.[3] The extract included here is from Aldrich's later book, *On the Edge of the War Zone*, published in 1917, and describes an outing to visit the site of the recent battle of Chambry with a view to decorating the soldiers' graves. Although she has no authority to enter the military zone, her anxiety on this score is unnecessary as it seems remarkably easy for Aldrich and her companion to drive freely through areas of recent fighting. Despite being a little voyeuristic, there is a poignance about her representation of the trip. Her status as a resident denies her objectivity, emphasising her sadness at what she sees, giving the reader a kind of insider's view of desecrated France.

In contrast, the 'letter' from Mrs Humphry Ward's propaganda book, *England's Effort* (1916), contains none of the sadness and contemplation, but a great deal more fiery optimism, as she describes touring the area close to the front line, as a guest of the military. Ward is full of praise for the efficiency of the military machine, the organisation of the military hospital, and the courage of all those participating in the great fight. Ward and her daughter are like tourists, motored from one chateau to the next, and, with the assistance of a variety of guides, allowed to see certain, edited aspects of the war. Yet even the most disturbing of these is cloaked in patriotic rhetoric, transforming the experience from human tragedy to human triumph. From a hilltop they are permitted to witness the actual fighting, though at too distant a range to make out clearly what is going on. They see just enough for Ward to claim authority through her writing; just enough to justify the patriotic argument without opening up the possibility of alternatives.[4]

For some women the battle front took on a different aspect. Many civilians found themselves behind enemy lines when war was declared in August 1914. Although not actually threatened by military bombardment, they were often placed in a hostile situation as 'enemy aliens'. Rosie Neale was a member of an all-female troupe of musicians and singers, called 'the Royal Brewsters', who arrived in Hamburg, Germany, on 27

---

[3] For a detailed discussion of this book see Claire Tylee, *The Great War and Women's Consciousness*, (London: Macmillan, 1990), chapter 1. Tylee discusses Aldrich's journalistic style in some detail, considering her history, her situation and her linguistic approach.

[4] For further information see Claire Tylee, '"Munitions in Mind": Travel Writing, Imperial Discourse and Great War Propaganda by Mrs Humphry Ward', *English Literature in Transition 1880–1920*, 39 (2); Helen Small, 'Mrs Humphry Ward and the First Casualty of War', in Suzanne Raitt and Trudi Tate, eds, *Women's Fiction and the Great War* (Oxford: Clarendon Press, 1997).

July 1914, for the first leg of a European concert tour. Unfortunately the outbreak of the war ensured that they never opened and also put them in a dangerous situation in an enemy country. Neale's journal, written in two stages, tells the story of their escape.[5] The climax comes as they reach the German frontier disguised as a party of American schoolgirls with the American member of the troupe playing the part of their mistress, speaking for them all. The neutrality of the United States in the first years of the war presented them with a ticket to freedom.

Flora Sandes and the Baroness de T'Serclaes provide examples of women's war experience on a different level. The Baroness, originally Mrs Knocker, together with her friend Mairi Chisholm, left their ambulance unit to set up a dressing station in the derelict village of Pervyse on the Belgian Front Line. As a result the pair, who became known as 'the Heroines of Pervyse', were exposed to the reality of the fighting in a very unusual way. The dressing station was a great success and it was during her work there that Mrs Knocker met and married the Baron de T'Serclaes.

Flora Sandes was a nurse who became separated from her unit in Serbia, only to end up joining the Serbian army, making her the only English woman to see active military service in the Great War. She rose to rank of sergeant, and was even decorated after being wounded in action.[6] Her early account of the experience, *An English Woman-Sergeant in the Serbian Army*, was published in 1916. Although Sandes's experience is remarkable, she gives no such impression in her account. There is little or no sense of danger as she reports a skirmish with the Bulgarian army on Mount Chukus. She seems more concerned with her failure to get any good photographs than with the possibility of injury or death. Sandes is in a position to illustrate a quite unique experience for women in the Great War, yet she sounds rather more like a tourist, or perhaps a girl guide, than a war hero. This could result from a problem of acceptable cultural representation. The book as a whole is patriotic and designed to inspire. In 1916 the concept of an actual woman soldier may have been very difficult for a reading public to take seriously. She was perhaps in danger of being perceived as an eccentric oddity rather than as a woman with a serious story to tell.

[5] Rosie Neale's 'Journal of the Royal Brewsters' is held in the Imperial War Museum. The first half was written while the girls were still 'trapped' in Germany, the second, upon their safe return to England.

[6] For further information on Flora Sandes see Tylee, *The Great War and Women's Consciousness*; Julie Wheelwright, *Amazons and Military Maids* (London: Pandora, 1989).

Mabel St Clair Stobart, however, presents a very different image of a woman in the man's world of the battle front. A veteran of the Balkan war of 1912, she was the first British woman to lead a Field Hospital Unit to the front line. Caught close to the fighting in Serbia, her units were forced to withdraw, along with thousands of Serbian civilians and defeated soldiers, fleeing across the mountains of Montenegro and Albania, pursued by an invading army. Throughout the retreat Stobart kept a tiny diary, jotting down her impressions on horseback as she led her unit over the precarious mountain paths.[7] The original document is virtually illegible, but its contents are strangely poetic, capturing the unique atmosphere of the experience. Even in the midst of the darkness, she is able to find some light. Stobart used her diary as a basis for *The Flaming Sword in Serbia and Elsewhere* (1916) which enabled her to give public voice to her views on the role of women in a political future devoid of the militarism which she felt had caused the war. Haunting fragments of the diary remain in the published text, giving it an aesthetic quality unexpected in such a political work.

It might be more reasonable to expect the home front to be the territory of women. But Sylvia Pankhurst's outcry against the closure of public houses to women and the decision to impose police supervision on the families of soldiers at the front, indicates that the notion of women dominating in the absence of men may be an inaccurate one.[8] The public face of the War was represented by displays of military technology and success, described here by schoolgirl Patricia Hanbury on a trip to London,[9] but for many women, particularly working-class women, the real battles were private; most particularly, the battle against the shortage of food.

'How *poor* people live is a mystery!' wrote Ethel Bilborough in January 1918. Contemporary journals were full of comments and ideas. Melvina Walker, writing for the socialist *Dreadnought* in March 1917, paints a dismal picture of life in the East End of London as women and children jostle for a meagre potato and profiteering retailers exploit their hunger. Ernestine Mills, writing for the less politically motivated *The Englishwoman*, offers some practical suggestions, arguing the clear benefits of

---

[7] The war diary of Mabel St Clair is held in the Imperial WarMuseum.

[8] For arguments concerning the social advancement of women during the Great War see Sandra M. Gilbert, 'Soldier's Heart: Literary Men, Literary Women, and the Great War', *Signs* 8 (3) (Spring 1983), 422–50, Margaret R. Higonnet et al., eds, *Behind the Lines: Gender and the Two World Wars* (New Haven and London: Yale University Press, 1987); Jane Marcus, 'The Asylums of Antaeus' in *The New Historicism* (London: Routledge, 1989): 132–51.

[9] Also see Trudi Tate, 'The Tank and the Manufacture of Consent', in *Modernism, History and the First World War* (Manchester: Manchester University Press, 1998).

communal kitchens to service the whole population. The tone is a little patronising, albeit unintentionally, and displays a naivety concerning the real situation of some of the working-class women whom she desires to help, but it is well-intended, and gives a humorous and interesting insight into how some women may have approached the War.

Although the women, and indeed the non-combatant men, who remained at home, could never hope to understand the violent experience of the War, each dreadful event reported to the waiting public had notable impact. Ethel Bilborough writes, 'On the 7th May [1915] all Europe was thrown into a state of consternation at a diabolical act of the German fiends!' She is referring to the sinking of the *Lusitania*, an American liner carrying nearly two thousand passengers, torpedoed by a German U-boat off the south coast of Ireland with a loss of almost 1200 lives.[10] Anti-German riots, already a problem, intensified as the news broke. Sylvia Pankhurst cries out against them, blaming the government for not satisfactorily and safely accommodating 'defenceless aliens' in appropriate internment camps.

G. B. Stern's fictional account of an anti-German riot from *Children of No Man's Land* (1919) presents a very sinister impression of the appeal of mob violence. Teenager Richard Marcus is swept along on a revenge attack on a German baker, a response to the *Lusitania* tragedy. At the moment of truth he is crippled by a guilty realisation of what he has become a part of, and runs in fear from the scene of the crime. But by the time he has put several streets between himself and the action, he is able, once again, to justify the behaviour of the mob. Stern's irony is manifested in the next chapter of the novel when Richard discovers that he is himself of German extraction and likely to be interned as soon as he comes of age. Through his inner conflicts, she represents some of the emotional turmoil of many people contained on the home front, at the mercy of propagandists, unable to participate in the real action.

The action must have felt very real indeed, however, for those people on the home front who had to suffer the nightly fear of air raids. This was one of the most significant new threats of the Great War. Never before had humankind possessed the technology to attack civilian populations from the air. Now the threat was very real, firstly in the form of Zeppelin

---

[10] For a more detailed account of the public impact of the sinking of the *Lusitania* and its effect of propaganda see, John Williams, *The Home Fronts 1914–1918* (London: Constable, 1972); Trudi Tate, 'War Neurotics', in *Modernism, History and the First World War*.

airships, later from two-engined Gotha aircraft.[11] By 1915 many British cities were watching the night skies. Areas containing military targets and munitions factories were in the greatest danger. The East End came off badly, as Sylvia Pankhurst noted.

For many women, this was the nearest they were likely to get to serious military action. Many chose to record their feelings and experiences. In the early hours of the morning, Nell Hague writes her impressions of a Zeppelin raid on Hull to her husband in London. Virginia Woolf is matter-of-fact in her description of being unexpectedly disturbed by a Gotha air raid on Barnes in 1917. But Woolf rarely refers to the mechanics of the war in her diary so the night must have made an impact.[12] Entertainer Vesta Tilley recalls how her show went on in the West End, despite the German attacks, noting it as 'a thrilling experience'; although this memory is tempered by an awareness of the dangers of being too close to the blasting bombs after the curtain had fallen. Ethel Bilborough watches in fascinated horror as British and German aircraft fight it out in the air above London, like 'fearful distorted mechanical birds'; a menace from the sky which appears untouchable from the ground.

One of the earliest assaults on the British mainland took place on 16 December 1914, when the German navy bombed the Yorkshire seaside town of Scarborough. The event took everyone by surprise. The destruction left many women and children homeless and provided useful propaganda material to encourage men to enlist. Phyllis Lunn was a schoolgirl in Scarborough at the time, and wrote an account of that night. For her, it feels rather like a big adventure, as she has no need to focus on the any more tragic aspect. The removal of the girls to York is organised and orderly, and spirits are high, 'just like a picnic'. Winifred Holtby's famous fictional account of the bombardment, taken from *The Crowded Street* (1924), was also based on her own experience. Holtby's heroine Muriel Hammond feels a euphoria comparable to that felt by some soldiers going into battle as she runs, with other refugees, from the burning town. But she is not blind to the trauma that the need to flee has caused for many of the unsuspecting civilians caught up in the blast: people running if they can, oblivious to the needs of others, desperate to escape an enemy they cannot see. But the greatest fear of all is that the enemy might

---

[11] See J. M. Winter, 'The Civilians' War' in *The Experience of World War 1* (London: Guild, 1988); John Williams, *The Home Fronts 1914–1918* (London: Constable, 1972).

[12] For a fictional account of a similar air raid see Virginia Woolf, *The Years* (London: The Hogarth Press, 1937).

become visible, might actually invade British shores. At all costs, the enemy must be kept abroad.

The women who worked abroad were, perhaps inevitably, in much greater danger of coming under fire. Many of those involved in nursing services operated very close to the front line which brought numerous hazards. Hospitals were close enough to come under fire from the same aircraft that threatened the soldiers in the trenches. Winifred Kenyon's description of the destruction of a Zeppelin during a raid on Verdun illustrates the close proximity of the threat.[13] But despite the danger, Kenyon is still distant enough from the actual fighting to be excited at witnessing the event. Outside of the operating theatre she and her colleagues can still become observers rather than participants.

Some hospital situations required nursing staff to be even closer to fighting, almost in the middle of it. Mary Ann Brown, nursing sister on a hospital ship in the Dardanelles during the evacuation of Gallipoli, did not have the luxury of an outsider's view. Indeed, it seems remarkable that she was able to write her diary at all. The fragmented nature of this text speaks volumes about the pressure she is under as the ship takes on board large numbers of wounded soldiers, all the while being pounded by the Turkish artillery only a few hundred yards away. This is not the kind of experience generally associated with women during the Great War. Technically, they were not supposed to get this close.

The piece by Mary Borden at the end of this chapter presents a different perspective. Taken from *The Forbidden Zone* (1929), 'Bombardment' views the destruction of a town by heavy artillery from the sky-borne view of an aeroplane. The reader follows the buzz of the insect-like aircraft watching, voyeur-like, as the town is repeatedly wounded by the bombardment. The town, personified in the attack, comes to represent firstly the individual, mutilated and contaminated by explosions, and, secondly, the whole of society, destroyed by weapons of its own making; a powerful technology which cannot be contained. Borden forces us to consider the notion of being 'under fire' in a wider context. The Great War places civilisation itself under fire, not simply the unfortunate individuals who happen to be in the firing line.

Mary Borden begins the next chapter with 'Conspiracy', a bitter and ironic comment on the role of the nurse in the Great War. Nursing was already an established female profession by 1914, while military nursing

[13] Winifred Kenyon's war diary is held in the Imperial War Museum.

services had grown up out of the role played by women in the Crimea.[14] Services like the Queen Alexandra's Imperial Military Nursing Service Reserve (QAIMNSR) and the Red Cross VAD continued to grow throughout the war years, making nursing one of the most popular war work options for young women. The women in question were all middle-class, as to be VADs they had to be able to pay for their own keep. It was often gruelling and traumatic, not at all the kind of occupation that Edwardian young ladies had been trained for. Their nun-like image was intended to perpetuate the Victorian image of the 'Angel of the House' in an environment where it was clearly quite inapplicable. Their uniforms resembled the habits of nuns, presumably in order to preserve the idea of innocence and chastity even as they were exposed to the forbidden and terrifying sights of men's naked and often mutilated bodies.[15]

Many of the women who were qualified medical professionals in 1914 offered their services to the military for the field hospital units, urgently required once the fighting had started. Prominent Scottish suffragist Dr Elsie Inglis was one such, proposing her medical teams as support for the British army.[16] When they rejected her offer, Inglis and the NUWSS formed the fourteen units of the Scottish Women's Hospitals which she sent abroad to work with the Allied armies instead.[17] In this essay from *The Englishwoman*, Inglis tells the story of the Scottish Women's Hospital in Serbia. It is a balanced piece, aimed at an audience of gentlewomen. In contrast, the extracts from the letters of Margaret Fawcett, a member of the unit in Russia and Roumania, give a more down-to-earth impression of the actual experience of nursing in the Serbian front line.

Nursing the wounded of the Great War took women closer to the experience of the fighting man than almost anything else. As Eleanora Pemberton writes in a letter to her father after her first real encounter with casualties, 'it brought war home to one in a way that nothing else, short of the actual battlefield could'. Mary Clarke, a nurse on a hospital ship is similarly shocked when she encounters the casualties from the Battle of Jutland

---

[14] For a complete history of military nursing from 1854–1914 see Anne Summers, *Angels and Citizens: British Women as Military Nurses 1854–1914* (London: Routledge, 1988).

[15] Sharon Ouditt discusses the problematic and contradictory role of the nurse in more detail in 'Nuns and Lovers' in *Fighting Forces, Writing Women: Identity and Ideology in the First World War* (London: Routledge,1994).

[16] Inglis was famously told by the War Office 'to go home and keep quiet' because the commanding officers 'did not want to be troubled by hysterical women' (Ray Strachey, *The Cause* (London: Virago, 1989): 338).

[17] For further information on Elsie Inglis and the Scottish Women's Hospitals see Leah Leneman, *In the Service of Life: The Story of Elsie Inglis and the Scottish Women's Hospitals* (Edinburgh: Mercat Press, 1994).

in June 1916.[18] 'I never saw such bravery in my life', she writes after having seen the burns inflicted by naval warfare. Writing over a decade later in *We That Were Young* (1932), the novel based on her own wartime experiences, Irene Rathbone uses the freedom offered by fiction to take these descriptions one stage further. She illustrates not only the wounded, but their treatment as well, in graphic detail. Disturbing though this is, it serves the dual purpose of emphasising the role of the nurse during the war, smashing the myths of innocence and attempting to put the women on equal terms with the men, at least in terms of their involvement with suffering.

As Rathbone's novel suggests, the hospitals in Britain saw their share of terrible casualties. Many soldiers did not stop again for medical care after they had left the casualty clearing stations behind the front line, until they reached the shores of 'Blighty'. Once they arrived at the hospital, the men were divided, officers to specially designated officers' wards, all the enlisted men to the rest. This brings into question the popular notion that the Great War broke down many existing barriers of social class. Enid Bagnold addresses this issue directly in her notorious book *A Diary Without Dates* (1918). Bagnold had been working as a VAD at the Royal Herbert Hospital at Woolwich until the publication of the book. Her account of hospital life was so unflinchingly brutal that she was dismissed by the matron for breach of military discipline as soon as the book appeared. She convincingly portrays the double standards of treatment for the officers and for the regular soldiers, which must have proved very uncomfortable for those in authority who condoned such action.

Bagnold attempts to describe life in the hospital from the point of view of the soldiers. She uses their own language, professing her own inadequacy when it comes to communicating with them. She explores the idea of pain from different angles and, when a dressing is changed, it is the song of the soldier that indicates the intensity of the experience to the reader rather than a straightforward description. It is also a contemplative book. Bagnold tries to analyse the need that the hospital fulfils in her, a need which may be at odds with that of the men. In this she echoes the deadly cycle of Mary Borden's 'Conspiracy'; vital though the nurses are, without the constant supply of the wounded the women who nurse them have no function, no purpose at all.

'The Masseuse' by G. K. Brumwell is stylistically similar to Bagnold's writing.[19] Brumwell wrote it in 1918 and tried to get it published in the

---

[18] The war diary of Mary Clarke is held in the Imperial War Museum.

[19] Mrs G. K. Brumwell's article 'The Masseuse' is held in the Liddle Collection, University of Leeds.

Daily Mail, but was unsuccessful. Like Bagnold she allows the men to speak for themselves, focusing on their experience rather than her own. But the tone of the piece is more light-hearted than is found in much similar Great War writing.

The final extracts in this chapter both deal with the experience of the untried and untested volunteer nurse. Vera Brittain gives a detailed description of the life of a VAD recruit, leaving home for the first time and learning to deal with the harsh conditions of the hospital, in her autobiography *Testament of Youth* (1933). Published fifteen years after the war, Brittain is able to look back at her wartime experience and ask questions about the issues of health and safety which, at the time, seemed secondary to the all-important war effort. But not all nursing volunteers lived lives of such hardship. Lady Cynthia Asquith worked very long hours when she dipped into the world of the hospital, but, unlike Brittain in her dismal hostel, Asquith's home circumstances were such that she didn't need to worry about not being able to have a bath. Her private lifestyle could continue very much as always. An older woman, with a husband and children, from an aristocratic family, she was able to control her war work without having to surrender her private life to military-style discipline. Perhaps this explains her excitement and satisfaction when she writes in her diary about nursing.

While nursing was a very popular way of 'doing one's bit', women were also involved in many other kinds of war work. Women's branches of all the major military services were established for the first time providing women with a new arena for wartime experience. The FANY, like the VAD, was a voluntary organisation which placed middle-class and upper-class young ladies on active service, usually driving ambulances, near the front line. Helen Zenna Smith's *Not So Quiet* ... deals directly with this experience. It is a particularly brutal novel, which intends to illustrate the hardships endured by women, and validate their suffering alongside that of their male contemporaries. Evadne Price, writing under the pseudonym Smith, based her narrative on the diary of a former ambulance driver, Winifred Constance Young (now unfortunately lost), and it aims to emphasise the difference between the women on active service and their patriotic families on the home front. She intends to shock, and the graphic detail does precisely that.

The second part of the extract serves a different purpose. As she drives her ambulance full of wounded soldiers along a pitch-black midnight road, Helen Smith tries to drown out the sounds of their hysterical dis-

pute with memories of her coming-out party. The contrast between the
horror of the ambulance journey and the ultra-feminine images of her
italicised thoughts emphasises the incompatibility of this Edwardian
young lady with the landscape of war. Price writes to create an effect, and
her text is extremely self-aware. It is interesting to compare it with the
'Base Notes' of Muriel Thompson, a real FANY, writing a kind of reflec-
tive postscript to her diary in 1918.[20] Thompson uses a rather detached
narrative technique, as though she is writing not about herself but about
a situation. Yet the impressions she creates are strikingly similar to those
found in *Not So Quiet ...* and there is a sense that Price's novel may not
be as extreme as some critics have supposed.[21]

Beyond these voluntary services, women carried out a great many
other roles during the Great War. Irene Rathbone writes in her diary of
work in a YMCA Camp in France, to which troops retired for rest periods
when they returned from the trenches. Beatrice Trefusis describes her
work in a wartime office. Mary Macleod writes to her mother and sister
about her work as a Land Girl. But perhaps one of the largest areas for
women's employment between 1914 and 1918 was in the manufacture of
munitions for the war effort.

The number of women employed in munitions and related industries
rose from 212,000 in July 1914 to 947,000 in November 1918.[22] F. Tennyson Jesse's essay from *The Englishwoman* describes the workings of a
French munitions factory in great detail. This was the world inhabited by
thousands of women, for very long hours throughout the War. It was hard
work and could be very dangerous. There was always the possibility of
explosion. Women working with TNT were in danger of contamination.
The substance turned their skin yellow, earning them the nickname
'canaries', and they were in danger of loosing their teeth and hair. Industrial accidents, such as the one described in the extract from Irene Rathbone's novel *We That Were Young*, were not uncommon.[23] But the wages
for munitions work were high, and the industry became a major
employer of working-class women, doing its bit to help along the end of

[20] The war diary of Muriel Thompson is held in the Liddle Collection, University of
Leeds.

[21] Mary Cadogan and Patricia Craig have argued, 'Social realism, the impulse to tell the
truth about war service and its aftermath, has given way to emotional melodrama and a
crude bid for the reader's attention' (*Women and Children First* (London: Gollancz, 1981):
42).

[22] Arthur Marwick, *Women at War 1914–1918* (London: Fontana, 1977): 166.

[23] For more information, see the discussion of the munitions industry in Oudit,
Fighting Forces. Oudit argues that fictional depictions of industrial accidents, such as
Rathbone's, intend to 'elevate their victims to the status of "soldier–women"' (76).

domestic service, as families could not afford to pay their servants a comparable wage.

There were women who worked in the munitions industry for reasons other than money. Rathbone's Pamela Butler wants revenge: to do something practical towards killing an unseen enemy responsible for the death of her fiancé. Lady Peggy Hamilton signed on for 'three years or the duration' intent on finding something different, useful and interesting to do and became very skilled by the end of the War. The extract from her memoir reproduced here, recreates not only a sense of working inside the Woolwich arsenal but also the overspill outside its gates. The carnival atmosphere of Woolwich Square represents the possible product of a large conglomeration of people. They are brought together by war, but it is life not death which is celebrated on the streets of East London, as the young pour out of work into leisure with money in their pockets and a motive to live fast.

7

The battle front

Mildred Aldrich
from
On the Edge of the War Zone

December 5, 1914.

We have been having some beautiful weather.

Yesterday Amelie and I took advantage of it to make a pilgrimage across the Marne, to decorate the graves on the battlefield at Chambry. Crowds went out on All Souls' Day, but I never liked doing anything, even making a pilgrimage, in a crowd.

You can realize how near it is, and what an easy trip it will be in normal times, when I tell you that we left Esbly for Meaux at half-past one – only ten minutes by train – and were back in the station at Meaux at quarter to four, and had visited Monthyon, Villeroy, Neufmontier, Penchard, Chausonin, Barcy, Chambry, and Vareddes.

The authorities are not very anxious to have people go out there. Yet nothing to prevent is really done. It only takes a little diplomacy. If I had gone to ask for a passport, nine chances out of ten it would have been refused me. I happen to know that the wife of the big livery-stable man at Meaux, an energetic – and incidentally, a handsome – woman, who took over the business when her husband joined his regiment, had a couple of automobiles, and would furnish me with all the necessary papers. They are not taxi-cabs, but handsome touring cars. Her chauffeur carries the proper papers. It seemed to me a very loose arrangement, from a military point of view, even although I was assured that she did not send out anyone she did not know. However, I decided to take advantage of it.

While we were waiting at the garage for the car to go out, and the chauffeur to change his coat, I had a chance to talk with a man who had not left Meaux during the battle, and I learned that there were several important families who had remained with the Archbishop and aided him to organize matters for saving the city, if possible, and protect the property of those who had fled, and that the measure which those sixty citizens, with Archbishop Marbeau at their head, took for the safety of the poor, the care for the wounded and dead, is already one of the proudest documents in annals of the historic town.

But never mind these things, which the guides will recite for you, I imagine, when you come over to make the grand tour of Fighting France, for on these plains about Meaux you will have to start your pilgrimage.

I confess that my heart beat a little too rapidly when, as we ran out of Meaux and took the *route départmentale* of Senlis, a soldier stepped to the middle of the road and held up his gun – *baionette au canon.*

We stopped.

Were we after all going to be turned back? I had the guilty knowledge that there was no reason why we should not be. I tried to look magnificently unconcerned as I leaned forward to smile at the soldier. I might have spared myself the effort. He never even glanced inside the car. The examination of the papers was the most cursory thing imaginable – a mere formality. The chauffeur simply held his stamped paper towards the guard. The guard merely glanced at it, lifted his gun, motioned us to proceed – and we proceeded.

It may amuse you to know that we never even showed the paper again. We did meet two *gendarmes* on bicycles, but they nodded and passed us without stopping.

The air was soft, like an early autumn day, rather than December as you know it. There was a haze in the air, but behind it the sun shone. You know what that French haze is, and what it does to the world, and how, through it, one gets the sort of landscape painters love. With how many of our pilgrimages together it is associated! We have looked through it at the walls of Provins, when the lindens were rosy with the first rising of the sap; we have looked through it at the circular panorama from the top of the ruined tower of Montlhery; we have looked through it across Jean Jaques Rousseau's country, from the lofty terrace of Montmorency, and from the platform in front of the prison of Phillippe Auguste's unhappy Danish wife, at Etampes, across the valley of the Juine; and from how many other beautiful spots, not to forget the view up the Seine from the terrace of the Tuileries.

Some time, I hope, we shall see these plains of the Marne together.

When we do, I trust it will be on just such another atmospheric day as yesterday.

As our road wound up the hill over the big paving-stones characteristic of the environs of all the old towns of France, everything looked so peaceful, so pretty, so normal, that it was hard to realize that we were moving towards the front, and were only about three miles from the point where the German invasion was turned back almost three months ago to a day, and it was more difficult to realize as we have not heard the cannon for days.

A little way out of Meaux, we took a road to the west for Chauconin, the nearest place to us which was bombarded, and from a point in the road I looked back across the valley of the Marne, and I saw a very pretty white town, with red roofs, lying on the hillside. I asked the chauffeur:

'What village is that over there?'

He glanced around and replied: 'Quincy.'

It was my town. I ought not to have been surprised. Of course I knew that if I could see Chauconin so clearly from my garden, why, Chauconin could see *me*. Only, I had not thought of it.

Amelie and I looked back with great interest. It did look so pretty, and it is not pretty at all – the least pretty village on this side of the hill. 'Distance' does, indeed, 'lend enchantment.' When you come to see me I shall show you Quincy from the other side of the Marne, and never take you into its streets. Then you'll always remember it as a fairy town.

It was not until we were entering into Chauconin that we saw the first signs of war. The approach through the fields, already ploughed, and planted with winter grain, looked the very last thing to be associated with war. Once inside the little village – we always speak of it as 'le petit Chauconin' – we found destruction enough. One whole street of houses was literally gutted. The walls stand, but the roofs are off and doors and windows gone, while the shells seem burned out. The destruction of the big farms seems to have been pretty complete. There they stood, long walls of rubble and plaster, breached; ends of farm buildings gone; and many only a heap of rubbish. The surprising thing to me was to see here a house destroyed, and, almost beside it, one not even touched. That seemed to prove that the struggle here was not a long one, and that a comparatively small number of shells had reached it.

Neufmortier was in about the same condition. It was a sad sight, but not at all ugly. Ruins seem to 'go' with the French atmosphere and background. It all looked quite natural, and I had to make an effort to shake myself into a becoming frame of mind. If you had been with me I should have asked you to pinch me, and remind me that 'all this is not yet ancient history,' and that a little sentimentality would have become me. But Amelie would never have understood me.

I was not until we were driving east again to approach Penchard that a full realization of it came to me. Penchard crowns the hill just in the centre of the line which I see from the garden. It was one of the towns bombarded on the evening of September 5, and, so far as I can guess, the destruction was done by the French guns which drove the Germans out that night.

They say that Germans slept there the night of September 4, and were driven out the next day by the French *soixante-quinze*, which trotted through Chauconin into Penchard by the road we had just come over.

I enclose you a *carte postale* of a battery passing behind the apse of the village church, just as a guarantee of good faith.

But all signs of the horrors of those days have been obliterated. Penchard is the town in which the Germans exercised their taste for wilful nastiness, of which I wrote you weeks ago. It is a pretty little village, beautifully situated, commanding the slopes of the Marne on one side, and the wide plains of Barcy and Chambry on the other. It is prosperous looking, the home of sturdy farmers and the small *rentiers*. It has an air of humble thrift, with now and then a pretty garden, and here and there suggestions of a certain degree of greater prosperity, an air which, in France, often conceals unexpected wealth.

You need not look the places up unless you have a big map. No guide-book ever honoured them.

From Penchard we ran a little out to the west at the foot of the hill, on top of which stand the white walls of Monyton, from which, on September 5, we had seen the first smoke of battle.

I am sure that I wrote some weeks ago how puzzled I was when I read Joffre's famous *ordre du jour*, at the beginning of the Marne offensive, to find that it was dated September 6, whereas we had *seen* the battle begin on the 5th. Here I found what I presume to be the explanation, which proves that the offensive along the rest of the line on the 6th had been a continuation simply of what we saw that Saturday afternoon.

At the foot of the hill crowned by the walls of Montyon lies Villeroy – to-day the objective point for patriotic pilgrimages. There, on the 5th of September, the 276th Regiment was preparing its soup for lunch, when, suddenly, from the trees on the heights, German shells fell amongst them, and food was forgotten, while the French at St. Soupplet on the other side of the hill, as well as those at Villeroy, suddenly found themselves in the thick of a fight – the battle we saw.

They told me at Villeroy that many of the men in the regiments engaged were from this region, and here civilians dropped their work in the fields and snatched up guns which the dead or wounded soldiers let fall and entered the fight beside their uniformed neighbours. I give you that picturesque and likely detail for what it is worth.

At the foot of the hill between Monyton and Villeroy lies the tomb in which two hundred of the men who fell here are buried together. Among them is Charles Péguy, the poet, who wore a lieutenant's stripes, and was referred to by his companions on that day as '*un glorieux fou dans sa bravoure*.' This long tomb, with its crosses and flags and flowers, was the scene on All Souls' Day of the commemorative ceremony in honour of the victory, and marks not only the beginning of the battle, but the beginning of its triumph.

From this point we drove back to the east, almost along the line of battle, to the hillside hamlet of Barcy, the saddest scene of desolation on this end of the great fight.

It was a humble little village, grouped around a dear old church, with a graceful square tower supporting a spire. The little church faced a small square, from which the principal street runs down the hill to the open country across which the French 'push' advanced. No house on this street escaped. Some of them are absolutely destroyed. The church is a mere shell. Its tower is pierced with huge holes. Its bell lies, a wreck, on the floor beneath its tower. The roof has fallen in, a heaped-up mass of *debris* in the nave beneath. Its windows are gone, and there are gaping wounds in its side walls. Oddly enough, the *Chemin de la Croix* is intact, and some of the peasants look on that as a miracle, in spite of the fact that the High Altar is buried under a mass of tiles and plaster.

The doors being gone, one could look in, over the temporary barrier, to the wreck inside, and by putting a donation into the contribution box for the *restauration* fund it was possible to enter – at one's own risk – by a side door. It was hardly worth while, as one could see no more than was visible from the doorways, and it looked as if at any minute the whole edifice would crumble. However, Amelie wanted to go inside, and so we did.

We entered through the *mairie*, which is at one side, into a small courtyard, where the school children were playing under the propped-up walls as gaily as if there had never been a bombardment.

The *mairie* had fared little better than the church, and the schoolroom, which has its home in it, had a temporary roofing, the upper part being wrecked.

The best idea that I got of the destruction was, however, from a house almost opposite the church. It was only a shell, its walls alone standing. As its windows and doors had been blown out, we could look in from the street to the interior of what had evidently been a comfortable house. It was now like an uncovered box, in the centre of which there was a conical shaped heap of ashes as high as the top of the fireplace. We could see where the stairs had been, but its entire contents had been burned down to a heap of ashes – burned as thoroughly as wood in a fireplace. I could not have believed in such absolute destruction if I had not seen it.

While we were gazing at the wreck I noticed an old woman leaning against the wall and watching us. Out of her weather beaten, time-furrowed face looked a pair of dark eyes, red-rimmed and blurred with much weeping. She was rubbing her distorted old hands together as she watched us. It was inevitable that I should get into conversation with her, and discover that this wreck had been, for years, her home, that she had lived there all alone, and that everything she had in the world – her furniture, her clothing, and her *savings* – had been burned in the house.

You can hardly understand that unless you know these people. They keep their savings hidden. It is the well-known old story of the French stocking which paid the war indemnity of 1870. They have no confidence in banks. The State is the only one they will lend to, and the fact is one of the secrets of French success.

If you knew these people as I do, you would understand that an old woman of that peasant type, ignorant of the meaning of war, would hardly be likely to leave her house, no matter how many times she was ordered out, until shells began to fall about her. Even then, as she was rather deaf, she probably did not realize what was happening, and went into the street in such fear that she left everything behind her.

From Barcy we drove out into the plain, and took the direction of Chambry, following the line of the great and decisive fight of September 6 and 7.

We rolled slowly across the beautiful undulating country of grain and beet fields. We had not gone far when, right at the edge of the road, we came upon an isolated mound, with a rude cross at its head, and a tiny *tricolore* at its foot – the first French grave on the plain.

We motioned the chauffeur to stop, and we went on, on foot.

First the graves were scattered, for the boys lie buried just where they fell – cradled in the bosom of the mother country that nourished them, and for whose safety they laid down their lives. As we advanced they became more numerous, until we reached a point where, as far as we could see, in every direction, floated the little *tricolore* flags, like fine flowers in the landscape. They made tiny spots against the far-off horizon line, and groups like beds of flowers in the foreground, and we knew that, behind the skyline, there were more.

Here and there was a haystack with one grave beside it, and again there would be one, usually partly burned, almost encircled with the tiny flags which said: 'Here sleep the heroes.'

It was a disturbing and a thrilling sight. I give you my word, as I stood there, I envied them. It seemed to me a fine thing to lie out there in the open, in the soil of the fields their simple death has made holy, the duty well done, the dread over, each one just where he fell defending his mother-land, enshrined for ever in the loving memory of the land he had saved, in graves to be watered for years, not only by the tears of those near and dear to them, but by those of the heirs to their glory – the children of the coming generations of free France.

You may know a finer way to go. I do not. Surely, since Death is, it is better than dying of old age between clean sheets.

Near the end of the route we came to the little walled cemetery of Chambry, the scene of one of the most desperate struggles of the 6th and 7th of September.

You know what the humble village burying grounds are like. Its wall is about six feet high, of plaster and stone, with an entrance on the road to the village. To the west and north-west the walls are on the top of a bank, high above the cross-roads. I do not know the position of the pursuing French army. The chauffeur who drove us could not enlighten us. As near as I could guess, from the condition of the walls, I imagine that the French artillery must have been in the direction of Penchard, on the wooded hills.

The walls are pierced with gun holes, about three feet apart, and those on the west and south-west are breached by cannon and shell-fire. Here, after the position had been several times stormed by artillery, the Zouaves made one of the most brilliant bayonet charges of the day, dashing up the steep banks and through the breached walls. Opposite the gate is another steep bank where can still be seen the improvised gun positions of the French when they pushed the retreat across the plain.

The cemetery is filled with new graves against the wall, for many of the officers are buried here – nearly all of the regiment of Zouaves, which was almost wiped out in the charge before the position was finally carried, – it was taken and lost several times.

From here we turned east again towards Vareddes, along a fine road lined with enormous old trees, one of the handsomest roads of the department. Many of these huge trees have been snapped off by shells as neatly as if they were mere twigs. Along the road, here and there, were isolated graves.

Vareddes had a tragic experience. The population was shockingly abused by the Germans. Its aged priest and many other old men were carried away, and many were shot, and the town badly damaged.

We had intended to go through Vareddes to the heights beyond, where the heroes of the 133rd, 246th, 289th, and of the regiment which began the battle at Villroy – the 276th – are buried. But the weather had changed, and a cold drizzle began to fall, and I saw no use in going on in a closed car, so we turned back to Meaux.

It was still light when we reached Meaux, so we gave a look at the old mills – and put up a paean of praise that they were not damaged beyond repair – on our way to the station.

As we came back to Esbly I strained my eyes to look across to the hill on which my house stands, – I could just see it as we crawled across the bridge at the Iles-les-Villenoy, – and felt again the miracle of the battle which swept so near to us.

In my innermost heart I had a queer sensation of the absurdity of my relation to life. Fate so often shakes its fist in my face, only to withhold the blow within a millimetre of my nose. Perhaps I am being schooled to meet it yet.

I brought back one fixed impression – how quickly Time had laid its healing hand on this one battlefield. I don't know what will be the effect out there where the terrible trench war is going on. But here, where the fighting turned, never to return – at least we believe it never will – it has left no ugly traces. The fields are cleaned, the roads are repaired. Rain has fallen on ruins and washed off all the marks of smoke. Even on the road to Vareddes the thrifty French have already carried away and faggoted the wrecked trees, and already the huge, broken trunks are being uprooted, cut into proper length, and piled neatly by the roadside to be seasoned before being carted away. There was nothing raw about the scene anywhere. The villages were sad, because so silent and empty.

I had done my best to get a tragic impression. I had not got it. I had brought back instead an impression heroic, uplifting, altogether inspiring.

By the time you come over, and I lead you out on that pilgrimage, it will be even more beautiful. But, alas, I am afraid that day is a long way off.

Mrs Humphry Ward
from
England's Effort: Six Letters to an
American Friend (no. 5)

I

Our journey further north through the deep February snow was scarcely less striking as an illustration of Great Britain's constantly growing share in the war than the sight of the great supply Bases themselves. The first part of it indeed led over solitary uplands, where the chained wheels of the motor rocked in the snow, and our military chauffeur dared make no stop, for fear he should never be able to start again. All that seemed alive in the white landscape were the partridges – sometimes in great flocks – which scudded at our approach, or occasional groups of hares in the middle distance, holding winter parley. The road seemed interminably long and straight, and ours were almost the first tracks in it. The snow came down incessantly, and once or twice it looked as though we should be left stranded in the white wilderness.

But after a third of the journey was over, the snow began to lessen and the roads to clear. We dropped first into a sea-port town which offered much the same mingled scene of French and English, of English nurses, and French *poilus*, of unloading ships, and British soldiers, as the bases we had left, only on a smaller scale. And beyond the town we climbed again on to a high land, through a beautiful country of interwoven downs, and more plentiful habitation. Soon indeed the roads began to show signs of war; – a village or small town, its picturesque market-place filled with a park of artillery wagons; roads lined with motor lorries with the painted shell upon them that tells ammunition; British artillerymen in khaki, bringing a band of horses out of a snow-bound farm; closed motor-cars filled with officers hurrying past; then an open car with King's Messengers, tall soldierly figures, looking in some astonishment at the two ladies, as they hurry by. And who or what is this horseman looming out of the sleet? – like a figure from a piece of Indian or Persian embroidery; turbaned and swarthy, his cloak swelling out round his handsome shoulders, the buildings of a Norman farm behind him? 'There are a few Indian cavalry about here,' says our guide – 'they are billeted in the farms.' And presently the road is full of them. Their

Eastern forms, their dark intent faces, pass strangely through the Norman landscape.

Now we are only some forty miles from the line, and we presently reach another town containing an important headquarters, where we are to stop for luncheon. The inn at which we put up is like the song in *Twelfth Night*, 'old and plain' – and when lunch is done, our Colonel goes to pay an official call at Headquarters, and my daughter and I make our way to the historic church of the town. The Colonel joins us here with another officer who brings the amazing news that G.H.Q. (General Headquarters) – that mysterious centre and brain of all things – invites us for two days! If we accept, an officer will come for us on the morning of March 1st to our hotel in ——, and take us by motor, some forty miles, to the guest-house where G.H.Q. puts up its visitors.

'*Accept*'! Ah! if one could only forget for a moment the human facts behind the absorbing interest and excitement of this journey, one might be content to feel only the stir of quickened pulses, of gratitude for a fur-ther opportunity so tremendous. As it was, I saw all the journey hence-forward with new eyes because of that to which it was bringing us.

On we sped through the French countryside, past a great forest lying black on the edge of the white horizon – (I open my map and find it marked Bois de Crécy!) – past another old town, with Agincourt a few miles to the east; and so into a region of pine and sand that borders the sea. Darkness comes down and we miss our way. What are these lines of light among the pine woods? Another military and hospital camp, which we are to see on the morrow – so we discover at last. But we have overshot our goal, and must grope our way back through the pinewoods to the sea-shore where a little primitive hotel, built for the summer, with walls that seem to be made of brown paper, receives us. But we have motored far that day and greet it joyfully. …

The following morning we woke to a silvery sunlight, with, at last, some promise of spring over a land cleared of snow. The day was spent in going through a camp which has been set down in one of the pleasantest and healthiest spots of France, a favourite haunt of French artists before the War. Now the sandy slopes, whence the pines, alack, have been cut away, are occupied by a British reinforcement camp, by long lines of hos-pitals, by a convalescent depot, and by the training grounds, where, as at other bases, the newly arrived troops are put through their last instruc-tion before going to the Front. As usual, the magnitude of what has been done in one short year filled one with amazement. Here is the bare cata-logue. Infantry base depots, *i.e.* sleeping and mess quarters for thousands of men belonging to the new armies; sixteen hospitals with 21,000 beds; three rifle ranges; two training camps; a machine-gun training school; a vast laundry worked by French women, under British organisation, which washes for *all* the hospitals, 30,000 pieces a day; recreation huts of all types and kinds, official and voluntary; a cinema theatre, seating 800 men, with performances twice a day; nurses' clubs; officer' clubs; a supply depot for food; an Ordnance depot for everything that is not food; new sidings to the railway, where 1000 men can be entrained on the one side, while 1000 men are detraining on the other, or two full ambulance trains can come in and go out; a convalescent depot of 2000 horses! – etcetera. And this is the work accomplished since last April in one camp.

Yet, as I look back upon it, my chief impression of that long day is an impression, first, of endless hospital huts and marquees with their rows of beds, in which the pale or flushed faces are generally ready – unless pain or weariness forbid – as a visitor ventures timidly near, to turn and smile in response to the few halting words of sympathy or enquiry which are all one can find to say; and, next, of such a wealth of skill, and pity and devotion poured out upon this terrible human need, as makes one thank God for doctors and nurses, and bright-faced V.A.D.s. After all, one tremblingly asks oneself, in spite of the appalling facts of wounds, and death, and violence, in which the human world is now steeped, is it yet *possible,* is it yet *true,* that the ultimate thing – the final power behind the veil – to which at least this vast linked spectacle of suffering and tenderness, here in this great camp, testifies – is *not* Force, but Love? Is this the mysterious message which seems to breathe from these crowded wards – to make them just bearable.

Let me recollect the open door of an operating theatre, and a young officer, quite a boy, lying there with a bullet in his chest, which the surgeons were just about to try and extract. The fine pale features of the wounded man, the faces of the surgeon and the nurses, so intent and cheerfully absorbed, the shining surfaces and appliances of the white room – stamp themselves on memory. I recollect too one John S——, a very bad case, a private. 'Oh, you must come and see John S——,' says one of the Sisters. 'We get all the little distractions we can for John.' 'Will he recover?' 'Well – we thought so – but –' – her face changes gravely – 'John himself seems to have made up his mind lately. He knows – but he never complains.'

Knows what? We go to see him, and he turns round philosophically from his tea. 'Oh, I'm all right – a bit tired – that's all.' And then a smile passes between him and his nurse. He has lost a leg, he has a deep wound in his back which won't heal, which is draining his life away – poor, poor John S—! Close by is a short plain man with a look of fevered and patient endurance that haunts one now to think of. 'It's my eyes. I'm afraid they're getting worse. I was hit in the head, you see. Yes, the pain's bad – sometimes.' The nurse looks at him anxiously as we pass, and explains what is being tried to give relief.

This devotion of the nurses – how can one ever say enough of it! I recall the wrath of a medical officer in charge of a large hospital at Rouen – 'Why don't they give more Red Crosses to the *working nurses*? They don't get half enough recognition. I have a nurse here who has been twelve months in the operating theatre. She ought to have a V.C.! It's worth it.' And here is a dark-eyed young officer who had come from a distant colony to fight for England. I find him in a former Casino where the Baccarat room has been turned into two large and splendid wards. He is courteously ready to talk about his wound, but much more ready to talk about his Sister. 'It's simply *wonderful* what they do for us!' he says, all his face lighting up – 'when I was worst there wasn't an hour in the day or night my Sister wasn't ready to try anything in the world to help me. But they're all like that.'

Twenty thousand wounded! – while every day the ambulance trains come and go from the Front, or to other bases – there to fill up one or other of the splendid hospital ships that take our brave fellows back to England, and home, and rest. And this city of hospitals, under its hard-pressed medical Chief, with all its wealth of scientific invention, and pain-saving device, and unremitting care, with its wonderful health and recovery statistics, has been the growth of just twelve months. The mind thinking of it wavers backwards and forwards between the two impressions – the hideous havoc of war, on the one hand; the power of the human brain, and the magical energies of human feeling on the other.

II

It was late on the 29th of February that we reached our next resting-place, to find a kind greeting from another Base-Commandant and final directions for our journey of the morrow. We put up at one of the old commercial inns of the town – (it is not easy to find hotel quarters of any kind just now, when every building at all suitable has been pressed into the hospital service) – and I found delight in watching the various types of French officers, naval and military, who came in to the *table d'hôte*, plunging as soon as they had thrown off their caps and cloaks, and while they waited for their *consommé*, into the papers with the latest news of Verdun. But we were too tired to try and talk! The morning came quickly, and with it our escort from G.H.Q. We said good-bye to Colonel S. who had guided our journey so smoothly through all the fierce drawbacks of the weather, and made friends at once with our new guide, the staff officer who deals with the guests of G.H.Q. Never shall I forget that morning's journey! I find in my notes: –

'A beautiful drive – far more beautiful than I had expected; over undulating country, with distant views of interlocking downs, and along typical French roads, tree- or forest-bordered, running straight as a line up hill and down hill, over upland and plain. One exquisite point of view especially comes back to me, where a road to the coast – that coast which the Germans so nearly reached! – diverged upon our left, and all the lowlands westward came into sight. It was pure Turner: – the soft sunlight of the day, with its blue shadows, and pale blue sky; the yellow chalk hills, still marked with streaks of snow; the woods, purple and madder brown; the distances ethereally blue; and the villages, bare and unlovely, compared to the villages of Kent and Sussex, but expressing a strong, old, historic life, sprung from the soil, and one with it. The first distant glimpse, as we turned a hill-corner, of the old town which was our destination, – extraordinarily fine! – its ancient church a towered mass of luminous grey under the sunshine, gathering the tiles roofs into one harmonious whole.'

But we avoided the town itself and found ourselves presently descending an avenue of trees to the eighteenth-century chateau, which is used by G.H.Q. as a hostel for its guests – allied and neutral correspondents, military attaches, special missions and the like. In a few minutes I was standing, bewildered by the strangeness and the interest of it all, in a charming Louis-Quinze room, plain and simple, in the true manner of the genuine French country house, but with graceful panelled walls, an old *armoire* of the date, windows wide open to the spring sun, and a half-wild garden outside. A *femme de ménage*, much surprised to be waiting on two ladies, comes to look after us. And this is France! – and we are only thirty miles from that fighting-line, which has drawn our English hearts to it, all these days!

A map is waiting for each of us downstairs, and we are told roughly where it is proposed to take us. A hurried lunch, and we are in the motor again, with Captain —— sitting in front. 'You have your passes?' he asks us, and we anxiously verify the new and precious papers that brought us from our last stage, and will have to be shown on our way. We drive first to Arques, and Hazebrouck, then south-east. At a certain village we call at the Divisional Headquarters. The General comes out himself, and proposes to guide us on – 'I will take you as near to the fighting line as I can.'

On we went in two motors; the General with me, Captain —— and D. following. We passed through three villages and after the first we were within shell range of the German batteries ahead. But I cannot remember giving a thought to the fact, so absorbing to the unaccustomed eye were all the accumulating signs of the actual battle-line: the endless rows of motor lorries, either coming back from, or going up to the Front, now with food, now with ammunition; reserve-trenches to the right and left of the road; a 'dump' or food-station, whence carts filled from the heavy lorries go actually up to the trenches; lines of artillery waggons, parks of ammunition, or motor-ambulances, long-lines of picketed horses, motor cyclists dashing past. In one village we saw a merry crowd in the little *place* gathered round a field kitchen whence came an excellent fragrance of good stew. A number of the men were wearing leeks in their ears for St. David's Day. 'You're Welsh then?' I said to one of the cooks – (by this time we had left the motor and were walking). 'I'm not!' said the little fellow, with a laughing look. 'It's St. Patrick's Day I'm waitin' for! But I've no objection to givin' St David a turn!' He opened his kitchen to show me the good things going on, and as we moved away there came up a marching platoon of men from the trenches, who had done their allotted time there, and were coming back to billets. The General went to greet them. 'Well, my boys! – you could stick it all right?' It was good to see the lightening on the tired faces, and to watch the group disappear into the cheerful hubbub of the village.

We walked on, and outside the village I heard the guns for the first time. We were now 'actually in the battle,' according to my companion, and a shell was quite possible though not probable. Again, I cannot remember that the fact made any impression upon us. We were watching now parties of men at regular intervals, sitting waiting in the fields beside the road, with their rifles and kits on the grass near them. They were waiting for the signal to move up towards the firing-line as soon as the dusk was further advanced. 'We shall meet them later,' said the General – 'as we come back.' At the same moment he turned to address a young artillery officer in the road. 'Is your gun here?' 'Yes, sir, I was just going back to it.' He was asked to show us the way. As we followed I noticed the white puff of a shell, far ahead, over the flat ditch-lined fields; a captive balloon was making observations about half a mile in front; and an aeroplane passed over our heads. 'Ah, not a Bosche,' said Captain —— regretfully. 'But we brought a Bosche down here yesterday, just over this village – a splendid fight.'

Meanwhile the artillery fire was quickening. We reached a ruined village from which all normal inhabitants had been long since cleared away. The shattered church was there, and I noticed a large crucifix quite intact still hanging on its chancel wall. A little further the boyish artillery officer, our leader, who had been by this time joined by a comrade, turned and beckoned to the General. Presently we were creeping through seas of mud down into the gun emplacement, so carefully concealed that no aeroplane over-head could guess it. There it was – how many of its fellows I had seen in the Midland and northern workshops! – its muzzle just shewing in the dark, and nine or ten high explosive shell lying on the bench in front of the breech. One is put in. We stand back a little, and a sergeant tells me to put my fingers in my ears and look straight at the gun. Then comes the shock – not so violent as I had expected – and the cartridge case drops out. The shell has sped on its way to the German trenches – with what result to human flesh and blood? But one did not think of that – till afterwards. At the time, the excitement of the shot and of watching that little group of men in the darkness held all one's nerves gripped.

In a few more minutes we were scrambling out again through deep muddy trench leading to the dug-out, promising to come back to tea with the officers, in their billet, when our walk was done. Now indeed we were 'in the battle.' Our own guns were thundering away behind us, and the road was more and more broken up by shell-holes. 'Look at that group of trees to your left – beyond it is Neuve Chapelle,' said our guide. 'And you see those ruined cottages, straight ahead – and the wood behind?' He named a wood thrice famous in the history of the war 'Our lines are just beyond the cottages, and the German lines just in front of the wood.' 'How far are we from them?' 'Three-quarters of a mile.' It was discussed whether we should be taken zigzag through the fields to the entrance of the communication trench. But the firing was getting hotter, and Captain —— was evidently relieved when we elected to turn back. Shall I always regret that lost opportunity? You did ask me to write something about 'the life of the soldiers in the trenches' – and that was the nearest that any woman could personally have come to it! But I doubt whether anything more – anything, at least, that was possible – could have deepened the whole effect. We had been already nearer that any woman, even a nurse, has been, in this war, to the actual fighting on the English line; and the cup of impressions was full.

As we turned back, I noticed a little ruined cottage, with a Red Cross flag floating. Our guide explained that it was a Field Dressing station. Some serious 'casualties' had been brought there the night before, and had not yet been removed. It was not for us – who could not help – to ask to go in. But the thought of it pursued me as we walked on through the beautiful evening. A little further, we came across what, I think moved me more than anything else in that crowded hour – those same companies of men we had seen sitting waiting in the fields, now marching quietly, spaced one behind the other, up to the trenches, to take their turn there. Every day I am accustomed to see bodies, small and large, of these khaki-clad men, marching through these Hertfordshire lanes. But this was different. The bearing was erect and manly, the faces perfectly cheerful; but there was the seriousness in them of men who know well the work to which they were going. I caught a little quiet whistling sometimes, but no singing. We greeted them as they passed with a shy 'Good luck!' – and they smiled back, surprised of course to see a couple of women on that road. but there was no shyness towards the General. It was very evident that the relations between him and them were as good as affection and confidence on both sides could make them.

I still see the bright tea-table in the corner of a ruined farm, where our young officers presently greeted us; the General marking our maps to make clear where we had actually been; the Captain of the battery springing up to shew off his gramophone; while the guns crashed at intervals close beside us – range-finding, probably – searching out a portion of the German line, under the direction of some hidden observer with his telephone. It was over all too quickly. Time was up, and soon the motor was speeding us back towards the Divisional Headquarters. The General and I talked of war, and what could be done to stop it. A more practical religion, 'lifting mankind again'? – a new St. Francis, preaching the old things in new ways? 'But in this war we had and have no choice. We are fighting for civilisation, and freedom, and we must go on till we win.'

III

It was long before I closed my eyes in the pretty room of the old chateau, after an evening spent in talk with some officers of the Headquarters' Staff. When I woke in the dawn I little guessed what the day (March 2nd) was to bring forth, or what was already happening, thirty miles away on the firing line. Zelie, the *femme de ménage*, brought us coffee, and bread and eggs, and by half-past nine we were downstairs, booted and spurred, to find the motor at the door, a simple lunch being packed up, and gas-helmets got ready! 'We have had a very successful action this morning,' said Captain ——, evidently in the best of spirits. 'We have taken back some trenches on the Ypres–Comines canal that we lost a little while ago, and captured about 200 prisoners. If we go off at once, we shall be in time to see the German counter-attack.'

It was again fine, thought not bright, and the distances far less clear. This time we struck north-east, passing first the sacred region of G.H.Q. itself, where we shewed our passes. Then after making our way through roads lined interminably, as on the previous day, with the splendid motor lorries laden with food and ammunition which have made such a new thing of the transport of this war, interspersed with rows of ambulances and limbered waggons, with flying-stations and horse lines, we climbed a hill to one of the finest positions in this northern land; an old town, where Gaul and Roman, Frank and Fleming, English and French have clashed; which looks out northward towards the Yser and Dunkirk, and east towards Ypres. Now, if the mists will only clear, we shall see Ypres! But, alas, they lie heavy over the plain, and we descend the hill again without that vision. Now we are bound for Poperinghe, and must go warily, because there is a lively artillery action going on beyond Poperinghe, and it is necessary to find out what roads are being shelled. On the way we stop at an air station, to watch the aeroplanes rising and coming down, and at a point near Poperinghe we go over a casualty-clearing station – a collection of hospital huts, with store houses and staff quarters – with the medical officer in charge. Here were women nurses, who are not allowed in the Field dressing-stations nearer the line. There were not many wounded, though they were coming in, and the Doctor was not for the moment very busy. We stood for a while on the threshold of a large ward, where we could not, I think, be seen. At the further end a serious case was being attended to by nurses and surgeons. Everything was passing in silence; and to me it was as if there came from the bowed heads of the distant group a tragic and wordless message. Then, as we moved lingeringly away, we saw three young officers all wounded, *running* up from the ambulance at the gate, which had just brought them, and disappearing into one of the wards. The first – a splendid kilted figure – had his head bound up, the others were apparently wounded in the arm. But they seemed to walk on air, and to be quite unconscious that anything was wrong with them. It had been a success, and they had been in it!

The ambulances were now arriving fast from the field dressing-stations close to the line; we hurried away, and were soon driving through Poperinghe. Here and there was a house wrecked with shell fire. The little town indeed with its picturesque *place* is constantly shelled. But all the same, life seems to go on as usual. The Poperinghe boy, like his London brother, hangs on the back of carts; his father and mother come to their door to watch what is going on, or to ask eagerly for news of the counter-attack; and his little brothers and sisters go tripping to school, in short cloaks with the hoods drawn over their heads, as though no war existed. Here and in the country round, poor robbed Belgium is still home on her own soil, and on the best terms with the English Army, by which indeed this remnant of her prospers greatly. As I have already insisted, the relations everywhere between the British soldier and the French and Belgian populations are among the British – or shall I say the Allied? – triumphs of the war.

In one street a company from a famous regiment, picked men all of them, comes swinging along, fresh from their baths – life and force in every movement – young Harrys with their beavers on. Then, a house where men have their gas-helmets tested – a very strict and necessary business; and another, where an ex-Balliol tutor and Army Chaplain keeps open doors for the soldier in his hours of rest or amusement. But we go in search of a safe road to a neighbouring village, where some fresh passes have to be got. Each foot now of the way is crowded with the incidents and appurtenances of war, and war is close at hand. An Australian transport base is pointed out, with a wholly Australian staff – 'Some of the men,' says our guide, 'are millionaires'; close by is an aeroplane descending unexpectedly in a field, and a crowd of men rushing to help; and we turn away relieved to see the two aviators walking off unhurt. Meanwhile I notice a regular game of football going on at a distance, and some carefully written names of by-paths – 'Hyde Park Corner' – 'Piccadilly' – 'Queen Mary's Road' – and the like. The animation, the life of the scene are indescribable.

At the next village, the road was crowded both with natives and soldiers to see the German prisoners brought in. Alack, we did not see them. Ambulances were passing and repassing, the slightly wounded men in cars open at the back, and the more serious cases in closed cars; and everywhere the same *va-et-vient* of lorries and waggons, of staff-cars and motor cyclists. It was not right for us to add to the congestion in the road. Moreover the hours were drawing on; and the great sight was still to come. But to have watched those prisoners come in would have somehow rounded off the day.

IV

Our new passes took us to the top of a hill well known to the few onlook-
ers of which this war admits. The motor stopped at a point on the road
where a picket was stationed, who examined our papers. Then came a stiff
and muddy climb, past a dug-out, for protection in case of shelling, Captain —— carrying the three gas-helmets. At the top was a flat green space
– three or four soldiers playing football on it! – an old windmill, and farm
buildings. We sheltered behind the great beams supporting the windmill,
and looked out through them, north and east, over a wide landscape; a
plain bordered eastwards by low hills, every mile of it, almost, watered by
British blood, and consecrate to British dead.

And as we reached the windmill, as though in sombre greeting, the
floating mists on the near horizon seemed to part, and there rose from
them a dark jagged tower, one side of it torn away. *It was the tower of Ypres*
– mute victim! – mute witness to a crime, that, beyond the reparations of
our own day, history will avenge through years to come. A flash! –
another! – from what appear to be the ruins at its base. It is the English
guns speaking from the lines between us and Ypres; and as we watch we
see the columns of white smoke rising from the German lines as the shells
burst. There they are, the German lines – along the Messines ridge. We
make them out quite clearly, thanks to a glass and Captain ——'s guid-
ance. Their guns too are at work, and a couple of their shells are bursting
on our trenches somewhere between Vlamertinghe and Dickebusche.
Then – the rattle of our machine guns – as it seems, from somewhere
close below us, and again the boom of the artillery. The counter action is
in progress, and we watch what can be seen or guessed of it, in fascina-
tion. We are too far off to see what is actually happening between the
opposing trenches, but one of the chief fields of past and present battle,
scenes which our children and our children's children will go to visit, lie
spread out before. Half the famous sites of the earlier war can be dimly
made out, between us and Ypres. In front of us is a gleam of the Zillebeke
Lake, beyond it Hooge. Hill 60 is in the band of shadow; a little further
east the point where the Prussian Guard was mown down at the close of
the first battle of Ypres; further south the fields and woods made for ever
famous by the charge of the Household Cavalry, by the deeds of the
Worcesters, and the London Scottish, by all the splendid valour of that
'thin red line,' French and English, cavalry and infantry, which in the first
battle of Ypres withstood an enemy four times as strong, saved France,
and thereby England, and thereby Europe. In that tract of ground over

which we are looking lie more than 100,000 graves English and French; and to it the hearts of two great nations will turn for all time. Then – if you try to pierce the northern haze beyond that ruined tower, you may follow in thought the course of the Yser westward to that Belgian coast where Admiral Hood's guns broke down and scattered the German march upon Dunkirk and Calais; or if you turn south, you are looking over the Belfry of Bailleul, towards Neuve Chappelle, and Festubert, and all the fierce fighting ground round Souchez and the Labyrinth. Once English and French stood linked here in a common heroic defence. Now the English hold all this line firmly from the sea to the Somme; while the French, with the eyes of the world upon them, are making history hour by hour at Verdun.

So to this point we have followed one branch – the greatest – of England's effort; and the mind, when eyes fail, pursues if afresh, from its beginnings, when we first stood to arms in August 1914, through what Mr Buchan has finely called the 'rally of the Empire,' through the early rush and the rapid growth of the New Armies, through the strengthening of Egypt, the disaster of Gallipoli, the seizure of the German Colonies; through all that vast upheaval at home which we have seen in the munition areas, through that steady and ever-growing organisation on the friendly French soil we have watched in the supply bases. Yet here, for us, it culminates; and here, and in the North Sea, we can hardly doubt, – whatever may be the diversions in other fields – will be fought, for Great Britain, the decisive battles of the war. As I turn to those dim lines on the Messines ridge, I have come at last to sight of whither it all moves. There, in those trenches, is *The Agressor* – the enemy who has wantonly broken the peace of Europe, who has befouled civilisation with deeds of lust and blood, between whom and the Allies there can be no peace, till the Allies' right arm dictates it. Every week, every day, the British armies grow, the British troops pour steadily across the Channel; and to the effort of England and her Allies there will be no truce till the righteous end is won.

But the shadows are coming down on the great spectacle, and with the sound of the guns still in out ears, we speed back through the crowded roads towards G.H.Q. One more scene – before the wonderful day is over. A message from an important Headquarters brings us to a halt there on our way back. The pleasant upper room in the old French house with its going and coming; the interest of watching the Army Commander himself – strong, weather-beaten figure! – as he stood receiving reports from his A.D.C.s, including the 'German wireless' just picked up, on the fighting of the morning; the happy bearing of the young officers, as they arrive in haste, one after another; the appearance in the group of a second General, whose name will be for ever associated with some of the most brilliant deeds of the war; and finally, the courtesy with which, at a first moment of leisure, on a day of action, a woman writer was received, merely for her errand's sake, as simply and kindly as though we had been all standing in Kensington or Belgravia: – these things remain engraved on memory. The fine grizzled heads of the older men; the radiant looks of the younger; the talk – reticent, quietly confident, humane: – they are with me still. It was war, one aspect of it, seen from close by, and in undress. An Englishwoman left it behind her, prouder even than before that –

> Chatham's language was her mother tongue,
> And Wolfe's great name compatriot with her own.

Now all that I have to do is to take you far away from the armies, into the homes whence our fighting men are drawn, and to shew you, if I can, very shortly, by a few instances, what rich and poor are doing, as individuals, to feed the effort of Britain in this war. What of the *young*, of all classes and opportunities, who have laid down their lives in this war? What of the families who reared them, the schools and Universities who sent them forth – the comrades who are making ready to carry on their work? You ask me as to the *spirit* of the nation – the foundation of all else. Let us look into a few lives – a few typical lives, and see.

Rosie Neale
The Escape of the Royal Brewsters

The next stop was the frontier. Here we all began to tremble. Looking out at this station one sees nothing but soldiers with fixed bayonets. We got into the custom house & had our hand baggage well looked into. When the custom officers found no ammunition we were politely handed over to the policemen to whom we had to show our passports. Here we tried to hold our tongues & only speak when absolutely necessary in our best American accent we could master, (which was very bad). Kit produced her passport & handed it over. One glance at it & the soldiers with the bayonets were ordered to lock all doors. Here the trembling & cross ques-

tioning began. We lived in holy dread of being sent back, or even worse
than that, to prison where we should be made to dig the ground & eat that
terrible black bread.

Now they wanted to know how five people could travel on one passport, so Kit told them that in America young girls didn't need passports
& another thing, she was a teacher with her four pupils & if he didn't let
her through she would inform President Wilson on her return to America. At this the poor man began to quiver & handed back the passport
telling her everything was quite all right. We all wanted to shout 'Bravo
Kit' but knew we dare not. But the danger wasn't over even yet, those
doors weren't unlocked & the big baggage had to be examined. It was the
time I most dreaded. Not that we were trying to smuggle anything. Oh
no! But our swords, supposing they should find them, our number would
be up. They would not think they were toys as we did for they had the dear
old crest on the hilts & could tell a long story for they have been through
the South African war. Eventually the baskets were closed and the boy's
letters were safe, those terrible doors unlocked & the soldiers with the
bayonets ordered to let the American school mistress and her young
ladies pass.

Oh what a sigh of relief. 'Success at last'. We who were feeling very sad
only five minutes before were now five of the happiest people in the
world.

Flora Sandes
from
An English Woman-Sergeant
in the Serbian Army

Later on the next day the sun put in an appearance, as did also the Bulgarians. The other side of the mountain was very steep, and our position
dominated a flat wooded sort of plateau below, where the enemy were.
One of our sentries, who was posted behind a rock, reported the first sight
of them, and I went up to see where they were, with two of the officers. I
could not see them plainly at first, but they could evidently see our three
heads very plainly. The companies were quickly posted in their various
positions, and I made my way over to the Fourth, which was in the first
line; we did not need any trenches, as there were heaps of rocks for cover,

and we laid behind them firing by volley. I had only a revolver and no rifle of my own at that time, but one of my comrades was quite satisfied to lend me his and curl himself up and smoke. We all talked in whispers, as if we were stalking rabbits, though I could not see that it mattered much if the Bulgarians did hear us, as they knew exactly where we were, as the bullets that came singing round one's head directly one stood up proved, but they did not seem awfully good shots. It is a funny thing about rifle fire, that a person's instinct always seems to be to hunch up his shoulders or turn up his coat collar when he is walking about, as if it were rain, though the bullet you hear whistle past your ears is not the one that is going to hit you. I have seen heaps of men do this who have been through dozens of battles and are not afraid of any mortal thing.

We lay there and fired at them all that day, and I took a lot of photographs which I wanted very much to turn out well; but, alas! during the journey through Albania the films, together with nearly all the others that I took, got wet and spoilt. The firing died down at dark, and we left the firing line and made innumerable camp fires and sat round them. Lieut. Jovitch, the Commander, took me into his company, and I was enrolled on its books, and he seemed to think I might be made a corporal pretty soon if I behaved myself. We were 221 in the Fourth, and were the largest, and, we flattered ourselves, the smartest, company of the smartest regiment, the first to be ready in marching order in the mornings, and the quickest to have our tents properly pitched and out camp fires going at night. Out Company Commander was a hustler, very proud of his men, and they were devoted to him and would do anything for him, and well they might. He was a martinet for discipline, but the comfort of his men was always his first consideration; they came to him for everything, and he would have given anyone the coat off his back if they had wanted it. A good commander makes a good company, and he could make a dead man get up and follow him.

That evening was very different to the previous one. Lieut. Jovitch had a roaring fire of pine logs built in a little hollow, just below what had been our firing line, and he and I and the other two officers of the company sat round it and had our supper of bread and beans, and after that we spread our blankets on spruce boughs round the fire and rolled up in them. It was a most glorious moonlight night, with the ground covered with white hoar frost, and it looked perfectly lovely with all the camp fires twinkling every few yards over the hillside among the pine trees. I lay on my back looking up at the stars, and, when one of them asked me what I was thinking about, I told him that when I was old and decrepit and done for, and had to stay in a house and not go out any more, I should remember my first night with the Fourth Company on the top of Mount Chukus.

Baroness de T'Serclaes
from
Flanders and Other Fields

Fight for an idea

We were busy, no denying that. We were used to being under fire, and we had shed a lot of illusions. But I was not at all satisfied. There was too little thought and too much scurrying about for its own sake. This could be very wasteful, as when an ambulance was sent on a longish journey simply to pick up a few bandages, perhaps largely as an excuse to take some visiting 'big-wig' on a sightseeing jaunt – for there was plenty of that in the early months of the war. People still thought it would all be over by Christmas, and I suppose they wanted to see as much as possible.

Hospital arrangements at Fumes were pitifully inadequate, partly in a convent and partly in a commandeered school. The chaos of the retreat had prevented any proper arrangements being made. All available doctors were frantically busy sawing off limbs and patching men up at forward dressing-stations. Fumes was just left to fend for itself – and this was before good hospitals had been opened at La Panne and Calais. The only hope was to send as many men as possible on to Dunkirk. It was a poor look-out for the rest.

During the Battle of the Yser 20,000 Belgians – about 35 per cent. of the army's total strength – were killed or wounded. Day and night, ambulances and wagons streamed into Fumes, packed with casualties. In the 'hospital' one doctor and one nursing sister, helped by drivers, troops in transit, anyone who was around and could bear to lend a hand (for the sights and stench were appalling), struggled against hopeless odds.

There were so many bodies – dead, dying, shockingly or slightly wounded – laid on the floor that it was difficult to walk without treading on them. Two small boys with a handcart took the dead to the burial-dump. They slid the corpses off the stretchers, and when they had balanced as many as they could manage, off they went. When our ambulances drove in with a fresh load we would have to get down to the loathsome task of clearing the dead to make space for the living. Once I roped in some passers-by – simply ran out into the street and hauled them in – and for four hours we toiled, just two to each stretcher, piling the dead in a field.

Sometimes I helped in the operating-room. Amputated limbs were simply swept or thrown out into the courtyard, and there was a frightful smell of rotting, gangrenous flesh. How that doctor and that sister kept going I will never know. For the first day or two my freshly starched Queen Charlotte's mind was shocked by what I saw, and I tried to protest.

Most of the men were so badly smashed that each needed a nurse to himself. I wrote in my diary: 'It is terrible to go into those wards at night. There are no big lamps, just little candle lamps which you carry in your hand. It looks no better than pictures I have seen of Florence Nightingale's hospital at Scutari – so dark and dreary. One hears groans and tears and faint cries, in French and German, from corners so dim that you cannot see who is making them. ...'

When every bed and every inch of floor was taken up the military ambulances, unable to stop, dumped their casualties on the pavements or in the street – not even on stretchers, for they were needed in the firing line – and drove off, trusting that some one would sort it all out. We heard cries of 'Water!', 'De l'eau!', and 'Wasser!' We wanted to have compassion, but it was best to stop one's ears and walk on; otherwise it would have meant running about with a water-bottle all day and probably going mad into the bargain.

I wanted to set up a first-aid station (or Advanced Dressing Station, as it was called) where the wounded could rest and recuperate before being jolted over the roads to the operating table. I had noticed how many of them died of superficial hurts, a broken arm, perhaps, or a gash. They 'died on the way to hospital,' or on the pavements or the floors, and I knew why this happened. They were the victims of shock – the greatest killer of them all. Months later, when I had proved my theory up to the hilt, I had a case of an officer who had accidentally been shot by a sentry. The officer was soon patched up – it was a mere graze – but it was the sentry I was worried about. The men laughed at me, of course, but I insisted that he was the one that most needed sympathy and treatment because of the shock and guilt he had suffered. How right I was! The wretched boy could not speak for days: he just lay in a corner of the cellar which was our dressing-station, staring up at the ceiling. We kept him warm and quiet, and he recovered. It takes a woman to know these things. Men are so blind, and often insensitive to suffering.

At first it seemed that I would never get even a cellar to work in. I went to Dunkirk to badger Sir Bertrand Dawson (later Lord Dawson of Penn), medical chief of the B.E.F., and talked to Prince Alexander of Teck. Both were sympathetic, and gave me all the support in their power then and later, but they were so busy with a multitude of things. Admiral Ronarc'h, who happened to be present when I was pleading with Sir Bertrand, scoffed openly, and became very angry when I persisted. He had never heard anything quite so absurd. Surely I knew that women were not allowed in the trenches? They had to be at least three miles behind the lines. If I chose to disobey orders I could expect no assistance, and that meant no rations and no medical supplies. The Admiral stated firmly, almost with relish, that because I was a woman (and, oh, how utterly disparaging those two words, *une femme*, can sound) I could not possibly stand the strain of Front-line life, and would only become an added worry and responsibility.

When he had finished I informed the Admiral as respectfully as I could manage that because I was a woman I could stand strain and hardship (I nearly asked him if he had ever heard of childbirth), and that as I firmly believed in my mission – for such it had become to me after much thought – I would go, with or without assistance.

I made my preparations, undeterred by the fact of Dr Munro's disapproval. The next thing was to find a suitable place to start a post. I was fortunate to meet a Belgian Army doctor, Dr Van der Ghinst, who fully agreed with my plan. He had spent weeks in Dixmude and knew that I was not talking out of the back of my head. He suggested that a village called Pervyse might be the spot, and we drove out there to have a look. I was sceptical, for a few days before I had been there and had noted '… we passed through Ramscappelle first. It was a wreck and a ruin, but nothing could ever equal Pervyse – there is not a house which one could even pig it in – it is just one huge fallen mass, heaped-up bricks and stones … the dead horses, cows, and sheep looked so pathetic. …'

Yet behind the intervening floods the Belgians had set about fortifying the place. The crude earthworks thrown up in the heat and hurry of battle were being linked and converted into a system of trenches and dugouts. Two houses, both with deep, damp but safe cellars, remained fairly intact. In one of them some Belgian officers had their quarters. The other one was offered to me, and with it went the good wishes and a promise of co-operation from the officers and men to whom Dr Van der Ghinst introduced me and explained my idea.

'Our house ' – for it was soon settled that Mairi Chisholm, who had proved herself brave and steady as well as being an excellent driver, should accompany me – was a woeful sight. There was not a pane of glass left whole, the roof had fallen in, the walls were ominously cracked, and everything that was any good had been taken or looted. It was right at the edge of the village, nearest the tottering church and the trenches, and the stream of shells which the Germans lobbed across the water meant that we should have to sleep, cook, and nurse in the cellar. I could not wait to move in!

The cellar was about ten feet by twelve, dimly lit by gratings set into the pavement above. Two soldiers, Alphonse and Desire, who had been sleeping there on some straw, rustled up a table and a few chairs for us, and some boards to surround our sleeping straw, which they renewed as often as possible. The stove sometimes smoked badly, but in that icy winter of 1914 we were able to overlook such trifles. We slept in our clothes, and cut our hair short so that it would tuck inside our caps. Dressing meant simply putting on our boots. Most nights Tom Woffington, our Cockney driver, and Alexandre, the eighteen-year-old cook who was assigned to us, slept in the cellar too.

Ablutions were infrequent and difficult. Alexandre sometimes managed to heat some ditch water, and we would try to wash down in a huge old copper while he kept watch at the top of the steps and prevented any new patients from coming down before we were decent. Now and again we would get to Furnes or Dunkirk for a good soak, but there were times when we had to scrape the lice off with the blunt edge of a knife, and our under-clothes stuck to us.

We were unofficial visitors, there on approval and expected to leave in a few days with our tails between our legs. Those who didn't actually disapprove of us regarded us as a passing eccentricity. When our ambulances drove into Dixmude the French Marines had greeted us with shouts of 'Les folles anglaises,' and though there were no such shouts at Pervyse, the thought was there. Nothing had been done, certainly, to encourage us to stay. There was no sanitation, and for some time we had to go down a convenient shell-hole to relieve nature while Alphonse or Desire kept guard. Later, this devoted couple brought us a magnificent commode which they had somehow managed to find, complete with a screen which they had made out of some old sheets. Disposing of soiled bandages was a problem, but after a while in Pervyse one forgot the niceties. The village had been taken and retaken several times in the Battle of the Yser, and the graveyard was choked with corpses of several nationalities, exposed by the heavy rains. Our only available water-supply ran through the middle of the courtyard, and even when it had been boiled it had a horrible taste.

We soon contrived to make the house cheery, by hanging on the walls the flags of Belgium, France, and Scotland, and a fine, defiant Union Jack. Spoons, forks, and crockery were discovered in a derelict farmhouse, and Alphonse and Desire scraped up some vegetables from the abandoned gardens. Alexandre boiled up a great soup stew in his copper in a lean-to outhouse at the back. Every night more horses were killed bringing up food and ammunition, and they provided the meat on the menu. Now that he had been appointed cook, Alexandre took on a new dignity. He was no longer a private – he was a chef, a man of importance.

The trenches were only five yards away, and in those first days we took jug after jug of soup or hot chocolate to the men on watch. When they were relieved the men would come over to the Cellar House, as it became known, and queue up with their mugs. At night we took hot drinks to the sentries in the outposts at the end of the causeways which ran out into the floods. An officer accompanied us through the icy and often misty dark-ness, giving the password as we were challenged. The machine-gunners had scooped a dug-out of sorts: a hand would emerge, grasp the jug, and draw it in. In a few seconds it would be returned empty. All was done in silence, and when the odd star shell curved down towards us inquisitively we would have to stand stock still.

The soup and the chocolate made us known and welcome, but they were only a sideline. The fearful winter of 1914 brought us more casual-ties than German bullets or shells. The men's clothes were hopelessly inadequate for the intense cold. Frostbite, pneumonia, and bronchitis fol-lowed nights of exposure, and I spent many a spare moment writing to friends and acquaintances at home begging for warm clothes. Men came in with festering sores after scratching themselves on barbed wire, or in agony with swollen, inflamed feet. Sometimes a soldier would have no obvious symptom, except that he was 'quite done-up' and incapable of any exertion. We put such cases of trench fatigue on clean straw in the corner, covered them with blankets, arranged a good supply of hot-water bottles, and let them sleep round the clock. More often than not they were new men when they got up.

There were curious accidents. One man fell down a deep crater in the dark, and gashed his head badly on a jagged piece of shell. Another came in with his hand in an appalling state: he had been wearing gloves at the time of the explosion, and bits of glove were mixed up with shredded flesh, and had to be picked out. Stray shrapnel and a moment of carelessness brought some horrible casualties. A piece of shell had penetrated one young fellow's head and blinded him.

News of our work spread like wildfire, and in the evenings officers from various parts of the Front would turn up to see 'these women' and drink a cup of tea. Sometimes they did not leave till midnight, and as we were on the alert all night and all day we did not welcome visitors, but I suppose it was what would now be called good public relations.

Mme Curie, who, with her daughter, was running an X-ray unit in Furnes, was most interested in the work, and did me the honour of visiting the Cellar House. She was only five feet tall, soft-spoken and gentle in manner. We had a long and most interesting technical talk about methods of treatment, and she agreed with me that the three great priorities of nursing were quiet, rest, and warmth.

The shelling got so bad that we were forced to move to the other house farther back in the village, while keeping our first cellar as a forward dressing-station. The Daimler ambulance was riddled with shrapnel, and we got quite sentimental over it, for it was like seeing an old friend wounded. Already we were thinking and acting like veterans. In my diary I was able to write, 'only a few stray *blesses*,' and, walking back from the advanced post at night, with the troops squelching past on their way to or from the trenches, I would feel at once lonely because they marched on without saying a word and perhaps sweeping me nearly off the road, and proud that I should be here sharing everything with them, and accepted as one of them. 'They don't know I'm not one of themselves,' I wrote with my stub of pencil, 'as they pass with their heavy, overloaded walk, with just the outline of their rifle above their heads as it is slung across their back. ...' Oh, how those words bring back to me those strange days, and my strange state of mind, the sense of sharing, of comradeship and identification, the hatred of the muddle and waste of war, and then, hard on its heels, the sharp gratitude for being there in the middle of it all to make a tiny corner of sanity!

Our daily work taxed us to the limit of our physical strength. Sometimes I smile now when I watch soccer on the television, and see a player being carried off the field by as many as six stretcher-bearers – all for a man wearing the lightest of clothes. Yet Mairi and I often went out to help bring in the wounded, and between us lifted a man in full field kit with rifle and tin-hat. There was the first wrenching jerk from off the ground to waist-level, and then the stumbling over mud and slush and cratered roads.

Many people, especially British officers, thoroughly disapproved of our being at Pervyse. It just did not fit in with their conventions, and they would start off by wasting a great deal of breath in arguments which simply ran like water off a duck's back. I let them get on with it, and then asked them to contribute something to keep the work going, instead of grumbling about it. Most of them responded very well with gifts of food and drink – much needed in the first months when we had to depend on scrounging for our own food: Alphonse once spent a whole day shooting twelve sparrows which he brought to us for supper. I specially remember the huge slabs of chocolate the naval officers brought from Nieuport. We broke chunks off with a hammer for chewing, and in bulk it made a marvellous hot brew.

Naturally I was more concerned about getting official approval for our mission. Sir Bertrand Dawson visited us several times and told me that he had noticed that wounded who had been nursed at Pervyse arrived at hospital in far better condition. He had put in a favourable report, he said, but it was now up to the Allied Council in Paris to decide whether or not to let us continue. Waiting for their decision was the worst suspense of the lot, for not only was I convinced that I was doing good work, but I was happier than ever before in my life, happy, perhaps, for the first time in my life.

Weeks later Sir Bertrand called. I was particularly busy bandaging a nasty chest-wound, and could not get away. I knew what his mission was, and he gave me such a wonderful warm smile that I guessed it was all right – and so it was. My work had been recognized, and in the most flattering terms. Mairi and I were to be allowed to stay where we were – the only exceptions on the whole of the Western Front. I was to have rations and any help I needed with medical supplies, and to be taken on the strength of whichever unit took over that part of the line.

Straight away I wrote to the British Red Cross Society, and from then on I had their full support, and could add the Red Cross flag to our array. They sent me a fine lot of equipment, even including a complete set of dental instruments. To my surprise I found them very easy to use. If you have a strong wrist, the right weapon, and a decisive mind the tooth comes out. My fame as a dentist spread far and wide, and I pulled out many teeth which were causing a lot of discomfort and even suffering. We had no anaesthetic, but for particularly nervous cases or tough pullings we would, if we had any, give the patient a swig of brandy or whisky.

Ours was an ever-open door. It was nothing unusual to be woken up in the early hours of the morning and to hear a voice saying, 'Wake up, Sister; I'm wounded!' Men often came up to me to ask me about their domestic troubles, and despite my own disastrous experience of marriage (it was about this time that I got word that my husband had died) I found that I was able to help them quite a bit.

Things were looking up in other directions, too. An excellent hospital had been opened by Dr de Page in a former luxury hotel on the sea-front at La Panne. The Royal Family was now living in a small villa at La Panne, which had become an important military centre, with drilling and manoeuvres taking place on the sands. Millicent, Duchess of Sutherland, a gay and brilliantly capable woman of great charm and beauty, had started a big hospital at Calais. The shambles of Furnes was a thing of the past.

Now that I was established, I was given a new job. Early in 1915 Colonel Edward Maitland of the Royal Flying Corps and Commander Harry Delacombe of the Royal Naval Air Service asked me if I would 'spot' for them, as I was right in the front line. They issued me with a field tele-phone and a wonderful pair of Zeiss binoculars, and made arrangements to alert me whenever a plane was going over our lines to Germany. I had to keep a check on the time, when the plane returned, etc., and give its direction and approximate height. It was a great responsibility, but often a sad one. Some of the little planes which went out so gaily never returned, or crashed near our lines. Their pilots had not seen, as I with my powerful glasses had, the scarlet flash of one of the planes of Baron von Richthofen's 'Circus' ready to swoop down on them from above the drift-ing clouds.

It made me almost envious to watch the flimsy-looking planes of those days wheeling about far above our squalid, muddy level. Now that the war of movement was over and trench systems were being elaborated from the Belgian coast clear across to Switzerland, aerial combat seemed to offer the only real scope for gallantry and individual daring.

The troops were as pleased as we were that we had taken root. They brought us souvenirs – cap-badges, German helmets and swords, and in their spare time would carve intricate designs on brass shell-cases and present them to us. I started my album of war artists, and gathered a remarkable collection of drawings and paintings by men of all ranks and several nationalities – some of them famous, like Bruce Bairnsfather and Heath Robinson, most of them quite unknown but so talented. Many of them were killed.

The most unusual memento was presented to me just after the church-tower at Pervyse, which had become more and more wobbly, was blown up for safety's sake. The clock had been carefully removed and was carried along the village street with great ceremony and propped against the walls of the Cellar House. We didn't know what to do with it, and finally I detached the heavy, rusty old iron hands and brought them back with me to add to the hoard of odds and ends that grew every time I visited England on leave or to raise funds.

An end to Pervyse

It happened on March the 17th, 1918, almost exactly a month after the triumphal matinée. The Germans were preparing a terrific bombardment, and something warned me that we should get up and put on our gas-masks. Remembering to manoeuvre round the trap-door, I roused Mairi and called Barker and Beaumont. Just as they came up from their funk-hole there was a tremendous explosion, and gas poured through the slit. We started to pull on our masks, but we were all coughing and choking so much that it seemed a bit pointless.

My head was swimming, and I felt horribly sick. The place was in complete darkness, and I could see little through the goggles of my mask. Just as I found my torch and switched it on I heard voices cursing and swearing in the lower dug-out, into which some would-be rescuers had fallen, through the trap-door. I managed to crawl over and wheeze out some instructions as to how to get out of this lower dug-out. One of the men had already located the ladder. I heard him coming, but had not the strength to get out of the way, and so got a splendid uppercut from his steel helmet.

I vaguely remember being carried to an ambulance. The driver was saying 'For Christ's sake hurry'; he wanted to get out of Pervyse and its shells. That is my last memory of the village where I had spent three and a half fantastic years.

We were taken to the hospital at La Panne, but I had no time to speculate about this, since I was coughing and gasping for breath, together with dozens of soldiers all around me, until I thought my lungs must burst or be torn from my body. Some one gave me an injection in my thigh, and I remember thinking how funny I must look with my breeches pulled down to my knees in the midst of all those soldiers. They were much too ill to notice such details.

A nurse came and stripped off all my clothes, explaining that they were impregnated with gas and must be destroyed. At that I felt utterly miserable and helpless. A soldier somewhere to my right tried to comfort me by saying, 'Cheer up, gal, you've just got to the fifth stage. When you get to the eighth you'll be all right.' I asked him to explain, and this was the sequence.

(1) The first shock. (2) The realization of what has happened and the panic. (3) The rescue – if you're lucky. (4) The dash to the casualty station. (5) The nasty demoralization of being just a lump of flesh that can be stripped, injected, lugged around, and expected to have no emotions. The sixth stage was when you were lifted up and carted away, either to the mortuary or to a ward bed; the seventh was when you came to and realized that you were getting better; the eighth was when you could appreciate the warmth of your nice neat bed and fall luxuriously asleep.

It was twenty-four hours before I woke up after that injection. Two days later I was moved to Lady Hatfield's hospital at Boulogne, and then transferred to a hospital in London. I was in no condition to put up much of a fight when I was firmly told that this time the post at Pervyse would have to close down – for good. Surrounded by comforts and expert nursing, I was more desolate and wretched than I had ever been in my life. Not even the flowers that filled my room or the kind phone-calls that came through from Queen Mary and Queen Alexandra could rally me. My life seemed to be in pieces, and I had not the heart to try to put it together again.

The most encouraging visit was from Major-General Sir Godfrey Paine, who told me that the Royal Naval Air Service and the Royal Flying Corps were to be amalgamated as from April the 1st, that he was to be Master-General of Personnel to the new force, the Royal Air Force, and that he was looking for suitable women to officer the Women's Royal Air Force. Was I interested? Up until then women had served either with the Army or the Navy, and there was, warned Sir Godfrey, strong resistance in the existing women's services (particularly among their leaders) to the idea of the W.R.A.F., which was going to take away a large slice of their membership.

Women of courage and integrity were needed, women whose record could command respect. It would be a tough job, but he thought I would do it well.

I knew that if I didn't get my teeth into something pretty soon I'd brood myself silly, so I was easily tempted. However, before getting into any sort of harness again, I wanted a complete rest and change of scene.

Mabel St Clair Stobart
The Retreat from Serbia

Wed Nov 3rd [begins 2 a.m.]
Hear endless rumbling of wagons like breaking of raging sea on distant shingly beach. World of shadows & dreariness. Some rain again. Is no one angry for all this? … Daybreak beautiful. Sunrise cloud colours marvellous. Golden clouds ag. dark purple hills with wool like folds of clouds in dist. to soften effect. One daring cloud like golden dragon spread out alone in the dark sky. Colours too delicate to call blue or gold or crimson. Glories & beauties everywhere. Is it all meaningless or waiting for us to catch meaning? While was thinking about this, the glories disappeared & I saw the eternal picture of drab dressed weary soldiers splashing with open feet in the sloppy mud. Sometimes stumbling & rising without murmur cov. with wet mud. Hleba [bread] None for 3 days I heard one say. Silence of voices, no singing no whistling, scarcely even talking. Sometimes horse stumbles over little flock sheep wh. drives along road for food. A tiny mouse indistinguishable in darkness ran across road. Was life going on as usual for it?

8

The home front

Sylvia Pankhurst

Insults to Soldiers' Wives and Mothers

Last week it was announced that public-houses were to be closed to women, though to men they are to remain open as before. To the average woman, though she may be disgusted by the smug impertinence of such an order to the more temperate sex, from the less temperate one, this regulation makes little practical difference. The average woman never thinks of spending her mornings in public-houses. The working woman whether she is a mother at home or a wage-earner in a factory, is much too fully occupied in any case, and the leisured woman, even when she has time to idle, has other ways of life. So the order for closing public-houses to women only will excite but little indignation although almost every woman pronounces it unjust.

But on Saturday was issued another order which is gravely dangerous and offensive, and is arousing very deep and bitter indignation.

It is an order to place families of soldiers under police supervision.

The order comes in the form of a memorandum from the Army Council, forwarded by the Home Office with a covering letter to Chief Constables which says: –

I am directed by the Secretary of State to say that the Army Council desire to have the assistance of the police in the measures being taken to provide for the with-holding of separation allowances, payable to wives or dependants of soldiers, in the event of serious misconduct on the part of the recipient. ... In addition to furnishing reports on the special cases in which complaints are referred to them, the police should, as opportunity offers, endeavour to check misconduct before it reaches a point at which it may become subject to official notice, by warning the offenders that its continuance will involve the stoppage of their allowances.

The War Office memorandum is headed: –

CESSATION OF SEPARATION ALLOWANCES AND OF ALLOTMENTS TO PAY THE UNWORTHY

It explains that separation allowances will be discontinued in cases of serious misconduct, immorality, conviction of criminal charges, and neglect of children.

The memorandum details the procedure to be followed in which the complaint of 'unworthiness' comes from, (1) the soldier, (2) his commanding officer, (3) a local committee, (4) other sources.

It is unfortunately, quite clear that all this means, that there is to be an attempt to put the dependants of the soldiers and sailors under police supervision, and we must protect against this attempt with all the power and earnestness we possess.

The wives of the soldiers and sailors differ in no way from other women, except that just now, they are all of them facing an agony of dangerous suspense.

They are drawn from every section of society, but, because the majority of our people are working people so too the majority of soldier's wives are sprung from the working class. Their strengths and virtues, their faults and failings are those of the majority of other women. Amongst every large body of faulty human beings, some will be found to do things which the majority of the others dislike or disapprove, and naturally some of these too will be found amongst the vast number of soldiers wives. But there is no shadow of reason or excuse for this attempt to place soldier's wives under police supervision. If any of these women break the ordinary law of the land and do things which are prohibited to others, ample means exist for checking them and bringing them to punishment; and if they do not break the law and do not do the things that are prohibited to others, it is unjust that they should be either punished or checked.

If their houses are unclean, the sanitary inspectors can deal with them, as with others, if their children are neglected, the law and the Society for the Prevention of Cruelty to Children – reinforced by neighbours – will bring them to book. If their children fail to go to school, the school attendance officers will have them punished. The police will arrest them, as they do others, and under the same conditions, if they get drunk or steal. If the Government is to have further power to compel persons to sobriety, thrift and the care of the home and children, those powers must be extended to embrace every individual in the State. It is intolerable that they should be enforced against a special class of women, because those women's husbands chance to be *earning* wages from the State.

Apart from the monstrous injustice of erecting a special code of conduct and morals to be forcibly riveted upon the soldier's wives, we must protest very specially also against the proposal to place these our country women under the supervision of the police. The police force is a body of men at least as fallible as these women whom it is proposed that they should supervise and control. The majority of them are probably very worthy men, still, in spite of the fact that their occupation brings them into perpetual contact with the more sordid side of life, and gives them a power over other human beings which is dangerous to the average faulty human character.

But it is impolitic to give any body of men large powers over the lives and surroundings of women, and there are some members of the force in whom those powers will produce peculiarly objectionable results. The management and traditions of the police force tend to shield the objectionable conduct of such men.

This was clearly illustrated by the case of Rex *v* Wetherall. In this case a policeman was prosecuted for assaulting a little girl of fourteen, with whose parents he had lodged. The defence was that the crime was committed, not by Wetherall, but by another police constable who was also a lodger in the house, and Wetherall was acquitted.

Appeals for the dismissal of the two constables who went into the witness box and swore that they knew of the immoral relations of one of their fellow constables with this child and yet did not report the matter, were made in vain. The child victim nearly lost her life in the serious illness which resulted, her father went out of his mind and died as an outcome of the affair; but the policemen remained members of the force, and they will be amongst those who will supervise and control the mothers, the wives and the little daughters of the soldiers at the front.

Patricia Hanbury
German Guns in St James's Park

November 3rd 1915
We went to London for our music lessons & afterwards we went to St James' Park to see the German guns captured by the British at different

battles during the war. They were most interesting. Some were battered, while others were very torn & shattered. There were a good many field guns & a few trench mortars. A great many of the field guns had been captured at Loos. On our way we had seen a troop of Horse Guards in full dress, – red coats & armour, on their lovely black horses. They looked so unreal when one had seen nothing but khaki for over a year.

We saw car-loads upon car-loads of wounded soldiers – Englishmen, Australians & New Zealanders, all jolly & splendid. One often saw a grand motor-car or a grand carriage, with beautiful horses, full of wounded Tommies, & then one would see quite a shabby brougham or small motor with a very smart lady inside! A great many of the motors are driven by ladies.

We then went to Wimbledon where we met Mother & Betty at the [d'Hendecourtes] house. They were all there, also Roger, who was on leave. He showed us the most thrilling photos of the land & trenches in Belgium taken from aeroplanes. Their sister who had been nursing in Belgium was there too & she was very interesting. On our way we saw some men just come straight out of the trenches, all muddy & torn. They looked dead tired but quite cheerful.

Ethel Bilborough
How Poor People Live Is a Mystery

January 1918:
Meat is getting scarce and we have had no butter or margarine for a fortnight! I am rather glad, because when one is struggling with a slice of horrid dry toast that rebels against going down, one really feels one is at last taking part in the war!! How *poor* people live is a mystery!

Virginia Woolf
Suddenly One Has Come to Notice the War

Saturday 5 January 1918.
… Then we took a tram to Kingston & had tea at Atkinsons, where one

may have no more than a single bun. Everything is skimped now. Most of the butchers shops are shut; the only open shop was besieged. You can't buy chocolates, or toffee; flowers cost so much that I have to pick leaves, instead. We have cards for most foods. The only abundant shop windows are the drapers. Other shops parade tins, or cardboard boxes, doubtless empty. (This is an attempt at the concise, historic style.) Suddenly one has come to notice the war everywhere. I suppose there must be some undisturbed pockets of luxury somewhere still – up in Northumbrian or Cornish farm houses perhaps; but the general table is pretty bare. Papers, however, flourish, & by spending 6d we are supplied with enough to light a week's fires.

Melvina Walker
The Potato Queue

It was Saturday market day in Chrisp Street, Poplar, and cold, miserably damp morning. It was only half-past nine, and many of the Jews' stalls and costers barrows were not yet set out. At ordinary times one never thinks of going to market before 10.30, but to-day large numbers of women were hurrying up the street with worried faces, and all talking at once about 'children,' 'starvation,' and 'potatoes.'

Suddenly they all began to run, and made one dash for a coster's stall. The owner had not arrived, but bags tied up were slung carelessly across the stall. The women felt the bags eagerly but to their disappointment, what they thought were potatoes turned out to be onions.

'Oh, my God,' said one woman, as she turned away from the stall and caught my eye, 'what shall I do if I can't get potatoes? It looks as if we were facing starvation.'

'Have you many children?' I asked.

'Many children? I should say so – I've only got seven, and not one of them able to bring me in a penny – that's where this War comes hard on the likes of us. It isn't them as lives up in the West End that's a going short! Why they're blooming well putting up the price of everything! It looks to me like this: there's food in the country and it looks as if they are putting up the price so as only the rich can buy it and the poor, those as has to do the blooming work has got to go without.'

'That's just it, missus,' I said, 'we women can see through this War.'

'Yes,' said my companion, 'and it's women that always has to suffer: it's the likes of us as always has to go without, and you can't get the men to see it.'

I was just going to tell her that men had a very different view now to what they had at the commencement, when suddenly the conversation was interrupted by a shout from the other women, who said that the man at the corner of Tetley Street was just beginning to weigh up potatoes. Off ran the women and with them my companion.

When I got to Tetley Street I saw that the women and children there already numbered about 400, and that a 'bobby' was making them stand behind one another, four abreast. The line reached a long way down the street. I wondered how long the little children would have to wait before being served, for it was perishing cold.

There were many more children than women, for the mothers had sent them to save their own time. They were poorly clad, and with poor boots or bootless, and thin, pale faces and sunken eyes, thin little necks and shoulders huddled up to ears nipped with cold. As I watched them, it dawned on me as it never had done before, that these were the children of the workers, the children of the men and women who, both in peace and war time produce the wealth of the country. There they were waiting in the gutter for a few potatoes. I should have liked men like Lloyd George, Carson and Winston Churchill to see this sight as I saw it.

A prominent tradesman tapped me on the shoulder and said: 'What do you think of it, Mrs Walker?' Before I had time to answer he referred to the children being poorly clad.

'Yes,' I said, 'I see, but this is England's greatness.'

He shrugged his shoulders and hurried away.

My thoughts wandered back to my school days and to one of the stories by which the school teachers tried to instil into our minds a belief in our country's greatness. This was the story of a black prince, who after Dreadnoughts, battle ships, arsenal, and so on had been shown to him, was received by Queen Victoria, of whom he asked that she would produce to him the secret of England's greatness at which he marvelled. The Great White Queen immediately brought forward the Holy Bible, and said: 'Herein doth lie the secret of England's greatness.'

To us, mothers of the human race, England's greatness consists neither in battleships nor vast dominions over seas, but in the freedom of its citizens to shape and mould their lives and the lives of their children. When every little child in this England of ours shall have a chance to live happily and all Christians realise the truth of the words: 'It is the will of my Father that not one of these little ones shall perish,' then, and only then will England be great.

Potato raid

There is an instinct towards Communal ownership in East London which readily finds expression at periods of pressure.

Last Friday, in the Roman Road, Bow, the potato shortage was acute, and women's eager minds were busily reviewing the possibilities.

The day before large supplies had been delivered at a fried fish shop; to the fish shop, therefore, the crowd went when all the greengrocers had been tried in vain.

Conflicting versions of what happened afterwards are given. Some say that the fried fish man, a Jew, was selling uncooked potatoes privately either to members of his own faith or to regular customers at a side door: some say that he was not selling uncooked potatoes to anyone, but that he refused to sell fried potatoes without fish, and that a customer who wanted chips without fish started the trouble by an altercation with his wife, which ended in blows: others again maintain that the business was carried on just as usual, and that the sole reason for interference was that the fried fish and chip mongers had potatoes enough to last for many days, whilst their neighbours could not buy any for that day's meal.

But whatever the preliminary causes may have been there seems to be no doubt that the crowd was determined to storm the fish shop if it could not get the potatoes in any other way, and that the police therefore directed the owner to come out and sell them for 1½d. per lb. from a stall placed opposite his door.

Ernestine Mills
from
Real Food Economy, The Englishwoman
no. 89, May 1916

The present need for economy in food and labour affords an excellent opportunity for urging a reform long overdue, a reform which has been advocated in every Utopia that has ever been imagined, and which we have been approaching indirectly for many years.

In the present crisis women are wanted in their tens of thousands to increase the productivity of the country. They are entering skilled trades in overwhelming numbers, they are engaged in professions, they are urged to work on the land to the number of 400,000, they are exhorted to throw their whole energies into the service of the State. And on the other hand women are urged to practise economy in housekeeping; well-intentioned gentlemen write to the papers almost every day, telling us all to make soup, to eat beans, to use margarine, to warm up coffee, and not to throw away scraps. Most of the economies advocated have always been customary in middle-class households, but in Wartime they can be sprung upon us as something new and strange – and housewives are too busy to protest.

As a matter of fact, no appreciable economy of food will be made until we adopt some system by which no private consumer buys any uncooked food at all.

Among the industrial classes the appalling prevalence of digestive disorders, decayed teeth, craving for drink, and other preventable ailments, is largely due to the fact that all their cooking is done by amateurs, usually under the most unhygienic conditions. But if every working man's wife were an enthusiastic and expert cook, with ample leisure to devote herself to the task, the lack of fuel and utensils – both expensive items – would tend to dishearten the most optimistic. It must be remembered that in the vast majority of working-class homes the cooking must all be done in the family living room, in many cases also the sleeping room. Let this fact weigh against the sentimental idea that there is any likelihood of 'homelife' being marred because the food is cooked elsewhere. Doubtless our great-grandmothers would have shuddered at the idea of 'baker's bread' (and indeed it often falls short of our ideal), but can any one really doubt that the general standard of bread consumed to-day in our large towns is higher than if every working-man's wife attempted to make her own? Or that the cost of labour, material, and distribution is not lessened on the whole by our bread being made by experts, and kneaded by clean machinery instead of by hand.

An army 'marches on its stomach' it is said – so does the health of the nation; and until the diet of the nation is studied intelligently we shall have no decrease in the number of citizens with impaired and enfeebled constitutions who suffer all their lives from amateur cookery.

The remedy for our wasteful habits of living and our miserably inadequate cooking is not to teach every woman to cook, but to forbid the vast majority of women to cook at all on any excuse whatever. Why should every woman learn cooking, any more than every man should learn tailoring? We all want food, we all want clothes, but cooking and tailoring are skilled crafts, and both are far better left in the hands of experts. We really discovered this long ago – before the first fried-fish shop provided cheap and wholesome suppers in the East-end, or the first barrack-like flats opened a common dining-room. We do not all like fried fish, nor do we all wish to live in flats, but there are many alternatives.

As the working woman suffers from lack of utensils and fuel, so the middle-class and professional women suffer from a dearth of cooks – a 'good plain cook' is fast becoming as extinct as the Dodo – and no wonder. With modern appliances one whole woman should not be required to devote her life to cooking for a single family, she could as easily cook for a dozen while she is about it. In a terrace of twenty houses we still find twenty basement kitchens, just as we did a hundred years ago, each with its wasteful range, its half-trained cook, its anxious mistress, its dozen tradespeople calling every day, and all – to what end? A single cook with modern appliances and a couple of trained assistants could cook for twenty families with ease. A steam roaster can cook dozens of joints without attention or waste, a washing-up machine can cleanse the crockery from a dozen meals in a few minutes – without breakage.

Then as to economy in distribution. The working-class woman, weary after her day's work in the factory or the home, must trudge from street to street in all weathers to seek the cheapest food, and must carry it home, to be stored usually in the family living room, for she rarely possesses a larder. Consider, again, the time and the energy expended even by the average middle-class woman who thinks it her duty to do her own marketing every day. Look into one of our large provision stores any morning and see numbers of worried women choosing their little wasteful bits of meat and other foodstuffs. Each of these has probably had a worrying interview with her cook already, and an undercurrent of worrying will run through her brain at intervals until her family have consumed the evening meal. And the next day it all begins again. True, many of these women have hitherto had nothing else to do, but can the country now afford to waste so much woman power? Do we realise the industrial revolution which is taking place? Our women are wanted in munition shops, in factories, in offices, on the land, they are for the first time entering skilled trades, from which they have hitherto been excluded by the men's Unions, hundreds of women are now doing what has hitherto been con-

sidered men's work – and doing it well. This large new industrial army
must be kept at work after the war, it will be our chief means of recoup-
ing our expenditure. It will not be suddenly demobilised, there will be a
development of industry which will absorb all these trained workers for
our extending commerce, and to repair the huge wastage of this hideous
war. But if this industrial production is to continue, if our women are also
to be employed on the land in large numbers, they must be fed, and their
families must be fed, without any extra exertion to themselves. It will be
to the benefit of the State if the energies of all working women can be
employed productively instead of being frittered away upon their own
personal concerns. No woman should be allowed to work for a wage
which is not sufficient to enable her to procure ample and wholesome
food without additional labour on her part.

There are many women in every class who are 'born housekeepers,' and
who can bring real talent and taste to bear upon the cooking and orga-
nizing of food supplies. These should be given ample scope and good pay
to use their abilities for the benefit of the community. There are also many
women who loathe the sight of raw meat, and who would rather live on
tea and toast for a week than cook a meal: why should they not be allowed
to devote themselves to other work in which they may be entirely useful
and happy? But 'Every woman ought to be able to cook' – in the name of
common sense – why?

If we were pioneers in a wild country it would be necessary, but then
we must also brew and wash, and return to a more or less primitive life,
toiling to produce the bare physical necessaries of existence. After all,
cooking is not so terribly difficult, there is no fear of its becoming a lost
art, and if need arose, a few weeks' training and a cookery-book would
give the pioneer knowledge which would carry her far. But in a civilised
community the mother can no longer profitably do personally all that is
required to feed, clothe, and educate her children according to progres-
sive standards, she must have expert assistance if she is to do the best for
them. The boy whose mother insisted on cutting his Sunday clothes
would certainly be at a disadvantage among his fellows, and 'Mother's
cooking' is responsible for a good deal of digestive trouble. It is a popular
idea that a man really likes his wife to be a cook, but as a matter of fact, if
a man is well fed, he will usually be quite indifferent as to who prepared
his food, and, on the other hand, no amount of affection will help him to
digest bad cooking.

The large amount of unsuspected illness among married working
women, which has been brought to light since the National Insurance Act

came into force, reveals the terrible strain endured by working mothers who, in addition to wage earning in factories, or on home work, spend long hours in cooking, marketing, and washing up; these women have been in the habit of working literally until they dropped. Miss Clementina Black, in her valuable book, *Married Women's Work*, dwells on the high percentage of infant mortality in districts where women are not wage earners, but where the domestic toil is heavy because the men of the family work on different shifts, and consequently require substantial hot meals at different hours. But the present crisis has brought a gleam of hope that at last these things may be remedied.

In a recent description of the cheery scene at the dinner hour in a refreshment hall of a munition factory, the writer says:

> Hundreds of men were filing across from the factory to the canteen. I pushed in with them and found a cheery scene. Scores of white tables, touched here and there with flowers and decked with shining cutlery, stretched away in long aisles. The comfort of it all was almost dramatic. You could see it reflected in the faces of the men as they dropped down into their seats at the table.

And again, speaking of the canteens at the docks for transport workers:

> The sole aim of all concerned was the comfort of the men, and their practical requirements were everywhere the first consideration. Nevertheless, through all, and over all, in these establishments there was a refining influence which it was impossible not to recognise, and which has its place in producing a certain atmosphere of restfulness.

Now, why should not all our industrial workers and their families dine in like comfort and restfulness every day, in peace as well as in war-time?

The problem is really a simple one. In villages a central kitchen could easily be run, with a cheerful room in which children from the schools and the mothers from the fields could meet for the midday meal, or if preferred could carry the cooked food home: an arrangement of hay-boxes easily keeps food hot. No woman working on the land ought to be expected to cook on her return home – no man would, why should the woman with less surplus energy? It is to be hoped that some such arrangement will always be made in the proposed village colonies for disabled soldiers, leaving most of the wives free to assist in farming and garden work.

In large towns, when once the idea is accepted, many enterprising firms could be found to organize catering for middle-class households, with a choice of foods as large as is now the choice of uncooked edibles. The meals could be delivered – as is now the raw material – or could be sent if necessary, and the used crockery returned to the central kitchen to be washed by one of the excellent labour-saving machines now on the market. Or even one house in every street could be set aside for cooking and catering.

The professional woman, struggling perhaps to produce some creative work, while equally anxious that her family should be comfortably fed, would feel she had wings indeed if the burden of the kitchen, and what an able American writer calls the 'transient stream of incapacity' in the shape of cooks, could be lifted from her shoulders. For it must be remembered that for the small minority of women in this country who keep servants at all (and it is only a small minority) it is not one cook, but an uncertain succession of cooks, that have to be dealt with. We all know the comfort that comes to a household which rejoices in faithful service extending over many years, but this becomes more and more exceptional as we get further away from the feudal system. Every year more and more of a woman's thinking time is absorbed, as the scarcity of domestic servants, the need for economy, and the uncertainty and growing instability of the present system increases.

The private kitchen is unhygienic, extravagant, and has nothing what-ever to recommend it but a vague sentimentalism, and an excuse for wasted female energy. Home-made clothes and home-made cooking are not really superior, and even if they were, the waste involved far out-weighs what in exceptional cases may be an advantage.

With no cooking except perhaps what could be done by each person at the table with a small electric heater, the domestic servant problem would be immensely simplified, basements, from which most of us unfortu-nately still suffer, could be made much more comfortable, and real econ-omy of food, in coal, in utensils, and in the disposal of refuse, would commence. There is ample proof that the sale of cooked provisions is a very profitable undertaking. Lady Angela Forbes, in an account of her canteens in France, says that out of 200*l.* taken in an average week, about 100*l.* is profit. True, much of her help is voluntary, but against that must be noted that the soldiers are only charged nominal prices for what they consume, and that more than wholesale prices are paid for the stores, which come from two New Bond Street and Oxford Street firms.

It is to be hoped that in the light of the present state of women's work, and the prospect of developments after the War, the instructive article 'Experiments in Cheap Catering' by Miss Sellers, which appeared in the *Nineteenth Century* for November, 1914, will now be widely read. She gives among other information, a detailed account of the 'Steam Kitchen' in Christiania, founded fifty-seven years ago, and rebuilt in 1900. Its working expenses are only 8'7 of its turnover – and its annual turnover seven years ago was 70,000*l*. It is frequented by all classes, meals at different prices can be eaten in the coffee or dining rooms, or carried home. The cheapest dinner, well served, with a choice of several dishes, enough for 'a big, strong hand-worker,' costs a fraction over four pence. If taken home, it costs a little less, and it can then be eked out with more bread, and divided among several children. And this undertaking pays more than six per cent.

The 'People's Kitchens' in Vienna, founded in 1872, seem to have been equally successful, and interestingly enough, the waiting in the dinner hour, during the first few years, was done entirely by voluntary lady helpers, just as it is being done now in our canteens. The late Dr Kuhn, who founded these valuable 'Kitchen Associations' assured Miss Sellers that 500*l*. would cover the full cost of starting a centre in which 500 persons might be self-supporting. Surely the time has now come for us to prepare to carry on the work which is now being proved to be so valuable in our munition factories, and which is doing so much to maintain and improve the stamina of our workers; can we not also extend these facilities to the middle classes who are, perhaps more than any other section of the community, feeling the need for 'War economy'?

We merely want business firms, expert cooks, and kitchens open to inspection. One possible danger to be avoided is lest the catering fall into the hands of 'cranks' or 'food specialist,' who would want to feed us all on powders and slops. But the problem is, as has already been pointed out, a simple one, especially when we realise that whatever its possible drawbacks, it cannot be more extravagant and inconvenient than our present arrangements are for the majority of working women.

A school teacher, after giving her class a learned lecture on diet, explaining the relative values of proteins, carbohydrates, and fats, asked whether any girl could now tell her three kinds of food necessary to health. A bright girl held up her hand. 'Well, Jane?'

'Please, teacher, yer breakfast, yer dinner, and yer tea.'

And really that is all most of us need trouble about.

Ethel Bilborough

The *Lusitania*

On the 7th May [1915] all Europe was thrown into a state of consternation at a diabolical act of the German fiends! They actually torpedoed (and sank) one of the largest liners, the 'Lusitania' coming from America; and twelve hundred civilians – American, English, and many other harmless and helpless people were ruthlessly drowned without a chance of escape.

Words entirely fail to express what all England – and America too – felt at this unparalleled outrage. The Americans talked a lot, and threatened Germany if such a thing 'ever occurred again', but it all ended in smoke, and was soon forgotten – except by the poor sorrowing relatives of the 1200 souls whose bodies lay at the bottom of the sea, all because Germany is at war. The relentless wickedness of such an act has not its like in all history I should think. But the Germans become more inhuman every day.

G. B. Stern

from

Children of No Man's Land

A woman was huddled on a doorstep, wailing loudly, openly, without any pretence of hiding her stark grief. Her wisps of grey hair were blown by the wind flat across her distorted face, which she neither burrowed in her arms nor covered with a handkerchief. For she had just received tidings that her daughter had gone down in the steerage of the Lusitania, and she wanted God and man to know it.

A knot of sympathizers, neighbours and casual passers-by stood dumbly around her, listening to the saga of Ethel Ann's childhood, and Ethel Ann's adolescence, and Ethel Ann envisioned powerfully but crudely as a human livid face, struggling, gulping, pleading for help … help refused. … They pushed 'em back into the water!' screamed the old crone. 'My little 'un. Curse the Germans! – Curse 'em! They watched 'er drowning, and they laughed: A-a-aaah …' articulation trailed away into a long-drawn-out cry of rage and mourning and hate. She strained her skinny arms in a tight line upward, as though in one gesture could be uttered all that her tongue had failed to say.

Richard felt it was impossible just to stand still and look on at this. He glowered about him in a spirit of desperate truculence. The others of the group were in exactly the same case, their eyes roaming stupidly up and down the narrow street, as though in search of some immediate measures. A carter leaning against his dray drawn up to the kerb opposite, spoke out fiercely:

'Ay. 'Uns. That's the sort they are. Wish I 'ad one or two under my fist now. I'd show 'em what for.'

'You *have* got 'em under your fist now – plenty – if you know where to look!' A lantern-jawed man with the hollow eyes of a fanatic, sprang onto the tail-board of the dray. At once he formed a vortex for all the loose and aimless emotions adrift in that street. Richard and Fraser found themselves in a wedge of men and women, women predominating, swaying with that sort of concerted drunken rhythm peculiar to all crowds. Even the mother of the drowned girl stopped her wails, and stared fixedly at the demagogue.

'Germans everywhere in this country – millions of 'em, laughing up their sleeves because we're such ruddy softs as not to chuck 'em out. Laughing now, I expect, over our women and children pushed back into the icy water; *English* women and children. Yes, it's a good joke, ain't it ? First-class! I 'ad a pal on the Lusitania – well, never mind that – there's some 'ere as 'ad more than pals. Are we going to stand it – that's what I want to know? Are we going on trading with murderers and cowards, living cheek by jowl with 'em, buying our very bread from 'em … *poisoned* bread! I tell you, there are Germans in the next street, in this street, and in a thousand other streets in England, with their dirty names over the shop-windows. Ask the Government! – ah! – they'll say they've took the proper measures of precaution. We don't want precaution, thank yer all the same. We want revenge on the foul scum what sank the Lusitania! We want revenge – not by and by, but *now*! We want revenge – and by the dying agonies of our children, and for the sake of those they've left, we'll have it!'

His hearers had been like empty bottles offering no resistance to the fiery liquid he poured into them. Yes – they wanted instant revenge; that was what they had sought by their vacant stares. With a scattered howl, from which the human element seemed long since to have been drained, they swirled up the street. Richard was borne along by the impetus of their fury. He had lost sight of Fraser, who, missing him, had probably

returned home; it did not matter; this was rather a lark – one of the Lusitania riots; they had been breaking out all over London since the news
had come through. No – not exactly a lark ... it swelled in to something
more formidable and animated by a spirit of deeper satisfaction than
warranted by the schoolboy description: this was action; this was war; he
was in direct contact with it at last. A gang of men in an ugly temper, running in a set direction ... he could feel purpose behind the lurching, staggering passage of the mob. They were on their way to punish the Germans
– coarse hulking giants who could laugh at Ethel Ann's drenched face
helpless in a green tumble of breakers. ... Brutes! damned brutes! we'll
show them! ...

This was all the jerky elated comment his brain could register during
the headlong stampede up the cramped alley; that – and a confused
impression of the women's faces here and there patching: the rest streaming hair, with the iron pins still clumsily caught in it; mouths open and
awry; damp red skins. Mob-women – they were hideous. ...

The lantern-jawed man, still leader, halted abruptly in front of a small
baker's shop. 'What about that?' denunciatory forefinger thrown out to
indicate the name painted over the window: Gottlieb Schnabel. The
crowd replied by another exultant howl ... it was beginning to merge its
separate identities into the Demos-beast, at once frightful yet silly; incapable alike of retreat or initiative; a beast that uttered meaningless
sounds; could be deflected hither and thither; a beast without logic or
coherence; but a beast that was out, very obstinately, to maul somebody
... the Germans. ...

'What about that?'

Those in the van swerved so sharply into the little doorway of the shop,
that their comrades immediately behind them could not restrain themselves from reeling past it by weight of impetus; then turned, and pressed
back, with a violent impact jamming the rearmost in the narrow aper-
ture; so that it seemed that dark menacing figures were springing out of
the shadows from all sides and directions, into the pallid flare of the gas-
jets singing forlornly over the counter.

The shop was deserted. Violent hands ripped down the curtains that
divided off the back-parlour, and about a dozen roughs hurled themselves up the stairs, chanting: 'Schnabel: Schnabel!' in hideous sing-song.
Their feet could be heard trampling the upper premises in search of the
owner: 'Come aht of it, yer bloody funk! Wot abaht the Lusitania?' ... The
shop-door swung backwards and forwards in the draughts of wind which
blew down the street; and at each oscillation, a little bell tinkled the warn-

ing of customers – an innocent tinkle, like a distant sheep-bell … inadequate tinkle that recurred thinly through all the chaos of heavier sound: Crash of splintered glass, as the scales and weights were sent flying through the front window of the shop. The majority of the avengers were working off their blood-lust by hullabaloo and wreckage; tossing about the buns and cakes; swinging and smashing the rows of big sweet-bottles; sending a hurricane of piled up bread-baskets over the floor. It had been a neat little interior, three minutes before … !

But Richard was impatient with all this monkey destruction; his imagination was a-sweat to vent itself upon Germans, not upon rolls and doughnuts. He raced up the back stairs – and down again; no Germans there; and the rioters engaged in the same stupid business of destruction. But the Germans … pointed steel helmets, puffed-out cheeks, and thick sensual lips – where had they contrived to stow themselves away? The notion had got started that they were here … somewhere … the excited boy did not stop to reason it out. He wanted to batter with his fists against a fat resisting carcase. Here? – of course they were; somebody had said so. Dodging the volley of loaves, he bolted out of the shop, and round the corner to the tiny yard at the back, unheeding whether he was alone or followed. The bakehouse! – must be one under the shop. Yes – beneath this wooden flap. Guided by the hot good smell of bread in the oven, he wrenched at the hinges; and rashly taking the ladder for granted plunged into the gaping black space. Fragments of tales relating to the Lusitania horrors were flying loosely about in his mind, like the loaves in the shop: sickening details gasped out by dazed survivors, and written up for the public in lurid journalese. Fighting – was that the Hun idea of fighting? – swine! cheats! butchers! – his turn to show them now. …

Richard bumped his feet on level ground; he blinked an instant in the red dimness of his surroundings … then, gradually, a face swam into his consciousness – a face over there, by the barrels – a face smeared with flour, and channelled by the drip of perspiration – a face that would have been ludicrous, were it not for its expression of deadly shivering fear … *trapped* fear. …

With knowledge of utter helplessness in his fascinated gaze, he confronted Richard. Beside him, a plump woman and two or three children crouched in a shadowy lump.

No army of Germans here. Only a little baker, Gottlieb Schnabel, and his family.

He started at Richard. Richard stared back. And then his swollen illusion was pricked and shrivelled. So this was the reality of what he had been vengefully hounding down, he and the bawlers overhead? this one peaked, unhappy little face, white with dabs of flour, white in the last extremity of panic.

Schnabel's dry lips moved convulsively … 'Ach, bitte,' he babbled; then, with an effort: 'Can – I – help – for – it?' …

Richard just caught the words. He recoiled; turned and stumbled up the ladder. … One must get away from that face. … Not so easy – some of the crowd had followed him after all, were swarming round the entrance to the bakehouse. 'There's no-one there,' muttered Richard; 'no-one there' … his voice was choked as though in a thick fog. 'No-one there –' But the main thing to do was to get out, into the street, before they began to do things – no, that did not matter, – but before he could *hear* them doing things. They were pressing him back again, down again. … 'There's no-one there, I tell you!' Blindly he buffeted right and left the heads which blocked his passage. Some of them, believing him, gave way … melted out of reach from his hard fists and powerful driving shoulders. Others went shuffling and clattering past him, down the wooden rungs. 'Schnabel! Schnabel!' – and a sharp scream. One must get away, quickly. …

A great surge of bodies in the yard. Thrusting forward, with his head low down, through a rank smell of boots and corduroys and rusty skirts, Richard got clear at last. Round the corner – into the street – a number of people running in his direction – three or four policemen. 'There's no-one there!' – half-sobbing, he dodged through a mews into a wider street; again that loud trample of feet beating towards him – would they never let him escape? he wanted to be free of mobs. What did this mob want? Schnabel? … No, it was only a helter-skelter of gnome-like urchins, shrieking hoarsely their late editions. He paused to draw breath; leant up against an adjacent wall; his cap had gone long ago, and the wind blew in hard, fresh gusts through his hair.

Presently he walked on again, slowly. Hysteria had evaporated, and was replaced by the usual shame. Now he came to think over the matter coolly, what had so upset him? The little rat of a baker had been in a funk, certainly; probably justified; probably the rabble had handled him fairly roughly. What of that? Ethel Ann, equally innocent, equally helpless, had met an infinitely worse fate.

Oh, he was not going to take part in the baiting himself. No sport in it. The wisest course to pursue had been to depart from the scene, as he had done. Had he 'departed from the scene' or made an exit – rather less dignified than that inferred? Well, he could hardly be expected to stay and look on. Nor could he have protected Schnabel – hang it! the man was a

German. Not 'the Germans' – but still a German. Richard, impatiently, classified the whole experience as 'quite a decent scrum'; and as such, stuck it up on a shelf in his memory, like a book with several pages safely gummed together. He proved to be in a completely strange neighbourhood; and devoted all his present faculties in discovering the whereabouts of Montegu Hall.

Sylvia Pankhurst
The East End Air Raid

To see the result of the German Air Raid, numbers of unaccustomed visitors came flocking to East London, well-dressed people in motor cars and taxis, journalists, photographers, high military officials, Red Cross nurses, policewomen, and travellers from all over the world.

Impatient passengers on the tops of buses were heard asking 'Is this the East End?' before they had got past Bishopsgate. Many of the sightseers stopped at a certain church, because rumour had said it had been set fire to by a bomb. But no damage could be seen. Crowds stood with chins uncomfortably stretched and eyes gazing on the steeple, arguing as to whether a lightning conductor was a crack. A constant stream of people passed for hours through the churchyard, a dense cluster always gathering around the old stocks, because some lingered to look at them from interest and others stopped to look over their shoulders to see if those who lingered were looking at a bomb.

Many West-Enders gave up their search here and went home disappointed but those who inquired of the people of the district easily learnt in what part of the East End the damage had been done.

In the by-ways leading from one of the meanest of all mean streets many bombs had done their work.

[People dressed in] flowsy garments thronged the road and squeezed past each other in the crowded alleys.

What a sight for the pretty ladies in dainty dresses with slender delicate throats, peering from taxi cabs and for the rather too comfortable looking business men and well-groomed officers in motor cars. Miserable dwellings, far from fit for housing human creatures, poorly clad women with sad work-worn faces, other women just covered, no more, in horrid rags, hopeless, unhappy beings, half-clothed neglected looking little children a sadder sight, this mean street that is always with us, even than the havoc of destruction wrought by German bombs. The windows of the first little house we saw, on which a bomb had fallen, were smashed, but no other damage could be seen from the outside. It was said that two children had been hurt there. A dense crowd was pressed close against the building, and a soldier in khaki stood on the doorstep to keep them back. The people who lived in the damaged house could scarcely manage to get in and out.

At the corner of a very narrow alley, was a baker's shop with a German name over it. It bore marks of a recent raid. The shutters, the door and window framework had been torn away, and the place now boarded round with new unpainted wood. Six or seven yards off, down the alley, a bomb had fallen on a brewery. The building was burnt out and there remained nothing but the outer walls and a mass of [charred wood] that had fallen on the cellar floor within.

One or two dwelling houses were burnt out almost as completely as this brewery, the twisted iron-work of the bedsteads, and the fire-irons alone showing what they had been. But the damage in most cases was slighter, at least to outward showing.

The streams of people showed the way to every injured building and big crowds, largely composed of women, collected at each one.

Everywhere were heard excited voices and the snatches of conversation that came from every group contained the same group of thoughts. 'We poor people are being made to pay for it.' 'Why is everything so dear?' 'Conscription.' 'Will they have conscription?' 'They can get all the poor fellows they want without.' 'They put off the poor fellows that have always had to work hard and tell them to give their lives.' 'There were little lights signalling telling them where to drop the bombs.' 'I saw taxi cabs driving up and down signalling.' 'Everywhere you'll find a bomb is dropped near to where one of their shops was wrecked.' (Those who say this forget that there is no place in the East End that is not near a raided German shop.) 'They should have been cleared out at the beginning of the war.' 'The Government has nowhere to put them: they go and give themselves up to the police, and they tell them to go home.'

In the main street there is a rushing and excitement. A German baker's shop has just been wrecked. 'They were serving bread there an hour ago.' says someone. Another answers: 'They buy bread from them and then they wreck the shop.'

The big windows are all smashed in, and only a few jagged bits of glass remain about the edges. The pavement is covered with glass and flour.

The counters have been cleared, and everything movable is gone from the shop. A policeman stands before the door. Two soldiers come out laughing and telling the people as they go through the crowd 'there is plenty of new bread downstairs if you want it. There is plenty of new bread downstairs, it'll only be wasted.'

Down the street people are blowing policeman's whistles. A big man in clothes dusty with flour is struggling in the grasp of several others, his mouth is full of blood.

A woman with streaming hair is grabbed at by many people. A big man, who has been drinking, throws her on the ground. Someone cries out: 'They are kicking her.' She is lost to sight in the midst of a struggling mass of people.

Somebody asks a soldier standing by to rescue her. He answers: 'What can I do?' 'You are a soldier, they will respect you, can't you help her?' 'What can *I* do?' 'Aren't you trained to fight? You can stop them.' He laughs and then becomes indignant. 'Why should I? There's another soldier. Why don't you get on to him?'

Somebody screams: 'Oh she's covered with blood.'

A big open motor car, in which is an officer in khaki and some men in plain clothes, stops in the middle of the road. Someone runs up to it. 'There is a woman being hurt here. Can you take her away in the car?'

There is a vacant seat but the officer answers: 'I don't think we can, we are on military business,' and the car goes off.

But they have got the woman up from the mass. Her face is white; and there is blood running down her arm, but she may not be dangerously hurt. They have sat her on a barrel. Someone is fastening up her hair. The feeling of the crowd turns to pity. 'I believe in all things being done in a proper manner.' someone says, and another adds: 'Killing the woman can't do any good.'

When the people realise that they have injured a fellow creature their rage passes quickly, compassion takes its place.

Now the trouble is over the police come. They hustle the crowd away, the woman who is hurt and the people who support her.

A crowd comes past from another direction. Two men are holding by the back of his collar a man in floury clothes. A stream of boys and youths are following. The men who are holding the captive by the collar wrench and jerk at it, although he goes quite passively and each time they do it, he says: 'All right gov'ner, all right,' in reasoning Cockney tones.

Prominent newspapers fill their columns with articles intended to inflame the populace to anti-German riots, articles which consume ignorant nervous excitable people with a suspicious terror that transforms for them the poor Hoxton baker and his old mother into powerful spies, able at will to summon fleets of Zeppelins.

The Government does nothing to stop, or even to deprecate the publication of such matter. The Government fails to protect defenceless aliens, and will not even give them the safe-keeping of an internment camp.

9
Under fire

Nell Hague

Zeppelins over Hull

7th June 1915
111 Cranbrook Avenue
Hull
1 a.m. Monday

My darling Husband,

We are having the strangest experience that has ever come our way. The Zeps! are here! and from Mother's bedroom window the whole town seems on fire.

Our darling child is peacefully sleeping among the infernal doings but we are wondering about others.

Last night was the second time since our arrival that the alarm whistles have blown; after the previous one we heard that they had been over Driffield but the reports in the press have been very meagre.

However last night (Sunday) they were blown again about 10 p.m. and about 11 we all went to bed. I did not feel afraid, but of course I longed to have you here, for you always bring such a sense of security to me.

In about half an hour's time they came! The noise is terrific and we heard the sounds caused by the dropping of bombs.

We all congregated into Mother's room and before long saw the fires – distinct ones flaming almost up to the sky. It was like the pictures of Quo Vadis and similar ones, for of course all else was in complete darkness.

As soon as things were quieter Mother and Father went along to Grandfather's to see that Mrs Reddish was alright, so Mrs Close and I are staying here. It makes one want to go along to see where the fires are and what the damage is.

I am glad to say I never felt calmer in my life though it is a dreadful thing to think of. Mother is in a state of nervous tension naturally, and she thinks the whole town is on fire, but however 'here we are again' as Arthur says.

Thank God for our safety, dearest, but I pray that no others will have to mourn because of the dastardly acts of those arch-fiends.

Let me have a letter soon dearest, for I am quite anxious about you. We feel far too wide awake to go to bed again. However we are in the hands of the Father and are loving you.

Your own
Nell

Virginia Woolf
Gothas over Barnes

Thursday 6 December 1917
When I wrote that we were only at the beginning of our day's work, last night, I spoke more truly than I knew. Nothing was further from our minds than air raids; a bitter night, no moon up till eleven. At 5 however, I was awakened by L. to a most instant sense of guns: as if one's faculties jumped up fully dressed. We took clothes, quilts, a watch & a torch, the guns sounded nearer as we went down stairs to sit with the servants on the ancient black horse hair chest wrapped in quilts in the kitchen passage. Lottie having said she felt bad, passed on to a general rattle of jokes & comments which almost silenced the guns. They fired very quickly, apparently towards Barnes. Slowly the sounds got more distant, & finally ceased; we wrapped ourselves & went back to bed. In ten minutes there could be no question of staying there: guns apparently at Kew. Up we jumped, more hastily this time, since I remember leaving my watch, & trailing cloak & stockings behind me. Servants apparently calm & even jocose. In fact one talks through noise, rather bored by having to talk at 5 A.M. than anything else. Guns at one point so loud that the whistle of the shell going up followed the explosion. One window did, I think, rattle. Then silence. Cocoa was brewed for us, & off we went again. Having trained one's ears to listen one can't get them not to for a time; & as it was after 6, carts were rolling out of the stables, motor cars throbbing, & then

prolonged ghostly whistlings which meant, I suppose, Belgian work people recalled to the munitions factory. At last in the distance I heard bugles; L. was by this time asleep, but the dutiful boy scouts came down our road & wakened him carefully; it struck me how sentimental the suggestion of the sound was, & how thousands of old ladies were offering up their thanks-givings at the sound, & connecting him (a boy scout with small angel wings) with some joyful vision – And then I went to sleep: but the servants sat up with their heads out of the window in the bitter cold – frost white on the roofs – until the bugle sounded, when they went back to the kitchen and sat there till breakfast. The logic of the proceeding escapes me.

Today we have printed, & discussed the raid, which, according to the Star I bought was the work of 25 Gothas, attacking in 5 squadrons & 2 were brought down. A perfectly still & fine winter's day, so about 5.30 tomorrow morning perhaps –

Lady De Frece
from
The Recollections of Vesta Tilley

During the dreadful days of the War, when air raids were frequent, I was playing at the London Coliseum. We were staying at the Savoy Hotel at the time, in order to be near the theatre, and I shall never forget the fearful time we had getting to and from the theatre. The maroons would sound and my maid and I would rush to the nearest likely-looking shelter, dodge from that to another, until we made the stage door of the Coliseum.

Then came the night when the air raiders were actually over London. I was in my stage costume ready for my turn, when we heard the warnings to take cover. Dear Lily Langtry, who was playing at Coliseum at the time, and occupied the next dressing-room to me, was in a pitiable condition, as indeed were most of the people around me, but the orchestra stuck to their places and I dashed on to the stage and began my performance as though nothing was happening. It was a thrilling experience, but the audience remained seated, and I managed to entertain them for the best part of an hour.

Worse was to come. When we reached the Savoy, and were partaking of a light supper, the waiter told us the alarm had again been given, and we should take cover in the basement of the hotel. We hurried down to find the rest of the residents and staff already in the concrete cellars, and after a miserable half-hour or so the all-clear signal was given and we gradually drifted back to our respective rooms. My sitting-room faced the Embankment, almost directly opposite the building known as Savoy Mansions. It was a fine clear night, and I drew the curtains slightly and looked over the Thames. The maroons started again, and I saw quite plainly a machine flying overhead. At the same moment there was a terrific explosion and I was hurled across the room as the windows cracked and blew in. Luckily I was not hurt, just bruised. We all escaped, although my maid was in hysterics. After a pause, we went to the window again, and saw a ghastly sight.

A bomb had dropped on Savoy Mansions, cutting the building clean in two. We could see the remains of the rooms. Providence must have been watching over us that night. If the bomb had fallen a few seconds earlier would certainly have struck the part of the hotel in which my rooms were situated. I did not sleep much that night, and next day we learned of the havoc caused at Odhams Printing Works in Long Acre, and elsewhere.

Ethel Bilborough
Fearful Distorted Mechanical Birds

7th July 1917
There was the peculiar steady drone of the German engines – loud enough for they were very low down, and then came the furious banging of the machine guns showing that our aeroplanes had attacked the enemy & were doing their best to bring some down. Gracious heavens what next! A wild fight in the air thousands of feet above the earth – in things like fearful distorted mechanical birds (only with no beauty) which were circling round each other & engaged in deadly combat; dodging – swerving, diving and soaring, while sometimes they would be lost sight of in a cloud of smoke.

Phyllis Lunn
The Bombing of Scarborough

Tuesday night the 15th December 1914 saw us all going to bed gay and happy and full of eager anticipations of to-morrow, for the 16th was to be our Bazaar day. Our class rooms were all decorated with red, white and blue, our stalls laid out with many treasures of warm comforts for our brave soldiers and sailors, and in the larder were piles upon piles of gorgeous home-made cakes for our sale. At 9 o'clock the waits came and I waltzed round the room to their cheery music. Somehow we did not sleep too well that night, we all of us felt that something was going to happen. Gertrude said 'Something is in the air, I don't know what.'

It was very dark when we were called and we asked the maid most anxiously if breakfast were not a little later than usual, but the inexorable reply was 'Half-past eight miss.' About two minutes afterwards there was a terrific crash, we thought it must be a sudden thunder, though the 16th December seemed a queer time of year for it – but when another crash came we rushed to the window and saw a lot of smoke filling the road and we all cried out 'It is the Germans.' We knew what to do, to get down stairs at once to our basement cloakroom, known to many generations of High Cliffians as the 'Vacuum', so we seized our dressing gowns and rushed down, and within three minutes of that first awful crash the whole school, mistresses and girls, had assembled in that place of refuge. As we went down we heard loud reports, like great explosions, and the whole house shook as if it were coming down about our ears. Everything was perfectly quiet and orderly, we might have been going down to breakfast, the Heads were on the low stairs dressed and looking as if a bombardment were the most everyday occurrence, but I thought their voices sounded rather queer. We spent the time in dressing and consuming bread and butter, being awfully hungry. Two of the wee girls hung on to me and said 'It isn't the Germans going to kill us' and I said 'No, it is our own battleships practising' because I felt sure that they were there, and we thought some of the appalling hammering must be our guns replying to the Germans. Two of our girls had seen a cruiser fire a broadside, and a shell burst over the house next to ours before they fled downstairs. We were so thankful we all knew what to do or we might have rushed outside and been killed. It would not be true to say nobody was frightened, but we did not let anyone know it till afterwards.

The bombardment began at three minutes past eight because I had just looked at my watch, it was over about twenty-five minutes to nine. Directly it was over we went upstairs to wash and pack our handbags which were in readiness in our cubicles, then came breakfast, and some of us eat an excellent one. After breakfast we put our rooms in order, had prayers and sang the Doxology with all our hearts, then we put on our rose coats and caps and waited in the library singing 'It's a long long way to Tipperary', the Guides' song and 'Admirals All' till the Heads were ready to walk with us on the way to York. It was no use trying to get any train at that moment as the station was black with people fleeing, and we could get no carriages, the horses were mad with fear.

We walked along the road and saw many doors and windows gone and several great holes in the road where bombs had fallen. It was a glorious morning, the first day of real sunshine for long enough, the trams had broken down, the telegraph wires were lying about and we had here and there to pick our way over heaps of bricks and stones. We walked two or three miles, and then carriages overtook us and we had a grand drive to Weaverthorpe station; it was just like a picnic because when once the strain was over we thoroughly enjoyed ourselves. The Heads tried at every village to telegraph to our parents but it was impossible to send any news till we reached Malton.

We had such a gorgeous time at York that we were rather pleased than otherwise that we had been in the firing line, we did not know then that people had been killed. The postman bringing our letters had been killed at the house opposite.

We thought our Headmistresses were absolutely splendid, they kept everything going so peacefully and it was not till we got to our homes that we realized through what awful danger we had passed. Everyone was so kind to us and we do feel rather proud of having been under fire and of having got away scatheless. It is sad to think that in consequence of this bombardment we shall have to leave our beautiful Scarborough, and that next term our school has to be removed inland.

Winifred Holtby
from
The Crowded Street

Crash!

As though the fury of a thousand thunderbolts had hurried, crashing against the house, the noise shattered the morning and then ceased.

So swiftly the quietness closed in again, it seemed as though the sound were but a jagged rent across the silence, letting into the world for a moment the roaring of the spheres. Yet, though this one blow crashed and then was still, Muriel felt as though such violence must last for ever, and silence became the incredible thing.

She lay quite still, her limbs relaxed in the flat darkness of the bed, her arms lying beside her, heavy with sleep. She did not believe that the sound had really happened. Her thoughts returned to their path. If Godfrey had been a man like Martin Elliott, someone in whom one could seek companionship of mind, with whom one could feel as much at home as with one's own thoughts. ...

Crash! Crash! Crash!

It really had happened then.

It was not an illusion. She drew one hand across her forehead that felt damp and cold.

Of course this was what Uncle George had said would happen. The noise was the noise of guns, big guns firing. This was what the little pamphlets had told them to prepare for. This was the War. Only it had no business to happen so early in the morning before they were properly awake.

Crash! Crash!

Huge sounds, flat and ugly, dropped into the silence of the room. Slowly she turned and sat up in bed. Her curtains were drawn aside, but she could see nothing through her window. The panes looked as though they had been painted grey. Solid and opaque, the fog blotted out the sea.

It seemed absurd that this blinding, shattering immensity of sound should yet convey no impression to the eye.

She lay back in bed, her mind completely calm and rather listless, but she could feel the perspiration from her armpits soaking her nainsook nightgown. That was curious.

'Muriel! Muriel!'

In an interval of silence her mother's voice called to her. The door opened. Mrs. Hammond in her dressing-gown of padded lilac silk stood by the bed.

'Muriel, are you there? Are you all right?'

'Yes. Of course I am all right. What is it?'

She wished that her mother would go away and let her lie there quietly.

'Get up, get up. Come to my room. You mustn't lie there, facing the sea.' There was a sharp note of anxiety in her mother's voice.

Facing the sea. Why shouldn't she face the sea? Slowly Muriel thrust her feet out of bed, her toes twitching in the cold air as she felt for her slippers along the carpet.

'Quick, quick, never mind your slippers. Ah!'

Another sound broke about them, sharper than any before, as though the whole world had splintered into fragments round them. Muriel still fumbled below the bed.

'I can't find my slippers,' she said stupidly.

'Look!' gasped Mrs. Hammond.

Muriel looked at the window. The shattered edges of the panes still shivered in the wooden frame. On the floor below broken glass lay scattered. The noise had become visible at last.

After that, a series of odd and ridiculous things all happened very quickly. Uncle George appeared in his shirt-sleeves, with one side of his face lathered for shaving.

'I'm going to the Garbutts'. Their car must take Rose. Get her ready.'

Mrs. Hammond and Muriel hurried to Aunt Rose's room. Muriel always remembered afterwards kneeling by her aunt's bed and drawing cashmere stockings, two pairs, over those fat legs, where blue veins ran criss-cross below the tight-stretched skin. It seemed to her a fantastic sort of nightmare that could bring her to such close contemplation of her aunt's legs. Then Uncle George returned, and they all bundled Aunt Rose's shawls downstairs into the car, hoping that she was still inside them, for they could see nothing of her.

As the door opened, and Muriel saw the blank wall of fog along the Esplanade, she felt as though she were standing on the world's edge, staring into the din of chaos. All the time the vast noise pounded on above them.

Then they were all running, Uncle George, her mother and herself, down a grey funnel with tall looming sides. They stumbled in a little tripping run as one runs in a dream. Muriel tried to tell herself, 'This is an immense adventure. The Germans are landing at Cayton Bay under cover of the fog. Or they are on the foreshore. This noise is a bombardment from battleships to cover the landing, and we are running for our lives to Seamer Valley. This grey funnel is a street leading to Mount Road. I am running for my life and I am not afraid.'

The noise crashed above them through the fog, as though a grey curtain of sound had shut out the light. Little knots of people in peculiar attire appeared from the grey mists, and blew like wandering smoke along the alley, only to vanish again into vapour.

'In another moment,' Muriel told herself, 'we may all be dead.' But she could not make herself feel really interested in anything except her stockings, which were sliding to her ankles, and felt most uncomfortable. She would have liked to stop and fasten them, but she felt that it would somehow not be etiquette, to stop to fasten one's stockings in the middle of a race for life. 'I was not brought up to adventures,' she told herself. 'I don't yet know the way to manage them.'

Then her mother stopped. 'I – I can't – run – any – more,' she panted. Her small fat figure in its fur coat had been bouncing along in little hops, like an india-rubber ball. Now she stumbled and clung on to a railing for support. 'You – go – on. I'll come.'

'Draw a deep breath, Rachel, and count three,' said Uncle George solemnly. He performed Sandow's exercises every morning before breakfast and was therefore an athletic authority.

Muriel watched them, while the running figures stumbled past, quiet beneath a canopy of sound.

'You – go – on,' Mrs. Hammond repeated.

'Now, Rachel, go steady. Breathe as I count. One, two.'

They were not afraid, any of them. They had a strange, courageous dignity, these two comical little people, standing beneath the desolation of deafening clamour and breathing deeply. 'Mother,' thought Muriel, 'is thinking of Father.' Uncle George was thinking of Aunt Rose. Muriel was thinking about herself, and the strangeness of it all, and how she was not afraid. For there was something that made each one of them feel stronger than the fear of death.

A woman rushing along the pavement with her perambulator pushed it into Muriel and nearly knocked her over. She sobbed as she ran and the two babies in the perambulator were crying.

'This is real,' said Muriel to herself 'This is a really great adventure, and none of us know this minute where we shall be tomorrow and nothing matters like success or failure now, but only courage. This must be why the soldiers sing when they go to the trenches. It's all so beautifully simple.' She wanted to die then, when life was simple, rather than face

Marshington again and the artificial complications that entangled her life there.

An elation possessed her. She could have sung and shouted. She stumbled down the rough road again, holding her mother's arm and talking to her foolishly about what they would have for breakfast when they awoke from this strange dream. She remembered saying that she would have kippers, although she knew that she really hated them and rarely ate more than toast and marmalade. But then she didn't run for her life every morning before breakfast. She saw Seamer as some goal of human endeavour, very far away in the distance. It did not seem to be an ordinary place at all.

Suddenly from their feet, the Mere stretched, flat and lifeless beyond tall reeds, clouded like a looking-glass on which somebody has breathed. The noise grew louder. Somebody called, 'Turn to your right. Your right. They're firing straight in front.'

And even then, Muriel was not frightened. They wandered in a vague, irrelevant place among heaps of garbage, and cabbage stalks, and teapot lids, and torn magazine covers. Just to their left rose a little hovel, the crazy sort of shelter that allotment holders erect to hold their tools. She looked at it, blinking through the mist and noise, and then, suddenly, it was not there. It just collapsed and sank quietly down in a little cloud of smoke, hardly denser than the fog. It seemed appropriate to the absurd nightmare of the whole affair that a board on a post should grin to them out of the mist, saying, 'Rubbish may be shot here.'

'Ha, ha!' laughed Uncle George. 'They're shooting rubbish, and no mistake.'

And Mrs. Hammond pushed back her hair feebly with one free hand and laughed too.

Then they were all leaning over a gate, unable for the moment to run further. As though for their amusement, a grotesque and unending procession passed before them on the road to Seamer. There was a small child, leading a great collie dog that limped forlornly on three legs; an old man, leading two pretty young girls with greatcoats above their nightgowns, who giggled and shivered as they ran. There were little boys pushing wheelbarrows, and waggons holding school children, and motor-cars, and bicycles, and ladies in fur coats and lacy caps. Then a girls' school came trotting, two and two, in an orderly procession, laughing and chattering as they ran. Then more cars and cycles and donkey carts.

Nothing was quite normal except the girls' school. Every one else was a little fantastic, a little distorted, like people in a dream.

All the time on the other side of the road, the soldiers were passing into Scarborough, some marching, some swinging their legs from the back of motor-lorries, some flashing past on motor-cycles. As they passed, some of them cheered the procession leaving the town and called, 'Are we down-hearted?' And the refugees shouted 'No!' And some cried and sobbed as they ran, and some shouted back and some said nothing, but plodded on silently looking neither to the left nor right.

A cheerful, round-faced man in pyjamas and a woman's flannel dressing-jacket nodded at Uncle George.

'Heard the news?' he shouted. 'They've got into the town. That's why the firing has stopped. Our chaps are giving 'em hell. I'll give 'em half an hour until the fleet comes up.'

Everybody talked to everybody else. And Scarborough was said to be in flames, and our men were fighting all along the foreshore, where the little cheap booths stood in summer. While they talked, the mist seemed to break, and the steep hills of Seamer shouldered up from the tattered cloaks of fog.

It was just then that a lorry swung by down the road, and stopped for a moment, blocked by the crowd. The officer in charge stood up to see what had happened, and Muriel saw, standing very tall and clear against the hills of Seamer, her lord and master, Godfrey Neale. He had seen Muriel. Their eyes met, and for a moment they became conscious of nothing but each other. He smiled at her and stooped down from the lorry.

'You are all right?'

'Quite. We're going to Seamer. We shall be all right.'

She thought that he was going to his death, and then the thought came to her that she loved him. Here at last she had found all that she had been seeking. The fullness of life was hers, here on the threshold of death. She knew that it must always be so; and she lifted her head to meet love, unafraid.

'Good luck to you!' she called, and smiled to him across the road.

'Good luck!' he said.

The words came back to her, 'Good luck have thou with thine honour. Ride on because of the word of truth of meekness and righteousness, and thy right hand shall teach thee terrible things.'

The lorry swept him away along the road.

Winifred Kenyon
An Air Raid on Verdun

22 February, 1916.
Rumours of a German attack expected – anyhow all civilians had been evacuated from Verdun. Very heavy guns Weds eve, but nothing came of it. The weather was pretty bad so we said perhaps that had upset arrangements.

Then came yesterday. We had a plating case in the morning, and at 11 o'clock we were busy in the theatre, when we heard guns quite close. No doubt practising at Revigny we told ourselves, and went on with our work. Presently in rushed De Waru – 'Bosche aeroplanes, and we are firing at them' – we flew out to see the sky above dotted with aeroplanes – about ten we thought they must have been – and all about little tufts of white where the shells had burst. We heard something whistle through the air quite close to us, and afterwards we found the top of a shell in the garden, which was no doubt it. And that top is now in my possession. Little pieces of shell came down too, and I suppose we ought to have fled to the cellars, but we didn't, and no harm was done us. …

Half way down we saw two long beams of light quite close – from Revigny as it turned out. We stopped and watched. Then full in one beam, we saw a long sausage shaped thing – a Zeppelin! Both the lights got it and a third went up, also incendiary shells again – like rockets without tails those were. Did we hear a noise or didn't we? Was it the searchlight engine or the Zepp itself or guns?

Then 'it's hit!' We saw it crumple in the middle of one half, then that end dropped down, next moment it burst into flames, turned end up and slowly slowly dropped through the sky, lighting up everything, and leaving a long flaming trail behind it. Oh the excitement, it seemed too wonderful to be true, and the luck to have seen the whole thing from the beginning. We cheered and clapped and laughed and ran about quite mad for the moment.

Mary Ann Brown
The Evacuation of Gallipoli

9/8/15, Anzac.

I was on deck at 5 a.m. The guns woke me up then, the Tanks were doing their morning *hate*, it was continual Boom Boom & crack crack. The whole morning we watched the fighting through field glasses, we saw about 50 of our men leave this trench & |march| for the Turks.

Some of the battleships beside us kept up a continual fire with big guns … during the forenoon, shells fired by the Turks went right over our ship into the sea. What a wild & useless bit of country, so many lives are being lost for, … before we got breakfast, a boat load of wounded came along-side & all day the boats were bringing them over. We dressed nearly 1000. … We were hard at it *all day*, had no time to pay attention to the fighting. The whole thing is too ghastly to write about. … We had 640 bad cases on at midnight & we had to send away three boat loads that we had no room for. … As I am writing this the shells are going whistling over our heads, they don't worry me, the noise of the guns so close worries me more. I am dead tired. …

Mary Borden
Bombardment

Poetic

The wide sweet heaven was filling with light: the perfect dome of night was changing into day. A million silver worlds dissolved from above the earth: the sun was about to rise in stillness: no wind stirred.

A speck appeared in the great immensity. It was an aeroplane travelling *mysterious* high through the mysterious twilight. The sound of the whirring of its engine was lost in the depthless air: like a ghost it flew through the impalpable firmament: it was the only thing that moved in heaven and earth.

The unconscious map lay spread out beneath it: the wide plain, the long white beach and the sea, lay there exposed to its speeding eye.

On the face of the plain were villages and cities; the dwellings of men who had put their trust in the heavens and had dared to people the earth.

The aeroplane turned in the sky and began circling over the town.

Bomb is omniopent, god like   *people insignificant on the earth*

ghostly, eery

The town far below was asleep. It lay pillowed on the secure shore; violet shadows leaned against its pale buildings; there was no movement in its streets; no smoke from its chimneys. The ships lay still in the deep close harbour; their masts rose out of the green water like reeds thickly growing with the great funnels and turrets of the warships like strange plants among them. The sea beyond the strong breakwater was smooth as a silver plate; there was no sound anywhere.

The aeroplane descended in slow spirals upon the town, tracing an invisible path through the pearly air. It was as if a messenger from heaven were descending upon the people of the town who dreamed.

Suddenly a scream burst from the throat of the church tower. For an instant the sky seemed to shiver with the stab of that wail of terror rising from the great stone throat. Surely the town would waken in a panic – and yet, no, nothing stirred. There was no sound or movement in any street and the sky gave back no sign.

The aeroplane continued to descend until it looked from the church tower like a mosquito; then there dropped something from it that flashed through the air, a spark of fire.

Silence had followed the scream.

The aeroplane, superbly poised now in the spotless sky, watched the buildings below it as if waiting for some strange thing to happen; and presently, as if exorcised by the magic eye of the insect, a cluster of houses collapsed, while a roar burst from the wounded earth.

The bombardment had commenced. The big gun hiding in the sand-dunes in Belgium had obeyed the signal.

Still, the neat surface of the wide city showed no change, save in that one spot where the houses had fallen. How slow to wake the town was! The daylight brightened, painting the surfaces of the buildings with pale rose and primrose. The clean empty streets cut the city into firm blocks of buildings; the pattern of the town spread out on the earth, with its neat edges marked by walls and canals, gleamed like a varnished map.

Then the siren in the church tower screamed again; its wail followed by a second roar and a ragged hole yawned in the open square in the middle of the town.

The aeroplane circles smoothly, watching.

And at last signs of terror and bewilderment appeared in the human ant hill beneath it. Distracted midgets swarmed from the houses: this way and that they scurried, diving into openings in the ground: swift armoured beetles rushed through the streets; white jets of steam rose from the locomotives in the station yard: the harbour throbbed.

Bird's eye view

Again there was a great noise, and a cloud of debris was flung into the air as from a volcano, and flames leapt after it. A part of the wharf with a shed on it reeled drunkenly into the sea with a splash.

The white beach was crawling now with vermin; the human hive swarmed out on to the sands. Their eyes were fixed on the evil flying thing in the sky and at each explosion they fell on their faces like frantic worshippers.

The aeroplane cavorted, whirling after its tail in an ecstasy of self-gratification. Down among the sand dunes it could see the tiny black figures of men at the anti-aircraft guns. These were the defenders of the town; they had orders to shoot to death a mosquito floating in boundless heaven. The little clouds that burst in the sunlight were like materialised kisses.

The face of the city had begun to show a curious change. Scars appeared on it like the marks of smallpox and as these thickened on its trim surface, it seemed as if it were being attacked by an invisible and gigantic beast, who was tearing and gnawing it with claws and teeth. Gashes appeared in its streets, long wounds with ragged edges. Helpless, spread out to the heavens, it grimaced with mutilated features.

Nevertheless the sun rose, touching the aeroplane with gold, and the aeroplane laughed. It laughed at the convulsed face of the town, at the beach crawling with vermin, at the ant people swarming through the gates of the city along the white roads; it laughed at the warships moving out of the harbour one by one in stately procession, the mouths of their guns gaping helplessly in their armoured sides. With a last flick of its glittering wings, it darted downward defiant, dodging the kisses of shrapnel, luring them, teasing them, playing with them: then, its message delivered, its sport over, it flew up and away in the sunshine and disappeared. A speck in the infinite sky, then nothing – and the town was left in convulsions.

10

Medical care

Mary Borden

Conspiracy

It is all carefully arranged. Everything is arranged. It is arranged that men should be broken and that they should be mended. Just as you send your clothes to the laundry and mend them when they come back, so we send our men to the trenches and mend them when they come back again. You send your socks and your shirts again and again to the laundry, and you sew up the tears and clip the ravelled edges again and again just as many times as they will stand it. And then you throw them away. And we send our men to the war again and again, just as long as they will stand it; just until they are dead, and then we throw them into the ground.

It is all arranged. Ten kilometres from here along the road is the place where men are wounded. This is the place where they are mended. We have all the things here for mending, the tables and the needles, and the thread and the knives and the scissors, and many curious things that you never use for your clothes.

We bring our men up along the dusty road where the bushes grow on either side and the green trees. They come by in the mornings in compa-nies, marching with strong legs, with firm steps. They carry their knap-sacks easily. Their knapsacks and their guns and their greatcoats are not heavy for them. They wear their caps jauntily, tilted to one side. Their faces are ruddy and their eyes bright. They smile and call out with strong voices. They throw kisses to the girls in the fields.

We send our men up the broken road between the bushes of barbed wire and they come back to us, one by one, two by two in ambulances, lying on stretchers. They lie on their backs on the stretchers and are pulled out of the ambulances as loaves of bread are pulled out of the oven.

The stretchers slide out of the mouths of the ambulances with the men on them. The men cannot move. They are carried into a shed, unclean bundles, very heavy, covered with brown blankets.

We receive these bundles. We pull off a blanket. We observe that this is a man. He makes feeble whining sounds like an animal. He lies still; he smells bad; he smells like a corpse; he can only move his tongue; he tries to moisten his lips with his tongue.

This is the place where he is to be mended. We lift him on to a table. We peel off his trousers and his boots. We handle his clothes that are stiff with blood. We cut off his shirt with large scissors. We stare at the obscene sight of his innocent wounds. He allows us to do this. He is helpless to stop us. We wash off the dry blood round the edges of his wounds. He suffers us to do as we like with him. He says no word except that he is thirsty and we do not give him a drink. We confer together over his body and he hears us. We discuss his different parts in terms that he does not understand, but he listens while we make calculations with his heart beats and the pumping breath of his lungs.

We conspire against his right to die. We experiment with his bones, his muscles, his sinews, his blood. We dig into the yawning mouths of his wounds. Helpless openings, they let us into the secret places of his body. We plunge deep into his body. We make discoveries within his body. To the shame of the havoc of his limbs we add the insult of our curiosity and the curse of our purpose, the purpose to remake him. We lay odds on his chances of escape, and we combat with death, his Saviour.

It is our business to do this. He knows and he allows us to do it. He finds himself in the operating room. He lays himself out. He bares himself to our knives. His mind is annihilated. He pours out his blood unconscious. His red blood is spilled and pours over the table on to the floor while he sleeps.

After this, while he is still asleep, we carry him into another place and put him to bed. He awakes bewildered as children do, expecting, perhaps, to find himself at home with his mother leaning over him, and he moans a little then lies still again. He is helpless, so we do for him what he cannot do for himself, and he is grateful. He accepts his helplessness. He is obedient. We feed him, and he eats. We fatten him up, and he allows himself to be fattened. Day after day he lies there and we watch him. All day and all night he is watched. Every day his wounds are uncovered and cleaned, scraped and washed and bound up again. His body does not belong to him. It belongs to us for the moment, not for long. He knows why we tend him so carefully. He knows what we are fattening and cleaning it up for;

and while we handle it he smiles.

He is only one among thousands. They are all the same. They let us do with them what we like. They all smile as if they were grateful. When we hurt them they try not to cry out, not wishing to hurt our feelings. And often they apologise for dying. They would not die and disappoint us if they could help it. Indeed, in their helplessness they do the best they can to help us get them ready to go back again.

It is only ten kilometres up the road, the place where they go to be torn again and mangled. Listen; you can hear how well it works. There is the sound of the cannon and the sound of the ambulances bringing the wounded, and the sound of the tramp of the strong men going along the road to fill the empty places.

Do you hear? Do you understand? It is all arranged just as it should be.

Dr Elsie Inglis

The Tragedy of Serbia

Looking back, the day we went to Lazaravatz in October seems typical of all the time we were in Serbia. We left Kragujevatz in the motor ambulance given to the Scottish Women's Hospitals by Welsh Suffragists. The day was one of brilliant sunshine – a glorious Serbian autumn day, but on the horizon hung black clouds, ominous and threatening. Hill and valley stood out in the bright, clear light, and the shadows chased one another across the landscape. Never had that beautiful country looked so beautiful. The woods and hedgerows glowed with the reds and yellows of the falling year, and the air had a sharp nip in it, very pleasant after the hot summer. Peace seemed to brood over the whole land; but all the time that black bank of cloud hung threatening above us, and after we left Topola it broke in a downpour of rain. In a very few minutes the road was a slithering mass of mud. Then the darkness came on and we suddenly skidded, not for the first time. Well for us that we had Miss Holm as chauffeur; just before lay one of the worst hills in Serbia, and though we were only about eleven kilometres from Lazaravatz we called a halt, hauled the car to the side of the road, and settled down for the night. Gradually the thunder of the rain on the roof lessened, and then we became aware of another sound – the boom, boom of distant cannon. Another storm was breaking

over Serbia, a storm that swept through the land and wiped out, that gallant little nation. For the guns we heard were bombarding Belgrade.

When we reached Serbia in May, she was lying in the sunshine. Two
storms had raged over her during the preceding months – the Austrian
invasion, and the terrific typhus epidemic. In our safe little island we can
hardly realise what either meant. In the end of 1914 the Austrian Empire
hurled its 'punitive expedition' across the Danube, a 'punitive expedition'
that ended in the condign punishment of the invader. But they left behind
them a worse foe than themselves, and the typhus which began in the
hospitals they left so scandalously filthy and overcrowded, swept over the
land.

Then came the long, peaceful summer, with the shadows of probable
advance chasing one another across the scene. The advance was always
coming – in ten days, in a fortnight, once in three days. One long threatening shadow was the report of the 'secret' treaty with Italy, which was to
give her, in return for her help, the stretch of country along the Adriatic,
inhabited by Serbs, which the Serbs looked on as not only theirs by right,
but of necessity, for it was becoming increasingly evident that they must
have an outlet to the sea. One Serbian woman said to me, bitterly, 'But
what does it matter what a little nation like us feel. You Great Powers are
settling it over our heads.' But that passed. The undying hopefulness of
the Serb could not long believe in any real final disaster, and they were
conscious that the 'Great Powers' owed them much. How often we heard
the words, said with such childlike pride and confidence, 'We are the only
one, as yet, who has beaten our enemy.' They knew what that beating had
cost them, and they knew too how much it had helped in the weakening
the line against Russia.

Not till September did any real sense of danger trouble them. Then the
clouds rolled up black and threatening on the horizon – Bulgaria arming,
and a hundred thousand Germans massing on their northern frontier.
They began to draw off the main part of their army from the Danube
towards the East to meet their old enemies. The Powers refused to let
them attack, and they waited till the Bulgarian mobilisation was complete. The Allies discounted the attack from the North; aeroplanes had
been out, and 'there are no Germans there.' 'There are no signs whatever
of any military movements,' so said the wiseacres. 'The only troops there
are untrained Austrian levies, which the Serbs ought to be able to deal
with themselves, if they are up to their form last year.'

Then the storm broke. The 100,000 Germans appeared on the Northern Frontier. The Bulgars invaded from the East, the Greeks did not come

in, and the Austrians poured in from the West. The Serbian Army short-
ened the enormous line they had to defend, but they could not stand
against the long-distance German guns, and so began to retreat.

Terror and despair were seen everywhere, despair for their dear Fatherland. 'What is coming to Serbia,' said a Serb to me, 'we cannot think!' and
then, hopefully, 'But God is great and powerful, and our Allies are great
and powerful too,' – a distribution of attributes that was almost startling
in its exact equality. Strong men could hardly speak of the disaster without breaking down. They looked at one so eagerly. 'When are your men
coming up?' they said. 'They must come soon.' 'We must give our people
two months,' the experts among us answered, 'to bring up the heavy
artillery.' We thought the Serbs would be able to hold the West Morava
Valley. 'It is too hilly for the German artillery to be of any use,' they said.
And the Serbs in their stormy history have, it is true, often made a stand
there. All hospitals and wounded were moved down; but again the calculations were wrong, for it was down this very valley that the Austrian
forces came. The Serbs were caught in a veritable trap, and that 160,000
of their gallant little Army was able to escape is a wonderful feat, and that
they already are keen to take the field again is but one more proof of the
extraordinary recuperative power of the nation.

The Scottish Women's Hospitals sent out their first unit to Serbia in
December, 1914, and it arrived just in time for the work following on the
great Serbian victories. A surgical hospital was opened in Kragujevatz – a
hospital perfectly equipped and adequately staffed, which did excellent
work up to the moment it was evacuated during the retreat in October,
1915. Within a fortnight of its arrival, however, our Committee received
a telegram asking for more doctors and more nurses. 'Dire necessity,' said
the telegram; and later we heard that the word 'dire' had been used in the
hope that the Censor would not know what it meant, for at that time the
authorities did not want the enemy to know to what a plight the country
had been reduced by typhus. We shall never know what the death rate was
during that epidemic; but this we know, that of the 425 doctors in Serbia,
125 died of the disease, and that two-thirds of the remainder had it. That
gives some idea of its ravages among the population. Gradually letters
came through telling of the terrible condition of the hospitals, of the dirt
and over-crowding, telling of the constant stream of funerals, of illness
and death among the personnel of the Foreign unit. Dr. Soltau, to her
undying credit, with her small staff, and, for the enormous work, her
inadequate equipment, took over No. 6 and No. 7 Reserve Hospitals, and
she and her doctors and nurses did yeoman service. The Scottish Com-

mittee hastened out supplies, doctors and sisters. For three months the epidemic raged, and all women may ever be proud of the way those women worked. It was like a long-drawn-out battle, and not one of them played the coward. Not one of them asked to come away. There were three deaths and nine cases of illness among the unit; and may we not truly claim that those women who died gave their lives for the great cause for which our country stands to-day as any man in the trenches?

Other British units took their full share of the work, notably Lady Paget's Hospital at Skopio, where two great blocks of barracks were taken over and equipped, and magnificently organized. Lady Paget herself later fell ill from the disease. Mr Berry's unit made their hospital a triumph in its sanitary arrangements. The British Red Cross unit, too, under Dr Banks, took more than its share of the burden. The comment of the man in charge of the American Hospital at Belgrade, Dr Ryan, was that Serbia would have been wiped out if it had not been for the work of the Foreign Missions.

There were several Commissions sent out by the Governments of the Allied Powers – a French Commission. which later undertook the inoculation of the whole country for enteric, and a British Commission under Colonel Hunter, which arrived during the typhus epidemic, and which did splendid service outside the hospitals in improving the sanitary conditions of the country, and by carrying out the disinfection of men coming down from the infected area in the north. They also inoculated the whole army against cholera, with such good results that not a case occurred in Serbia during the whole summer. The American Commission, under Dr Strong, arrived in April, with the whole wealth of the Rockefeller Institute at their backs, and they, the French, and the British, divided the country into three sections for sanitary purposes. By May the epidemic was practically over.

A scheme was developed for forming medical hospitals close behind the Army to block up any infectious disease that might break out and prevent it spreading all over the country as the typhus had done. The Scottish Women's Hospitals were asked by Colonel Grutitch, Head of the Serbian Army Medical Department, to undertake two of these hospitals, one at Valjevo, and one at Mladenovatz, both under canvas.

To Mladenovatz we sent the unit that had been working at No. 6 Reserve Hospital, Dr Beatrice McGregor being sent out from home to take charge. We were given a fine site, above the village of Mladenovatz, with a glorious view across to the Kosmaj, the mountain which gives its name to one of the battles of the autumn before. Mrs Haverfield, our able

Administrator, planned out the camp, and it was in all its arrangements worthy of being a British Camp Hospital. Colonel Grutitch had asked for 400 beds, but it was never found necessary to open more than 200, the summer was so healthy. The Hospital was close behind the Second Army, and through the whole summer took in ordinary medical cases: malaria, relapsing fever, rheumatism, and pneumonia. To Valjevo was sent the Second Scottish Unit, under Dr Alice Hutchinson, who had already made a name for herself in Calais as an organizer and physician. It also was under canvas, and came out expecting to nurse typhus. However, long before it reached Serbia the typhus epidemic was over, for when it arrived in Malta it was commandeered by Lord Methuen, the Governor of the Island, to help with the pressure of cases from the Dardanelles.

The Hospital at Valjevo was all that we expected it to be under such a chief, and Sir Ralph Paget, the British Commissioner in Serbia, to whom all the Red Cross work in Serbia, and especially the British Hospitals owe so much, wrote that he had 'nothing but praise' for it. It was a beautiful camp, perfect in every detail. Dr Hutchinson used to be found prowling about the camp at 5.30 in the morning. She said it was an excellent time to 'find out things that were wrong.' Naturally, under these circumstances, there was seldom anything wrong in that camp. Their 200 beds were also filled with medical cases – these from the first army. Five cases of paratyphoid occurred among the staff, and Sister Sutherland died. She was buried in the quiet little cemetery above the town – another life given in a great cause. The hospital was sent out with a laboratory, very completely equipped, Dr Porter in charge, and it was of use far beyond that of its own confines of Valjevo.

We thus had three hospitals at work, the original hospital at Kragujevatz, which had gone on steadily with its surgical work, through all vicissitudes. Dr Chesney and Dr Laird worked there untiringly all through the summer, mainly occupied with old cases of wounds, badly treated or neglected during the *sturm und drang* that followed on the great battles of the preceding December. The little hospital with its hundred and fifty beds was one of the most perfect hospitals in Serbia. A modern operating theatre was made, with a concrete floor, and white walls oil-painted. It was furnished almost entirely with things made on the spot; for instance, the iron stands for the basins were made at the Arsenal and the instrument cupboard by the local carpenter. The X-ray room could have held its own with any X-ray room in Europe, and the work done there by Dr. Macdougal was excellent.

Then we were asked to undertake a new scheme. All these three hospitals were our own Scottish Women's hospitals, carried on in our own way and equipped by our own Committee. But now we were asked to staff a Serbian hospital, using their equipment, and running on their lines. Sir Ralph Paget approved very highly of the idea, and thought much could be achieved if it could be widely carried out. He promised to supplement the equipment, and so did Colonel Soubetitch, Head of the Serbian Red Cross. The plan was possible at the moment, because owing to the Mladenovatz Hospital not requiring its full four hundred beds, we had doctors and sisters who could be spared. The first invitation came from Jagodina, but Colonel Grutitch negatived this, and sent the contingent to Lazaravatz. Dr Holloway was chief medical officer and Mrs Haverfield administrator, Lazaravatz was the railway line between Mladenovatz and Valjevo. It is a village, and had been the centre of one of the great battles. The houses still showed the signs of bombardment. The hospital was scattered through the village in the gasthouses (inns), or in ordinary dwellings. When we first went there it had about four hundred cases, chiefly medical. We took over about half of these, and the store and laundry. Later we made arrangements for opening a dressing-room at the station and a surgical hospital with a theatre, Colonel Soubetitch supplying us with the steriliser, instruments, &c., from the Red Cross stores at Nish. It was obvious that all these hospitals on the branch line to Valjevo would be forced to undertake surgical work, if there was fighting on the Danube, and with the continued rumours of an advancement of a German attack, we hastened to develop this side of all the centres. The Committee sent out Dr. and Mrs Hope to Valjevo as surgeons, and a full surgical equipment to Mladenovatz.

Our only thought was that of a victorious campaign on the Danube, and we congratulated ourselves that all three hospitals, placed as they were, could perform real service to the Serbian Army. Then the black bank of clouds on the horizon began to roll up, and broke like a devastating storm over the whole country.

The first of our hospitals to be moved was Mladenovatz. They got their orders on the Sunday, and by Tuesday evening their whole equipment was packed and on the train, a feat of which the whole unit, and their administrator, Miss Pares, may well be proud. By Colonel Grutitch's orders they came to Kragujevatz, took over the Artillery Barracks, and opened a dressing station and hospital of 600 beds for the slightly wounded. At the same time the Valjevo unit got order to prepare to evacuate the hospital there, and towards the end of the week they moved to Poshega at the western end of the West Morava Valley, thence to Nevatzha Bania.

The English Missions were all gradually being collected in this valley, and the wounded who could move were sent there also, to Charchak.

To our surprise the hospital at Lazaravatz got no orders to move, and the unit as a whole sincerely hoped they had been forgotten, for they one and all wanted to hold on to the post as they stood. Suddenly, however, a week later they also got orders to move to Kruchevatz at the eastern end of the valley, at the junction of the broad and narrow gauge lines of railway.

At the time we were puzzled as to why Mladenovatz which was at the one end of the Valjevo line, and Valjevo itself at the other should have been so quickly evacuated, while Lazaravatz which lay between the two should be left. However, later on it became clear. Mladenovatz, which was on the direct line from Belgrade, had obviously to be cleared as soon as Belgrade fell. Valjevo was evacuated because the Serbs withdrew from that district – without fighting – in order to shorten their enormous front, while Lazaravatz lay just behind the ridge of hills where they hoped to make a stand.

As has been said, however, it was impossible for the Serbs to stand caught as they were between three fires, and the Lazaravatz Hospital got a few hours' notice to move. They got away bringing all their wounded and their entire equipment complete. The lines were blocked with transport and refugees, and after a three days' journey of incredible discomfort and delay arrived at Kruchevatz and were sent up to the Serbian Military Hospital.

Meantime Dr MacGregor's unit was moved to Kraljevo, a place about the centre of the West Morava Valley, where she opened another dressing station on the same lines as Kragujevatz.

During all this time the Surgical Hospital at Kragujevatz was full to overflowing. Dr Chesney cleared the hospital as soon as the wounded from Belgrade began to arrive, all those who could move being evacuated to Charchak. The 125 beds we had run all through the summer increased to 150, and as the cry was still for more beds, we filled the corridors, packed the wards and reached 175. One Director, Major Protitch, urged us to put three men in two beds, but this we decided against as long as possible. We took over two gasthouses, 140 beds in all, and into them we moved each morning every case which needed only dressing, not nursing. Matron took over the supervision of these buildings, they were cleaned and warmed, and a sufficient supply of blankets provided. Men who had been the spoilt children of the hospital during the long quiet summer did not in any way approve of the change, 'Ne dobra' [not good], they said to us reproachfully when we went in.

As far as possible we kept every wounded man in for twenty-four hours before sending him to the gasthouses or Charchak. Occasionally men with obviously slight wounds were sent straight to the gasthouses. The men came in batches from the train, any number from fifteen to, on one day, seventy. They went straight to the bathroom on arrival, and then in their clean unbleached cotton pyjama suits – which the Serbs prefer to any others for hospital garb – to the Priialista – or room for dressings – and then to their comfortable beds in the wards. Bad cases went straight to the wards, and were washed and dressed there. And so we solved the problem as far as our own little bit of it was involved. We never refused a case, we never got unmanageably overcrowded, and we never got dirty. Dr. Curcin, under whose kindly care all the Foreign Missions worked in Serbia, thought we were going to fail when he heard that we would not put three men in two beds. 'That,' he said, 'is the difference between the Serbian and English point of view. The Serbs take in every case that comes, and the hospitals, it is true, will get dirty and overcrowded, but all the men will be in. But the English will only take in as many as they can properly manage, and they will be beautifully nursed and cared for, and the rest will remain in the street.' Which shows how difficult it is for even a sympathetic admirer to understand another nation. We exclaimed in horror, 'But that is exactly what would not happen. Nobody lies in the street under English management.' 'What would you do, then?' he asked. There were about 3000 wounded in Kragujevatz at the moment, and what we would do, with true British muddleheadedness, we could not say. After all, it is difficult to solve a problem when even the stating of it was not given. But we solved it practically in our own little corner.

We hoped against hope that we would not be moved from Kragujevatz. But the experts told us that is was a good tactical move to place all the hospitals in the West Morava Valley, where base hospital would be useful till the Allies came up; and when we got our orders to evacuate on October 23rd, we obeyed. All the wounded who could move were sent to Charchak, and the others left with three Serbian doctors, Major Protitch in charge, at Kragujevatz.

We left on the afternoon of the 25th, all our equipment – thanks to the energy of Mr Smith – our excellent Secretary – being saved. About twenty men were left in hospital, – and after everything was packed and gone, one patient had a severe secondary haemorrhage. Not a single instrument was still unpacked, and the only thing to do was to put on a tourniquet and send him up to the Military Hospital. Two of the sisters volunteered to stay behind and do the day's dressings; and the four of us left by the evening train, Mr Smith having refused to go until the whole unit was out before him. Just before we started we ran back with cigarettes for the men. Such a changed place the little hospital was, untidy with the morning's packing, the ward in which the remaining cases had been collected already dirty, only untrained Serbian orderlies in charge, for the Austrian orderlies with whom we had worked all the summer had been sent southwards. One man with a fractured femur and with extension apparatus applied was sitting up, taking off his bandage. Another man with both feet amputated and paralysed on one side was sitting in the corridor singing at the top of his voice. We vowed that nothing would induce us again to leave patients for whom we were responsible until they were well.

So ended our work in Serbia *free*. It seemed to some of us impossible to leave her in the hour of her catastrophe. We had come out to help, and now that our help was most needed it was our clear duty to stand by. Sir Ralph Paget gave his consent to those staying who wished to. It was the good fortune of some of us that we were able to work for Serbs in a Serbian hospital, as long as there were Serbs to work for. Others of us, who desired only the same lot, were fated to spend dreary weeks as prisoners in Austria.

If we had learnt to love the Serbs, during the quiet summer days, for their gentleness and courtesy, for their generosity towards us, and their idealism, in those hard dark times that followed we came to admire them still more for their grit and their pluck and their wonderful power of rebound. They have their very obvious faults, the faults of any people who have spent five hundred years under Turkish domination. But remember, during all those five hundred years, each year they kept as a fast day the anniversary of the battle of Kossovo – that day on which they lost their independence. And when at last they threw off the Turkish yoke, that day was still observed, no longer now with fasting, but with feasting. A people with such a vivid sense of nationality, with such unquestioned courage behind it, must ultimately win through. 'What we are fighting for,' they used to tell us, 'is for liberty. Six millions of us are free now, but thirteen millions are not, and all Serbs must be free.'

In the hospital at Krushevatz, in the middle of the night on their New Year's Eve – our 12th of January – we were wakened by the shouting of the Serbian National Hymn by a score of young Serbian voices. And the Austrian Guards were standing outside the windows. Worthy sons, indeed, these Serbs, of the men who through the long, dark centuries still remembered the time when Serbia was free.

Margaret Fawcett
from
First World War Papers, 'Extracts from my letters'

Monday July 16 1917. Reni.

I have just started my month's night duty. Lady Decies is in charge, and I am the second. We have had quite a busy time; if it is like this all the time, we shall not be dull. To start with, five sisters arrived from 'B' Hospital and had to be fed. They were very bad tempered, as they had had to walk from the station.

Now we have had something far more exciting – a soldier walked in with his arm in a sling and looking like a ghost. He was so ill that I fetched Dr Laird. After she had come, I took the bandages off his arm, and found that more than half his arm had been blown away. He had been shot by a sentry. His arm is to be amputated directly after roll-call in the morning.

Dr Inglis is in Odessa trying to arrange matters with the Serbs. It is possible that we shall go to the Galician front.

Afternoon, Tuesday July 17. When I finished my letter last night our adventures were by no means over. After the poor boy had been in bed for about an hour he started to haemorrhage. I fetched Dr Laird, and she said that she would amputate at once, so I fetched the theatre sister and Murphy for the anaesthetic, and the operation took place at 4 a.m. It was my first op, and I thoroughly enjoyed it.

It is just too difficult for words, sleeping in the daytime, because of the heat.

Wednesday July 25 1917. S.W.H. Reni.

The firing at the front has been going on steadily for the last three days and nights. We can distinctly see the flashing from the bursting shells after dark.

Our two Armoured Car men will be leaving us soon – we shall be awfully sorry to lose them, as they are both very nice boys. We hear that their people have had a good many casualties lately.

Tuesday August 7 1917. S.W.H. Reni.

I am still on night duty, and am getting rather tired. It is too hot to sleep in my tent this evening, so I am lying outside in my pyjamas trying to get cool. My night duty is nearly over. Matron, who is an awful idiot, will try and persuade me to go on with it as I know the work. That is the sort of reason she gives for everything she does. On the whole I have quite enjoyed my time, although days when they operate at five in the morning – the only cool part of the day, and just at my busiest time – are not nice. They are operating tomorrow morning – bother them.

We are still waiting for orders from the Serbs. They may be coming down to this front.

Yesterday we had the biggest thunderstorm we have had at all. Murphy and I were down by the Danube. For a long time we sat under a willow tree hoping that the torrents of rain would stop, and getting wetter and colder every minute. Finally we decided to make a bolt for it. By the time we got to the hospital we looked as though we had fallen into the Danube. As we came back the water was tearing down the hill in mighty torrents. We have always wondered what made the huge gorges that are all along the steppe and lead into the valleys – we imagined it must be the thaw after the snow. However, when we saw the thaw it was quite gentle, and not nearly enough to cut gorges – but now we see that it is thunderstorms that cause the damage.

Friday August 17 1917. S.W.H. Reni.
There is no time for a long letter today, as we are in the midst of an immense rush of work – there are two hundred and twenty cases in hospital, all badly wounded, and every precious minute off duty has to be spent in sleep. Wright and I are in charge of the Dressing Room, a very strenuous but very interesting job. The first day of the rush, the day after I came off night duty, we did sixteen hours, with barely time for meals. Now [that] things are settling down a bit and people are getting used to working in double quick time, we have arranged to divide our work into shifts so things will not be so strenuous. The cases are by far the worst we have had since we have been here, and we get a huge percentage of deaths. This is very depressing, but is due to the fact that the majority of cases are men who are too ill to be sent on – those who are not so seriously ill are sent on to Odessa. On an average since the rush we have evacuated about twenty slight cases per day and admitted as many serious ones. You can imagine how the number of bad dressings to be done every day accumulates. We have all four of our doctors here, so dressings go on all the time. Whilst the 'B' Hospital doctors operate, our own do dressings, and vice versa.

My last letters from you were dated Feb. and March. This you will observe was the time of the first Revolution. We were told at the time that they were keeping our letters in Petrograd so they needn't censor them.

Sunday August 26 1917. S.W.H. Reni.

At last there is a lull in the work. For the last fortnight we have been rushed to death with as many as two hundred wounded in at a time. This meant that, besides the usual hundred beds in the hospital, we had eight big marquees full. Then we were evacuating every day, so that there were more than two hundred dressings to be done every day. Dr Laird and Dr Ward were simply splendid, and ripping to work for; they worked all day and much of the night. For about a week this was their programme:

8 – 10	Dressings
10 – 12	Operations
12 – 12.30	Lunch
12.30 – 4.30	Dressings
6 – 7.30	Operations

Then after supper they dressed all the new cases that came in.

The new patients hardly ever started to arrive till after supper when we were supposed to have finished work. This meant all the bathing and everything had to be done that night. One night the day sanitars refused to stay on and help with the bathing and stretcher bearing; and as there were only perhaps half a dozen night sanitars for the whole hospital, we set to and did all the bathing ourselves. For stretcher bearers we had to rely on an ex-patient named Andrea, who often helped us, a Russian Jew who was our accountant at the time, and two of the Austrian prisoners, who came on without a murmur.

I unfortunately had to take a day off duty in the middle of the rush with malaria, which was particularly unfortunate as all the sisters were new.

Today and tomorrow we have to evacuate the entire hospital, as we have orders to join the Serbian Division at Hadji Abduli, a place half way between here and Bolgrad. This is very trying – we have been at Reni for eight months with really hardly enough to keep us busy, and now that there is lots of work to be done, we have to leave.

The other day I was desperate for a swim, so attached myself to one end of a long bandage, and got someone to hold the other end, and went in. It was ripping.

To show you how well we are being fed, I will give you a typical day's menu.

Breakfast. Two eggs, black bread and real butter, tea and sugar.
Dinner. Meat; two vegetables; pudding.
Tea. Scones; home-made blackberry or plum jam.
Supper. Meat dish; pudding.

The fleas are terrible. I caught eighteen in my sleeping bag this morning, but one morning after a night in hospital Armstrong caught eighty-two. We never see them on the men, so they must come out of the wood.

The Germans in hospital have been most troublesome – they treat us like dirt under their feet. The only decent one among them died.

Eleanora Pemberton
Casualties

To Dad. 2/11/14

That night we took in 26 new cases which filled up our 40 beds and they all had to be undressed and washed ready for the doctors. It took us till about 2.30 as it is not a quick job when you have to be so careful about moving them and also when you have to change the water about 4 times for each case on account of the grime. Most of the men had not washed for weeks, many had their socks sticking to their feet, all the clothes were filthy, clotted with blood and very odoriferous and it was just a joy to get them off and the poor fellows a bit clean and fairly comfortable, but it brought *war* home to one in a way that nothing else, short of the actual battlefield could. The horrible, horrible side of war which sent us these travesties of the fine, strong husbands, fathers, lovers, sons who had gone forth so proudly how short a time ago. When you turn down the blanket to wash an arm and find no arm only a soaking bandage that was once white, or you go to feed 'no. 14' and find that he has only half a face and cannot swallow but tries to speak and you strain to understand. It fills you with a fury against the devillish ingenuity which conceived the perfection of the weapons which have caused this devastation and a loathing of the man who set loose these fiends of hell.

Mary Clarke
After the Battle of Jutland

2nd June 1916.

News at last & of the most exciting kind! We received orders early to proceed down to the Forth Bridge & prepare to take in patients as the ships come in. There has been a tremendous battle & I am afraid we have lost a good many ships, including some say the 'Queen Mary', but I do hope that is not true.

As we got to anchor the ships began to come in, the Lion, the Tiger, the Princess Royal, the Southampton, the Birmingham, the Birkenhead ... [the Inconstant] who was to have been our next appointment besides Destroyers, etc., etc., steamed passed us & our crew gave them cheer on cheer. They did not look much the worse except for a few ominous looking holes, but inside some of them had been inferno but a few short hours before. Crowded on the decks in most varied rig, were survivors from the poor lost ships. The men all looked cheery even at that hour & one could hardly believe all that they must have gone through. I much regret that I did not take any photographs as they came in, but we were expecting patients at any moment, so did not dare go away.

Soon they began to arrive, drifters by the dozen six or seven deep on the port and starboard sides waiting to unload their sad burdens. Poor men, they almost all had their faces and hands tied up. We started about 11 & by 12.30 had taken in over 100 & they said the worse ones, at least 90 cot cases, were still to come. We got them into bed as quickly as possible, no easy job sometimes, and fed them with beef tea & the bad ones with brandy and left them to settle down a bit before we attempted their dressings. We rushed & snatched a little lunch as we could, then the bad cases began to come in, poor things it was pitiful to see some of them, with legs off & arms off, & some fearfully burnt, face, arms, legs & body. We even had destroyers up alongside discharging patients directly on board. A tremendous thunder storm came on in the afternoon, which didn't assist matters as everything got wringing wet; by about 3.30 they were all on board with the exception of a few isolated cases, so we were able to get to work & see what we had got.

I had the most in my ward with 46 acute cases besides the supervision of 'B' which was full up too. We started about 5 to do the dressings, Dr Iles, Dr Aitken, Ward S.B.S. & myself with one St John's man each to wait on us & each took so many beds to do. Some of the poor things hadn't been touched since wed[nesday] night when the first fight took place & had only the first picnic dressings on their burns. It must have been agonies taking the dressings off, but very few of them made a moan. I never saw such bravery in my life.

We worked hard until about 11 with a short interval for dinner. Dr Aitken was called away to give anaesthetics as poor Jordan had about 10 cases in the theatre from various wards, besides her own to look after. Happily I only had one officer, gas poisoning & not very bad, or I don't know how I should have got done, but they all went to Lady Beatty's yacht the 'Sheila', which took only officers, including Sub-Lieut. Miller from the P.R.

3rd June.
The smell of burns is awful, one gets almost nauseated sometimes, but Dr Iles is using Eucalyptus & olive oil, so that is taking away the worst of it. The poor things have nearly all to be fed as nearly all have both hands tied up & masks on their faces & their poor eyes are so bad in most cases, it takes a long time.

4th June.
I am thankful! & more thankful that we happened to be here & got all the work ... After waiting all through the war for 'the Day' I should have been sick if we had missed it, or it had come after I left the Ship.

Irene Rathbone
from
We That Were Young

The dressing proceeded.

And the next, and the next, and the next. From bed to bed all morning. Lifting and holding mangled limbs; wringing out fomentations; carting away dirty dressings; washing, boiling, trundling the trolley up and down the ward; keeping alert to be Sister's second pair of hands, her other half, to divine what she wanted almost before she knew herself, to be, in fact, the perfect V.A.D.

There was McIvor, the jaw-case, who, when his innumerable and complicated bandages were removed, revealed flat holes plugged with gauze where a nose had been, and pendulous shapeless lips. The stench which rushed forth as the last dressings dropped off was just humanly endurable, and only just. It had an acrid, putrefying quality, unlike that from other wounds. McIvor sat up in bed against his mass of pillows, and gave little grunts – he couldn't form his words. He was stouter and older than the other men, and was known by those on either side of him as 'Dad.' But that did not necessarily mean that he was very old, only that most of the British Army at that time was in the heyday of youth. Anyone over thirty was apt to be called 'Dad.'

With the forceps Sister slowly pulled out the two twists of pus-dripping gauze from the nose-holes, and dropped them into the dish held by Joan. One side of the jaw was a mass of little broken bones and teeth. The cheek was swollen like a bloated orange. The whole thing had to be most carefully irrigated, and very little water used at a time so that it could be coughed out again. Finally, he was plugged up with clean gauze and bandaged. The bandaging was a miracle of competence on Sister Ewart's part. Joan watched admiringly. Openings were left for the eyes, and a larger opening for the mouth; otherwise the head was a white ball.

Joan often thought about McIvor, that whatever expression had been obliterated around his mouth leapt into his eyes – eyes that were questioning and fearful at the same time. And she was always aware, too late, of having registered the horror for those pathetic eyes to devour – no doubt wounding his spirit afresh.

Then there was Turner with a smashed right arm, and Tubbs with a smashed left arm – each arm bound to a padded rectangular splint. They lay in neighbouring beds, and ragged each other the whole time.

There was Sergeant King with his left leg amputated within an inch or two of the hip, who kept his lips in a thin line and never uttered a word. He was six feet tall, and belonged to the famous '29th' – last year in Gallipoli, this year in France.

And lastly there was little O'Leary, not wounded, but badly burnt by liquid fire.

Little O'Leary, aged nineteen, made no attempt at heroics – either of the grim or of the joking sort – while he was being dressed. His whole body was a mass of burns; and piece by piece the lint had to be peeled off him while he whimpered like a rabbit, and slow tears ran down his cheeks. It took endless time and patience, and the smell here was of another order – the stomach-heaving smell of charred flesh. As each bit of lint was removed a new bit, coated thick with boracic ointment, was instantly applied; for under these conditions it was dangerous to leave more than the smallest area of the body exposed.

Sister left Joan to 'finish off' this patient alone. She knew that the girl was careful, and that there was nothing to go actually wrong.

'All right, Pat. Never mind. We're getting along beautifully. Now listen while I tell you a funny thing that happened this morning.' And Joan chattered on while she did her nauseous job, trying to keep the boy's attention off the pain.

When it was all over, and he had been covered up and made comfortable, he smiled at her weakly – his eyes still wet with tears.

'Thank you, Nurse. You're a foine nurse. Oi'll be all right now.'

'*You*'ll be all right now!' she said, smiling down at him, and longed to give him a kiss. That being impossible, she rattled off with the trolley down to the annex.

The mental atmosphere of the ward might have been described as one of cheery pessimism. On the whole the men seemed fairly hopeful about the success of the offensive, and their spirits were good; but always it was the same tale. 'When we came out there were only twenty of us left.' 'Fifty alive out of a battalion of eleven hundred,' 'Only one man turned up at role-call,' and so on. The same monotonous repetition of losses. It looked as though three-quarters of Kitchener's army – that incredible young civilian army which England had raised in under two years, and flung against the German military machine – were out of action. No previous casualty-lists had even approached in length those now appearing in *The Times*. Every day one or more of the girls at the 1st London would hear of the death of a brother or a fiancé, be granted two days' leave, and then return and carry on. Oh, a fine time to be young in, that summer of the Somme!

As Joan went off duty at about 8.15 – the last man having been washed, the last dressing done – she looked down the ward. Almost every other bed was raised into a tunnel-like shape by a protective cage under the bed clothes, or else looked gallows-like with some strange arrangement of wood and cord supporting the shattered arm of its occupant. And here and there a German spiked helmet hung on the wall above; and here and there on the bedside lockers lay German watches, buttons, coins – trophies of war taken only a few days ago at la Boissell, Fricourt or Mametz; at Longueval, Thiepval or the ghastly Delville Wood.

Enid Bagnold

The Boys

So now one steps down from chintz covers and lemonade to the Main Army and lemon-water.

And to show how little one has one's eye upon the larger issues, the thing that upset me most on coming into a 'Tommies' ward was the fact that instead of twenty-six lemons twice a day for the making of lemonade I now squeeze two into an old jug and hope for the best about the sugar.

Smiff said to-day, 'Give us a drop of lemon, nurse. ...' And the Sister: 'Go on with you! I won't have the new nurse making a pet of you. ...'

I suppose I'm new to it, and one can't carry on the work that way, but, God knows, the water one can add to a lemon is cheap enough!

Smiff had a flash of temper last night. He said: 'Keepin' me here starin' at green walls this way! Nothing but green, nine blessed mouth!'

His foot is off, and to-night for the first time the doctor promised that he should be wheeled into the corridor. But it was forgotten, and I am too new to jog the memory of the gods.

It's a queer place, a 'Tommies' ward. It makes me nervous. I'm not simple enough; they make me shy. I can't think of them like the others do, as 'the boys'; they seem to me full-grown men.

I suffer awfully from my language in this ward. I seem to be the only V.A.D. of whom they continually ask, 'What say, Nurse?' It isn't that I use long words, but my sentences seem to be inverted.

An opportunity for learning to speak simple Saxon ...

'An antitetanic injection for Corrigan,' said Sister. And I went to the dispensary to fetch the syringe and the needles.

'But has he any symptoms?' I asked. (In a Tommies' ward one dare ask anything; there isn't that mystery which used to surround the officers' illnesses.)

'Oh no,' she said, 'it's just that he hasn't had his full amount in France.'

So I hunted up the spirit-lamp and we prepared it, talking of it.

But we forgot to talk of it to Corrigan. The needle was in his shoulder before he knew why his shirt was held up.

His wrath came like an avalanche; the discipline of two years was forgotten, his Irish tongue was loosened. Sister shrugged her shoulders and laughed; I listened to him as I cleaned the syringe.

I gathered that it was the indignity that had shocked his sense of individual pride. 'Treating me like a cow ...' I heard him say to Smiff – who laughed, since it wasn't his shoulder that carried the serum. Smiff laughed: he has been in hospital nine months, and his theory is that a Sister may do anything at any moment; his theory is that nothing does any good – that if you don't fuss you don't get worse.

Corrigan was angry all day; the idea that 'a bloomin' woman should come an' shove something into me systim' was too much for him. But he forgets himself: there are no individuals now; his 'system' belongs to us.

Sister said, laughing to Smiff the other day, 'Your leg is mine.'

'Wrong again; it's the Govermint's!' said Smiff. But Corrigan is Irish and doesn't like that joke.

There are times when my heart fails me; when my eyes, my ears, my tongue, and my understanding fail me; when pain means nothing to me. ...

In the bus yesterday I came down from London sitting beside a Sister from another ward, who held her hand to her ear and shifted in her seat.

She told me she had earache, and I felt sorry for her.

As she had earache we didn't talk, and I sat huddled in my corner and watched the names of the shops, thinking, as I was more or less forced to do by her movements, of her earache.

What struck me was her own angry bewilderment before the fact of her pain. 'But it hurts. ... You've no idea how it hurts!' She was surprised. Many times a day she hears the words, 'Sister, you're hurtin' me. ... Couldn't you shift my heel? It's like a toothache,' and similar sentences. I hear them in our ward all the time. One can't pass down the ward without some such request falling on one's ears.

She is astonished at her earache; she is astonished at what pain can be; it is unexpected. She is ready to be angry with herself, with her pain, with her ear. It is monstrous, she thinks. ...

The pain of one creature cannot continue to have meaning for another. It is almost impossible to nurse a man well whose pain you do not imagine. A deadlock!

One has illuminations all the time!

There is an old lady who visits our ward, at whom, for one or two unimportant reasons, it is the custom to laugh. The men, who fall in with our moods with a docility which I am beginning to suspect is a mask, admit too that she is comic.

This afternoon, when she was sitting by Corrigan's bed and talking to him I saw where her treatment of him differed from ours. She treats him as though he were an individual; but there is more in it than that. ... She treats him as though he had a wife and children; a house and a back garden and responsibilities; in some manner she treats him as though he had dignity.

I thought of yesterday's injection. That is the difference: that is what the Sisters mean when they say 'the boys.' ...

The story of Rees is not yet ended in either of the two ways in which stories end in a hospital. His arm does not get worse, but his courage is ebbing. This morning I wheeled him out to the awful sleep again – for the third time.

They will take nearly anything from each other. The only thing that cheered Rees up as he was wheeled away was the voice of Pinker crying, 'Jer want white flowers on yer coffin? We'll see to the brass 'andles!'

From Pinker, a little boy from the Mile End Road, they will stand anything. He is the servant of the ward (he says), partly through his good nature and a little because he has two good arms and legs. 'I ain't no skivvy,' he protests all the time, but every little odd job gets done.

Rees, when he wakes, wakes sobbing and says, 'Don't go away, nurse. ...' He holds my hand in a fierce clutch, then releases it to point in the air, crying, 'There's the pain!' as though the pain filled the air and rose to the rafters. As he wakes it centralizes, until at last comes the moment when he says, 'Me arm aches cruel,' and points to it. Then one can leave him.

It was the first time I had heard a man sing at his dressing. I was standing at the sterilizer when Rees's song began to mount over the screen that hid him from me. ('Whatever is that?' 'Rees's tubes going in.')

It was like this: 'Ah ... ee ... oo, Sister!' and again: 'Sister ... oo ... ee ... ah!' Then a little scream and his song again.

I heard her voice: 'Now then, Rees, I don't call that much of a song.' She called me to make his bed, and I saw his left eye was full of tears.

O visitors, who come into the ward in the calm of the long afternoon, when beds are neat and clean and the flowers out on the tables and the V.A.D.'s sit sewing at splints and sandbags, when the men look like men again and smoke and talk and read ... if you could see what lies beneath the dressings!

When one shoots a wooden figure it makes a hole. When one shoots at a man it makes a hole, and the doctor must make seven others.

I heard a blackbird sing in the middle of the night last night – two bars, and then another. I thought at first it might be a burglar whistling to his mate in the black and rustling garden.

But it was a blackbird in a nightmare.

Those distant guns again tonight. ...

Now a lull and now a bombardment; again a lull, and then batter, batter, and the windows tremble. Is the lull when they go over the top?

I can only think of death to-night. I tried to think just now, 'What is it, after all! Death comes anyway; this only hastens it.' But that won't do; no philosophy helps the pain of death. It is pity, pity, pity, that I feel, and sometimes a sort of shame that I am here to write at all.

Summer. … Can it be summer through whose hot air the guns shake and tremble? The honeysuckle, whose little stalks twinkled and shone that January night, has broken at each woody end into its crumbled flower.

Where is the frost, the snow? … Where are the dead?

Where is my trouble and my longing, and the other troubles, and the happiness in other summers?

Alas, the long history of life! There is that in death that makes the throat contract and the heart catch: everything is written in water.

We talk of tablets to the dead. There can be none but in the heart, and the heart fades.

There are only ten men left in bed in the ward. Sometimes I think, 'Will there never be another convoy?'

G. K. Brumwell
The Masseuse

'Nurse! Sister! Well who the 'ell are they?' A poor puzzled patient gazes after the white clad figure, with a badge picked out in red, white and blue – a badge of wings, a cross and a wheel and quite a portion of the alphabet included, 'A.P.M.M.C.'

'Why that's the gal wot comes and rubs you, mate. Wait till you've had some – "All Patients Most Murderously Cured", the letters stand for.' This the man in the next bed murmurs to the interested arrival of the last convoy. 'See that big bloke over there,' pointing to a six-footer, 'Wal that bit of fluff don't 'alf put it across 'im – see 'er bend that stiff knee it's as good as a play to watch 'is face – You'd never think they could do it. But thank Gawd I shall give it a miss this trip.' This last added with great sincerity.

Yes! We really do exist and that is rather the attitude of Tommie towards us, but the masseuse who knows her job makes friends with her patient before it is time to introduce those painful movements of stiff and sore joints. Then it is often, 'Carry on, Sister! I can stick it, but I'm blowed if I'd let anyone else do it but you.'

We do get to know our patients quite well for that half-hour each morning, when perched on the edge of the bed, we rub and chat. The latter being a really necessary part of the business, and not just for sheer amusement as some imagine; for in talking of home, friends and common interests, Tommie forgets that after all 'massage' does not just consist of gentle strokings.

The photographs, generally of the post-card variety, that are produced during treatment and duly admired – sometimes a bit difficult to know just the right thing to say. Once lost for words, I gazed upon an obviously blushing bride, clutching in one hand a bouquet, and hanging on the arm of my patient, who is hardly recognisable in frock-coat, silk hat and button hole. Now white and worn, with a few days' growth on his chin, he lies tucked away among his blankets, and remarks, 'My! Sister, that was a day.'

They are great dears, these men who have suffered so much, and are so grateful for the smallest kindness shown them. One hates to hurt them again, but it is unavoidable at times, though we do get our silver lining when you come across two patients comparing notes as to how much better their poor limbs are since they have been under treatment.

'Why, Bill, I can get out afternoons now, if it is a bit of a hobble, it's a jolly sight better than spending all my time in this blessed old ward, so I just don't mind that little massager putting me through it and giving that "buckshee" bend of hers for luck.'

Vera Brittain
from
Testament of Youth

Camberwell Versus Death

After the solid, old-fashioned comfort of the Buxton house, it seemed strange to be the quarter-possessor of a bare-boarded room divided into cubicles by much-washed curtains of no recognisable colour, with only a bed, a wash-stand and a tiny chest of drawers to represent one's earthly possessions. There was not, I noticed with dismay, so much as a shelf or a mantelpiece capable of holding two or three books; the few that I had brought with me would have to be inaccessibly stored in my big military trunk.

As soon as I had unpacked in the cold, comfortless cubicle, I sat down on my bed and wrote a short letter to Roland on an old box-lid.

'I feel a mixture of strangeness and independence and depression and apprehension and a few other things to-night. Though I am really nearer to you, you somehow feel farther away. Write to me soon,' I implored him. 'London – darkest London – sends you its love too, and wishes – oh ever so much! – that it may soon see you again.'

Now two insignificant units at the 1st London General Hospital, Camberwell – the military extension of St. Bartholomew's Hospital – Betty and I had reported to the Matron that afternoon. We were among the youngest members of the staff, we learnt later, only two of the other V.A.D.s being 'under age.' The nucleus of the hospital, a large college, red, gabled, creeper-covered, is still one of the few dignified buildings in the dismal, dreary, dirty wilderness of south-east London, with its paper-strewn pavements, its little mean streets, and its old, ugly houses tumbling into squalid decay. Formerly – and now again – a training centre for teachers, it was commandeered for use as a hospital early in the War, together with some adjacent elementary schools, the open park-space opposite, and its satellite hostel nearly two miles away on Champion Hill.

To this hostel, as soon as we had reported ourselves, Betty and I were dispatched with our belongings. Our taxicab, driving through Camberwell Green over Denmark Hill and turning off the summit of Champion Hill into a pleasant, tree-shaded by-road, deposited us before a square, solid building of dirty grey stone, with gaping uncurtained windows. Closely surrounded by elms and chestnuts, tall, ancient and sooty, it looked gloomy and smelt rather dank; we should not be surprised, we thought, to find old tombstones in the garden.

At that stage of the War the military and civilian professional nurses who had joined Queen Alexandra's Imperial Military Nursing Service or the Territorial Force Reserve were still suspicious of the young semi-trained amateurs upon whose assistance, they were beginning to realise with dismay, they would be obliged to depend for the duration of the War. Only about a dozen V.A.D.s had preceded the batch with which I was sent, and the arrangements made for our reception were typical of the spirit in which, as a nation, we muddled our way through to 'victory.'

It still seems to me incredible that medical men and women, of all people, should not have realised how much the efficiency of over-worked and under-trained young women would have been increased by the elimination of avoidable fatigue, and that, having contemplated the addition of V.A.D.s to the staff for at least six months before engaging them, they did not make the hostel completely ready for them before they arrived instead of waiting till they got there. But in those days we had no Institute of Industrial Psychology to suggest ideal standards to professional organisations, and a large proportion of our military arrangements were permeated with a similar unimaginativeness. On a small scale it undermined the health and even cost the lives of young women in hospitals; on a large scale it meant the lack of ammunition, the attempt to hold positions with insufficient numbers, and the annihilation of our infantry with our own high-explosive shells.

Each morning at 7 a.m. we were due at the hospital, where we breakfasted, and went on duty at 7.30. Theoretically we travelled down by the workmen's trams which ran over Champion Hill from Dulwich, but in practice these trams were so full that we were seldom able to use them, and were obliged to walk, frequently in pouring rain and carrying suitcases containing clean aprons and changes of shoes and stockings, the mile and a half from the hostel to the hospital. As the trams were equally full in the evenings, the journey on foot had often to be repeated at the end of the day.

Whatever the weather, we were expected to appear punctually on duty looking clean, tidy and cheerful. As the V.A.D. cloak-room was then on the top floor of the college, up four flights of stone steps, we had to allow quarter of an hour for changing, in addition to the half hour's walk, in order to be in time for breakfast. This meant leaving the hostel at 6.15, after getting up about 5.45 and washing in icy water in the dreary gloom of the ill-lit, dawn-cold cubicle. After a few grumbles from the two eldest of the room's five occupants, we accepted our unnecessary discomforts with mute, philosophical resignation. When the rain poured in torrents as we struggled up or down Denmark Hill in the blustering darkness all through that wet autumn, Betty and I encouraged each other with the thought that we were at last beginning to understand just a little what winter meant to the men in the trenches.

Many chills and other small illnesses resulted from the damp, breakfastless walk undertaken so early in the morning by tired girls not yet broken in to a life of hardship. After I left I heard that a V.A.D. living at the hostel had died of pneumonia and had thus been responsible for the establishment of morning and evening ambulances, but until then no form of transport was provided or even suggested. Neither, apparently, did it occur to the authorities who so cheerfully billeted us in a distant, ill-equipped old house, that young untried women who were continually in contact with septic wounds and sputum cups and bed-pans, and whose constantly wet feet became cumulatively sorer from the perpetual walks added to the unaccustomed hours of standing, required at least a daily bath if they were to keep in good health.

At the hostel, to meet the needs of about twenty young women, was one cold bathroom equipped with an ancient and unreliable geyser. This apparatus took about twenty minutes to half fill the bath with lukewarm water, and as supper at the hospital was not over till nearly nine o'clock, and lights at the hostel had to be out soon after ten, there was seldom time after the journey up Denmark Hill for more than two persons per evening to occupy the bathroom. So temperamental was the geyser that the old housekeeper at the hostel refused to allow anyone but herself to manipulate it. While the tepid water trickled slowly into the bath she would sit anxiously perched beside the antique cylinder, apparently under the impression that if she took her eye off it for a moment it was bound to explode.

Any gas company could probably have installed an up-to-date water-heater in half a day, but it had not occurred to anybody to order this to be done. As several Sisters also slept in the hostel the V.A.D.s had seldom much luck in appropriating the bath, so in the bitter November cold we did our shivering best to remove the odours and contacts of the day with tiny jugfuls of lukewarm water. Later a second bathroom was installed, a process which, as I told Roland a few weeks afterwards, 'for some reason or other requires the cutting off of the entire hot water supply. ... It is rather an amusing state of affairs for the middle of London.' Never, except when travelling, had I to put up with so much avoidable discomfort throughout my two subsequent years of foreign Service as I endured in the centre of the civilised world in the year of enlightenment 1915.

Much subsequent reflection has never enabled me to decide who was really responsible for our cheerless reception. Probably, in the unfamiliar situation, responsibility was never formally allocated to anyone by anybody, and, human nature being incurably optimistic and fundamentally hostile to assuming any work not established as its own by long tradition, each person who might have shouldered the task of organisation hopefully supposed it to have been performed by one of the others.

Organisation and regulation of another sort existed in plenty; it was evidently felt that, without the detailed regimentation of their daily conduct, amateur intruders would never fit into the rigid framework of hospital discipline We went on duty at 7.30 a.m., and came off at 8 p.m., our hours, including three hours' off-time and a weekly half day – all of which we gave up willingly enough whenever a convoy came in or the ward was full of unusually bad cases thus amounted to a daily twelve and a half. We were never allowed to sit down in the wards, and our off-duty time was seldom allocated before the actual day. Night duty, from 8 p.m. to 8 a.m. over a period of two months, involved a twelve-hour stretch without off-time, though one night's break was usually allowed in the middle. For this work we received the magnificent sum of £20 a year, plus a tiny uniform allowance and the cost of our laundry. Extra mess allowance was given only on foreign Service, but at Camberwell the food, though monotonous, was always sufficient.

Those of us whose careers survived the Denmark Hill conditions gradually came, through the breaking-in process of sheer routine, to find the life tolerable enough. We all acquired puffy hands, chapped faces, chilblains and swollen ankles, but we seldom actually went sick, somehow managing to remain on duty with colds, bilious attacks, neuralgia, septic fingers and incipient influenza. It never then occurred to us that we should have been happier, healthier, and altogether more competent if the hours of work had been shorter, the hostel life more private and com fortable, the daily walks between hostel and hospital eliminated, the rule against sitting down in the wards relaxed, and off-duty time known in advance when the work was normal. Far from criticising our Olympian superiors, we tackled our daily duties with a devotional enthusiasm now rare amongst young women, since a more cynical post-war generation, knowing how easily its predecessors were hoodwinked through their naive idealism, naturally tends to regard this quality with amusement and scorn.

Every task, from the dressing of a dangerous wound to the scrubbing of a bed-mackintosh, had for us in those early days a sacred glamour which redeemed it equally from tedium and disgust. Our one fear was to be found wanting in the smallest respect; no conceivable fate seemed more humiliating than that of being returned to Devonshire House as 'unsuitable' after a month's probation. The temptation to exploit our young wartime enthusiasm must have been immense – and was not fiercely resisted by the military authorities.

Lady Cynthia Asquith
Night Nurse

Thursday, 9th May

John and his governess took me to the station – it is an ordeal behind me. Arrived at Stanway for luncheon found Mary S., Miss Wilkinson, and Sister Orde – the night nurse I was to go on duty with. My apprehension was fully aroused by Mary's gruesome stump talk ... of course, I have come just after a very bad amputation.

I rested and motored over to the hospital with Orde in a blue funk, feeling the mixed sensations of a 'new boy', a night traveller, and an actress on her first night. There is a sort of supper meal at eight, but I didn't have any – I washed up the things and stood about. Lights are put out in the ward at nine o'clock, and occasionally one walks round the dim lantern-lit room. It is rather creepy – surrounded by all those huddled forms sleeping aloud. The porridge is put on early and has to be stirred all through the night, and one has to stoke the furnace. When there is nothing to do we sit quite comfortably in the little sitting room talking, reading, or writing. The queer anomalous meals are great fun in the setting and the eating: at about twelve one has what I suppose represents lunch (something is left in the larder in the nature of eggs, sardines, and so on, and one drinks what one likes, such as Horlicks, tea, cocoa, or coffee) and at four one has a delicious meal of porridge and so on – the porridge is far the best I have ever tasted.

The pet and the interest of A Ward now is poor little Harris, who has got his leg off right high up. A few days ago he had to have a lot more taken off his stump and he has nearly died of haemorrhage ever since. He is much better now, but still a very bad colour. He is such a darling – so brave and always smiling. It's still very painful – pray God I never have to see that stump naked!

My first night was eventful. At about eleven there came a knock at the door. In burst Nurse Ewing, who is alone in B Ward (where they are supposed not to have bad cases). She was white as paper and told us one of her men (obviously a case of bad shell shock) was quite unmanageably walking in his sleep – thinking he was at the Front, poor fellow – hurling missiles about in the delusion that they were bombs and labouring under the impression that his companions were Germans. He was 'hollering' like anything and Nurse Ewing said she couldn't be left alone with him.

Away went Nurse Orde with her, leaving me quite alone in that snoring ward. I was in terror lest Harris should have a haemorrhage or something, but after a time they – to my intense relief – returned.

I went back under blazing starlight at about five, quite revived by delicious porridge and tea. Talked to Orde till about six when we call the men and the bustle begins. Breakfast has to be got ready for them and I take washing materials round to the bedridden ones. After their breakfast the dressings are done, at which I have to help, holding bowls and running to fetch things of whose whereabouts I have no idea – one feels anxious and foolish. A wag – Matthews – is a wonderful helper and enjoyed bringing boiling hot fomentations: I didn't mind the three dressings at all – the wounds were quite inoffensive. My only trial was attending to poor dear Harris. Thank God we didn't undo his stump! But we had to wash him and pull the draw sheets. The slightest movement is agony to his stump and it made me feel sickish, but I was able to function all right. We had screens round us. He was so sweet, and when we left him in peace, spent ages with the brush, comb, and glass making his hair curl. They are a delightful lot of men. My favourite is a K.R.R. called Morris, who does beautiful elaborate embroidery with an admiring audience standing round – one man seems to do nothing all day but thread needles for him. They are very friendly to one – ambitiously facetious a great many of them: one joke is to ask one to start the gramophone when one creeps round the ward in the dark. I felt my identity disappearing into 'Nurse' and my one absorption was to satisfy the Sister and please the men.

I felt excited and not in the least tired at eight when Mary arrived in the pony-cart which was to drive me home. I am glad I decided to do this. My self-esteem is much reinforced.

11

Other war work

Helen Zenna Smith
from
Not So Quiet …

Oh, come with me, Mother and Mrs. Evans-Mawnington. Let me show you the exhibits straight from the battlefield. This will be something original to tell your committees, while they knit their endless miles of khaki scarves, … something to spout from the platform at your next recruiting meetings. Come with me. Stand just there.

Here we have the convoy gliding into the station now, slowly, so slowly. In a minute it will disgorge its sorry cargo. My ambulance doors are open, waiting to receive. See, the train has stopped. Through the occasionally drawn blinds you will observe the trays slotted into the sides of the train. Look closely, Mother and Mrs. Evans-Mawnington, and you shall see what you shall see. Those trays each contain something that was once a whole man … the heroes who have done their bit for King and country … the heroes who marched blithely through the streets of London Town singing 'Tipperary,' while you cheered and waved your flags hysterically. They are not singing now, you will observe. Shut your ears, Mother and Mrs. Evans-Mawnington, lest their groans and heart-rending cries linger as long in your memory as in the memory of the daughter you sent out here to help win the War.

See the stretcher-bearers lifting the trays one by one, slotting them deftly into my ambulance. Out of the way quickly, Mother and Mrs. Evans-Mawnington – lift your silken skirts aside … a man is spewing blood, the moving has upset him, finished him. … He will die on the way to the hospital if he doesn't die before the ambulance is loaded. I know. … All this is old history to me. Sorry this has happened. It isn't pretty to see a hero spewing up his life's blood in public, is it? Much more romantic to see him in the picture papers being awarded the V.C., even if he is minus a limb or two. A most unfortunate occurrence!

That man strapped down? That raving, blaspheming creature screaming filthy words you don't know the meaning of ... words your daughter uses in everyday conversation, a habit she has contracted from vulgar contact of this kind. Oh, merely gone mad, Mother and Mrs. Evans-Mawnington. He may have seen a headless body running on and on, with blood spurting from the trunk. The crackle of the frost-stiff dead men packing the duck-boards watertight may have gradually undermined his reason. There are many things the sitters tell me on our long night rides that could have done this.

No, not shell-shock. The shell-shock cases take it more quietly as a rule, unless they are suddenly startled. Let me find you an example. Ah, the man they are bringing out now. The one staring straight ahead at nothing... twitching, twitching, twitching, each limb working in a different direction, like a Jumping Jack worked by a jerking string. Look at him, both of you. Bloody awful, isn't it, Mother and Mrs. Evans-Mawnington? That's shell-shock. If you dropped your handbag on the platform, he would start to rave as madly as the other. What? You won't try the experiment? You can't watch him? Why not? *Why not?* I have to, every night. Why the hell can't you do it for once? Damn your eyes.

Forgive me, Mother and Mrs. Evans-Mawnington. That was not the kind of language a nicely-brought-up young lady from Wimbledon Common uses. I forget myself. We will begin again.

See the man they are fitting into the bottom slot. He is coughing badly. No, not pneumonia. Not tuberculosis. Nothing so picturesque. Gently, gently, stretcher-bearers ... he is about done. He is coughing up clots of pinky-green filth. Only his lungs, Mother and Mrs. Evans-Mawnington. He is coughing well to-night. That is gas. You've heard of gas, haven't you? It burns and shrivels the lungs to ... to the mess you see on the ambulance floor there. He's about the age of Bertie, Mother. Not unlike Bertie, either, with his gentle brown eyes and fair curly hair. Bertie would look up pleadingly like that in between coughing up his lungs. ... The son you have so generously given to the War. The son you are so eager to send out to the trenches before Roy Evans-Mawnington, in case Mrs. Evans-Mawnington scores over you at the next recruiting meeting ... 'I have given my only son.'

Cough, cough, little fair-haired boy. Perhaps somewhere your mother is thinking of you ... boasting of the life she has so nobly given ... the life you thought was your own, but which is hers to squander as she thinks fit. 'My boy is not a slacker, thank God.' Cough away, little boy, cough away. What does it matter, providing your mother doesn't have to face the shame of her son's cowardice?

These are sitters. The man they are hoisting up beside me, and the two who sit in the ambulance. Blighty cases ... broken arms and trench feet ... mere trifles. The smell? Disgusting, isn't it? Sweaty socks and feet swollen to twice their size ... purple, blue, red ... big black blisters filled with yellow matter. Quite a colour scheme, isn't it? Have I made you vomit? I must again ask pardon. My conversation is daily growing less refined. Spew and vomit and sweat ... I had forgotten these words are not used in the best drawing-rooms on Wimbledon Common.

But I am wasting time. I must go in a minute. I am nearly loaded. The stretcher they are putting on one side. Oh, a most ordinary exhibit, ... the groaning man to whom the smallest jolt is red hell ... a mere belly full of shrapnel. They are holding him over till the next journey. He is not as urgent as the helpless thing there, that trunk without arms and legs, the remnants of a human being, incapable even of pleading to be put out of his misery because his jaw has been half shot away. ... No, don't meet his eyes, they are too alive. Something of their malevolence might remain with you all the rest of your days, ... those sock-filled, committee-crowded days of yours.

Gaze on the heroes who have so nobly upheld your tradition, Mother and Mrs. Evans-Mawnington. Take a good look at them. ... The heroes you will sentimentalise over until peace is declared, and allow to starve for ever and ever, amen, afterwards. Don't go. Spare a glance for my last stretcher, ... that gibbering, unbelievable, unbandaged thing, a wagging lump of raw flesh on a neck, that was a face a short time ago, Mother and Mrs. Evans-Mawnington. Now it might be anything ... a lump of liver, raw bleeding liver, that's what it resembles more than anything else, does-n't it? We can't tell its age, but the whimpering moan sounds young, somehow. Like the fretful whimpers of a sick little child ... a tortured child ... puzzled whimpers. Who is he? For all you know, Mrs. Evans-Mawnington, he is your Roy. He might be anyone at all, so why not your Roy? One shapeless lump of raw liver is like another shapeless lump of raw liver. What do you say? Why don't they cover him up with bandages? How the hell do I know? I have often wondered myself, ... but they don't. Why do you turn away? That's only liquid fire. You've heard of liquid fire? Oh, yes. I remember your letter. ... '*I hear we've started to use liquid fire, too. That will teach those Germans. I hope we use lots and lots of it.*' Yes, you wrote that. You were glad some new fiendish torture had been invented by the chemists who are running this war. You were delighted to think some German mother's son was going to have the skin stripped from his poor face by liquid fire. ... Just as some equally patriotic German mother rejoiced when she first heard the sons of Englishwomen were to be burnt and tortured by the very newest war gadget out of the laboratory.

Don't go, Mother and Mrs. Evans-Mawnington, ... don't go. I am loaded, but there are over thirty ambulances not filled up. Walk down the line. Don't go, unless you want me to excuse you while you retch your insides out as I so often do. There are stretchers and stretchers you haven't seen yet. ... Men with hopeless dying eyes who don't want to die ... men with hopeless living eyes who don't want to live. Wait, wait, I have so much, so much to show you before you return to your committees and your recruiting meetings, before you add to your bag of recruits ... those young recruits you enrol so proudly with your patriotic speeches, your red, white and blue rosettes, your white feathers, your insults, your lies ... any bloody lie to secure a fresh victim.

What? You cannot stick it any longer? You are going? I didn't think you'd stay. But I've got to stay, haven't I? ... I've got to stay. You've got me out here, and you'll keep me out here. You've got me haloed. I am one of the Splendid Young Women who are winning the War. ...

'Loaded. Six stretchers and three sitters!'

I am away. I slow up at the station gate. The sergeant is waiting with his pencil and list.

I repeat, 'Six stretchers and three sitters.'

'Number Eight.'

He ticks off my ambulance. I pass out of the yard.

Number eight. A lucky number! A long way out, but a good level road, comparatively few pot-holes and stone heaps.

Crawl, crawl, crawl.

Along we creep at a snail's pace ... a huge dark crawling blot on the dead-white road.

Crawl, crawl, crawl.

The sitter leans back motionless. Exhausted, or asleep, after the long journey. His arm is in splints, his head bandaged, and his left foot swaddled in a clumsy trench slipper. He leans back in the darkness, his face as invisible as though a brick wall were separating us. The wind cuts like a knife. He must be numbed through, for he has no overcoat and his sleeve is ripped up. He has draped the Army blanket cloak-wise over his shoulders, leaving his legs to the mercy of the freezing night. It is snowing again. Big snow-flakes that hiss as they catch the radiator. I tell the sitter he will find a cigarette and matches in the pocket of my coat nearest him. I have placed them there purposely … my bait to make him talk. I want him to talk. He does not reply. I want him to talk. If I can get a sitter to talk it helps to drown the cries from inside. I discovered that some time ago. I repeat my offer, a trifle louder this time. But he makes no reply. He is done. Too done to smoke even. No luck for me to-night.

Crawl, crawl, crawl.

How smoothly she runs, this great lumbering blot. How slowly. To look at her you'd never think it possible to run an ambulance of this size so slowly. …

Crawl, crawl, crawl.

Did I hear a scream from inside? I must fix my mind on something. … What? I know – my coming-out dance. My first grown-up dance frock, a shining frock of sequins and white georgette, high-waisted down to my toes. … *Did I hear a scream?* … Made over a petticoat … *don't let them start screaming* … a petticoat of satin. Satin slippers to match, not tiny – my feet were always largish; so were my hands. … *Was that a scream from inside?* … Such a trouble Mother had getting white gloves my size to go above the elbow. … *Was it a scream?* … My hair up for the first time … *oh, God, a scream this time* … my hair up in little rolls at the back … *another scream – the madman has started, the madman has started. I was afraid of him. He'll start them all screaming.* … Thirty-one little rolls like fat little sausages. A professional hairdresser came in and did them – took nearly two hours to do them while Trix and Mother watched, and Sarah came in to peep. *Don't let him start the others; don't let him start the others.* … Thirty-one little sausages of hair, piled one on top of the other, and all the hair my own too, copied from a picture post card of Phyllis Dare or Lily Elsie. Now, which one was it? … *The shell-shocked man has joined in. The madman has set the shell-shocked man howling like a mad dog.* … Lily Elsie, I think it was. … *What are they doing to one another in there?*

'Let me out. Let me out.'

The madman is calling that. Lily Elsie, I think it was. Lily Elsie. …

'Stop screaming. You're not the only one going through bloody hell.'

A different voice that one. That must be one of the sitters. … Satin slippers with buckles on the toes – little pearl buckles shaped like a crescent. Aunt Helen or Trix gave me those.

'Shut up screaming, or I'll knock hell out of you with my crutch, you bastard. Shut up screaming.'

What was that crash? They're fighting inside. They're fighting inside. ...
Scream, scream, scream. ...

'I'm dying. Oh, Jesus, he's murdered me. I'm dying.'

What are they doing? Are they murdering one another in there? I ought
to stop the ambulance; I ought to get out and see. I ought to stop them.
... I ought. A driver the other night stopped her ambulance, and a man
had gone mad and was beating a helpless stretcher case about the head.
But she overpowered him and strapped him down again. Tosh, that was.
But Tosh is brave. I couldn't do it. I must go on. ...

They are all screaming now. Moaning and shrieking and howling like
wild animals. ... All alone with an ambulance of raving men miles from
anywhere in the pitch blackness, ... raving madmen yelling and screaming. I shall go mad myself. ...

Go and see ... go and see ... go and see.

I will not. I cannot ... my heart is pounding like a sledge-hammer. My
feet and hands are frozen, but the sweat is pouring down my back in
rivulets. I have looked before, and I dare not look again. What good can I
do? The man who spewed blood will be lying there dead, ... his glassy eyes
fixed on the door of the ambulance, staring accusingly at me as I peep in,
... cold dead eyes, blaming me when I am not to blame. ... The madman
will curse me, scream vile curses at me, scream and try to tear himself
from the straps that hold him down, ... if he has not torn himself away
already. He will try to tear himself from his straps to choke the life from
me. The shell-shocked man will yammer and twitch and jerk and mouth.
The man with the face like raw liver will moan. ... I will not go and see. I
will not go and see.

Crawl, crawl, crawl.

Number Eight, where are you? Have I missed you in the monotony of
this snow-covered road. I have been travelling for hours. Am I travelling
too slowly? Am I being over-careful? Could I accelerate ever so slightly ...
cover the distance more quickly? I will do it. A fresh scream from someone as I jolt over a stone ... I've hurt someone. I slow down again.

Scream, scream, scream. Three different sets of screams now – the
shriek of the madman, the senseless, wolfish, monotonous howl of the
shell-shock case, and now a shrill sharp yell like a bright pointed knife
blade being jabbed into my brain. One, two, three, four, ... staccato yells.
Which one is that? Not the little fair-haired boy. He is too busy choking
to death to shriek. Another one has joined in ... inferno. They are striking one another again ... hell let loose. Go and see, go and see. ...

I will not go and see. I will not go and see.

Crawl, crawl, crawl.

The sitter sleeps through it all. A pool of snow has fallen in his lap. We have missed Number Eight. I must have missed the turning in the snow. The black tree-stump on the left that leads to Number Eight ... snow-obscured. I must have missed the turning in the snow.

Crawl, crawl, crawl.

The screams have died down, but a dreadful moaning takes their place. Oo-oo-oh ... oo-oo-oh ... dirge-like, regular, it rises above the sound of the engine and floats out into the night. Oo-oo-oh ... oo-oo-oh ... it is heart-breaking in its despair. I have heard a man moan like that before. The last moans of a man who will soon cease moaning for ever. Oo-oo-oh ... the hopelessness, the loneliness. Tears tear at my heart ... awful tears that rack me, but must not rise to my eyes, for they will freeze on my cheeks and stick my eyelids together until I cannot see to drive. Even the solace of pitying tears is denied me.

Crawl, crawl, crawl.

I have given up all hope of reaching Number Eight by now. I will go on until there is a place to turn.

Crawl, crawl, crawl.

The moans have ceased. I strain my ears. The madman is shouting again, ... a hoarse vituperative monologue. I cannot catch his words. I do not want to catch his words. But I strain to catch them just the same. He will start the others again. ...

Crawl, crawl, crawl.

If only I could find a place to turn. The road seems to grow narrower. How many journeys shall I make to-night? Was it a big convoy? I didn't notice at the station. ... I always forget to notice. Perhaps I shall have shrapnels next time ... shrapnels, too exhausted from the loss of blood to scream. A sitter who will talk and smoke. ... The madman is screaming again ... he will start the others.

Crawl, crawl, crawl.

Is that a light? No ... yes! Number Eight! The big canvas marquee gleaming dully in the darkness ... the front entrance flaps already parted ... white-capped nurses waiting in the doorway. They can see my lights. The orderlies are standing by. ... Number Eight. ... Number Eight. ... I am there at last. The tears are rolling down my cheeks ... let them. Let the tears freeze my eyelids together now ... let them freeze my eyelids. ... It doesn't matter now ... nothing matters now. ...

Muriel Thompson
Base Notes

Black darkness all around, the smell of the sea & of the rain – first in front a semi-circle of light [blown] by the ship's lamps, showing up the wet sails on the quay, & shining on the deep space below. Twinkling in the distance other lights, & at regular intervals ambulances arriving & stopping by the gangway, while slowly – carefully, four limp forms on stretchers are drawn out one after the other, lowered for a moment to the ground, then raised, & carried on board.

The light shines on the M.O.'s face; his clerk steps to the stretcher, cuts a white label from the patient's coat, & calls briskly, 'gunshot wound, left thigh, sir' – 'Ward B,' says the M.O., & the bearers carry on.

Not even the darkness hides the white head on the next stretcher, it shows up startlingly as the lamp light strikes it – no particle of human face is seen – only holes, in a white mask, 'severe burns, sir,' intones the orderly – 'Ward A' is the reply – & another load of bitter human suffering, heroically endured, goes silently away.

The next ambulance stops, the driver looks round & calls through the little window behind her 'all for Blighty boys, out you get,' & out they stumble, limping, slipping, on the wet quay, painfully yet cheerily – six 'C & D' cases as the R.A.M.C. puts it – able to sit up and sometimes to walk. They hop, limp, hobble & crawl up the gangway; & take their places in the semi-circle of light, showing up the black darkness of the early winter morning.

Four a.m. – a chilly November day, with a channel crossing before them & like as not, a Boshe souvenir inside them, '——— it all, there's Blighty only an hour away – who cares.'

So the onlooker watches, & sees the crowd, of broken men, most in khaki, a few in hospital blue, sometimes a [foreman] cap proudly worn, some with Scottish head-gear & some with wide Australian hats & keen, lean faces beneath them. At last the stream of cars comes to an end, & the driver of the last car hands a strip of paper to the section leader on the quay – 'last car' she says – the gangway is withdrawn, & the ship pulls out for home.

Not always so! 'All cars back to the ship' comes the order sometimes, & every girl flies to her starting handle, & the convoy goes sadly back. 'Poor boys, how disappointed they'll be. ' Courtesy hospital duties are vouchsafed the drivers –

'Why mayn't we go Sister?'

'Because it's too rough you see.'

'We don't mind as long as we get to Blighty! We don't care, we've been over the top!' with a downward glance at a bandaged arm, & a touch of pride.

'I bet you have' says Sister 'but that [is] no reason why you should go to the bottom!'

At this feeble joke they laugh, & ask to be taken for a joy-ride. A gramophone is unearthed by the drivers, & taken to check the dreary hours of waiting, & this produces a fervent letter of thanks, & apology for some small damage inadvertently done to the machine.

'Yours till hell freezes' the letter ends & the convoy feels their efforts are appreciated by the New Zealand writer.

Afternoon now, a pale lemon-coloured sky with a rose flush, & behind it an ink-black dome of rain clouds driving up – all faces skywards – it's worth while to stop & gaze too – a crack avi-man is up, & as you look your heart stops – Sheer against the lemon sky he drops, head first, down, down like a stone – it must be an accident – he can't fall so far on purpose you think – But you are wrong – at the last moment the Belgian ace rights himself, & sails away on the sun-like air till he is lost to sight amid the black clouds beyond.

One dreadful day – 'four cars wanted at once. Serious accident.' Eighteen miles off. The cars go down to the shore, draw their full complement of stretchers & blankets, & are off regardless of any speed limit that ever was, save that imposed by the capacity of the engines. One thought only – 'please God I don't puncture!' No need to ask the way on nearing the village, anxious soldiers at every corner point it out & the summer sun shines down on a terrible sight, & the drivers struck with sudden horror at the thought of such suffering.

They helped to raise the stretchers, & get the poor, burned, blackened bits of men into the ambulances, & then set out on the nerve-racking return journey.

Terrible cries from within, & a stop for water to moisten parched lips. 'Sister, I can't bear it, I can't bear it!' moaned one man with both eyes gone – 'Man you're bearing it fine – you're a Scottie' the girl called back, she [adding] her voice with a brave effort, while tears poured down her face, & the horror-struck French villagers looked on pityingly.

None of the drivers will ever forget that day, or the horror of seeing the cars unloaded. A Padre stood by the hospital door, no novice either.

'My God! What is it?' was all he could find to say.

Two months later, two men were carried onto the Blighty boat, sole survivors of that terrible day.

Another picture – black darkness again, & a blue-white fierce light biting into the blackness above, a towering shape, & now, when the light strikes, a twisted, distorted mass – tubes, wheels, cogs, blades – incredible, misshapen remains of what was but a few hours back, a living destroyer.

One third of her lies at the bottom of the channel; but the rest floated, reached the harbour, & now lies dry-docked, her dazed, battered crew already working to prepare her for the repair gang.

A sad sight, a broken ship.

Next day – two gun carriages & two coffins. Bareheaded survivors on either side. French blue jackets bringing up the rear of the sad procession, and two more English boys 'go West'.

Irene Rathbone
The YMCA Rest Camp

22 June 1918, Saturday.

This was the last day of this camp. We shut down the club at 6, & all went up to the final concert at 8 in the entertainments hut. It was packed. … We all six went & sat on the stage. … Why should these men who suffer such unimaginable horrors month after month be called upon to cheer us, who came out & do a little & suffer not at all for them. The whole thing is out of proportion & unfair. All this clack about what the women of England are doing makes me sick. However on this particular occasion, I think the men enjoyed seeing us sitting there beaming, & showing their appreciation of us.

There was a thrilling atmosphere about the whole gathering, but as a *concert* the thing was flat. … I was called upon, & gave them the waltz song out of the Maid of the Mountains, & 'Black-eyed Susans' which went very well, of course that sort of song always goes well. … It was Kit, however, who had the success of the evening. She sang two ridiculous songs – 'Goodbye-ee' and another, & the men simply shouted & whistled & yelled with joy … this [break up] was about 10.30, & at 2.30 we were to open the tent & serve them with tea; and at 4.30 they were to march away – back *there*.

Beatrice M. Trefusis
The Censor's Office

March 1915

I have got, through Major Cockerill, a post at the censor's office as examiner of private correspondence – at £2 a week. Major C. is head of all that Intelligence Dept at the War Office.

It is 8 hours a day for 6 days in the week. I started it on Mar 24th.

It is interesting & not a little exciting. All very secret, of course. You are not supposed to tell any but the necessary people that you are even working there – of course no mention of anything of the work that goes on there is allowed outside. We (there are 3 or 4 rooms full of lady examiners in private correspondence alone) are working at Salisbury House, London Wall. We examine correspondence between this country & all neutral countries in Europe.

Perhaps it would be as well not to write here anything farther about it until after the war – & perhaps not even then – or mention names of anyone else in it. One certainly derives lots of amusement from the work, & a certain amount of insight into the 'feeling' in various countries. And it's fun to be doing War Office work.

Mary L. Macleod
The Land Army

July 13th [Letter no. 33 to sister Betty]

I think I will wait and start Pelman at the same time as you in Cambridge. Flanders Nurseries is luxury compared with this place. It would be ripping if it did not rain so much. Land Army boots have arrived, enormous clumping army ammunition boots, really not worth the money paid, as they'll be impossible to wear in normal society ... a wash in cold water 'as far down as possible and as far up as possible' ... sleeping in a tent ... there are 7 of us, 5 being 'sweet girl undergraduate hefty types' ... very Haw, Hawish to begin with. I have to use my holdall as a head raiser and either put my clothes in it as come off or else, put them on top of my feet ... in night when it rains, streams of water trickle under the sides of tent and wet your mattress … we are all feeling fitter than we have done for months. It is 100 yards to the washing marquee and about 300 to the other necessary, from our tent at the end of camp. We belong to a cycling gang, about ¼ hours ride to the flax … it is supposed to be a nine hour day, but you can subtract about two hours for rests, as it has been showery we have extra. Work is moderately strenuous … had stiff wrists, most people complained of backs and legs. Food is good and should be plentiful, but such a lot of hungry people about 150 to each of four mess tents, and only one dish to serve from, sometimes the first get served scrum for seconds before others have had any … undisciplined girls refuse to obey orders. The waste is pretty bad. Some people are faddy and leave piles on their plates then go to Y.W.C.A. and stodge cakes etc. As we are allowed only ½lb bread per day it seems unpatriotic … do well for butter and cheese. Someone heard a Yeovil citizen complaining. Personally enjoying it better than being indoors sewing. The Y.W.C.A. does a lot for us it does seem funny to be using its hospitality instead of dispensing it.

July 14th [Letter no. 34 to Mother]
Sending things off to be washed … want them back as soon as possible to keep things clean or keep rules of hygiene … when 7 of you are dossing down in one Army tent … impossible to be coherent whilst waiting in a crowd at a Public hotel for a hot bath. Bed … an army blanket laid on boards, superimposed by a mattress cover stuffed with chaff, holdall full of clothes as pillow, covered by my 'imitation flea bag' and 2 or 3 blankets and my macintosh down side nearest the tent … to keep out streams of rain. 2 inches from nose on right side … satchel containing dressing gear and a hand basket containing eating gear. My writing case serves as an extension for Bunch to put her pillow on. Lower down rolled up overall are garments just taken off. At foot of my mattress a suitcase draped with towel. … It is some squash. We have lunch and tea on the field, which is pleasant. Please send hockey boots and galoshes … thought the Army boots would have served but … heavy and galumping and cannot go walking in them.

F. Tennyson Jesse
The Sinews of War – France

It is almost easier for the proverbial camel to perform his feat of passing
through the eye of a needle than for a layman – who is a laywoman and a
foreigner at that – to penetrate into one of the great factories where the
sinews of wars are forged; therefore I felt that luck had not quite deserted
me when I was taken by the Under-Secretary of State for Munitions on a
'personally conducted tour' round the famous Renault works.

They stand in a dreary, working-class quarter outside Paris, where the
dirty white houses seem stained by the weeping of years; huddled shoulder to shoulder, peering with blind eyes from beneath lowering brows.
They have no gardens, only here and there a patch of ground where linen
hanging limply from a line, takes the place of flowers; but all down the
streets are plane-trees that in summer must make grateful blots of fresh
green against so much staleness, but that now, mere symbols of themselves, need the eye of faith to see their potentialities. Past them scream
the trams, rocking on the steel lines that make thin threads of chill bright-
ness along the brown and greasy cobbles. Yet once inside the high walls,
sentry-guarded, of the works, one is in such a world apart that these surroundings, outcome of the industry though they are, sink away from the
mind.

The Renault factory started in 1899 for the manufacture of autos; it
employed six workmen and occupied some sixty square metres. Now it is
a little city in itself, a city peopled by many thousands of workers, of
whom three thousand are women. Even before the war there was a small
number of women employed, but only in the work of verification, which
consists of testing, with special instruments, every piece of shell or engine
made in the factory, to see that it is mathematically correct. This work,
though requiring care and accuracy, is not in any way hard. Now, though
in the face of much opposition, for the iron casters' syndicate was jeal-
ously opposed to the employment of women – there are twelve departments in which women work, sometimes alone, sometimes with men.

Women cast the balls for shrapnel; cut them off from the connecting
stalk of metal on which they are cast; make the moulds of specially prepared sand which serve to fill in the air-spaces when aeroplane engines are
cast; make the fuses both for high explosive shells and shrapnel, a labour
as delicate as watch-making, for there are twelve different parts, of which

some are very fine. One piece alone, the *porte-charge* of the fuse, has to go through six different processes. Women can also make various pieces of rifles; turn shells on the electric lathes, though it was prophesied to begin with that the work of placing the shells in the movable carrier would be too heavy. Women work on the caps of shells, which they shape, perforate, turn on lathes, polish, &c. They charge the shell cases with shrapnel, disposing the ball evenly and pouring resin to keep them fixed, except in the cap, where they place the bullets in a wooden mould to prevent them disturbing the fuse. Women solder various parts together by means of a blowtorch, burning acetylene and oxygen, which plays on the object to be soldered as it turns on a lathe which requires both skill and endurance to work correctly. And in addition to all this, women still verify every piece of every article made in the factory.

Now, all this has not come about without much shaking of doubtful heads and wagging of foreboding fingers. The labour problem, always complicated by an inflow of new workers, is not one which can be altogether satisfactorily re-arranged at a time like the present. The men workers are fearful of a future invaded by women, but they are the strongest advocates of equal payment, lest the masters should prefer to employ women because of the lower wage. Nevertheless, in many cases where women are doing men's work they are getting less pay, chiefly because it would cause an automatic rise in all departments of women's work, which is normally less well-paid than men's. For it should not be forgotten that labour can be divided into three kinds – that which only men can do; that which only women can do; and that which either can do equally well. If the scale of women in the last class are suddenly raised, it would cause a sudden dearth of workers of the second class, which mostly consists of trades that could not afford to raise wages at a time like this, however to be hoped for ultimately such an end may be. The Renault factory however is noteworthy for having both the same hours of work and the same rates of pay for workers of either sex. They are paid by the piece, and the wage usually works out at about nine francs a day, though some of the women have attained to twelve francs, a thing never achieved by the men. The manager who showed us round began by saying that the official report was that the women's work was quite as satisfactory as the men's; he went on to say that, speaking from what he had personally noticed, he considered it superior. He gave various reasons for this, one being that the essentials in work of this kind are observation and patience, both of these qualities he considered were displayed in a finer degree in ordinary life by women than by men! Another great factor is that the women live more reasonably out of the factory. The working day of twenty-four hours is divided into three shifts of eight hours each, and there is only one half-day's rest in the fifteen, when the day and night workers exchange. Every one works for fifteen days and nights in alternate phases, with this one half-day off in between. When those women who are on the night shift go home in the morning they go at once to bed, only perhaps sallying forth on a little shopping expedition in the afternoon; but the men go first of all to a restaurant, where they have a *café* and then perhaps a *pousse-café*, then on to another restaurant for a chat or a game; in the afternoon comes a walk with friends, and then in the evening it is the turn of the restaurants again, and lo and behold! sleep-time has gone and work-time has come again. The women always arrange everything round their sleep, so to speak; but then in France the club-habit – which is what the café-habit amounts to – has no attractions for women.

The chief difficulty in work such as that at a munitions factory, where each person always does one thing, so that fuses are made in one department and bullets in another, and so on is to ensure that one department is not kept hanging back by another; if it once occurs the balance may not be set right for weeks. It this does happen, it is found that women do better set on a new job than do the men, for they have a greater flexibility of mind and muscle which makes them adapt themselves more quickly. The man's instinct, if he knows he is hurried, is to become tense and taut, which militates against swiftness; but women, who are less highly-strung, less nervous organisms, do not lose suppleness in the same way. The manager told us he had often, at the beginning of the experiment, pretended to busy himself with something in the workshops, while he watched the men and women; and he discovered that the women had greater economy of movement. And, after actual brute strength, economy of movement is the most invaluable quality in a worker. It means less wear and tear both of worker and material and a greater output; it is the essence of success. The women have attained such a perfect synchronism with their machines that every movement means something, and not a hair's-breadth of action is wasted in air.

Thus the Secretary; but there was one respect, he confessed, in which there was no doing anything with the women! He had been anxious to bring into use a simple uniform consisting of a combination suit and a cap of grease-proof material, as with so much oil that the very air is thick with it, work is excessively dirty. But the women continue to do their hair with paste slides and to wear nothing more shielding than a velvet ribbon round their necks. The manager considers this a '*coquetterie mal propre.*'

The women have come well enough out of the whole experiment, and the authorities are enthusiastic; but nevertheless, to one not a feminist (whatever that may be) or, indeed, any kind of an 'ist,' one little thought would obtrude, and that was all these machines with which the women worked, the great moulds into which they pour their liquid metal, the hundreds of wheels which whirr in the grip of driving belts, the steam-hammers that come thundering down on the red-hot metal – all these things have been invented and made by men. One can be deeply pleased that women should be proved not only so well-intentioned, but so capable, without losing a sense of proportion; but it remains for us to wonder what part women, now initiated, may take in the engineering developments of the future. The cohesion of creation and continuous work is, however, profoundly impressive. And so I found when, after listening to discussion of the work and woman problem, I went on through the factory and saw that vivid pictorial side of it, which, to the economics both of cause and result, is as the body is to the soul.

I have said that the munitions works were like a city – a city enclosed and guarded like some walled town of old, but that was all of antiquity about it. There was never anything more fiercely modern, so modern it seemed all the time to be trying to project itself into the future, forestalling inventions yet to come. Streets, up and down whose muddy lengths motor lorries came churning, stretched this way and that by the tall sheds, and new buildings were springing up, some with the finishing touches still being given, but the machinery already installed and the men at work within, some still mere skeletons of iron framework, painted with vermilion lead paint – towering lines and cross-lines of vivid scarlet against all the greyness.

As we approached the first shed a medley of harsh noises swelled to meet us, and when we entered sprang upon us full blast, a roar so great it passed the limit of a single sense and forced on the mind such a confusion that the very air seemed to darken with it; for there is always a point where any one sense becomes so intensified it fuses with others, and that point had been achieved for the sense of hearing in this shed.

Overhead, black against the dim panes of the roof, whirred a forest of driving-belts, horizontal and perpendicular, revolving so fast they seemed merely to tremble as they stood – long, deadly ribbons of things, like some nightmare growth in a tropical jungle. On either side of the narrow alley down which I walked, skirts gathered close, steam-hammers slid up and came crashing down with a thunder that one could feel vibrating through the earthy floor; gusts of heat came out from the tortured metal that was held, red and glowing, beneath the descending slabs which beat it into shape. Bursts of fire that licked the ground in a burning pool for a moment, or showers of tinsel that pulsed and died, came flashing out across the alley-way at every stroke, lighting the dimness with violent flares of orange-hued light; while clouds of steam that wavered up here and there were a pearly white, irradiated from below with a warmer tinge. It seemed incredible to an ignorant onlooker that people could work in this inferno of heat and noise, with so many belts whirring past their heads and creatures of steel springing out and back like fierce beasts on a leash, without accidents occurring, and frequently; yet, besides the women, I saw quite small boys working, seizing red-hot shell-caps in long pincers and holding them under crashing blows from the steam-hammers that must have jarred all up their little arms. Other boys were holding rings of metal about the size of bracelets, under hammers, then flinging them aside on to a pile of them, some already dead, some still red and glowing, but fading to blackness as one looked.

Further on, men were slipping the fiery shell-cases, so hot as to seem almost transparent, into place beneath the machines which pierced down through them, while, being impregnated with oil, the metal literally blazed at the friction. Then the tube, still a transparent orange, was picked up in a pair of pincers and borne away. We went on to where women stood by vats brimming with what looked like quicksilver but was really lead and antimony maintained at a heat of eight hundred degrees Centigrade. They ladled out this unholy brew with big ladles, as unconsciously as though it had been soup, and poured it into the wooden instruments before them, where a narrow division with scalloped edges showed down the middle. A swift movement of the handles and the mould opened out, letting a row of shrapnel balls, welded to a parent stalk, fall through into a trough. Next to the ball-moulders other women were seated before machines, into a groove of which they slid these shrapnel stalks, and with a clicking noise all the balls were shaved off and ejected to one side, while the flat and crumpled stalks fell out on the other.

In the next shed comparative quietness reigned, for the chief work was the making of the moulds which are used in the casting of aeroplane engines. These moulds are made of sand mixed with sugar as a binding agent, which grotesquely recalls the alleged practices of grocers. The women cast these moulds in other moulds made of wood, which, having packed them closely, they turn upside down and break with a mallet till the sand-mould drops out, for all the world like some fantastic 'pudding' made by children on the beach. Some of the sand-moulds or '*noyaux*,' as they are called, are quite big and complicated, and then they have to be reinforced with wire and nails just as concrete is reinforced with iron. It is a whole department of labour to clean them out when the engine is cast but luckily, once the metal is poured round them, the *noyaux* soon disintegrate – the marvel, to the uninitiated, is how they are firm enough to withstand the onslaught at all. I saw some great pieces newly cleansed of sand; they were made of aluminium and, in spite of their bulk, could easily be lifted.

Making the sand moulds is comparatively clean work, but turning the shells covers the workers with a film of oil, which drips from the machine at every point and seems to permeate the air. The work on various parts of rifles, though at large, oily machines, is far cleaner, the point of attack, where contact is established with whatever tiny nozzle or nut of brass is in progress, being wonderfully minute. All around the girls as they work the floor is strewn with hair-fine shavings of aluminium, like the frosting on a Christmas card, or with a powdering of brass as pale as gold. The cleanest work of all is the verifying, which chiefly consists of measuring all the pieces made by means of large compasses, on whose head a needle swings to the maximum and minimum points allowed, according to the angle of the application. Anything, even to a shrapnel bullet, that is not absolutely true, is rejected either for correction or complete melting down. Even the tools made for use in the factory are both verified and corrected by women, to ensure the angles at the sharpened end being mathematically accurate.

The aeroplane engines, when completed, are mounted on high platforms so that the propeller projects, and the noise when two or three are being tested is more appalling than all the other sounds in the works put together. The air vibrates with their harsh screaming, as though angry at their own impotence, chained there wingless, while the propellers are mere circling blurs. Aeroplanes are the most romantic things in the world, but there is something rather pathetic about the engine alone, like a bee whose wings have been stripped off by some callous child. But there is always a thrill to be expected on looking at the screaming engines whose propellers, though at the moment vainly threshing the air, will so soon be rising, solid weight of metal as they are, up into the sky.

Another thing of particular interest that I saw was the chassis of a huge motor lorry, weighing ten tons, of which the front and back wheels can work independently, so that if either pair are hopelessly stuck, the other can extricate the whole affair. In spite of the huge size and weight of this motor, I found wheel and levers comparatively easy to handle. But, on the whole, nothing seemed to me as interesting as the shells, because one could follow their progress from the mere shapeless lumps of metal to the fitting of the cap and the copper band near the base of the shell itself, which is such a necessary addition. For it is that smooth but outstanding band which allows the shell to spin on its wild rush through the ribbed interior of the gun, and in that rush this smooth ribbon of copper becomes deeply fluted, as we are now so used to seeing it on the fragments of shell that adorn so many mantelpieces at home. They were, of course, still smooth, the copper ribbons on those attacks of complete shells I saw, for the shining, blunt-nose creatures they girdled were virgin still, though to the eyes that had seen their progress from their red-hot inception, so instinct with a dire potency.

Irene Rathbone
from
We That Were Young

Rows of blue-overalled girls in unbecoming jelly-bag caps sat or stood all day in the long light shed of Staple and Studd's munition works at Willesden. Two hundred and fifty girls divided into sections according to the different jobs they were doing; three hundred men in other parts of the same vast shed. From eight to five, with an hour's break for lunch, they worked unceasingly.

Many of them came long distances. Liz Fanshawe, whose people kept a small shop in Brixton, took an hour to come. Nellie Crewe, ex-kitchen-maid in a boarding-house, took about the same time from her crowded home in Battersea. Pamela Butler, who sat between them, was luckier. If she caught the right trains and trams she could do the distance from her aunt's door in Curzon Street to the door of the 'shop' in forty-five minutes.

These three, with twenty-seven others, sat at the drilling machines. Perched on high stools, their feet on the cross-bar of the bench in front of them, their left hands held pieces of steel, six inches square, which were to become the backs of signal-lamps; their right hands worked the levers which drilled into the plates five holes on five marked places. From the machine up to the ceiling ran broad leather belts which flapped and whirred. The noise made by all the belts together was like a flock of nightmare birds. Added to it was the noise of the drilling of the plates; and from all parts of the shop came a mixed din of rasping, filing, cutting, hammering. Clang, clang, zzz, whrr. Clang, clang, zzz, whrr. Deafening, stupefying, brain-shattering.

Down came Pamela's lever: once, twice ... five times. The plate was thrown on to a pile beside her. Another was picked up, held steady, punched, dropped. She could do thirty to the hour now, like Liz Fanshawe on her right; for the first fortnight she had only been able to do twenty-four. The present pace meant keeping hard at it. Incidentally it meant extra pay on to one's £3 a week, and that was not to be despised.

A foreman wandered past, and paused behind Liz Fanshawe's stool. He was a jovial man, with a straw-coloured moustache, and was known as 'Father.' He was apt at times to bully, and at times to be familiar, but on the whole he was decent enough.

''Ello, Liz, wot's up with you this morn'n? Taking it easy, my girl? 'Ad one over the eight last night?'

'Go on, Father!' she shouted through the roar of the machinery. 'Don't 'and me out a lot of 'ole balsam! My work's orl right.'

'Now, *Saucy!*'

The foreman came behind Pamela, looked over her shoulder, and moved on without addressing her.

''Ear that?' Liz screamed when he had gone. 'Comin' in with a lot of ole madam! 'Oo does 'e think 'e is? Does 'e think I'm a penny-in-the-slot machine? Bin on this blasted job now six weeks. So've you. *You* know wot it's like!'

Pamela nodded sympathetically. The muscles of her fore-arm were aching. Another hour till lunch-time.

'Yer don't look too grand yerself terdye,' Liz bellowed at her. 'Worst of me is, when I'm feeling all in I don't show it same as others do.'

Nor did she. Her peony-coloured face and coarse black hair proclaimed triumphant health even at her lowest moments. She was a good-natured creature, if a bit foul-mouthed at times, and it was impossible not to like her; and Pamela, who hated making the exertion of raising her voice, had evolved a whole series of facial expressions with which to carry on conversation with her cheery neighbour.

The buzzer sounded through the shop. Twelve o'clock. The machines were turned off. The belts slowed down, flapped, stopped. Blessed silence! Pamela climbed off her stool, bent and stretched her right arm several times, and followed the blue chattering stream of other girls to the canteen. This was fifty yards away, up a bit of bad road churned into mud by the passing lorries. The late September air struck chill after the heated fuggy atmosphere of the shop, where ventilation was regarded with horror by the majority of the workers. Inside the canteen it was just pleasantly warm.

An excellent lunch could be procured here for a shilling. The catering had lately been taken over and feeding arrangements reorganised by Miss Dixon, the Supervisor, a woman of great competence, brusque hearty manners, and knowledge of all grades of humanity. The men and girls were devoted to her, and among some of them she went affectionately by the name of 'Dick.'

Pamela sat with a little quiet girl, a Miss Fenton, the daughter of a country vicar of small means and numerous progeny. Miss Fenton made no bones about the usefulness of the money she was earning. She was living at present with relations in London. She had several brothers at the Front. Pamela and she, finding much in common, had clung together from the first.

In work hours the other girls treated them in a friendly natural manner, neither with suspicion nor jealousy, neither with undue reserve nor undue familiarity; in off hours they left them tacitly alone.

'The only thing that I feel I *may* not be able to stick,' Pamela confided to her companion at lunch, 'is the awful lavatory arrangement!'

'I know,' said Miss Fenton, in her unemotional little voice. 'This morning I waited outside the doors quite ten minutes in the giggling crowd, and when at last one of the doors did open and let out a girl – Elsie Thompson it was – and I slipped in, I found there were two or three more inside. Elsie hadn't told me, she'd just let me pass. Extraordinary, isn't it!'

'M'm.' Pamela's expression was of controlled distaste. 'I'd never before imagined that that particularly private business could be carried on communally, had you?'

'The places are thoroughly cleaned out you know,' Miss Fenton remarked by way of consolation.

'I know … but even then … ! Well, I never *sit* on the seat myself – not actually – do you?'

They smoked their cigarettes. All the workers smoked after lunch – it was the only moment when they were allowed to. Then they trooped back to the shop.

Clang, clang, zzz, whrr. Clang, clang, zzz, whrrr.

Liz Fanshawe broke into song.

'"*Gawd* send you *back* to maee, *Owver* the rowling sea,"' she wailed, as she punched and levered. '"*Dearest*, I love you so-ow."'

Several girls joined in. Some sang what they called 'second,' but what was really growling and irrelevant bass.

'Now then, Liz, stop that!' came Miss Dixon's firm cheery tones. 'You know that song's not allowed.'

'Ow, Dick, it *does* 'elp!'

'Nonsense, it hinders. Your work slows down to its pace. Try another with a smarter rhythm, and keep time to *that*! ... All right, Butler?' she asked, passing Pamela's stool, and received a smiling nod.

Miss Dixon strode on in her long white coat. Seeing to the welfare of two hundred and fifty girls of all types was no easy job, but she was cut out for it. And just as no malingerer could bluff her, so no ardent martyr could carry off sickness by pretending to be well. She saw through either. It was her business to keep her varied troop hard at it and yet healthy.

'Ow, Dick,' yelled Liz, 'when are them new caps coming you promised us?'

'Next week, I hope,' was the reply.

'These 'ere things make us look like Jack-in-the-Green! Look at Nellie Crewe there! 'Ers is so big it makes 'er seem like a rat looking out of a sink-'ole!'

At three o'clock tea was brought round, thick cups of strong brown liquid. You paid a penny a cup. Pamela never took it. At the best of times she disliked tea, and only drank it if it was expensive china, and extremely weak. Liz swallowed hers at a gulp.

'That's better!' she sighed. 'Now come on, girls! "*Take* me back to dear ole *Bli-ighty*, Tum te, tum te, tumte, tum te, *tum*." Lor', that tea ain't 'alf made me 'ead sweat! Funny! Think I'll take me cap orf for a minute. Where's ole Dick? Don't want '*er* after me body!'

She pulled off the detested head-gear – though it was strictly against orders – and fluffed out her wiry black hair. The breeze from the flapping belt above her blew pleasantly on her hot forehead. She seized her lever.

'"Tiddely-iddely-ighty, carry me back to *Blighty, Blighty – is* the – *place – for – me*."' The last five notes were slightly slowed down to enable her to punch her plate in time to them.

'Put your cap on again!' shouted Pamela; but the din from the whole shop, and Liz's strident singing, drowned her cry. She waved her hand, pointed to her neighbour's head, and then to her own. Liz saw the gesture, but only laughed.

'Not much! I shan't be seen! I feel fine like this!' Her hair was blowing about. '"Birmingham, Leeds, or Manchester, I *don't – much – care*!"'

In a second it had happened. She had leant a fraction too far forward, and the wind from the flapping belt had blown her hair into the wheel of the drilling-machine. There was a yell which pierced even the usual racket of the shop, and the big Liz was on her feet, her eyes staring from their sockets, both hands to her head. The front part of it – from the forehead back – had been ripped raw.

The belt whirred on. The wheel continued to revolve; but now it had grown a wiry black beard which at each revolution flicked up into sight.

'All right, Liz,' cried Miss Dixon, who had materialised from nowhere, and was holding the screaming girl beneath the arms. 'Steady, steady now. You're all right.'

The girls round about had leapt to their feet; Pamela being nearest was best able to give assistance. But they were all ordered off.

'Get back to your stools!' thundered Miss Dixon, in the voice of a sergeant-major. 'All right, Liz. I'm with you.'

The next minute Liz, with a long moan, had crumpled up, and two St John Ambulance men, arriving from other parts of the shop, lifted her and carried her away.

Work was resumed. But, on Pamela's left, little Nellie Crewe, having moved her lever weakly once or twice, slid from her stool and staggered off. Pamela punched on in a frenzy, fighting her nausea. One did not faint. If one had any stamina, any pride, one – did – not – faint. Work must go on – and quicker than ever now. Anything to forget that bare raw strip of scalp – like the strip made by a reaping-machine in a field of corn; any-thing to forget those eyes – the eyes of a panic-stricken beast. In fifteen minutes Nellie was back on her stool. Pamela shot a glance at her. Both their faces, though they didn't know it, were white as paper.

'All right now?'

Nellie nodded. She had been quietly sick in one of the lavatory basins, where the old woman in attendance had held her head; and now she was able to go on.

At five o'clock the machines whirred down to silence. The girls trooped to the cloak-room, took off caps and overalls, put on outdoor things, and poured out into the dirty purple twilight to catch their trams.

Peggy Hamilton
from
Three Years or the Duration: Memoirs of a Munition Worker 1914–18

And so for months we toiled. The days were long and we slept like logs. I would have missed my first air raid if Joan had not awakened me. Of course, once I was properly awake the noise was deafening. The Zeppelin was almost overhead, we could see it very clearly in the searchlights and there was an anti-aircraft battery quite close to us. The Zeppelin was not very high and the shells were bursting all round it; then one seemed to explode very close to it and the Zeppelin turned and made off. We returned to bed and instantly to sleep.

There were so many workers in the New Fuse shop that I never got to know any except the girl on the machine next to me, my dear fitter Bert, the works manager, Mr Dynes, the foreman, and two girls Joan had met before. There was not much time to talk, except in the lunch hour as we hurried along to the canteen in the Square, or in the tea knock-off when we took sandwiches and a thermos to our cloakroom. The street was always teeming with people, workers, soldiers and sailors from all over the world. One day, running along the road to catch the bus with a friend who had been given a rose and was wearing it in her buttonhole, we came across two or three dashing young Australians, with high boots and ostrich feathers in their hats. One of these glamorous young men blocked our way and, clasping our friend to his manly bosom, said, 'What a beautiful rose,' buried his face in it, and walked on.

On Saturday night Woolwich Square was a wonder and a delight. Teeming with people of every race and colour, in and out of uniform, the crowd would swell to bursting point as the workers streamed out of the Arsenal to gather round the stalls and the tub-thumpers for an evening's amusement. There were barrels of whelks and winkles to be eaten with pins, coloured men selling silk shawls, jewellery, clothing, patent medicines. Teeth were extracted 'painlessly', conjurers performed, and every kind of slick selling guy went through his repertoire. One Saturday night we found a man selling little bottles of patent medicine, and as we squeezed ourselves within earshot he was saying, 'Three times I've been in jail, I 'ave, and for why? I'll tell you why, because I cured a woman when the physicians they couldn't.' In spite of the heat and our weariness, we were often too fascinated to tear ourselves away, but elbowed our way round from one attraction to another in the sweltering summer night. Then, having at last had our fill, we would push our way home to our lodgings and the supper which our good landlady always had ready for us. Her husband was a nightshift worker and she fed us all splendidly, but when she herself slept I never found out. One night a stack of shell-cases fell on her husband and he was incapacitated for life.

Part IV

THE END

... one will at last fully recognise that the dead are not only dead for the duration of the war. (Lady Cynthia Asquith, *Diaries 1915–18*)

The Armistice came into force on 11 November 1918. The War was over, but it took nearly two years to negotiate peace throughout Europe.[1] The end of the War was not heralded with the same kind of revelry as its outbreak. There was too much weariness; too much had been lost for victory to feel victorious. On top of four years of slaughter, the influenza epidemic of 1918–19 killed more people than the War itself. The two decades which followed brought instability and uncertainty to all the countries of Europe, with a legacy of extremist politics and further war. Those who had survived the War would be for ever tainted by the memory. The next generation reached maturity with a determination to live life to the full, just in case someone decided to take it away early.

Accounts of the end of the War have a tendency to be understated, cautious, even suspicious of the future. Many women writing in the decade following the end of the War allowed their words to be permeated with a distinct sense of loss, a 'lonely generation', haunted by the fear that it could all so easily happen again. Schoolgirl Patricia Hanbury expresses excitement as her studies are interrupted by the news of peace, but she is disappointed by the level of public celebrations and the day is clouded for her by drunken soldiers. Yet it is easy to imagine the number of people who might have been drinking to forget.

Hilda Craven has a more positive experience among the cheering

---

[1] The peace treaty was not signed until 28 June 1919 at the Palace of Versailles. The civil war continued in Russia between the Bolshevik government and the remnants of the White Army with Western Allies. A further five treaties were signed in the fourteen months following the Treaty of Versailles (Winter, 1988: 202). Also see: Alan Sharpe, *The Versailles Settlement: Peacemaking in Paris, 1919* (Basingstoke: Macmillan, 1991); Trevor Wilson, *The Myriad Faces of War: Britain and the Great War 1914–1918* (Cambridge: Polity, 1986); Eric Hobsbawm, *The Short Twentieth Century 1914–1991* (London: Michael Joseph, 1994).

crowds outside Buckingham Palace, waiting for an appearance by the King and Queen.[2] But for both Virginia Woolf and Beatrice Webb, the crowd of Armistice Day in London holds much less appeal. In her diary for the 11 November 1918 Webb writes:

> Peace! London to-day is a pandemonium of noise and revelry, soldiers and flappers being most in evidence. Multitudes are making all the row they can, and in spite of depressing fog and steady rain, discords of sound and struggling, rushing beings and vehicles fill the streets.

For Woolf, writing in her diary on 12 November 1918, 'the heavens disapproved' as the grey wet November weather seems to typify the anticlimax. The moment has meaning, it has emotion, but there is 'no centre, no form at all for all this wandering emotion to take'. No one is clear of their direction any more. No one seems to know what to do next.

Well, almost no one. *Britannia*, the mouthpiece of Emmeline and Christabel Pankhurst, takes a predictably more positive approach to the end of the War. In 1918 the first goal of the Suffrage Movement had been achieved as some women were given the vote.[3] During the War women had justified their right to citizenship with their enormous contribution to the war effort. They had carried out almost every conceivable social and professional role, with the exception of actually fighting. Having achieved a moderate success, *Britannia* could afford to be emphatic in its cries of 'no mercy' for the defeated German enemy. This publication shows no fear that an overly harsh peace settlement might cause more trouble in international politics. Nor does it predict the powerful move to push women back into their prewar roles, as men returned looking for their old jobs. It is perhaps ironic that *Britannia* fights so emphatically against any political movement, such as Bolshevism, which might threaten the stability of a democratic government capable of offering women a vote: the same democratic government against whom they had fought for so long. It would be ten years before all women were enfranchised and there was still a lot of work to do.

As soon as the dust settled women began to look to the future; to the rebuilding of a world in which a lasting peace could be established. Enid

---

[2] The war diary of Hilda Craven is held in the Liddle Collection, University of Leeds.

[3] The 1918 Representation of the People Act gave the vote to women of property over the age of thirty. For further information on the Act see: Sandra Stanley Holton, *Feminism and Democracy: Women's Suffrage and Reform Politics in Britain 1900–1918* (Cambridge: Cambridge University Press, 1986); Martin Pugh, *Women and the Women's Movement in Britain 1914–1959* (Basingstoke: Macmillan, 1992).

Bagnold's novel *The Happy Foreigner* (1920) illustrates both the fragility of the world that must be reconstructed and the optimism of some of those who have survived to carry out the task. Her heroine, Fanny (a member of the FANY) drives across the devastated battlefields of France finding the beginnings of new life growing from beneath the destruction. Fanny is a modern woman, a product of the Great War. She is the woman who, throughout the years of fighting, has had the opportunity to obtain new levels of freedom. She represents all those women who have learnt new skills, proved themselves in trade and commerce, faced the horrors produced by the battlefields, and come through. She can leave the broken landscape behind her, but she approaches the future with new values and keen sense of living for the moment.

But not all women can leave the past behind. Cynthia Asquith suffered a nervous breakdown at the end of the War. Her final diary fragment leaves the impression that the pain is only just beginning. Vera Brittain waited a long time before she was able to write her own war experience through *Testament of Youth*. In *Honourable Estate* (1936) she addresses, in fiction, those feelings of desolation which accompany the realisation of the dead. Heroine Ruth Allendyne recalls not only personal loss but the loss of all humanity as she surveys an Italian war cemetery. By 1936, Brittain, an ardent pacifist involved with the League of Nations, was doubtless growing more and more anxious about the threat of another war. She allows Allendyne to share this fear, 'if another such doom were to come upon the world, mankind would live no more'. In the light of the enormous impact of the Great War on the society and culture of the early twentieth century, this would seem to be the only reasonable conclusion to reach.

12

Armistice and aftermath

Patricia Hanbury

Armistice Signed

I was in the middle of an essay on Garibaldi & I just stopped & wrote Armistice in big letters across the page! Mother, [Missban] & I went over to our dear little church to which we had pleaded Friday after Friday for 'war intercession' for such terrible years. One couldn't pray – one's heart was just overwhelmed with a big 'thank God!' & nothing else mattered. We knelt there with guns booming, bugles blowing & church bells ring-ing & the whole air filled with a great joy & thankfulness. …

[Missban] & I hung out a big bundle of flags & tied bits of red, white & blue ribbon to everything. In the afternoon I went by train to Windsor to meet Rachel & drive home in the car with her. At Taplow station a crowd of M.O.'s & Tommies from the hospital were overwhelmingly happy & cheered the train that was taking them up to rejoice in 'the Big City.' Windsor was beautiful – a perfect maze of different flags meeting across the narrow streets. In the morning the Guards' band processed round the town with Eton boys on their arms – exchanging hats with them! Rachel & I couldn't go to bed ordinarily, so we first went to a very nice service, consisting of nearly all psalms & hymns in our little church, with the alter decorated with flags, & we then walked to Maidenhead to see what was happening there! The lamps had been washed & therefore shone brightly on the garlands of flags across the street. We saw an ambulance crowded with orderlies & convalescents waving flags & making odd noises with trumpets, megaphones etc. etc. Beyond a few cheers there was nothing exciting & our rejoicings were rather damped when we came across sev-eral hopelessly drunk Tommies. It seems so sad that getting drunk should be their way of rejoicing.

Hilda Craven
The Great Day of Days

Monday November 11th 1918
The great day of all days. Armistice signed by the Germans at 5.00 o'clock a.m. Heard the news at 10.00 which we didn't altogether believe but 11.00 the guns went off proclaiming peace at last and we all nearly went mad. Flags appeared very quickly from somewhere and everyone full of smiles once again. On duty in gym in afternoon. Only 7 patients left so nothing much to do. Sgt. May in Boreham treated us to champagne and then I had a hand of bridge with King, Reinert and Goodfellow. Rushed off at 7.45 with Bolingbrook and Sister Thompson and all went off to town by the 8.40, also Sister McNaught. Win and D. had gone up earlier in afternoon. London mad with joy and it was grand to see the lights full on again and to hear good-hearted cheers – crowds round Buckingham Palace where we made for and as luck would have it we only had to wait 20 minutes before the King, Queen, Princess Mary and the Duke of Connaught appeared on the balcony. Oh, it was a grand sight and the crowd seemed to cheer them from their very hearts. It's a sight I shall never forget and I am very glad I have been as near London and able to see it

Tuesday November 12th 1918
It's hard to realise that after 4 years of terrible anxiety and slaughter the war is over at last and the fighting finished with. The heavy clouds which always hung over us on waking up are rolled away and there is a different feeling over everything and everybody. D., Win and self went up to town again to see the rejoicing. The streets very gay and much beflagged. Captured guns in the Mall, motor lorries packed with girls and soldiers singing and dressed up, officers acting silly and dressing up in restaurants etc. and a general noise everywhere. Win went to Prisoners of War and was told all parcels were stopped and the prisoners were being sent back as soon as poss. so she is very happy to think that Geo. will soon be back amongst them again. Had tea at Maison Lyons and then went to see 'The Boy' at the Adelphi – oh, what a sight in The Strand. One surging mass of people and a very orderly crowd too, enjoyed the piece very much and Berry was a treat – came back by 11.20 – rather tired.

December 25th 1918
'Victory' Christmas in hospital. Colonel allowed all fit men to go home for 12 days but B top being such a happy floor had 30 stayed behind and all other floors only 6 and 12. B ground joined with A ground so B top was left alone in the block and a very jolly time we had too. 4 wards open, 10, 11, 13, 14, – all beautifully decorated, also the corridors. I got a raffle with 5 prizes which mother and auntie sent and got to £2, then father sent me £1 so I was able to buy for each man – tablet of soap, writing block, matches, chocolate, handkerchief, Xmas card and a toy – some had pipes and pouches instead of block which father sent me. I bought [Nassiban] Hagar Brandon and Glenn toys and we had great fun over them. Christmas morning started well by much noise and kissing which for the patients was great fun.

The whole staff was caught even I was again under the mistletoe which they had been told beforehand not to use but our expostulations were to no avail and they kept the game up until dinner time – we daren't go in our wards to dust!! 1.00 o'clock great dinner over in A block for patients – turkey, plum pudding, jellies, crackers galore. Afternoon each floor gave separate teas and B top surpassed the lot – patients dressed up and we had a huge tea in ward 10 – 51 sitting down together and lots of visitors. Everyone very jolly, dancing in B ground; after 7.00 o'clock we went to quarters, dressed in fancy dress (I as Miss Matty) and then we had a huge dinner at Ecclesbourne – great spread and very nice too. Sister Glover as a sweep got first prize then we all went back to Crescent and danced till 11.30. All had a great time and thoroughly enjoyed the day – patients say never had a better time in their lives. Got some lovely presents – mother, watch; father pendant; 16 hankies, hankey sachet, pin cushion, needle cases etc, cards and a PC from N. J. Craven which pleased me ever so much.

Virginia Woolf
The Aspect of Peace

Monday 11 November 1918
Twentyfive minutes ago the guns went off, announcing peace. A siren hooted on the river. They are hooting still. A few people ran to look out of the windows. The rooks wheeled round, & were for a moment, the

symbolic look of creatures performing some ceremony, partly of thanksgiving, partly of valediction over the grave. A very cloudy still day, the smoke toppling over heavily towards the east; & that too wearing for a moment a look of something floating, waving, drooping. We looked out of the window; saw the housepainter give one look at the sky & go on with his job; the old man toddling along the street carrying a bag out [of] which a large loaf protruded, closely followed by his mongrel dog. So far neither bells nor flags, but the wailing of sirens & intermittent guns.

Tuesday 12 November 1918
We should have done well, I think, to be satisfied with the aspect of peace; how the rooks flew slowly in circles, & the smoke drooped; but I had to go to Harrison, & I think we were both conscious of a restlessness which made it seem natural to be going up to London. Disillusionment began after 10 minutes in the train. A fat slovenly woman in black velvet & feathers with the bad teeth of the poor insisted upon shaking hands with two soldiers; 'It's thanks to you boys &c. &c.' She was half drunk already, & soon produced a large bottle of beer which she made them drink of; & then she kissed them, & the last we saw of her was as she ran alongside the train waving her hand to the two stolid soldiers. But she & her like possessed London, & alone celebrated peace in their sordid way, staggering up the muddy pavements in the rain, decked with flags themselves, & voluble at sight of other people's flags. The heavens disapproved & did their utmost to extinguish, but only succeeded in making feathers flop & flags languish. Taxicabs were crowded with whole families, grandmothers & babies, showing off; & yet there was no centre, no form at all for all this wandering emotion to take. The crowds had nowhere to go, nothing to do; they were in the state of children with too long a holiday. Perhaps the respectable suppressed what joy they felt; there seemed to be no mean between tipsy ribaldry & rather sour disapproval. Besides the discomfort tried every one's temper. It took us from 4 to 6 to get home; standing in queues, every one wet, many shops shut, no light yet procurable, & in everyone's mind the same restlessness & inability to settle down, & yet discontent with what ever it was possible to do.

Beatrice Webb
Peace in London

November 11th. [1918] – Peace! London to-day is a pandemonium of noise and revelry, soldiers and flappers being most in evidence. Multitudes are making all the row they can, and in spite of depressing fog and steady rain, discords of sound and struggling, rushing beings and vehicles fill the streets. Paris, I imagine, will be more spontaneous and magnificent in its rejoicing. Berlin, also, is reported to be elated, having got rid not only of the war but also of its oppressors. The peoples are everywhere rejoicing. Thrones are everywhere crashing and the men of property are everywhere secretly trembling. 'A biting wind is blowing for the cause of property', writes an Austrian journalist. How soon will the tide of revolution catch up the tide of victory? That is a question which is exercising Whitehall and Buckingham Palace and which is causing anxiety even among the more thoughtful democrats. Will it be six months or a year?

From Britannia, *no. 22 vol. VII, 15 November 1918*
The War Is Won
We Have Now
to Win the Peace

In other words we must:

1. Defeat German attempts to spread Bolshevism and Anarchy in this century, remembering that so far as that is concerned such Germans as Scheidemann and his colleagues are as dangerous as the Kaiser himself.

2. Prevent any kind of Compromise Peace with the Germans, whether under their present Government or any other, remembering that it is the savage and aggressive spirit of the German people that has been the real cause of this war and constitutes the danger of future war.

3. Prevent any Compromise Peace with the associates of Germany in the war, remembering that they have shown themselves the spiritual affinities and guilty accomplices of the Germans, and that they have

proved themselves to be merciless and dangerous enemies of our Allies as well as ourselves.

Enid Bagnold
from
The Happy Foreigner

Ahead lay the terrible miles. She seemed to make no gain upon them, and could not alter the face of the horizon, however fast she drove. Iron, brown grass – brown grass and iron, spars of wood, girders, torn railway lines and stones. Even the lorries travelling the road were few and far between. A deep loneliness was settled upon the desert where nothing grew. Yet, suddenly, from a ditch at the side of the road, a child of five stared at her. It had its foot close by a stacked heap of hand grenades; a shawl was wrapped round it and the thin hands held the ends together. What child? Whose? How did it get here, when not a house stood erect for miles and miles – when not a coil of smoke touched the horizon! Yes, something oozed from the ground! Smoke, blue smoke! Was life stirring like a bulb under this winter ruin, this cemetery of village bones.

She stopped the car. The child turned and ran quickly across a heap of dust and iron and down into the ground behind a pillar. 'It must have a father or mother below –' The breath of the invisible hearth coiled up into the air; the child was gone.

A man appeared behind the pillar and came towards the car. Fanny held out her cigarette-case and offered it to him.

'Have you been here long?' she asked.

'A month, mademoiselle.'

'Are there many of you in this – village?'

(Not a spar, not a pile of bricks stood higher than two feet above the ground.)

'There are ten persons now. A family came in yesterday.'

'But how are you fed?'

'A lorry passes once a week for all the people in this district – within fifty miles. There are ten souls in one village, twenty in another, two in another. They have promised to send us huts, but the huts don't come. We have sunk a well now and it is drinkable, but before that we got water by lorry once a week, and we often begged a little from the radiators of other lorries.'

'What have you got down there?'

'It is the cellar of my house, mademoiselle. There are two rooms still, and one is watertight. The trouble is the lack of tools. I can't build anything. We have a spade, and a pick and a hammer, which we keep between the ten of us.'

'Take my hammer,' said Fanny. 'I can get another in the garage.'

He took it, pleased and grateful, and she left this pioneer of recolonisation, this obstinate Crusoe and his family, standing by his banner of blue smoke.

Lady Cynthia Asquith
The Prospect of Peace

I am beginning to rub my eyes at the prospect of peace. I think it will require more courage than anything that has gone before. It isn't until one leaves off spinning round that one realises how giddy one is. One will have to look at long vista again, instead of short ones, and one will at last fully recognise that the dead are not only dead for the duration of the war.

Vera Brittain
from
Honourable Estate

And all at once, as she stood above that valley of death, her memories of the War and its aftermath came back to her in a torrent of recollection. She pictured again the dead buried in the sands of Gallipoli; she recalled her dying patients in France after Loos and the Somme and Passchendaele; she remembered the devastated villages of Volhynia, the forgotten German cemetery in a Polish wood, the stiff frozen bodies in Buzuluk churchyard; she now saw before her the fifteen thousand graves of American soldiers gathered together at Romagne from the trackless undergrowth and dark ravines of the Argonne Forest. How vast, illimitable and incalculable was the desolation which the War had brought! Stretching across the earth from America to Russia, from Flanders to Gallipoli, were the hidden whitening bones of a generation of men. Civilisation had barely survived their loss; if another such doom were to come upon the world, mankind would live no more. Surely, then, we cannot permit it; surely the instinct of self-preservation must override humanity's diabolical capacity for self-destruction!

'The light is fading,' she said to herself. 'I must face it now.'

Notes on the authors

JANE ADDAMS (1860–1935) was an American philanthropist who founded the Hull House social settlement in Chicago – a settlement for immigrants to the USA. She was President of the Women's International League for Peace and Freedom from its foundation, following the Hague Conference in 1915, until her death.

MILDRED ALDRICH (1853–1928) was a retired American journalist, living about twenty miles outside Paris in 1914. Her first book, *A Hilltop on the Marne* (1915), gives a detailed account of the early threat to Paris. *On the Edge of the War Zone* (1917) further describes the scenes she witnessed.

ELIZABETH VON ARNIM (1866–1941) was born Mary Annette Beauchamp in Sydney, Australia, but was brought up in England. In 1890 she married Count Henning August von Arnim and lived with him in Prussia until debt forced them to move in 1908. She wrote twenty-two books, the most famous of which was the first, *Elizabeth and Her German Garden* (1898). Her war novel, *Christine*, which draws upon her experience of living in Germany, was published in 1917.

LADY CYNTHIA ASQUITH (1887–1960) was the third child of Hugo Charteris, Lord Elcho (later 11th Earl of Wemyss). She married Herbert Asquith, son of Prime Minister Herbert Asquith, in 1910. She kept her diary from 1915 to 1918, giving a detailed account of her lifestyle, wartime and family activities. She lost two brothers in the Great War. After the War she became secretary to J. M. Barrie, continuing in that role for twenty years.

ENID BAGNOLD (1889–1981) spent some of her childhood in Jamaica. At nineteen she moved to Chelsea and became an art student at Walter Sickert's school of drawing and painting. In 1914 she went to work as a VAD nurse at the Royal Herbert Hospital, Woolwich. *A Diary Without Dates* (1918) records her experiences. Later she joined the FANY as a driver in France. Her letters home provided the basis for *The Happy Foreigner* (1920). In 1920 she married Sir Roderick Jones, Chairman of Reuters. She continued to write novels and plays.

ETHEL MARY BILBOROUGH was a civilian living in Chislehurst, Kent, with her husband.

MARY BORDEN (1886–1968) was American by birth but married General Sir Edward Spears to become Lady Spears. She had her own money, enabling her to set up a hospital unit close to the French lines, in which she worked as a nurse for the duration of the War.

VERA BRITTAIN (1893–1970) worked as a VAD nurse during the War. She kept a diary, later published as *Chronicle of Youth* (1981), which formed the basis for her ground-breaking autobiographical record of the War, *Testament of Youth* (1933). She lost her brother, her fiancé and her closest friends in the War. In the following years she became an ardent pacifist and worked for the League of Nations.

MARY ANN BROWN (1883–1968) trained at Paisley Hospital and joined QAIMNSR as an officer in January 1915. She served in the Mediterranean, at Gallipoli and Salonika, then in India and Mesopotamia, being mentioned in despatches and decorated by the Serbian Military. After the War she became a nursing sister with the Anglo-Iranian Oil Company (later BP). She married Cyril Spencely Cleverly in 1934 and remained in the Middle East for most of the Second World War.

G. K. BRUMWELL worked as a masseuse during the Great War. She wrote this piece in 1918 and tried, without success, to have it published in the *Daily Mail*.

EMILY CHITTICKS met her fiancé Will Martin on 9 August 1916 just as he was about to begin his army training. He was killed in action on 27 March 1917. She never married.

MARY CLARKE, biographical information unobtainable.

LADY KATE COURTNEY (1847–1929) was the sister of Beatrice Webb. In 1883 she married Leonard Courtney, later Lord Courtney of Penwith. They shared many like-minded friends in the political, academic and intellectual worlds. Extracts from her war diary were published privately in 1927.

HILDA CRAVEN lived at Ribby Hall in Lancashire with her parents and six brothers and sisters. Her diary suggests that the War only rarely intruded into her affluent life until she became a VAD nurse at Crescent Military Hospital, Croydon 1918–19. There are very few entries for this period.

LADY DE FRECE (1864–1952) better known as Vesta Tilley, was born Matilda Alice Powles. After a first stage appearance at the age of three, she became a celebrated male impersonator. Her image as a khaki-clad Great War soldier was a popular one. In 1890 she married Sir Walter de Frece. Her autobiography *The Recollections of Vesta Tilley* was published in 1934.

MARGARET FAWCETT was an orderly with a unit of Dr Elsie Inglis's Scottish Women's Hospitals who served in Romania and Russia.

A. T. FITZROY (Rose Allatini, 1890–1980) was born in Vienna, but later moved to England. She wrote romantic fiction using the name Rose Allatini. When she published *Despised and Rejected* (1918) under the pseudonym A. T. Fitzroy, reviewers assumed the author was a man. In 1921 she married composer Cyril Scott. They separated in 1941 and Allatini spent most of the rest of her life living with a woman, Melanie Mills, at Rye. Between 1941 and 1978 she published many novels under the name Eunice Buckley.

NELL HAGUE, biographical information unobtainable.

RADCLYFFE HALL (Marguerite, 1880–1943), lesbian poet and novelist who served as an ambulance driver during the War. The largely autobiographical novel *The Well of Loneliness* (1928) deals with this experience. The novel was suppressed after an obscenity trial, being one of the first works to deal openly with lesbianism. Hall also used her war experience for a collection of short stories, *Miss Ogilvy Finds Herself* (1934).

CECILY HAMILTON (1872–1952) was a former actress and dramatist who had become active in the suffrage campaign. During the War she worked as an administrator in a French Military hospital and later helped to organise wartime entertainment. She wrote three war books, *Senlis* (1917) which describes the destruction of the French town and its population, *William an Englishman* (1919), a novel which won the Femina Vie Heureuse prize in that year, and *Theodore Savage* (1922), a dystopian novel.

MARY AGNES HAMILTON (1884–1966) was a novelist educated at Newnham. She was a Labour MP for Blackburn (1929–31) and a governor of the BBC (1933–37). Her war novels were *Dead Yesterday* (1916) and *Special Providence* (1930).

PEGGY HAMILTON (b. 1895) worked in munitions factories from 1915 to 1918. Her brother was killed in an aviation accident on 10 November 1918.

PATRICIA HANBURY was a schoolgirl during the Great War. Her father was a director of Bank of England and Chairman of Guardian Assurance Co. She later became Lady Patricia Cunningham Grahame.

EMILY HOBHOUSE, biographical information unobtainable.

GERTRUDE HOLLAND was a member of Mrs Mabel St Clair Stobart's Hospital Units in Belgium and Serbia.

WINIFRED HOLTBY (1898–1935) was a Yorkshire-born novelist, dramatist and journalist. She interrupted her degree at Somerville College, Oxford, during the War and served in the WAAC. Returning to Somerville in 1919, she became close friends with Vera Brittain. They were both active campaigners for pacifism and women's rights. Her novel *The Crowded Street* (1924) includes semi-autobiographical wartime experiences such as the account of the German bombing of Scarborough.

ELSIE INGLIS (1864–1917) grew up in India. She received her Medical Diploma in 1892 and worked in a number of hospitals in London and her native Scotland. In 1900 she joined the NUWSS and in 1906 founded the Scottish Women's Suffrage Federation. Together with the NUWSS, Inglis formed the fourteen units of the Scottish Women's Hospitals which she sent abroad to work with the Allied armies. She worked abroad with the units until her death in 1917.

F. TENNYSON JESSE (1888–1958) was an English novelist and dramatist. She worked as a war correspondent during the war and much of her journalism was later published in *Sword of Deborah: First-hand Impressions of the British Women's Army in France* (1919). She later wrote crime fiction.

WINIFRED KENYON (1892–1990) was the daughter of Major-General Edward R Kenyon. During the war she served as a VAD at the Urgency Cases Hospitals at Bar-le-duc and Le Faux Miroir, Revigny. In 1921 she married Herbert Williamson, and moved to Oxford, England.

PHYLLIS LUNN was a schoolgirl and a student during the War.

ELIZABETH A. MACLEOD and MARY L. MACLEOD (twin sisters born 1897) were members of a Cambridge family. Their father was a lecturer at Cambridge University who addressed recruiting rallies and wrote patriotic articles. Their mother was a hospital visitor. They had two brothers in the army. The sisters both worked as VADs and then joined the Women's National Land Service on flax pulling and market gardening projects.

MERE MARIE GEORGINE was a nun in the Ursuline Convent, Thildonck, Wespelaer, Belgium, during the German occupation.

CATHERINE MARSHALL (1880–1961) was an activist in the Women's Movement who became a principal organiser of the NUWSS. A dedicated pacifist, she opposed the Great War by working to set up the international Women's Committee for Permanent Peace and organising the Hague Women's Peace Conference of 1915, although she was unable to attend as the government would not issue the necessary passports. She was also active in the No-Conscription Fellowship. After the war she worked with the League of Nations and assisted refugees from fascism.

ERNESTINE MILLS (1871–1959) was a metal worker, enameller and artist exhibiting both in Britain and abroad. She designed artwork, badges, pendants and jewellery for the WSPU and contributed to magazines such as *The English-woman* and *Apollo*. Examples of her work can be found in a number of collections including the Victoria and Albert Museum, the Royal Collection, Leighton House and the Army Museum in London. She also enamelled memorial tablets for both World Wars which can be found in churches, hospitals and institutions in Britain and abroad.

ELLEN LA MOTTE (1873–1961) was an American nurse, specialising in TB, who was working in Paris when the War broke out. From 1915 onwards she worked in a French military hospital close to front line at Ypres. She recorded her experiences as fragments in *The Backwash of War* (1916). It ran to several editions in the United States before being suppressed in 1918, considered bad for morale. It did not appear in Europe until after the War. La Motte published other medical writings.

ROSIE NEALE was a member of an all-female troupe of musicians and singers who embarked upon a European tour in the summer of 1914.

CHRISTABEL PANKHURST (1880–1958) was a daughter of Emmeline and a leader of the WSPU. With the outbreak of the War she turned her attention to campaigning for the patriotic cause. She worked with Lloyd George to persuade the government to allow women to work in munitions. After the War she continued to fight for women's rights.

EMMELINE PANKHURST (1858–1928) was founder and leader of the WSPU. She worked with her daughter Christabel throughout the War and following years.

ESTELLE SYLVIA PANKHURST (1882–1960) was a daughter of Emmeline Pankhurst. She broke with her mother and sister before the War and focused her attention on the social conditions of families in the East End of London. Throughout the War she was an outspoken pacifist and continued her work with the poor.

ELEANORA B. PEMBERTON (1885–1994) worked as a VAD in France from 1914 to 1917. Following this she returned to England and worked for the Metropolitan Police until the end of the War. She was later awarded the OBE in recognition of her wartime work. She never married, and cared for her parents until their deaths in 1934 and 1938. Much of her life was dedicated to charitable work.

IRENE RATHBONE (1892–1979) was born in Liverpool. She moved to London and began a career as an actress but this was cut short by the outbreak of the War. She worked in a YMCA rest camp at Boulogne, then as a VAD nurse at the 1st London General Hospital. In 1918 she returned to work for the YMCA in France. She wrote a number of novels, including *We That Were Young* (1932), which was based on the wartime experiences of herself and her friends.

FLORA SANDES (1876–1956) was the daughter of a Scottish clergyman. She joined an ambulance unit on the Serbian front in 1914. When the front collapsed she became separated from her unit and joined up with the Serbian army instead. She remained in the army as a Sergeant, and was eventually commissioned as a lieutenant and a captain. She was wounded and decorated for her bravery. Sandes was the only British woman to see active military service during the Great War. She recorded her experiences in *An English Woman-Sergeant in the Serbian Army* (1916) and *The Autobiography of a Woman Soldier* (1927.)

MAY SINCLAIR (1863–1946) was a successful novelist, critic and essayist, who became an important part of the modernist movement. She wrote four war books, *A Journal of Impressions in Belgium* (1915), an account of her three weeks working with a Field Ambulance Corps at the beginning of the war, and three novels, *Tasker Jevons* (1916), *The Tree of Heaven* (1917) and *The Romantic* (1920), all of which reflect her patriotic views. She became disillusioned in the years following the War.

HELEN ZENNA SMITH (Evadne Price, 1901–85) was born in Sydney, Australia, to English parents. She moved to London and worked firstly as an actress, then a journalist. She became a popular children's writer in the 1920s with the 'Jane Turpin' stories. As Helen Zenna Smith, she wrote *Not So Quiet ... Stepdaughters of War* (1932) in response to the success of Erich Maria Remarque's *All Quiet on the Western Front* (1929). It was followed by four further Helen Zenna Smith novels. She also wrote romantic fiction, plays and screenplays.

G. B. STERN (Gladys Bertha, 1890–1973) was born of Jewish parents and is best known for five novels about the Rakonowitz family. Her novel *Children of No Man's Land* (1919) deals with problems of ethnicity and marginality in wartime British society. She converted to Catholicism in 1947.

MABEL ST CLAIR STOBART (1862–1954) founded the Women's Sick and Wounded Convoy Corps in 1907 in order that women might be ready to prove themselves in time of war. She first took the corps into action in the Balkan War of 1912 and wrote *Women and War* (1913) to articulate her views on the position of women in warfare and in politics. In 1914 she went to Belgium and was captured during the German invasion. She only just escaped being shot as a spy. She subsequently set up a hospital staffed by women for the Belgian Red Cross before moving her operations to Serbia in 1915. She served as a Commandant of a hospital unit during the Serbian retreat later that year. *The Flaming Sword in Serbia and Elsewhere* (1916) gives a politicised account of this experience.

BARONESS DE T'SERCLAES, formerly Mrs Knocker, went to Belgium with a Field Ambulance Corps in 1914. With her friend Mairi Chisholm, she later left the unit to set up a dressing station in the derelict village of Pervyse on the Belgian front line. The pair became known as 'the Heroines of Pervyse'. The dressing station was a great success and it was during her work there that Mrs Knocker met and married the Baron de T'Serclaes. In March 1918 she was wounded in a gas attack and forced to return to Britain where she became an officer in the newly founded Women's Royal Air Force. *The Cellar House at Pervyse* (1916) and *Flanders and Other Fields* (1964) both give accounts of her experiences in Belgium.

MURIEL THOMPSON worked as a FANY in the St Omer Motor Ambulance Convoy. She left diaries and notes from 1918.

BEATRICE MORWENNA TREFUSIS (b. 1884) was a professional pianist prior to 1914, having trained in Leipzig and Dresden. During the War she worked in a censor's office In 1919 she married her cousin Schomberg Kerr Trefusis despite family opposition. In later years they ran a nursery garden in Buckinghamshire.

MRS HUMPHRY WARD (1851–1920) was a successful novelist, philanthropist and intellectual figure. She campaigned for higher education for women, but strongly opposed women's suffrage. She was a supporter of the War, and this is evident in all her war writing.

MELVINA WALKER, biographical information unobtainable.

BEATRICE WEBB (1858–1943), sister of Lady Kate Courtney, was a diarist, social reformer and political writer.

VIRGINIA WOOLF (1882–1941) novelist, essayist and critic, remained in London and Sussex during the War. Her diaries record some of the things she witnessed. Her later novels *Jacob's Room* (1922), *Mrs Dalloway* (1925) and *To The Lighthouse* (1927) all incorporate the War as a theme.

Select bibliography

Memoirs and letters held by the Department of Documents, Imperial War Museum

Bilborough, Ethel Mary, Unpublished Diary, MS.

Brown, Mary Ann, Unpublished Diary, MS.

Chitticks, Emily and Martin, William, Unpublished Letters, MS.

Clarke, Mary, Unpublished Diary, MS.

Holland, Gertrude, Unpublished Diary, MS.

Kenyon, Winifred, Unpublished Diary, TS.

Marie Georgine, Mère Unpublished Memoir, MS.

Neale, Rosie, Unpublished Memoir, MS.

Pemberton, Eleanora Blanshard, Unpublished Letters, TS.

Rathbone, Irene, Unpublished Dairy, MS.

Stobart, Mrs Mabel St Clair, Unpublished Diary, TS.

Memoirs held by the Liddle Collection, The Brotherton Library, University of Leeds

Brumwell, G. K., 'The Masseuse', Unpublished Article, TS.

Craven, Hilda, Unpublished Diary, MS.

Hague, Nell, Unpublished Letter to her Husband, 7 June 1915, MS.

Hanbury, Patricia, Unpublished Diary, MS.

Lunn, Phyllis, 'A Schoolgirl's Experiences of the Bombing of Scarborough', Unpublished Account, TS.

Macleod, Elizabeth Aileen, Unpublished Memoir, TS.

Macleod, Mary Lillias, Unpublished Memoir and Letters, TS.

Thompson, Muriel, 'Base Notes', Unpublished Diary, MS.

Trefusis, Beatrice Morwenna, Unpublished Diary, MS.

Primary sources

Aldrich, Mildred, *On the Edge of the War Zone*. London: Constable and Co. Ltd (1918).

Allatini, Rose ('A. T. Fitzroy'), *Despised and Rejected*. London: GMP (1988). (First published 1918.)

Asquith, Cynthia, *Diaries 1915–18*. London: Hutchinson and Co. (1968).

Bagnold, Enid, *A Diary Without Dates*. London: Virago (1978). (First published 1918.)

Bagnold, Enid, *The Happy Foreigner*. London: Virago (1987). (First published 1920.)

Borden, Mary, *The Forbidden Zone*. London: William Heinemann Ltd (1929).

Brittain, Vera, *Testament of Youth*. London: Virago (1992). (First published 1933.)

Brittain, Vera, *Honourable Estate*. London: Victor Gollancz (1936).

Cahill, Audrey Fawcett, ed., *First World War Papers of Margaret Fawcett*. Pietermaritzburg: Wyllie Desktop Publishing (1993).

Courtney, Lady Kate, *War Diaries*. Privately published (1927).

De Frece, Lady, *The Recollections of Vesta Tilley*. London: Hutchinson and Co. (1934).

Hall, Radclyffe, *The Well of Loneliness*. London: Virago (1994). (First Published 1928.)

Hamilton, Cicely, *William an Englishman*. London: Skeffington and Son Ltd (1919).

Hamilton, Mary Agnes, *Dead Yesterday*. London: Duckworth and Co. (1916).

Hamilton, Peggy, *Three Years or the Duration: The Memoirs of a Munition Worker 1914–18*. London: Peter Owen (1978).

Holtby, Winifred, *The Crowded Street*. London: Virago (1981). (First published 1924.)

La Motte, Ellen N., *Backwash of War*. London: G P Puttnam's Sons (1919).

Pankhurst, E. Sylvia, *The Home Front*. London: Hutchinson and Co. (1987). (First published 1932.)

Price, Evadne ('Helen Zenna Smith'), *Not So Quiet … Stepdaughters of War*. London: Virago (1988). (First published 1930.)

Rathbone, Irene, *We That Were Young*. London: Virago (1988). (First published 1932.)

Sandes, Flora, *An English Woman-Sergeant in the Serbian Army*. London, New York and Toronto: Hodder and Stoughton (1916).

Sinclair, May, *A Journal of Impressions in Belgium*. London: Hutchinson and Co. (1915).

Sinclair, May, *The Tree of Heaven*. London: Cassell and Co. (1917).

Stern, G. B., *Children of No Man's Land*. London: Duckworth and Co. (1919).

T'Serclaes, Baroness, *Flanders and Other Fields*. London: Harrap (1964).

Von Arnim, Elizabeth, *Christine*. London: Macmillan (1917).

Ward, Mrs Humphry, *England's Effort*. London: Smith Elder (1916).

Webb, Beatrice, *Beatrice Webb's Diaries 1912–1917*. London: Longmans (1952).

Woolf, Virginia, *Diary of Virginia Woolf, Volume 1, 1915–1919*. London: Hogarth Press (1977).

Secondary sources

Beauman, Nicola, *A Very Great Profession.* London: Virago (1983).

Blodgett, Harriet, *Centuries of Female Days: Englishwomen's Private Diaries.* New Brunswick: Rutgers University Press (1988).

Braybon, Gail, and Summerfield, Penny, *Out of the Cage: Women's Experiences in Two World Wars.* London: Pandora (1987).

Buitenhuis, Peter, *The Great War of Words: Literature as Propaganda 1914–18 and After.* London: B. T. Batsford Ltd (1987).

Bussey, Gertrude, and Tims, Margaret, *Pioneers for Peace: Women's International League for Peace and freedom 1915–1965.* Oxford: Alden Press (1980).

Cadogan, Mary, and Craig, Patricia, *Women and Children First: The Fiction of Two World Wars.* London: Victor Gollancz Ltd (1981).

Cahill, Audrey Fawcett, 'From Sitting Still to Making History: Elsie Inglis's Russian Unit 1916–1917'. Paper given at the Annual Conference of the Women's History Network, University of Natal, South Africa, 1994.

Cecil, Hugh, and Liddle, Peter, H. eds, *Facing Armageddon: The First World War Experienced.* London: Leo Cooper (1996).

Condell, Diana, and Liddiard, Jean, eds, *Working For Victory.* London: Routledge (1987).

Cooke, Miriam, and Woollacott, Angela, eds, *Gendering War Talk.* Princeton: Princeton University Press (1993).

Cooper, H. M., Munich, A. A., and Squier, S. M., eds, *Arms and the Woman.* Chapel Hill and London: University of North Carolina Press (1989).

Eksteins, Modris, *Rites of Spring: The Great War and the Birth of the Modern Age.* New York: Bantam Press (1989).

Elshtain, Jean Bethke, *Women and War.* London: The Harvester Press (1987).

Figes, Eva, *Women's Letters in Wartime 1450–1945.* London: Pandora (1994).

Florence, Mary Sargant, Marshall, Catherine, and Ogden, C. K., *Militarism versus Feminism.* London: Virago (1987) (First published 1915.)

Fussell, Paul, *The Great War and Modern Memory.* Oxford: Oxford University Press (1977).

Goldman, D., ed., *Women and World War I: The Written Response.* London: Macmillan (1993).

Hartley, Jenny, *Hearts Undefeated: Women's Writing of the Second World War.* London: Virago (1994).

Higonnet, Margaret R., Jenson, Jane, Michel, Sonya, and Weitz, Margaret C., eds, *Behind The Lines: Gender and the Two World Wars.* New Haven and London: Yale University Press (1987).

Holton. Sandra Stanley, *Feminism and Democracy: Women's Suffrage and Reform Politics in Britain 1900–1918.* Cambridge: Cambridge University Press (1986).

Hynes, Samuel, *A War Imagined.* London: The Bodley Head Ltd (1990).

Leneman, Leah, *In the Service of Life: The Story of Elsie Inglis and the Scottish Women's Hospitals.* Edinburgh: Mercat Press (1994).

Liddington, Jill, and Norris, Jill, *One Hand Tied Behind Us: The Rise of the Women's Suffrage Movement*. London: Virago (1978).

Liddle, Peter, *The Worst Ordeal: Britons at Home and Abroad 1914–1918*. London: Leo Cooper (1994).

MacDonald, Lynn, *The Roses of No Man's Land*. London: Penguin (1980).

Macdonald, S., Holden, P., and Ardener, S., eds, *Images of Women in Peace and War*. London: Macmillan (1987).

Marwick, Arthur, *Women at War 1914–1918*. London: Fontana (1977).

Onions, John, *English Fiction and Drama of the Great War, 1918–39*. London: Macmillan (1990).

Ouditt, Sharon, *Fighting Forces, Writing Women: Identity and Ideology in the First World War*. London: Routledge (1994).

Raitt, Suzanne, and Tate, Trudi, eds, *Women's Fiction and the Great War*. Oxford: Clarendon Press (1997).

Sebba, Anne, *Enid Bagnold: The Authorised Biography*. London: Weidenfeld and Nicolson (1986).

Simons, Judy, *Diaries and Journals of Literary Women from Fanny Burney to Virginia Woolf*. London: Macmillan (1990).

Strachey, Ray, *The Cause*. London: Virago (1989). (First published 1928.)

Summers, Anne, *Angels and Citizens: British Women as Military Nurses 1854–1914*. London: Routledge (1988).

Tate, Trudi, *Modernism, History and the First World War*. Manchester: Manchester University Press (1998).

Tylee, Claire M., *The Great War and Women's Consciousness*. London: Macmillan (1990).

Vellacott, Jo, *From Liberal to Labour with Women's Suffrage*. Montreal: McGill-Queen's University Press (1993).

Vellacott, Jo, *Bertrand Russell and the Pacifists of the First World War*. London: Harvester (1980).

Wiltsher, Anne, *Most Dangerous Women*. London: Pandora (1985).

Winter, J. M., *The Experience of World War 1*. London: Guild (1988).

Winter, J. M., *Sites of Memory Sites of Mourning: The Great War in European Cultural History*. Cambridge: Cambridge University Press (1995).

Index

Page numbers in **bold** refer to contribution; those in *italics* refer to illustrations